Dreams of the Heart

The Autobiography of
President Violeta Barrios de Chamorro
of Nicaragua

Violeta Barrios de Chamorro

with
Sonia Cruz de Baltodano and
Guido Fernández

Simon & Schuster

SIMON & SCHUSTER
Rockefeller Center
1230 Avenue of the Americas
New York, NY 10020

Simon & Schuster and colophon are registered trademarks
of Simon & Schuster Inc.

Designed by Jeanette Olender
Photo insert designed by Paula R. Szafranski
Manufactured in the United States of America

Unless otherwise credited, all photos are from
President Chamorro's personal collection.

1   3   5   7   9   10   8   6   4   2

Library of Congress Cataloging-in-Publication Data
Chamorro, Violeta.
Dreams of the heart: the autobiography of President Violeta Barrios
de Chamorro of Nicaragua/Violeta Barrios de Chamorro
with Sonia Cruz de Baltodano and Guido Fernández.
p. cm.
Includes index.
1. Chamorro, Violeta.   2. Nicaragua—History—1937–1979.
3. Nicaragua—History—1979–1990.   4. Presidents—Nicaragua—Biography.
I. Fernandez, Guido.   II. Cruz de Baltodano, Sonia.   III. Title.
FI528.22.C53A3   1996   972.8505′3′092—dc20
[B]   96-32253   CIP
ISBN 0-684-81055-7

ACKNOWLEDGMENTS

I would like to give special thanks to my daughter, Cristiana, for encouraging and guiding me in telling my story; to Sonia Cruz de Baltodano for generating and promoting the idea of this book; and to Reid Boates, my literary agent, who represented us and kept us on course for five years.

I am also grateful to Guido Fernández and Sonia for helping me put my feelings into words. Guido produced a first-draft Spanish manuscript that was augmented by Sonia, who provided the historical context for the book with the help of Cristiana. Sonia then wrote the book in the English language and fine-tuned it with me, with the help of Cristiana and Bob Bender, senior editor at Simon & Schuster.

Because of my busy schedule it was not easy finding time to write this book and I appreciate the help that I have received. I am very grateful to the friends and family members who read draft chapters and offered suggestions, including Dr. René Sandino, Dr. Fernando Zelaya, Rodrigo Cruz, and José Antonio Baltodano.

I am also thankful to all those who assisted me in my efforts, especially Margarita Dorn at the office of the President, and Julio Leon at the library at *La Prensa,* both of whom put in a lot of extra hours helping Sonia and Cristiana with the research.

Most of all I give thanks to the people of Nicaragua who rose in protest when my husband was killed and placed their trust in me when I ran for president. It is for them that I have written this book. It is for them that I have lived this unpremeditated political life.

To all those who will become presidents of Nicaragua after me, I say: Never forget that a life in public service is not a simple undertaking. Our actions must always be guided by a spirit of self-sacrifice, honesty, and competence.

To my departed husband,

Pedro Joaquín Chamorro Cardenal,

and my grandson Marcos Tolentino,

who taught me a lesson in love and courage

that I will never forget. And

to my grandchildren,

Valentina, Sexto Pedro Joaquín, Sergio Antonio,

María Andrea, Violeta Margarita,

Fadrique Damian, Mateo Cayetano,

Cristiana María, and Antonio Ignacio,

Luciana Fernanda, Andrés Fernando,

Christiana María, and Antonio Ignacio,

so that they will one day feel inclined

to contribute, in whatever measure,

to helping Nicaragua be as free and beautiful

as their grandparents wished it to be.

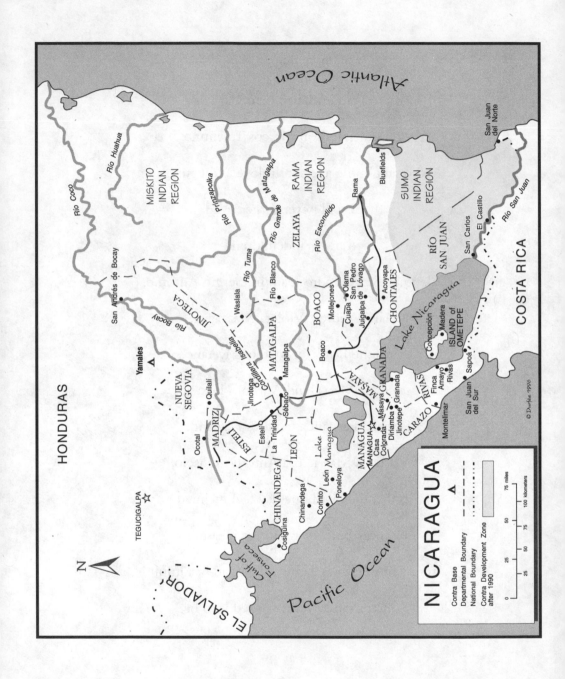

NICARAGUA

▲ Contra Base
--- Departmental Boundary
--- National Boundary
······ Contra Development Zone
after 1990

```
0    25   50   75 miles
0   25  50  75  100 kilometers
```

© *Durkee 1996*

HONDURAS

TEGUCIGALPA ☆

N

EL SALVADOR

Gulf of Fonseca

Pacific Ocean

Atlantic Ocean

Río Huahua

Río Coco

MISKITO INDIAN REGION

Río Prinzapolka

Río Grande de Matagalpa

ZELAYA

RAMA INDIAN REGION

SUMO INDIAN REGION

Bluefields

Rama

San Juan del Norte

Río Escondido

Río San Juan

RÍO SAN JUAN

San Carlos

El Castillo

COSTA RICA

San Andrés de Bocay

Río Bocay

JINOTEGA

Río Tuma

Waslala

Río Blanco

Cordillera Isabelia

Jinotega

MATAGALPA

Matagalpa

BOACO

Boaco

Mollejones

Cuapa

Olama

San Pedro de Lóvago

Juigalpa

Acoyapa

CHONTALES

Lake Nicaragua

Concepción

Madera

ISLAND of OMETEPE

Sapoá

Yamales ▲

NUEVA SEGOVIA

Quilalí

Ocotal

MADRIZ

Estelí

ESTELÍ

La Trinidad

Sébaco

CHINANDEGA

Cosigüina

Chinandega

Corinto

León

LEÓN

Poneloya

Lake Managua

MANAGUA

MANAGUA ☆

Casa Colorada

Diriamba

Jinotepe

CARAZO

MASAYA

Masaya

GRANADA

Granada

Finca Amayo

Rivas

RIVAS

Montelimar

San Juan del Sur

Chapter One

THE IDEALS OF THE REVOLUTION HAD BEEN betrayed. Nicaraguans were at war with themselves, caught in a downward spiral of violence that had left thirty thousand dead and the economy bankrupt. And if the Sandinista leaders were to prevail, the roots of communism would spread throughout the land, strangling freedom forever. This is the situation I entered into when I accepted the nomination of the Nicaraguan Opposition Union in September 1989 to run for president and oppose the Sandinista political juggernaut in the elections of February 1990, the first free and fair presidential election to be held in our country since 1934.

Why did I run? Because I was driven to fulfill my late husband, Pedro's, dream that Nicaragua become a truly democratic republic. My metamorphosis—from mother and wife to widow of a slain opposition leader and, finally, in February 1990, to democratically elected president of a country—was the ultimate result of a series of unyielding acts of defiance against a military dictatorship. This defiance led to Pedro's assassination and propelled me, as the custodian of Pedro's dream, into the center of Nicaragua's political arena.

One could also say that I embarked on this path the day I was born into a family of men who had led the secessionist charge in 1811 against the Spanish crown and fought in the 1821 War for Independence: I was called upon to fulfill the republican dreams of my forefathers. The day I met Pedro, a passionate advocate of freedom who swore to redeem Nicaragua at any cost from the Somoza tyranny, my destiny was sealed.

Twice I have been summoned to help defeat dictatorships: first as a symbolic figure of the revolution against Anastasio Somoza Debayle,

Pedro's longtime foe; and then as leader of the opposition against the Sandinistas, my former colleagues, who had betrayed our revolution. Each time I have been motivated by a desire to see my slain husband's dream realized, a patriotic ideal he carried in his heart like a burning obsession. Pedro confessed it to me for the first time soon after we met. He said his patriotism hung on his shoulders like a mantle God had placed upon him. This dream inspired all his thoughts, guided all his choices, though he knew it would cost him his very life. "Afterward," he told me, "as a result of my death, Nicaragua will be changed forever."

I should have known then that I would never be free to pursue an ordinary life, because from the time I met Pedro, the risen specters of our forefathers seemed intent on cutting a path for us in the history of our country. In fact, over time, I have come to comprehend that there was nothing coincidental in our meeting. I believe we fell in love as the unwitting subjects of a force that would drive us to fulfill a destiny from which we would not be able to extricate ourselves and that would join us together till death would part us.

Pedro and I are the descendants of men who were in the top echelons of Nicaragua's social structure, which was still in place when I was born, on October 18, 1929. Ours was a ruling class of European-blood criollos (children of Spaniards born in America) in which birth determined status. We were landowners and generals—masters of the white-and-Indian mixed-blood, or ladino, farmers, most of whom were of either Nahuatl or Chorotega Indian ancestry.

I remember as a child hearing the gloomy meditations of various family members as they discussed our nation's political follies at my parents' home. Why, they wondered, did everything in Nicaragua always seem to worsen? When everyone felt things could sink no lower, we always appeared doomed to repeat the bloody mistakes of our past. Why, while our neighboring countries were able to forge a national spirit, define their heritage, defend their borders, were we nothing more than an ideal, an aspiration that never managed to take form? Amid the disturbances of civil war, we had barely begun the march toward becoming a nation. "Sometimes," I would hear my father say, "we seem to be nothing more than an amalgamation of families, Liberals and Conservatives, and not the sum of many parts totaling a great country." Though I could not comprehend it then, I know now what my relatives found impossible to realize: that our failures as a republic have been a direct result of the devastations wrought by military rule and the socioeconomic inequities that have existed in Nicaragua. In addition the perpetuation of the colonial culture of victors and vanquished has fueled the mercurial swings in our nation's fortunes.

The tale of my family begins in 1762, with my Spanish great-great-great-great-great-grandfather Don Francisco Sacasa, taken prisoner by an English corsair during a brief period of British occupation in Florida and incarcerated for seven months in the fort at St. Augustine. He arrived in Nicaragua via Havana, Cuba, accompanied by a group of Spanish noblemen. At that time Nicaragua was a land still largely unexplored by Europeans, inhabited by a rich diversity of Indian tribes. The fledgling Spanish colonies of Granada and León were isolated spots of European civilization, and the vast plains, mountains, and lakes of the country were there for the taking.

The Nicaraguan poet Pablo Antonio Cuadra Cardenal, my husband's cousin, romanticizes the assertions of geologists with respect to the formation of the Americas and describes Nicaragua as rising from the oceans "like a Botticelli Venus" as a link between North and South America. The story goes that at first there appeared a crescent-shaped plot of land, the Mombacho volcano, which floated like an island in what was probably an enormous gulf. Thousands of years later, in one powerful seismic surge, this region became the two-hundred-mile-long Pacific rim of Nicaragua, lined by a chain of volcanoes: Cosigüina, San Cristóbal, Telica, Cerro Negro, Momotombo, Masaya, Mombacho, Concepción, and Madera. And it was then that the great lakes Xolotlán (later known as Lake Managua) and Cocibolca (later known as the Great Lake Nicaragua) came into being as interlocking bodies of water. Lake Managua receives the waters of as many as eight rivers pouring in from the north and the east. This confluence of waters empties into Lake Nicaragua, from which the San Juan River flows to the Atlantic Ocean. It has been speculated that the sweet waters of Lake Nicaragua and the river are rife with sharks, dolphins, manatees, sea turtles, and alligators, because once upon a time there was a connection to the Pacific Ocean through a region where the city of Rivas is now located, the city where I was born.

Some people say that because it lies at the core of the isthmus that joins North and South America, Nicaragua is the true center of the Americas. This claim is corroborated by the lushness of our flora and fauna—cougars and pine forests, typical of the northern countries, blend indiscriminately with the jaguars and wild boars that roam the humid jungles of the tropics—and in the profusion of Indian tribes that, not so peacefully, coexisted in our territory. There were the tobacco-smoking Subtiavas, the dictatorial Nahuas, and the more civilized Chorotegas, who allegedly came down from California and are believed to be related to the Sioux tribes of North America. The Pacific coast tribes prevailed over the more peaceful coca-chewing Ramas, Sumus, and Miskitos, reputed to have migrated to our Caribbean coast from Colombia and other South American regions.

It was into this dizzying array of ethnic cultures, climates, and landscape that my ancestor Don Francisco Sacasa entered, in 1762, as he negotiated the rapids of the San Juan River to take charge of the Fort of the Immaculate Conception. The previous superintendent, Don José Herrera y Sotomayor, another Spaniard, had perished of dysentery during an extended siege of the castle by the British, leaving his nineteen-year-old daughter, Rafaela, to oversee the defense of the citadel. As the story goes, in the last four days of the battle subordinate soldiers were about to surrender the fort when Rafaela, in a display of extraordinary character, fired the cannons and rallied the men back to arms until they successfully repelled the invaders.

According to family accounts, when Don Francisco, braving the rapids of the San Juan River and its inopportune sandbanks that had grounded many vessels, came upon El Castillo, he was awestruck by the area's beauty and by the sight of the stately fortification, majestically perched on a mountaintop. It was halfway up the course of the San Juan, described in 1852 by E. G. Squier in his book on Nicaragua as an earthly paradise with "trees rising like gothic columns." But being the commander of El Castillo was not an easy task; it involved repelling periodic invasions by English pirates and admirals desirous of conquering the wealthy city of Granada nearby.

Don Francisco's excellent performance in defending El Castillo led him, in 1784, to achieve a higher political position, in the Spanish city of Granada, where he moved with his wife, Doña Lucía Marenco López del Torral—a criolla, daughter of a magistrate and landowner of Genoese birth—whom he had met in that beautiful city. They were accompanied by their three children: Josefina, born in 1748, who married Joaquín Chamorro Fajardo (a distant relative of my husband, Pedro); Doña María del Pilar, born in 1749, who married Manuel Antonio Arana; and Roberto, born in 1751, who became governor general of Granada at the age of twenty-three.

Roberto remained in Granada, marrying Doña Paula Parodi, the daughter of an adventurous Genoese sea captain named Giovanni, who had voyaged to the Atlantic coast of Nicaragua. Roberto and Paula (my great-great-great-great-grandparents) had only one son, José Crisanto Sacasa y Parodi, born in 1779. Many years later, the family moved to the capital of the Royal Province of Nicaragua—León. The baroque city of León that my ancestors lived in was not the original settlement. The previous township, known as León Viejo, a few miles east, lies buried in the ashes of an eruption of the Momotombo volcano in 1610. The current city of León is also pummeled by the periodic eruptions of a (much younger) volcano.

José Crisanto Sacasa y Parodi, a colonel of the royal army, rose to political prominence and was appointed administrator of León. He married Doña María de los Angeles Méndez Figueroa, a criolla. They had eight children.

After 1808, when Napoleon Bonaparte evicted the Bourbon king Ferdinand VII and installed his brother Joseph on the Spanish throne, in the colonies the bonds of allegiance to the crown were irreparably torn. Several years later, the ferment of independence invaded the spirit of Don Crisanto, as he was known, and caused him to lead the secessionist charge. After the long War for Independence, the Central American colonies proclaimed their independence on September 15, 1821, and were loosely united in a brief confederacy comprising the republics of Guatemala, El Salvador, Honduras, Nicaragua, and Costa Rica. This organization prevailed until 1838, when a war of "all against all" broke out throughout the isthmus.

In all his military endeavors Don Crisanto was accompanied by my great-great-grandfather Francisco Sacasa y Méndez, his third child and oldest son, a physician. The gruesome scenes of wounded men expiring in the heat of battle and the raw ambition he beheld in the aftermath pushed Francisco away from politics forever. In 1826 he retired to the frontier town of Rivas, accessible only through the Great Lake Nicaragua, where he established a medical practice and was a gentleman farmer until the day he died.

My great-great-grandfather, his heart devastated by the barbarism of war and politics, tried to teach his children to turn their backs on the violent and treacherous quarrels that were part of everyday life in the cities of León and Granada, the centers, respectively, of Liberal and Conservative politics.

By contrast, my great-great-grandfather's youngest brother, Juan Bautista Sacasa y Méndez, produced a line of presidents. His son Roberto Sacasa y Sarria in 1889 became president of Nicaragua. And *his* son Juan Bautista Sacasa y Sacasa followed in his footsteps in 1932.

The chaos created by the War for Independence was to last a hundred years. The constant warfare and anarchy were not just the result of the power vacuum that was left in the absence of the Spanish crown, but also the consequence of the divergent political philosophies of the Conservatives and Liberals. The former believed in the importance of constitutional order, the preservation of family traditions, and the role of the Catholic church, which they believed should participate in government, while the Liberals believed the church should limit its influence to the spiritual sphere. In addition, the Liberals were regarded as bourgeois intellectuals and anarchists who, lacking the family ties and wealth of the Conservatives, wanted to abolish Nicaragua's aristocratic past.

In the years between 1827 and 1850 the clash between these two warring classes produced no fewer than thirty-eight civil uprisings and seventeen presidents, who alternated, in establishing government, between León and Granada. So in 1852, Managua, originally a fishing village between the two cities—it had been founded in 1846 as part of the district governed by the municipality of Granada—was declared the seat of government, but not the capital of the country. That would come later.

By then Managua was an emerging city that had begun to rival Granada and León in economic importance. The reason for its change of fortune was coffee, which was introduced by a group of Conservative families in the second half of the nineteenth century, into the cool and humid highlands that surrounded the city. Coffee quickly became a cash crop that enriched the area.

Amid the turmoil of the intermittent civil war, in 1853, emerged a commanding figure, Fruto Chamorro—the great-granduncle of my husband, Pedro Joaquín Chamorro Cardenal—an indomitable general who was willing to fight to the last drop of blood until the battle was won.

Fruto Chamorro, the illegitimate son of a European father and an Indian mother, was a mestizo who triumphed over the circumstances of his birth to become a respected political figure, founder of the Conservative Party and the first president of Nicaragua. Before his time they were called heads of state. He enacted the first set of laws to bring order to the chaos in Nicaragua. Opposing him in this effort was his great rival, the Liberal Máximo Jerez.

After a year of fighting, during which a terrible cholera epidemic broke out in Granada that killed Fruto and most of his men, the Liberals sent agents to California to hire a mercenary army. Thus, in 1855, as Fruto was dying, William Walker entered into the Nicaraguan conflict.

Walker was a physician, lawyer, and journalist from Tennessee with an audacious personality and, of course, ambition. In his previous excursion as a soldier of fortune, he had attempted the conquest of the Sonora territory in northwestern Mexico. Upon failing, he moved on to Baja California, where he was captured and sentenced to prison for having broken international law. After his release, he entered Nicaragua with a contingent of 150 men. Supported by American politicians who wanted to add new states to the Confederacy and establish slavery in Nicaragua, and with the help of the Liberals, he quickly took over the country, defeated the Conservatives, and burned the city of Granada. Soon afterward he had himself elected president.

This assault on our sovereignty by a foreigner released a strain of patriotism in the hearts of all Nicaraguans, who organized a Central American army of eighteen hundred men, led by General José Dolores Estrada, who defeated Walker on September 14, 1856, at the battle of San Jacinto and banished him from Nicaragua (though not forever). In the general's name I created the ceremonial order José Dolores Estrada in the first year of my presidency. It is the order I bestowed on King Juan Carlos of Spain, President Jimmy Carter, and others who have worked for peace and democracy in Nicaragua.

After Walker was expelled, a joint government of Liberals and Conservatives, represented by Generals Máximo Jerez and Tomás Martínez, ruled Nicaragua for a time. In 1875 the constitution was amended, the presidential term was set at four years, and Managua was declared the capital. This at last put an end to the rivalry between León and Granada. The period that followed was a golden age of entente, in which there was unparalleled economic progress. We refer to it as the Thirty Years of Conservative Peace.

In 1876 Pedro Joaquín Chamorro Alfaro, Pedro's great-grandfather, half brother of Fruto, became president. Don Pedro Joaquín labored to complete great civic projects, such as the construction of the first railway. This was followed by a hospital with all the modern conveniences, a wharf on Lake Managua, a new central market, and a National Library, which was in part administered by a child poet from León by the name of Rubén Darío, who would become Nicaragua's great national poet. As a final gift to the nation Don Pedro built a telegraph system, which allowed the country to communicate internally and with the rest of the world.

On August 6, 1889, the vacant presidency (the previous president had died suddenly) was filled by the Conservative senator Roberto Sacasa y Sarria, my great-granduncle. His first act as president was to establish an urban police. Elegantly uniformed and well instructed by a Costa Rican neighbor living in Nicaragua at the time, Federico Mora, its members were carefully selected from a group of people known for their honesty and good habits and inclined toward civil service.

On July 25, 1893, Don José Santos Zelaya (who was also related to my husband) marched into Managua from León at the head of a Liberal revolution. Afterward, a governing junta ruled for a brief period until the newly composed congress produced a new constitution that embraced the Liberal agenda of Zelaya and allowed him to push his colleagues out of power and turn his regime into a military dictatorship, thereby creating the prototype for all the subsequent Liberal tyrannies of our country.

This was about the time that my husband's grandfather Pedro Joaquín Chamorro Bolaños, the third son of the former president Pedro Joaquín Chamorro Alfaro, married his cousin Doña Ana María Zelaya Bolaños. He became a zealous defender of the Conservative Party. It is said he was a reclusive man who, even on the rare occasions on which he spoke, never revealed much about himself. But his life stands as a testament to his heroism because for most of it he was engaged in opposing his cousin José Santos Zelaya. In spite of this blood tie, Zelaya did not hesitate to imprison his cousin, shackling him to the point that his diabetic legs bloated, subjecting him to the most excruciating pain. He died as a consequence of his deteriorated health at the age of forty. He left a seven-year-old son, Pedro Joaquín Chamorro Zelaya, my husband's father.

The young boy went to live with his father's relatives, a family that offered him a stable home, social distinction, an intricate network of kinfolk, and—the important reference point—a tradition of public service. The greatest male influence in his life was his uncle Mariano Zelaya Bolaños, with whom he lived in exile in San Salvador for a period of time. Mariano stimulated his academic interest and exposed him to politics as an unavoidable part of his life. In 1909 Pedro Joaquín Chamorro Zelaya returned to Nicaragua, but it would be some time before he would take his rightful place in the politics of our country.

I am told that as a grown man, my husband's father was calm and reflective. Initially he was more interested in writing than politics. In 1923 he married Doña Margarita Cardenal of the Cardenales de Granada family, a well-to-do Conservative family of strict Catholic upbringing. They had five children: Pedro in 1920, Ana María (Anita) in 1927, Ligía in 1930, Xavier in 1932, and Jaime in 1934. In the early years of their marriage, the family lived frugally on the rent produced by a hacienda in Chontales that Doña Margarita had inherited from her parents.

They moved to Managua in 1925 when Don Pedro was elected to the Senate, where he distinguished himself for the integrity of his positions and the cold logic of his educated mind. It was at this time that Don Pedro became involved with the recently founded conservative newspaper *La Prensa*. In 1932, when Juan Bautista Sacasa was elected president and Anastasio Somoza García rose to power as chief of the Guardia Nacional, Don Pedro purchased *La Prensa*. In time Don Pedro would become Somoza García's chief critic.

In 1945 my husband, Pedro Joaquín, then a young law student, began his activist career by leading a student revolt against Somoza García's third bid for the presidency of Nicaragua. He was beaten, incarcerated, and then expelled from the university. So that he could complete his law studies, my in-laws sent him to Mexico. There he would often meet with other exiles and have political discussions. Among the exiles were my relative Juan Bautista Sacasa and Pedro's relative Emiliano Chamorro.

A year later, in 1946, Pedro's parents were also forced into exile by Somoza García. During this period, the family moved to New York, where they endured many hardships.

Being a girl from an isolated province, I don't remember much of the Managua of fifty and more years ago. But Pedro would tell me it was a city with broad boulevards lined with trees, which would turn yellow in the heat of summer. He was especially fond of recalling the ice cream parlors and juice stands that, as a young boy, he would frequent with friends to quench his thirst after an exhausting day at the local roller-skating rink or after a day of hunting alligators on the shores of Lake Managua. A local band would play every afternoon. Men wore tidy clothing, favoring light linen jackets and, for more informal occasions, guayaberas, loose cotton shirts with fine pleats stitched across the front. The women wore the prevalent fashion of gauzy silk dresses cut to the knee.

In Pedro's family there are so many daring men that in Granada it was said that "there could never be a Chamorro born without nerve." I would add that the Chamorros are also very intelligent and possess deep convictions, a love of freedom, unflinching honesty, and devotion to family and country. On the negative side, I would point perhaps to a certain tendency to be arrogant in the face of danger and obstinate in the face of reason, as well as a strong inclination to be autocratic. I would add that, though they were in positions of power an astonishing number of times, it was always through democratic means, with only one exception: Pedro's "granduncle" General Emiliano Chamorro.

Emiliano Chamorro is said to have been the last of the great Central American military strongmen known as caudillos. He was revered by his followers for his personal valor, demonstrated in a score of battles, for the firmness of his principles, and for an impetuous, unrelenting ambition.

Don José Santos Zelaya's preferences for European bankers and his stalwart opposition to the expansion of American interests in Nicaragua did not curry favor with the U.S. president of the time, William Howard Taft. So in 1909, when Zelaya's enemies formed a coalition of Conservatives and Liberals under the leadership of General Emiliano Chamorro, General Juan José Estrada, and Don Adolfo Díaz, Taft offered his support. Because of this what I term the second U.S. military invasion of our country occurred, following that of William Walker in 1855.

On this occasion the Americans materialized in the form of a battalion of four hundred marines, who disembarked on our Atlantic coast at the port of Bluefields to assist the rebels. The ostensible justification for this blatant intervention was to defend the lives and property rights of American citizens. It was this action that legitimized the rebel movement and ultimately catapulted the Conservatives back into power on August 29, 1910, in the person of General Juan José Estrada.

In 1916, in free and fair elections, Emiliano Chamorro became president. (In previous years, the American presence in Nicaragua had not only continued but had also expanded.) In 1924 Emiliano Chamorro's Conservative faction was defeated by an independent coalition of Liberals and Conservatives led by Carlos José Solórzano and my relative Juan Bautista Sacasa y Sacasa.

The American marines left Nicaragua in 1925. Two and half months after their departure, on October 25, 1925, the persistent Emiliano, unhappy with his electoral defeat, seized power by laying siege to the presidential palace and obtaining the immediate resignation of the peaceful Solórzano.

Claiming a constitutional right to succeed Solórzano, Juan Bautista Sacasa flew to Mexico to garner support and organize an invasion with the objective of reclaiming the presidency. The American marines returned to Nicaragua to force a truce between the warring factions in exchange for a guarantee of free elections.

Years later my husband, Pedro, would point to this episode as the reason why the party of his forebears, the Conservatives, lost their preeminence in Nicaraguan politics. As a young man Pedro would often chide Emiliano for his political blunder. In return, Emiliano would upbraid him for not declaring himself a bona fide member of the Conservative Party and for declining to play a role in the partisan politics of the country.

It was during one of these partisan struggles that my Conservative grandparents, landowners of solid Catholic stock, fled Nicaragua. My grandparents were not politicians, but in those days, as today, you couldn't avoid being involved one way or the other. Exile scattered our family to the four winds. On my mother's side, the Torres family went to Costa Rica, as Pedro and I would do many years later, victims of the same prejudice and intolerance that exist today and infest every stratum of society in our country.

On the Barrios Sacasa side, they traveled farther north, to New York, with seven children in tow. This is how my father came to be raised in New York and to have the opportunity to study at the Massachusetts Institute of Technology. Unfortunately, he was unable to graduate because his father died and he was called upon to manage a family hacienda called Santa Rosa, a huge spread of land, where he learned to speak Spanish among the cowhands and learned what it meant to be a Nicaraguan. He discovered that nationality is an extraordinary gift denied to those who live in exile.

In 1927, with the promise that fair elections would be held, all parties agreed to a fragile peace. The one exception was a young military officer, Augusto César Sandino. He remained at large in the mountains of Nicaragua, fighting the U.S. Marines for a long time to come. Pedro taught me to respect Sandino as a nationalist and a patriot. He was never a Communist, as the Sandinistas later claimed.

The long and bloody war Sandino waged against the marines developed his political consciousness. From being an opponent of the Conservatives, critical of his fellow Liberals' surrender, he became a fierce opponent of the Yankees, who decimated the ranks of his insurgency force during the seven years in which they engaged in battle. For his brawny defiance of imperialist forces, he became a hero to socialists and anti-imperialists the world over. Decades later he would be the inspiration for the Sandinista political movement.

(When my husband, Pedro, was still a schoolboy, he would be taught in history class about Sandino. But the story he heard was not about a heroic *guerrillero* who defended his country against an invasionary force and died at the hands of the treacherous Somoza García. He was told Sandino was a bandit. Pedro felt otherwise. He was an admirer of Sandino, whom he considered an idealist and a patriot, and in our home he insisted on hanging a portrait of him.)

The election of 1928 was peaceful and honest, and resulted in General Jose María Moncada becoming president.

In 1932 my husband's mother, Doña Margarita Cardenal de Chamorro, a typical lady of her times in her dedication to home and children, sold the small hacienda in Chontales she had inherited from her parents and gave the profits to her husband, Pedro Joaquín Chamorro Zelaya. He used this money to purchase the Conservative newspaper *La Prensa,* which had been operating since 1926. As was her custom, Doña Margarita did not question the prudence of his acts but simply supported all of her husband's endeavors. But from the moment the newspaper was purchased, it became the source of political confrontation between the entire Chamorro family and the Liberal government—and even with a phalanx of Conservatives whose desires were that *La Prensa* become a partisan daily. The constant assault and persecution they were subjected to from all sides was a trial Doña Margarita and her children learned to bear with dignity.

It was in this period that Anastasio Somoza García married Salvadora Debayle Sacasa, a distant cousin with whom I never had any acquaintance, since this is a blood tie I would much rather disavow. Exhibiting a great measure of political shrewdness, Somoza García propelled himself into the political scene. He was a plumbing supplies inspector turned car salesman turned general, whose most significant credential was a working knowledge of English. But coursing through his veins was the savage blood of the warlord Bernabé Somoza, who had terrorized the country during the presidency of Don Fruto Chamorro until he was captured and hanged, which put an end to a bloody career. It was probably this ancestry that best qualified Somoza García to be the head of a crude instrument of oppression like the National Guard, a post to which he was appointed in 1932 by Juan Bautista Sacasa y Sacasa when he was elected president.

The final withdrawal of American forces in Nicaragua came a year later, in 1933. Left in place was a two-thousand-strong army called the National Guard. Allegedly it was to be an apolitical force. But in the hands of Somoza García it became an instrument of oppression operating with the seeming indifference of the U.S. Department of State.

Pedro's father wanted to make *La Prensa* the pulpit from which to express his religious and political ideas. He spent most of his time at *La Prensa* or locked in his study, surrounded by dusty books, which he would often discuss with his brother-in-law Carlos Cuadra Pasos, also a great political thinker. Together they pondered the possibly nefarious consequences of General Somoza García's rise to power. They were worried by what was already a "coarse display of greed for wealth and a ruthless inclination for power." They felt that with his "corrupted heart" Somoza García would prove to be incapable of serving the country well.

Somoza García was ambitious, crafty, and politically sly. He understood the value of patience and knew how to reward his friends and punish his enemies. In short, he possessed all the qualities of a banana republic dictator.

His first victim was his fellow Liberal General Augusto César Sandino. He ensnared the rebel on February 21, 1934. At five o'clock that afternoon, Sandino and his lieutenants traveled to attend a banquet at the presidential palace to celebrate the accords that would bring peace between President Sacasa and Sandino. For the last time in his life the rebel soldier saw the afternoon turn into evening on Managua's horizon.

Forty-five minutes later General Somoza García called the American ambassador, Arthur Bliss Lane, to his residence. In anguished tones, he recounted to him the accords signed between President Sacasa and General Sandino. He termed them a threat and an insult to the independence of the National Guard. He went on to say he was being pressured by high officials in the army to do away with Sandino and was meditating on a course of action. But he promised he would do nothing without consulting the ambassador first.

The reception at the presidential palace started at 7 P.M. sharp. General Sandino was smiling and loquacious, but he warned Sacasa, "The way things are, Mr. President, you have only the appearance of power; ultimate power lies in the hands of the army. They are the supreme dictators in Nicaragua, and because they are possessed by greed and hate, I very much fear that they will strike against us and the peace we have just forged." It was common knowledge on the streets that though Somoza García had extended Sandino assurances of amnesty and safe passage throughout the country, something nefarious was being planned against the *guerrillero*.

The party ended around 9:30 P.M. Sandino bade farewell to his host. He climbed into his car with his aides and his driver. There were a total of six people in Sandino's car, some of them fatally marked. Immediately they noticed a sudden flash of light coming from the balcony of the presidential palace—a signal for the ten men lying in ambush farther ahead. These men captured Sandino and several of his aides. They took them away to the outskirts of Managua, where they opened fire with their machine guns and killed them.

From that point, plotting against his wife's uncle, President Sacasa, was a small matter for Somoza García. He first plotted a military revolt against Sacasa, then called for national elections, in which he was the only candidate. Sacasa fled to Mexico, where he died in anonymity. The U.S. government backed the actions of Somoza García and the generation of Somozas that followed in the years to come. Learning at the knee of the dictator were his sons, Luis and Anastasio Somoza Debayle, who would each one day control a piece of the pie, the former as president of the National Assembly, the latter as head of the National Guard.

As a boy my husband, Pedro, could not understand the princely attitudes of the two Somoza brothers, Luis and Anastasio. He knew what their father had done to Sandino and Sacasa and felt they should bow their heads in shame.

Pedro told me that when they were still twelve-year-old boys and Somoza García's increasing wealth was already becoming a topic of discussion, he heard a schoolmate ask Anastasio why his father liked being president. The answer was "For the money, of course." On Pedro's side, the idea that a person could live his life for nothing more than greed was contemptible. Pedro was an idealist who had a great deal of integrity and courage.

The son of devout Catholics, Pedro was raised within the confines of the strictest Catholicism. The first years of his life took place in a rigorous moral environment; his parents, strict disciplinarians, punished him severely if he lied and constantly pointed out to him the difference between good and evil. So it was that Pedro came to be increasingly on the side of the oppressed and rejected those who exploited and were corrupt.

Pedro battled three Somozas in all. The first one, Anastasio Somoza García, ruled for sixteen years. He rose to power in 1932 as head of the army and was gunned down at the height of his powers in 1956. Upon his death he was immediately succeeded by his eldest son, Luis, who ruled for six years, until May 1963. He was succeeded briefly by his handpicked candidate, René Schick. Luis died of a heart attack in 1967, months before Anastasio Somoza Debayle (Tacho), his younger brother, took office, which he held until 1979. Tacho ruled for nine years, with an interruption between 1972 and 1974. This was a short period in which Somoza allowed a puppet junta, composed of the Conservative Fernando Agüero as well as a Liberal and a general from the military.

⋙ ⋙

The record speaks of a Somoza dynasty that lasted forty-two years, but in reality one should include the years in which Somoza García held reign over the National Guard, because even though Sacasa was the nominal head of government, it was Somoza who, with the assistance of his gringo allies, held Nicaragua by the neck in what became the longest political pilferage in Central America.

Pedro and I were ashamed of the Somozas' alliance with the Americans and of the Americans' involvement in Central America. But most humiliating to us was the knowledge that whenever the imprint of the American warrior was found on Nicaragua's soil, it almost certainly was in response to the desperate cries of a Nicaraguan "compatriot" of dubious merit.

Today I can understand that when my political rivals scurry to hide under the skirts of the U.S. Congress or the White House, demanding sanctions against our country, they are operating under an impulse that originates deep in our past. But this does not absolve them of their crime. It has been clear since the days of William Walker that opening the doors to foreign intervention only betrays our sovereignty.

This is the history Pedro and I shared with each other, our common heritage. Together we admired the valor of our forefathers, who struggled to free us from the dominion of the Spanish crown and abhorred foreign interventions. We marveled at our ancestors' heroic achievements, their steely determination, their inexhaustible capacity to endure punishment, and their obsessive dedication to politics. But most important, we came to understand that the calm and deep wellspring of familial love can sustain a person through years of tempest and that through tolerance and respect we can be one nation. These early lessons in history predisposed us toward fighting oppression and incited us to rebel against dictators. But they also spoke to us about the value of unity in all our endeavors.

Chapter Two

MY FATHER, CARLOS BARRIOS SACASA (CHALE to his friends and family) was a man of the land, a rancher who inherited several large spreads from his parents, Don Manuel Joaquín Barrios and Doña Carmen Sacasa Hurtado. My father's great-grandfather, Dr. Francisco Sacasa y Méndez, was founder of the Sacasa branch of the family in Rivas, a veteran of the War for Independence.

By the time Father was born, politics had left a profound mark on his family, and perhaps some bitterness too because of the exiles the family had to endure. He would always say to us that they extracted some important lessons from adversity, such as the merits of a good education and the importance of flexibility in human relations. They understood that when people are forced to disperse they can be sustained by parental love, unity, and family traditions. "Persecution," Father would say, "can deprive you of your patrimony, but it cannot separate you from your moral principles and your personal talents."

I suppose that is why Father worked so hard to provide us with the necessary comforts and the advantages of a good education. He was always away trying to keep the family afloat. Though he owned several properties, it was Santa Rosa, in the Guanacaste region, that most occupied his time. His trips involved days and days of travel on his pedigreed horse, staying at inns along the way or traveling by schooner from the nearby port at San Juan del Sur on our Pacific coast. At one time Nicaragua's territory extended much farther south and north than it does today. In the south, the republic embraced all of the provinces of Guanacaste and Nicoya. But we lost them, as we also lost the lands between the Coco and Patuca rivers in the north at a much later time.

For each of Father's trips, Mother would minister to his every need. She would prepare medicines, food, and the clothing he most liked to wear in the countryside: khaki breeches, long-sleeved plaid shirts, and his spit-and-polish leather boots, which squeaked when he walked through the house. But I know his trips were a heavy burden on Mother. She was an incurable romantic and missed Father terribly in the months he would spend completely cut off from us. Sometimes I would hear Mother pleading with him, "Chale, why don't we sell Santa Rosa so you can remain closer to us?" But Father wouldn't hear of it.

So, with Father's all-consuming responsibilities, it was left to Mother to carry out the task of educating five children. She was rigorous but gentle in the application of her norms, expressing high expectations with regard to all of us. She never allowed us to submit to failure and never accepted any imperfections in our chores. All of this she conveyed to us in the gentlest of ways. It was from Mother that I learned one could be strong in substance while moderate in one's style of expression. "Conviction in one's beliefs," she would often say, "must be stated with the greatest of courtesy."

I remember it was Father, motivated by a desire to win us over after his long absences, who was most apt to buckle under pressure from his children. His kindness, however, we never mistook for weakness; it was clear to us that Father was a man of strong convictions who commanded authority and had the respect of those who came into contact with him. From Father I learned that "authority is better exercised through persuasion and becomes sacred only when it is borne through example."

Rivas, the quaint colonial city in which I was born and lived until my marriage, was not too different from today's Rivas. The city lies on a narrow plain, halfway between the Pacific bay of San Juan del Sur and the port of San Jorge on Lake Nicaragua. Its ancient orthogonal plan, which created a city of approximately fifteen square miles, remains virtually unchanged. On its eastern edge, rising in the distance, are the two mighty volcanoes Concepción and Madera on the island of Ometepe in the middle of the Great Lake Nicaragua. Because of them a person in Rivas can always know exactly where he is with respect to the cardinal points of the compass.

The city grid has four main axes intersecting at a large public square, or *plaza mayor*. This square is the key to the whole city. Its size regulates the dimensions of the blocks immediately surrounding, which are quarter sections of the *plaza mayor*. The units into which each of the sections is cut are called *solares*. One was assigned to the town parish, *la parroquia*; the others were sold to the leading settlers. Our house was across the street from the *parroquia* in Rivas, on a corner opposite the *plaza mayor*. Down the street lived my Torres grandparents, directly in front of the plaza, and at the far end was the Barrios Sacasa clan. It was a world that followed the slow rhythms of rural life and was devoid of any artificiality. Church and family were the pillars of our existence.

Our house, I am told, was built when I was born, in 1929. My aunts, who were more conservative and austere than Father, criticized him for his modern ways and for what they considered to be his lavish spending. Though in Rivas we were considered a family of means, Father took great care not to fall into an offensive opulence, conscious of our position of "privilege" in the midst of a less fortunate populace. But Father, who grew up in the United States, represented a shift in social attitudes because he was not willing to forgo certain elemental comforts. "A modern house is what I want," he told the architect who came from Managua to build it. Years later, when I had the opportunity to travel to the United States, I discovered to my surprise that our home could not really be termed modern. It was an eclectic mix of Spanish Colonial and American Greek Revival.

Fascinated by our house as they were, people in Rivas judged Father poorly for not building a house designed in the Spanish tradition, with the walls projecting all the way to the perimeter of the sidewalk, a porch that protects its front elevation from rain and sun, and a central patio around which the rooms are organized.

Unlike the Spanish perimeter housing, our home was set back from the street, which allowed a small fragrant garden of white roses to be cultivated in the front yard. The house had a five-foot wall surrounding it to ensure privacy. One gained entry through a pathway of mosaic tiles that looked like a front-hall rug rolled out all the way to meet the entrance. Unlike the Spanish houses, ours did not sit directly on the ground but was raised on a plinth, which gave us a view from the veranda over the garden wall to the *plaza mayor* and the park.

• • •

Until Father built our house, Rivas was a town that had a homogeneous appearance. Location and certain elaborate touches distinguished the homes of the oligarchy from those of the simple folk. There was no confrontation between luxury and poverty. Walls were whitewashed and built of adobe to a height of twenty feet, which was considered the minimum for proper air circulation. All the homes lacked plumbing and were dependent on latrines and water drawn from a well artfully placed at the center of an open-air courtyard, or patio. My grandmother, whom we called Macaca, lived in a house that I remember had a family of iguanas living in the patio. On rainy days the water would inundate the corridors and wash the floors clean. Afterward Felicidad, my grandmother's maid, would dry them to a shine that allowed me to see my cloudy reflection on the mosaic tiles. The rooms were equipped with shutters that were shut all day to keep out the soporific hot air, then opened at night to let the cool, fresh air in.

On Sundays, the midday meal was always a formal affair that involved the entire family. In a dark cool room with a high ceiling that made their voices echo in a strange way, the family discussed the vicissitudes of their everyday life, the complaints of old age, their illnesses and cures.

Inside, our house followed the Spanish plan, with two front rooms for formal occasions. One of them held the big Stroud piano Father imported from New York for me to take my first lessons on. But most interesting to me were the rooster and the six hens that provided us with fresh eggs every morning. There were staff quarters too; a laundry, where Otilia would iron and fold our clothes in huge aluminum tubs; and stables, where the wagons pulled by oxen unloaded the calves, pigs, and lambs that the cook grilled with exotic herbs and spices.

I am told that when Father decided to install toilets in our home it was perceived to be too ostentatious. "How crass, Chale," my aunts would say. "So much expense on those toilets!" Father didn't care; he prided himself on being a progressive thinker. I, on the other hand, have always preferred the old way of doing things. I have an affection for horses and nature.

Father loved to travel. He was especially fond of going to South America to visit the site of the Inca empires and the old colonial cities of the viceroys. But because he was afraid of airplanes, he would take long cruises in Mother's company.

• • •

On those occasions, my brothers—Carlos, whom we also called Chale; Ricardo; Manuel Joaquín, whom we called Maquín; and Raúl—and I would stay under the care of Mimí Ruiz, the woman who had come as a girl from Amayo on the day my parents were married, to be in Mother's employ.

The year I was to receive my First Communion, a great event in a child's life in Nicaragua, a great calamity occurred. It would be the first, but not the last, sadness in my life.

The School of the Angels in Costa Rica my brother Ricardo attended with Chale was in the process of completing a slide. The boys would rashly hurl themselves down the slide at a vertiginous speed. Because the ladder was still missing, to repeat their heroic feat the boys would climb back up the slide's steep incline. A classmate of Ricardo's hurled himself down without realizing that Ricardo was on his way up. From the collision Ricardo fell to the ground on his head, fracturing his skull. He was pronounced dead on arrival at the hospital.

I remember how we received the bad news. At the time I didn't particularly believe in presages. But since that day, I am ever vigilant about feelings that alight on my subconscious carrying a concealed pain. The day it happened, Mother awoke feeling sad. She worried all day without knowing why. In the afternoon, unable to bear the anxiety any longer, she resolved to get out of the house and pay a visit to Macaca. As was my custom, I accompanied her, and together we walked down the street hand in hand. The house was only two blocks away, on the far end of the plaza. When we arrived we were surprised to find the door ajar and everything engulfed in darkness. The gasoline-powered generator that usually lit Macaca's home was not working. A solitary gas lamp illuminated the entranceway, giving a somber appearance to the house that further depressed Mother. With regret, she begged Macaca to excuse her for not staying and confessed to feeling too overwhelmed by sadness to be in anybody's company. Quickly, we made our way back home, passing by the home of one of my aunts. Mother made excuses for not stopping to chat. She was feeling more dismal by the moment. When we arrived home, Mimí Ruiz received us at the door and accompanied us to Mother's bedroom to help her prepare for bed. When Father was away I always accompanied Mother and we recited the rosary together at the foot of her bed. We were about to finish the rosary when we were startled by a knock on the front door. It was a messenger, who carried in his hand three radiograms. Mother asked, "Why so many?" "I believe it is bad news, señora," he said. Wishing to keep the pain at bay, Mother said to the man, "You read it, please." *"Perdone,* señora, this is news you should read yourself." I will never forget Mother's enormous grief. She buried her face in her hands after she had finished reading. Through her fingers and her sobs Mother said to me, "Ricardo has been in a grave accident," then she ran screaming next door, where the Najarros lived. "Dennis, Dennis, Ricardo is dead." At that instant I blocked my ears. I did not want to hear another word.

The next few days were filled with action. Because there were no landing strips in Rivas, a pasture was cleared so Ricardo's body could be brought back to us on a plane Father hired. Ricardo's body was accompanied by Father, my brother Chale, a few priests, some of his teachers, and a profusion of flowers. After the funeral, though it pained him very much, Chale went back to Costa Rica to the school where Ricardo had died. The following year, however, he returned to Nicaragua and was enrolled in Granada at Colegio Centro América.

Though time has dulled the pain, my mind has vivid memories of that final good-bye. I remember feeling unreasonably calm at the time, as I have been with all the other deaths I've lived through—a spectator standing outside time and circumstance, insulated from the pain of grieving. But from it all I have learned there is danger in everything we do. Death will come anyway, and until it does we must not be paralyzed by fear of it.

I was educated at Colegio Francés, a boarding school in Granada run by French nuns, who taught me that God gave each person certain gifts and that if you use them appropriately, you will travel on a trajectory made explicitly for you. To aid us in that process of discovery the nuns taught us history, arithmetic, geography, Spanish literature (which included the poetry of our compatriot Rubén Darío, whose poems we had to memorize and recite), and music, which I loved. This, I thought, was my gift. Under the guidance of the esteemed Evelio Pérez Aycinena, I learned to play many Strauss waltzes and delicate Mozart sonatas, which I would perform with the school ensemble. I learned that ensemble music is best made when pieces are interpreted with group discipline, even at the expense of individual virtuosity. Performers must remember to serve the music and be the conduits for ideas larger than themselves. (Politics should be no different. For me it is not about power, ego, or appetite, but about knowledge, wisdom, and the desire to achieve things for the greater good of one's country.)

The trip from Rivas to Granada involved crossing the Great Lake Nicaragua on an old steamship called *El Victoria*. It was a long and arduous journey. The vessel had reached a venerable old age navigating the tame waters of the Río San Juan. Now in this fragile stage of its life it was being asked to confront the fury of a lake that the Spanish conquistador Gil González Dávila called a "freshwater sea."

In those days, because of the slowness of travel, separations were never for short periods of time but extended into long absences that went on indefinitely. For me this meant I had to resign myself to spending holidays far away from home as a guest in the one-story mansion of Doña Engracia Carazo, the mother of my friend and classmate María Jesús Chamorro Carazo.

The streets in Granada were wider than in Rivas, with grand multiple squares dispersed throughout the city. When our elders permitted it, we would entertain ourselves by going to the music shell in the *parque central,* where a local band would play concerts the whole town would attend, seated under the mango trees.

That first Christmas, in 1938, that I spent away from home, I consoled myself with warm thoughts of my family and the last vacation we had spent with Ricardo, at our summer home in our hacienda at Amayo on the shores of the Great Lake Nicaragua.

The trip from Rivas to Amayo took five hours to complete. Father, Chale, Ricardo, Maquín, and I, all seasoned equestrians, rode on horseback, overcoming the wide currents we sometimes encountered as we crossed several rivers on the way. Mother and my younger siblings, Raúl and Clarisa, who were still babies, rode with the maids in two covered wagons and a carriage sent from Amayo to fetch them. I remember how the farmhands had to clear a path through the dense brambly bush with a machete and how, every so often, the wheels of the wagons would give way on the steep incline, which made the servants curse as they labored to free the wagons.

I was then seven years old and had a liking for an impudent pony by the name of Torpedo, which the manager of the hacienda in Amayo did not like me to ride because of his fondness for taking off like a bullet with me riding on his back, hardly stopping to breathe until we had reached the great house. No sooner did we dismount in Amayo than we plunged into the sweet waters of the Great Lake. Heedless of warnings about sharks and alligators, we swam and played as often as four times a day.

The big house of Amayo nestled against a hill overlooking the lake. From it we could see the majestic curves of the Concepción and Madera slumbering in the distance. For us they were a stirring and ominous sight that followed us everywhere we went. They were the subject of constant discussion among our elders because in the past century Rivas had been destroyed by an earthquake reputed to have been caused by eruptions from the Concepción volcano.

According to local folklore, all the trouble in Nicaragua can be traced back to the day when these two colossal volcanoes emerged. The Indians tell it this way: When Nicaragua was devoid of people and all that existed was land, lakes, lagoons, and rivers, there were only fish that swam in the water; crabs that played on the sandy beaches; humming-birds that buzzed around the flowers; lizards that scurried between the rocks; iguanas that lolled in the sun's warm rays; coyotes, rabbits, and mountain lions that errantly wandered through the woodlands; and crows that perched in the branches of shady banyans, tall cedars, and beautiful poincianas. It was the animals, insects, and reptiles that were the owners of everything. They lived in tranquillity and happiness until the two volcanoes appeared to cook up a storm of lava and spout great clouds of smoke, which caused the earth to rumble and burn.

My memory of the relationship between my parents is one of intimate affection and love. From the time they met they were enamored of each other, though social custom prevented young couples from establishing a direct romantic relationship. Until it was determined by their elders that their sentiments were not a passing fancy and that an engagement could be announced, the strictest reserve had to be maintained.

These restrictive conditions limited the knowledge couples could have about each other before marriage. The longing experienced during those days of furtive glances and waiting often transformed the lovers into illusory figures, endowed with improbable virtues and sentiments, which in my opinion must have been the cause of unhappy marriages. Later these customs would change.

My mother once told me that life in Rivas began to change after the second invasion, with the arrival of the U.S. Marines who brought Vicks VapoRub into our homes. She said the smell of camphor replaced the homemade remedies, like lemongrass and *tiszana,* that had been used since time immemorial. Vicks seemed to have a revolutionary effect on the minds of the young, because this novelty was soon followed by the appearance of the Charleston in the local dance halls and at society balls, where once Strauss waltzes had reigned supreme. But none of these innovations was adopted by my mother's family. She was the product of an old-fashioned upbringing, the only daughter of prosperous merchants, taught to have great deportment regardless of the kind of behavior others might be exhibiting.

Hers was an education that, like Confucianism, was largely based on respect for one's elders and the great achievements of one's ancestors, coupled with the most rigorous discipline, which in the absence of psychology was enforced by a *tajona,* a homemade cat-o'-nine-tails.

I remember Mother as always being beautiful, fine featured, slim as a reed, with auburn hair, skin the color of pale honey, dark eyebrows, and green eyes. She possessed indescribable grace, moving like a gazelle through our home. But it was when she covered herself with her white, thick lace mantilla to attend six o'clock mass every morning that she seemed especially lovely to me. All through my childhood and adolescence people would say I was a Barrios in every way, tall like my father, with the same dark hair and eyes. Now that I am nearly sixty-seven, with white hair, my children tell me I look exactly like my ninety-four-year-old mother.

As a child, I was fond of observing my mother as she sat solemnly, following the mass in a leather-bound, gilt-edged missal full of colored pictures of the apostles and martyrs, while I heard the mass sung in Latin. In those moments her pure, svelte form was transfigured against the mystical music into something unearthly.

She tells me she never loved a man other than my father, that the first time she saw him, as she was coming out of church, walking between her father and her mother, she felt a seductive force that drove her to turn around. There, just a few feet away, stood my tall handsome father fixing her with a dark gaze. From that moment on she was caught in the hopeless fervor of first love. She had found the man she was going to marry. They always respected each other; never was there an argument or a discord, never a complaint. They were an example to me—with mutual respect, love can be strong and everlasting.

After graduating from primary school, I went to a boarding school in Managua, the Academia de la Virgen Inmaculada, taught by the same order of nuns as Mother Cabrini's. There I was to start my first year of high school. Throughout the entire trip from Rivas, on the train to the capital, all I could think of was that each time I was moving farther and farther away. At the time, I didn't recognize the finality of the events as they were unfolding, but when we finally reached our destination, I put my arms around Mother's neck and fought back my tears. The farewell with Father was more contained. He embraced me and gave me one last piece of advice: "Never discuss politics or religion, and you will see you will get along with everyone." And so it was. I made many friends who, like myself, were from remote regions of Nicaragua, and my time at La Inmaculada proved to be a happy one.

I was a good student, got medals, honorable mentions, and such, though I suffered during exam periods. Sports and music were what I really loved. But I never stopped missing my parents and would await eagerly their annual visit in September for the celebration of the *Fiestas Patrias,* the holiday in which we commemorate our independence and the defeat of the American invader William Walker.

Every year on this date, La Inmaculada, like all the other schools in Managua, would take part in a parade. I remember the school had a marching band, and we advanced in step with the sound of bugles, cymbals, and drums. The second year I was in the school, the sisters asked me to lead the parade. Being too embarrassed to assume such a prominent role, I refused. Then they suggested I play the clarinet, an offer Mother advised me to reject because she believed my lips might become monstrously deformed from all that blowing. They countered with an offer to play the drums. But I turned that down too because I didn't want to be the source of a sound that would reverberate offensively in everyone's ears. Finally they said, "Violeta, won't you at least carry the flag?" "That assignment," I said, "I will accept for its patriotism."

I remember that for the occasion I got to wear a special costume, not the vaporous white pleated affair the other girls were obliged to wear with straw boater hat and gloves. Mine was a tailored outfit—a blue jacket and skirt worn with a white shirt and a tie, black lace-up shoes, and yellow knee socks. Even then I had a marked preference for a straightforward simplicity.

We marched from the gates of the school on Avenida Bolívar down to the Plaza de la República, where the girls assembled in rows of six. Up Avenida Roosevelt we went, in cadence with the drumroll and the trumpets, toward the Parque Rubén Darío, where the foreign dignitaries were seated with the president of the republic, Anastasio Somoza García, against whom the Chamorro Cardenal family had launched a campaign in their newspaper, *La Prensa.*

Somoza García had announced his intentions to amend the constitution for a second time. His clear objective to remain indefinitely in power was being widely criticized. Pedro Joaquín Chamorro Zelaya, Pedro's father, opposed the action and wrote scathing articles vehemently denouncing Somoza's tyranny. It was 1944. Pedro was then twenty-four and beginning to organize mass demonstrations against the regime.

In 1945 Pedro's overt actions against Somoza García landed him in jail for three weeks and ultimately led to the expatriation of his entire family and the closing of the paper for one year. His parents and his two younger sisters, Ana María and Ligía, resettled in New York, where Pedro's father, a historian by training, worked at the New York Public Library, and the proud, aristocratic Doña Margarita worked as a seamstress in a clothing manufacturing shop. His brothers Xavier and Jaime remained with their Cardenal grandmother in Granada. Pedro went to Mexico to complete his law studies; there he came into contact with the exiled Nicaraguan community, among them Emiliano Chamorro and Juan Bautista Sacasa.

At the time, Harry Truman had become president of the United States. In stark contrast with his predecessor, Franklin Roosevelt, Truman found the American alliance with Somoza García embarrassing. Thus he gave instructions at the Department of State to warn the tyrant that the United States would not go along with his plans for reelection. Somoza García, always mindful to maintain a positive relationship with his American *patrones,* or bosses, initially tried to please them. He publicly renounced his candidacy and restored civil liberties for a time.

After I had been at La Inmaculada a couple of years, my parents decided it was time for me to perfect my English in an American boarding school. My concern was that, not knowing the language, I would not be able to keep up with the rest of my class. My parents assured me I had no reason to worry; I would pick up the language in no time at all. Not being one to argue, I did pretty much as I was told and prepared myself for another, much longer good-bye.

The plan was that after school in the United States I would go on to England, then Switzerland, to complete my education. I knew I would not return to Nicaragua for a long time. So I asked Father to let me experience one more time the majesty and harshness of Amayo. He agreed to the trip but wanted me to ride in the comfort of his new Packard. To please him, I consented to go the final half of the trip in the car, after we had crossed the Río Vergel on horseback—where the currents might grab hold of you and tear your heart out if you didn't approach carefully. For me this was one of the highlights of the journey.

That was August 1944, the last time I went to Amayo with Father. Afterward, I boarded a Pan Am flight to Brownsville, Texas, and alighted with my trunks in a city that was more civilized than anything I had ever seen. But I was not impressed. My fascination was reserved for a paradise of tree-covered mountains, menacing volcanoes, azure lakes, flowing waters, and spirited horses, a kingdom in which there is no horizon because water and sky melt into each other in shades of blue. How could I have been stirred by the modernism of urban living?

We rented a car in Brownsville and drove to San Antonio, where we met my brother Chale, who went with us to Our Lady of the Lakes, the boarding school I would be attending. It was close to Austin, where Chale was completing his studies. This proximity was not a coincidence but a requirement, because a young girl of fourteen like myself couldn't simply dispossess herself of her family and take up living in a foreign country. It had to be done in a controlled fashion, with a close relative nearby whom one could be entrusted to. For my parents there was no better candidate for the job than my older brother.

My passage through Our Lady of the Lakes would not be a very long one. Though I excelled in softball because of my speed, basketball because of my height, and choir because of my musical background, I found learning English impossible. On campus there were eighty Latin American girls speaking Spanish at all times. I thought with nostalgia of my companions at La Inmaculada, who were completing their junior year and would be graduating the next year. I, on the other hand, was falling irremediably behind in my studies. These feelings of utter waste I conveyed to my parents in a tearful letter. They wrote back not to worry, that everything would be arranged when they came to Austin for Chale's graduation from engineering school the following year.

When my parents arrived, the four of us went searching for a new academic setting for me. Because of Father's aversion to airplanes, we traveled to New York by first-class train. We spent four days and three nights on a train. It is an experience I never want to repeat.

Father's sister Julia was living in New York. She helped us rent an apartment so that we could be comfortable and have the opportunity to visit several colleges. The idea was that I could attend school in New York or somewhere near Boston. But we arrived too late. It was already June and in most places they had already made their commitments for the coming academic year.

We found a school named Blackstone in Virginia, a one-and-a-half-hour drive from Richmond. We had hoped for a Catholic school, which Blackstone was not. But I had few options, and my parents thought that to attend a school with a mixture of Catholics and Protestants would promote in me respect for the ideas of others. And so it was. On Sundays students walked to town to attend the service of their choice and then, free of any religious biases, amicably socialized in the dances and concerts organized by the school. This American lay education was quite compatible with the way I had been raised at home. The two years I spent at Blackstone served to reaffirm my respect for pluralism, something I have tenaciously adhered to all my life.

My English was not too good. I spoke in halting sentences but somehow managed to make myself understood and even write term papers. My first roommate was Silvia Sánchez, the daughter of a Cuban diplomat. It was not a good idea for us to be together because, try as we might to avoid it, we couldn't help speaking in the tongue we were most comfortable in. So I asked to be moved into a room with an American girl. That is how I met Marie Guarini.

The experience of rooming with Marie was decisive in the formation of my character. Though we were from different worlds, Marie became my friend, companion, confidante. With the greatest enthusiasm we shared classwork, correspondence, dreams, and expectations, the medium through which women express to each other reciprocal feelings of trust, loyalty, respect, and support. I recall fondly how when one of us was feeling temporarily despondent, the other was quick to raise her spirits with an encouraging word of optimism or through innocent teasing. Both Marie and I were extremely attached to our families. We both came from stable homes, had loving parents, a strong Catholic upbringing, and a positive attitude toward life. We discovered that except for some minor cultural differences, our values were essentially the same. Marie liked to smoke Pall Malls, while I didn't like to smoke at all. She wore brand-name pleated skirts, while mine were tailored straight and assembled piece by piece by my seamstress in Rivas. I liked Bach and Mozart, while she perhaps enjoyed listening to Louis Armstrong or Benny Goodman. But this American girl and I weren't that different at all.

The school was very beautiful—Jeffersonian-style redbrick buildings on several acres of rolling hills with trees and grass that turned emerald in the spring, where we played field hockey and softball and rode horses, which brought to mind memories of Father and me herding cattle in Amayo from sunrise to sunset.

The food, served on tables covered in elegant linen, was very good. After the meal we would retire to the solarium for dessert and tea. It was a very refined environment. But in my second year the longing to go home became unbearable. I had a feeling that if I didn't return soon I would not see my father alive again because he was going to die.

That June, in 1947, my parents arrived for their annual summer visit. I'll never forget that vacation. Chale and I noticed that Father was suffering from a persistent cough that seemed to get worse when he smoked an occasional cigar. Under pressure from us, he agreed to submit to a routine examination. He decided to have it done at Lenox Hill Hospital in New York because his old classmate from MIT was an attending physician there. It fell to this old school friend to reveal the saddest news to Father: at the age of fifty, Father had terminal lung cancer.

We had already experienced the painful loss of Ricardo, but this threat to Father's life was even more wrenching; it came as a complete surprise because in those days we didn't associate tobacco with cancer. But what worried Father most was the solitary life he knew Mother would lead without him, though she was only forty.

The following three months brought an incredible transformation in Father. Accustomed to looking up at him because of his superior height, I was not prepared to look down upon him on a hospital bed, withering before my eyes, his strong jaw slack with pain, his neat mustache suddenly turned gray with anguish. Each morning I would hesitate before the closed door of his hospital room, wondering whether I would have the strength to confront the invalid in his impeccable pajamas lying between the starched hospital sheets. The days were all the same, Mother and I praying at the foot of the bed while they took him away to perform tests and treatments. But soon there was no hope. The time came when the doctors felt there was nothing to do but discharge him. I wanted to return with my father and mother to Rivas. But my parents, who gave no quarter to adversity, persuaded me to stay, assuring me that everything would be all right. They promised to return in December, confident, I suppose, that a miracle would take place. Part of me, of course, wanted to believe that too.

Reluctantly I returned to Blackstone that fall, but I had a difficult time concentrating on my studies, as I was always thinking of Father. Thanksgiving came. I spent it with Chale in Pennsylvania, where he was in a long training program with Westinghouse in Pittsburgh. Then Christmas arrived. Because Mother and Father were not able to come, Marie Guarini invited me for the holidays to her home in Jersey City.

The Guarinis lived in a brick Georgian house on Britton Street. Marie and her brother, Frank, were the only two children of a successful criminal attorney. Both of them looked a lot like their father, who had blue eyes and dark hair. Frank, I remember, was studying at Dartmouth to be a lawyer, like his father. During my visit he squired us around, escorting us to parties in New York City and to the theater. It was turning out to be a good visit until New Year's Eve came around. The Guarinis that night had a family party in which we were all toasting with champagne, and I, as I do every year, found myself thinking that I had survived Ricardo by a decade. Painful as his departure was, I had finally come to accept it.

But weighing heavily upon me was Father's state of health. Reports from home were good, but my instincts told me otherwise. I began to wonder how to excuse myself from the party. I couldn't explain my fear and I was afraid my morose feelings would ruin the evening for the others, when suddenly the tears started rolling down my cheeks. I took a deep breath and with some composure explained to the Guarinis that I wasn't feeling well and really needed to lie down. Mrs. Guarini was very kind and attentive but nothing could lift my thoughts. Upstairs, alone in Marie's room, I lay in the dark listening to the noise coming from below, thinking there was no one who could comfort me. Rocking back and forth I fell asleep. The next day I awoke feeling even more upset. All night I had dreamt of Father—that he had sat next to my bed, held my hand, and told me he had come to say good-bye. In the last moments of my dream I had clung to the last threads of sleep to avoid facing the calamity that my premonitions boded. At breakfast, though I had decided not to share my experience with the family, I am sure my anxiety was apparent.

We were still sitting at the table when the maid at the Guarini household announced a visitor. It was Tío Manuel, my father's brother. As soon as I saw him I knew my dream had not been mere fantasy.

"Tell me, Tío Manuel, is Father dead?"

"How did you know this?" he asked, unable to hide his shock. When I told him of my dreams, he was visibly perturbed. After recovering his composure he said to me, "Your brother Chale is already on his way back. He has asked that you return with us after you have purchased a mourning wardrobe."

Immediately I bade farewell to Marie and thanked her parents, believing that I would never see them again. I knew that from that moment on my life would take a totally different turn because, with the death of Father, Mother would renounce living.

Lamentably, I arrived too late for the funeral in Rivas. In New York I came down with such a case of bronchitis that I was forced to stay in bed in a hotel room for three weeks. Chale, who after Father's untimely death had abandoned a promising career as an electrical engineer and occupied himself primarily with the management of Amayo, was there to meet me at the airport.

With the passing of Father the house came under the rule of death. The doors of the house were closed and did not open except to receive intimate friends. Mother withdrew into the four walls of her bedroom, where she built an altar with Father's photograph and a candle that remained permanently lit. For the longest time she refused to go out even to glimpse the garden from the threshold of her home. So it fell to me, the eldest daughter, to replace Mother in her various domestic and familial roles. She delegated to me full authority in running the house. With all of my eighteen years I assumed this responsibility unflinchingly.

A complete period of mourning for women in those days was never

❧   ❧

less than two years. The first year was carried out so stoically that the widow and her daughters wore only black. In the sweltering heat of Rivas this was a trying ordeal. In the second year, the widow would continue in her black rigor but the daughters were allowed to wear half-black, half-white garbs, or *medio luto,* until the final stage, a year later, when the mourners could wear all white. The same social measure, however, did not apply to men. The day after the funeral they could attend the cinema.

Despite this double standard, I don't believe female austerity in the observance of the mourning period was arbitrary. It was a genuine expression of a deep sorrow experienced by the families who had been wrenched apart from their beloved through the finality of death. It was a symbol of their unity and the bonds that existed between them, which in the old days were considered to last for life.

So when my brother Maquín completed high school at Colegio Centro América, it was I who had to accompany him to the ceremony when he received his diploma. I remember I had nothing that was elegant enough for the occasion and had to have one of Mother's dresses altered. It was a simple and beautiful dress with draping across the front. Chale, Maquín, and I traveled to Granada in Father's new silver-gray Packard, which he had purchased on his last trip to New York. We stayed in my friend María Jesús's home. When they called Maquín's name I marched protectively down the aisle with him.

After the ceremony there was a party. Chale introduced me to some of his old classmates—Enrique Pereira, Luis Cardenal, Paco Castro, and Pedro Joaquín Chamorro, his pal. There always existed a great camaraderie between Chale and Pedro. Now that Pedro had returned from Mexico and was working at *La Prensa,* they agreed to try to see each other on those occasions when Chale was in Managua searching for provisions.

Perhaps it was my distracted state of mind, but on that night my sixth sense did not alert me to the fact that I was in the presence of the man I would marry. My memories of this first encounter with Pedro Joaquín Chamorro are quite vague. I thought Pedro an attractive, intelligent, and likable young man—but not more so than any of the others I met that evening.

Chapter Three

ONE DAY IN NINETEEN FORTY-EIGHT, ON ONE of his expeditions to the capital, Chale again ran into Pedro Joaquín Chamorro while traveling down Avenida Bolívar. The two friends decided to go together to the local watering hole, Gambrinus. Over a glass of beer, Pedro asked Chale what he was planning to do over the weekend.

My brother innocuously replied that he was going to Amayo that weekend. That is when Pedro made his devious proposal.

"You know, Chale, I don't want to impose," he said, "but since I got back from Mexico, I've had this urge to go hunting. My mother is spending the season at the beach in San Juan del Sur, and I was thinking of paying her a visit."

Chale, always the gracious friend, eagerly extended the invitation Pedro obviously wanted. "Well, Pedro, if you feel in the mood, come by our place and I'll take you to Amayo! But how are you thinking of getting there? Do you have a car?"

"No, I don't. I was planning on taking the Santa Fe Express."

"That'll take you to the old market in Rivas. I'll pick you up if you like."

The following day, back home in Rivas, Chale informed us that a friend of his was coming in from Managua on the Santa Fe and that he was rushing off to the old market square to meet him.

My brother suggested that I join him and his friend on their hunting expedition, a proposal to which I assented; I had not visited the old ranch in several weeks.

After loading the car with the necessary supplies, Chale departed to pick up Pedro, leaving me with explicit instructions: "When I honk, Violeta, you should come out. It's getting late and I want to get to Amayo before sundown."

Mother then ordered me to run into the backyard, where the chickens and hens ran wild, and to grab one of them for our supper. A short while later I heard the honking outside. So I kissed Mother good-bye and ran out like a rustic country girl, carrying the chicken in one arm and a can of Fleet insect repellent in the other.

I must have made quite an amusing sight. Pedro confessed to me years later that when he saw me, dressed in black pants and a plain white shirt, my pigtails flapping to and fro, and clutching that fat hen, the love that was simmering inside of him came to a boil. Apparently, since the day Chale had introduced us at Maquín's graduation, Pedro had been attracted to me. But now those latent and repressed feelings had exploded, causing him to experience all of the telltale symptoms of adolescent lovesickness: a rapid heartbeat, clammy hands, and a nervous agitation that left him fidgeting in his seat.

Unfortunately for Pedro, I did not share in his rapture and climbed into the back of the Packard, heedless of his protestations that I ride in the front by his side.

By car, the trip to Amayo took roughly an hour, giving us ample opportunity to observe the scenery. It was March, and the inclement tropical sun had scorched the grassy fields and produced unbearable droughts that drained the country's lakes, leaving them muddy, murky, and a miserable brown.

When we arrived at Amayo, the ranch manager, Jesús Marchena, came out to greet us. The old gaucho loped over with his boots unlaced, his revolver with the yellow grip dangling from his hip holster, and a long knife pressed tightly against his body. He faced us with his back to the lake, where the sun was setting, a thin line of orange that split the blue expanse of water and sky. I noticed he was wearing the gold-rim eyeglasses of Father's that Mother had given him after Father's death, along with an old pair of Father's trousers.

The sight of Father's clothing on someone else cast a sense of finality over his passing that constricted my heart and evoked memories of a time of unadulterated happiness that would never return. Marchena, sensitive to the somber mood that had fallen upon us, broke the silence by calling our attention to the sunset.

"Look, *patroncitos.*" He gestured to us with a hand missing two fingers. "The pastures are burning. The rabbits will come flying out of their holes—and the armadillos too, because no matter how thick their shells are, they hate fire. It should be a good *cazada* tonight."

Then, eagerly, Chale followed Marchena to the stables to see to the saddling of the horses, while I took Pedro around the porch where the rocking chairs were. The air, I recall, was thick with a dust that stuck like pinole on our skins. So Pedro and I went over to a small white sink attached to the railing on the porch and washed ourselves. Then he turned to me and asked expectantly, "What shall we do?"

In those days, we did not have electricity in Amayo, and although the route to the ranch was lit with kerosene lamps, the rest of the house was pitch dark. So, lighting a candle and filling a lamp, I suggested, "Let's play cards."

As I recall, the game was poker. Using turtle shells as chips, Pedro and I played several hands, never really gambling, of course. Nonetheless, I consistently beat him. In fact, I don't believe I lost to Pedro once.

Now I am by no means a card shark, but by defeating him, I believe, I gained Pedro's respect to a certain extent. Perhaps he thought he had at last found in me a formidable female adversary, a woman who could stare him in the eyes without being awed by his position or mystique. And although the game was as trivial as cards, I think Pedro realized then that he had found a companion who was every bit his equal. Pedro Joaquín Chamorro had met his match.

As special as our moment was, however, it was ever so transient. Just as we finished our twelfth hand, the rest of the hunting party, carrying rifles and lamps, came to take Pedro away for the evening's hunt. As he dropped his cards on the table, he bade me farewell and departed for the evening, leaving me behind to lay fresh white sheets on the cots he and Chale would return to sleep on before sunrise.

The next morning we breakfasted on *gallopinto,* the rice and beans that are typical country food in Nicaragua. Then we bathed in the fresh waters of the lake. When it was time to leave for Rivas, Pedro invited us to go with him to San Juan del Sur to visit his mother. But I refused, considering it inappropriate entertainment for someone who was still under the rigors of mourning. Chale, however, went with him. After they dropped me off, I bade Pedro farewell without ever imagining that the friendship we established in Amayo would lead to anything more. But by the following weekend, Pedro's emotions and intentions were fully evident.

Without any of us knowing, he organized two carloads of young people from the capital to go to Rivas under the pretense that Chale and I were offering to host them in Amayo. We were quite taken aback when he showed up with his friends. But gracefully we agreed to accompany them and took with us our cousin Amalita Torres, Mother's niece and namesake.

From that day, for a whole year, Pedro did not take his eyes off me. He arrived in Rivas every week, accompanied by one of his friends.

They came on a motorcycle or a rattletrap bus and stayed in the hotel in the old market. Invariably, I took notice of Pedro's gallant romancing. Still, I did everything in my power to push him away. In retrospect, I was lucky he was so persistent. Conversely, I am equally sorry that I wasted so much of the time we spent together rejecting his advances.

In a town where people's affairs were made public instantly, rumor soon spread that Violeta was being courted, and a rivalry was unleashed among the possible pretenders to my hand. Many wealthy suitors appeared, including, I might add, another Chamorro, from Granada, who was as insistent as Pedro.

Never one to be swayed by money, I had no interest in any of them, and I grew impatient with the noisome and indiscreet commentary flowing from the lips of our relatives and friends. As I saw it, they had no right to interfere in my life.

Although Pedro's intelligence, his affable nature, and the intensity with which he pursued his goals had made him a popular man in Managua, in Rivas nobody knew who he was. All they could observe was that this was a Chamorro of rather slovenly appearance who did not possess his own method of transportation.

The other Chamorro, however, did meet with their approval. He always arrived impeccably dressed, like a fastidious gentleman scholar, behind the wheel of an elegant car with whitewall tires. He was elegant, indeed, but perhaps too conscious of being so. Father's sister Amalia Barrios would accost Mother: "Amalita, why does Violeta receive this Pedro Joaquín Chamorro when the other is a dream of a man?"

In my personal view, though, both were unwanted suitors. Yet having no experience in these matters, I was confused and distressed, uncertain as to how far to go in discouraging their attentions without offending them.

So every weekend, accompanied by cousin Amalita, I submitted to their visits on the veranda of our home, where we could look out at the plaza. We frequently entertained ourselves by watching the activities transpiring in the heart of Rivas. Sometimes the two Chamorros would meet by chance, and, flattered by the double homage they were paying me, I would sit between them and wickedly refer to them as "my two angels."

Other times I would invite them for a spin around town.

"Who wants to drive?" I would ask, dangling before them the keys to the family Packard. I was, of course, aware both men wished to impress me with their driving prowess. Perhaps an even greater incentive was the fact that the driver would sit in the front seat next to me. Playfully, I would toss the keys up in the air and let Pedro and his distant cousin compete over them. I know that it was wrong, but as I said to myself, If I am going to be courted, I might as well afford myself the opportunity to be occasionally amused.

On Pedro's fifth visit, he declared his love to me. The two of us were sitting on wicker chairs on the veranda, watching the orange-and-pink sunset of Rivas. For a moment, the intensity of his words pleased and stunned me. But then, inexplicably, I hardened toward him, and my response was a categorical rejection that disappointed him deeply.

"Don't waste your time with me, Pedro. Our family is still in mourning. I haven't left this house since Father died. I don't even know Managua all that well. What makes you think I'd want to marry and settle there with you for the rest of my life? Besides, although I am of an age to fall in love, I am not in love with you."

He shook his head as if refusing to understand, and lifted his hand to touch my hair. But in one swift movement I cocked my head back and stood up to put an end to the tender moment that I found myself unprepared to deal with.

As Pedro departed, he remarked in an amused tone, "You're a strange girl, Violeta." And then, lowering his voice to a faint whisper, he said, "But I love you. I'll be back next week as usual. So wait for me."

Looking back, I now understand there was a great deal of coyness in my rejections. Though I was not conscious of it, for a resolute man like

Pedro my rejections acted as an invitation for him to become even more insistent.

So it was that Pedro came to have an intimate knowledge of my comings and goings. My daily jaunts were, of course, quite predictable. I lived in what I would term a social limbo. Up every day with the first crow of the roosters at five. Then to church at six. After mass, the cook and I would make our way to the market with our baskets to purchase our vegetables, then return to the house to dispose of the day's affairs. Later in the day I would spend my leisure time playing the piano in the parlor or practicing my typing.

In Rivas in 1948 there was only one telephone. It was at the local hospital, and all incoming calls quickly became a matter of public knowledge. Imagine my horror when, without fail, every Thursday Pedro would call to inquire if he could come pay me a visit. Each time the messenger from the hospital would knock on our door and announce that a call from Managua was waiting for *"la niña Violeta."*

And off I would have to go to the hospital to receive my call, furious at Pedro for placing me in this embarrassing situation. In turn, I would receive a flood of inquiries from curious relatives. "Are you sweethearts yet?" my aunts would ask, prompting me to respond with a furious "No!"

I suppose that behind my denial I hid a fear of making myself vulnerable and exposing myself to a torrent of emotions that I could not control. I was even more concerned, however, with the feelings that might flow out unedited by my conventional sense of propriety. So I would completely repudiate Pedro. "Don't come!" I would instruct. "I am not interested in you."

My words, however, seemed to mean nothing to him. Come Saturday, there he'd be, waiting on our doorstep. On Sundays, uncertain as to what mass I would attend, he would spend the entire day sitting on a bench in the *parroquia* waiting for me to appear.

With each passing day, my displeasure with Pedro's advances grew into exasperation. I felt completely crowded by his ever-present love, which in light of my desire to remain single and in the service of my family seemed more like a menace to our stability than a joy. But Pedro would persist in his siege, writing countless love letters—"Do you love me, Violeta? Because I love you. I follow your every step. I know sometimes you come with Chale to Managua and don't call me. Don't you care about me? Violeta, I am serious about my desire to form a home with you and have children."

"Don't waste your time with me, Pedro," I would write back. "I have no intention of committing myself to anyone, least of all to a boy from Managua. Besides, in the capital there are girls who are much prettier than me."

In his responses there was sometimes anger and pain, and for a fleeting second I would doubt whether I really wanted him to go away for good. But I said nothing to change my original stance.

According to the protocol for romantic engagements, confronted with such categorical rejections he should not return. At least for a time.

So the day came when Pedro did not visit me, and the phone calls and letters stopped. Alone again, cloistered within the privacy of my single life, I began to miss him. Afterward, when I awakened to the magnitude of what I felt for Pedro and realized how much I longed for him, I knew I had entangled myself in my own net. Somehow, without realizing it, he had stopped being the hopelessly obsessed suitor and had become the husband I was bound to marry. At night, in the cool darkness of my room, I would lie awake and think of Pedro. I repented for the sorrow I had inflicted on him, and I feared that I had finally succeeded in pushing him away.

Luckily, Pedro took it upon himself to end the moratorium. Some weeks after we had separated, I got notice from Mother that Doña Margarita, a friend of hers, had called to ask if she and a group of young women could come and stay with us during a society ball at the casino in Rivas. Though we were still in mourning and could not participate in the event, Mother consented and instructed me to attend to the preparation of the rooms for our guests: "Violeta, see to it that beds are made up for our friends and that food is prepared to welcome them."

All this I attended to with due haste and in good humor. But when I was told that accompanying one of the girls to the ball was a young man named Pedro Joaquín Chamorro, my jealousy knew no bounds.

My silent pain, however, was dissipated when it became clear to me that Pedro, in escorting the girl, had merely seized upon an opportunity to see me. That evening, when the boys arrived, outfitted in dark suits to escort the girls to the party, Pedro and I greeted each other with restrained courtesy, but soon it became obvious to me that Pedro did not want to leave my side. He kept suggesting excuses to linger a little longer and finally came right out and said, "Either you come with us or I stay with you."

It was something that was totally out of the question. And I reasoned with him, "Pedro, you have come here to escort this girl. There is no way you can stay behind without offending her, and I simply cannot go. Do your duty. Go to your party and we will talk later."

My conversation with Pedro was interrupted by Doña Margarita, who was talking to Mother. "Oh, Amalia, I have come here to chaperone these girls, but I am having such a good time chatting with you that I don't want to leave right now."

I quickly responded, "Don't worry, Doña Margarita. You can stay with Mother all you want. Maquín and I will drive you over to the casino anytime."

No more words passed between Pedro and me, though I was aware that he remained alert to everything that was being said. Then they all left for the party. But Pedro, I later learned, did not have a moment's peace. He spent the entire night listening for sounds in the driveway of the casino, certain that I would arrive any minute.

The casino was a beautiful structure in the middle of a huge lawn, with ample porches all around it. Inside there were several large rooms. When we arrived, the band was playing "Blue Moon," but Pedro wasn't dancing. He was standing on the porch, waiting. After Doña Margarita alighted with Maquín, he jumped over the low wall that surrounded the casino and came flying into the front seat of my car.

"Here I am at your disposal. Let's go so you can tell me once and for all. Do you or do you not care for me?"

"No, not now," I said. "You have a date and have to go back in there. Besides, here comes Maquín, and I have to leave with him right now."

"So, promise me you'll see me tomorrow."

"Yes, tomorrow will be fine."

"Tomorrow when?" he insisted.

"I don't know yet. We'll see."

With that, he demanded no more of me and returned to the casino. Driving home with Maquín, I kept thinking of the contradictions in my attitude. Before, I had chased Pedro away. Now, suddenly, I wanted very much to be with him. Several hours later, in Mother's room, I was still awake thinking about Pedro when I heard the girls returning from the party. They were all aghast by what they said was the rude behavior of Pedro Joaquín Chamorro!

". . . and how he ignored poor so-and-so . . . when it was he who had asked her out. To lead her on like that when he knew full well she had a crush on him!"

"Yes, this whole trip has been a disaster," another voice interjected. "Why don't we all pack up and leave right now?"

I dreaded to find out what Pedro could possibly have done to prompt such drastic action from these girls. But on the other hand, I was flattered because I knew that whatever Pedro had done, he had done for me.

The next morning I was at eight o'clock mass when Pedro pushed his way through the aisle until he was by my side. "Do you want me to get on my knees to beg you to accept me?" he asked. When I didn't answer, he carved a heart on the pew in front of us with his key and asked again, "Do you or don't you love me?"

Still, I refused to answer him while the mass was in progress. After the service, in front of the church, Pedro and I talked to my aunts. Periodically, he would tug on the sleeve of my blouse, saying, "I want to speak with you alone."

I invited him to accompany me to the house. There on the veranda, where he had courted me so many times, I waited eagerly to speak to the man whom I had once repudiated. But Chale, my brother, was always around, and we never had a moment's privacy. The mass had let out at nine, and it was nearly ten when Chale informed us that he needed to go to Amayo to tend to business there. Pedro and I decided to accompany him instead of remaining in Rivas.

Amayo proved to be a most idyllic setting. As we stood on the beach of the Great Lake Nicaragua where I had swum and played with my brothers under the shadow of the twin volcanoes, Pedro Joaquín proposed marriage to me.

His first request was to ask if he could continue to visit me in Rivas. "I want to keep coming to see you," he said very respectfully, "so we can get to know each other better." Each of his entreaties I would answer with a nod of my head. Timidly he would go on.

"I want to talk to your mother and your brother Chale."

"For what?"

"So that they know I am seriously thinking of marrying you and to get their permission."

I was amused by his courtly respect for my family. I didn't imagine him to be capable of such traditional behavior. I respected my brother very much. Since Father's death he had become the titular head of the household, and though I planned to inform Chale and Mother of Pedro's declaration, I saw this merely as a formality and not a matter that required their blessing. To see a vibrant and eloquent man like Pedro, who had a free way about him, reduced to speaking in timid, halting phrases was so endearing I wanted to prolong his misery a little bit longer. So I teasingly remarked, "And who wants to get married, Pedro?"

"Well, me, of course, and you, I hope, as well."

"Then ask me outright, Pedro. Why are you suddenly afraid?"

"Violeta, do you want to be my wife?"

I don't remember if I accepted him with a resounding "Yes!" or if it was a simple movement of my head. But I do recall that we kissed. With this began a relationship in which we would share a life for twenty-seven years and be apart for however long God decides. But I can assure you of this: I will never marry again. I don't think a beautiful love like ours can ever be repeated.

We were engaged on March 19, 1949, and married twenty-one months later on the twelfth anniversary of my First Communion, December 8, 1950, the feast of the Immaculate Conception, which I believe brought many blessings to our union. I remember Pedro arrived for our engagement dressed in white linen, and he who had said he did not believe in rings brought me a small one, which I still keep.

Why, between the two Chamorros, did I finally accept Pedro? Perhaps, in the end, I was impressed by his constancy and his passion, because Pedro was also a man of great tenderness and exceptional gallantry. Once, when I was staying with Mother at my *tía* María's house in San José, Costa Rica, long before I had accepted him, he sent me a bouquet of red roses. I have no idea how he knew where I was. But he had a vast and intricate network of friends who served as his espionage system and allowed him to keep a close watch on my every step. He not only learned the address where I was staying but had a complete itinerary of my trip. Upon my return, he was waiting for me at the airport.

"I am your welcoming committee," he said with a triumphant smile.

Pedro also possessed unusual charisma. He was an interesting storyteller, and I suppose, too, that deep in my heart I admired that. After a four-hour trip from Managua, he would arrive at his hotel, wash, dress, and without stopping to eat, appear at my home for however long I wished to have him. Because I hadn't accepted him formally, I thought it far too intimate an act to invite him to eat with the family. So I never gave him more than a glass of juice on the veranda. I still don't know how he managed to subsist without eating for long hours during those weekends in Rivas.

The rules were so strict then. Everything had to be done according to protocol because evil-minded neighbors were quick to misinterpret a situation. But sometimes traditions bordered on the ridiculous. For example, if the admirer asked for a photo, one was obliged to deny it until a formal declaration of sentiments had been made and a commitment was agreed upon. To present the photo gave a delicate signal that an understanding had been reached, just as a return of the photo symbolized the unequivocal rupture of the relationship.

Courtship is no longer pursued so strictly. Boys don't take the time to declare their feelings romantically to a girl, nor do they desire to adopt the formality of agreeing to visit with each other for a while. Even less so do they have the patience to embark on a long engagement period. But when I recall the innocent encounters between Pedro and myself, I am still moved with emotion.

I remember that soon after I had accepted Pedro we were strolling on the beach and Pedro had brought along his camera. "At last I will have a photo of you," he announced gaily as he trained his camera lens on me. It seems silly now, but for a long time I was at a loss how to respond properly to Pedro's many advances, obsessed as I was with repressing any unsuitable emotion until we had received the holy blessing.

So whenever he asked, "Did you miss me?" I simply nodded, without confessing that I too felt love gnawing like a hungry animal. But I do recall that in December, a week before we married, as proof of the sweet affection I felt for him I sent Pedro a box of chocolates with the picture he took of me on the beach that day concealed at the bottom, because all men can benefit from a little sweetening.

Father's absence detracted from the joy of my wedding. Just as at my First Communion (which was so soon after Ricardo's death), all of us were too deeply involved in our pain to be in the right celebratory mood. But Chale and Mother stoically insisted on seeing me off by having a party with all the trimmings. I recall telling them that Pedro and I preferred to have the money rather than an expensive party catered all the way from the capital.

My family was insistent, however. The food was prepared by a lady who is still alive today and is the owner of an excellent bakery, Doña María Alaníz. The cake itself was baked by Doña Carlotita Argüello de Pasos, who was my mother-in-law's neighbor on Calle El Triunfo, a neighborhood that was reduced to dust by the earthquake of 1976.

In those days the Panamericana highway had been inaugurated, but it was only gravel. On this bumpy road came the truck from Managua with all the rented tables and chairs, wineglasses, and plates. Even the waiters came on that truck. The cake was supposed to come on that journey as well. But as luck would have it, they forgot to pick it up from Doña Carlotita's. Realizing what had happened, Doña Carlotita, being an astute woman, promptly dispatched it with two maids in a taxi.

In most village weddings, the trip to the church is a long procession on foot. A child dressed as an angel walks ahead, carrying a paper Star of David covered in tinfoil. Then the bridesmaid, flower girls, and bride follow with the large entourage of guests behind them. I, however, did not want any of that fanfare and intended simply to walk across the street on Chale's arm. But the mayor of Rivas, Don Paco Gallegos, who was a relative of ours, wouldn't have it. He ordered the dirt roads of the city covered in sand especially for my wedding, and I couldn't simply disregard his kind gesture without offending him. So I agreed to follow custom and marched down the street, my brother Chale by my side, Raúl in angel wings carrying a Star of David ahead of us, and my only sister, Clarisa, as my bridesmaid.

Chale bought my wedding dress, underthings, and shoes on a chance trip to Dallas, Texas. The dress was made of white satin, cut in a very simple line that was much to my liking and fit me perfectly. All through the procession Mother, veiled and dressed from head to toe in black garb, cried disconsolately, "Oh! how Chale would have loved seeing her." For me the day was charged with as much joy as pain. I was caught between two opposite poles of emotion, which in my life strangely complement each other.

In those days it was tradition that the groom's family decorate the church. So Pedro's mother, Doña Margarita, had huge arrangements of white lilies placed at the altar and a bolt of white cloth rolled down the aisle to the church steps.

Everything looked pristine and beautiful, but without affectation of any sort. The only complication was that I had never worn sandals before that day, and during the procession the sand on the streets had worked itself between my toes, making me exceedingly uncomfortable.

Waiting for me at the main altar was Pedro, dressed in a black tuxedo that gave him an air of elderly sagacity. Next to him stood his father and the priest who had come from Managua to officiate at the ceremony. It was not the custom to celebrate a wedding with a mass. But we had told Padre Federico that during the ceremony we wanted to receive Communion. By then I had reached a point of total certainty where my love for Pedro was concerned. I wished to seal my marriage eternally with the most sacred of Catholic rites, receiving the Body of Christ. The experience was further enhanced by the voice of a soprano who had been commissioned by Doña Margarita to sing the *Ave Maria* during the consecration and as we received the Eucharist.

By the time we had arrived at our home, the cake was there, though in its broken state it was a comical sight. However, no one other than I really seemed to notice. Everyone commented on the excellence of the wedding reception, which was attended by people from all parts of Nicaragua—Granada, Diriamba, Managua, and even León. In a sense my wedding was something of a historic event. You could say it was the "first reconciliation," because there at the same table sat Granadinos and Leoneses, the two opposing sides in the civil wars that had bloodied the country ever since independence. Their wounds healed and their anger dissipated, they were able to toast Pedro's and my own happiness without coming to blows with each other.

Long before the ceremony, Pedro and I had been discussing our honeymoon plans. He would offer me trips to all parts of the world—the United States, Europe, Asia, and so forth—but I always knew that we would go no farther than the Hotel Magestre in Diriamba. Mother lent us the Packard for the trip, which lasted roughly two weeks. We honeymooned by making stops along the way to our final destination, the home of Pedro's parents on Calle El Triunfo in Managua, where we would live.

We left on the afternoon of the wedding, after sharing a tearful good-bye with Mother, Chale, Maquín, Clarisa, and little Raúl. From home we headed north, traversing the cattle lands of Rivas, across the mighty Río Ochomogo, which irrigates the agricultural plains of Nandaime, until we finally reached Diriamba. There, Pedro and I spent our first night together. Though I had come to my wedding with no experience in love, I was not a prude. I knew from watching the stallions chase the mares what was to come. I needed no explanations. Pedro was a man of strong impulses and I gave myself without fear.

The following day we vacationed in Casa Colorada, the coffee-growing region in the *sierritas* of Managua. We stayed at the home of one of Pedro's uncles, Don Carlos Cardenal, called Las Tejitas. One of Mother's maids was sent out ahead of us to cook and clean for us. We were there for seven days. Then we left with another pair of newlyweds, Enrique Pereira and Daisy Solórzano, for the beaches of Pochomíl. Don Pedro Joaquín and Doña Margarita, as I recall, came to visit us there. Afterward we all left for Managua. Unfortunately, I did not return to my home in Rivas until our second child, Claudia Lucía, was about to be born.

And so, that is how I became part of the intense and polished Chamorro clan, where twenty people would sit down to a meal and the women never served the food. There was among them an air of imperial haughtiness and an obsession with politics that consumed the family to its last breath. All this contrasted markedly with my joyful effusiveness and the simple, unpremeditated way in which I had led my life.

It was then that I ceased to be Violeta Barrios—or, more formally, Violeta Barrios Torres Sacasa Hurtado—and became Violeta de Chamorro.

At the time I did not realize the significance of this change, but it would later become apparent. It was like emerging from a cocoon to live in a very different world, a world with infinitely more obligations—not just where my husband or my children were concerned, but also for what I came to feel was my larger family, all Nicaraguans.

Chapter Four

THE DAY I DECIDED TO ACCEPT PEDRO I WAS motivated by only one emotion: love. Nothing else mattered. I harbored great dreams for the new life we would begin, the home we would make for ourselves, the children we would have. I never suspected what would come afterward—our lack of financial independence, the difficulties that would arise from living with the Chamorro Cardenal family for what seemed an interminable seven months. For Pedro there would be years of imprisonment and torture. In the twenty-seven years we were married, he served four years in prison and one under house arrest. It was only through the strength of my invincible love for him that I was able to overcome these obstacles to happiness.

It was also very difficult to leave the city where I had been born and the splendor and freedom of my country life, things that were so strongly rooted in me that for years I felt a great homesickness. With great nostalgia I would recall the palm trees in the park; morning service in the *parroquia* across the street; and traveling by train or car from Rivas to Managua at the end of each school year, passing the Mombacho on the way, watching the undulating cow pastures that stretched for endless miles and the many shades of green and the textures of the landscape and the volcanic soil ripe with crops of rice, beans, sugarcane, and watermelons.

All of this simple and honest beauty I gave up to be with Pedro, a man I did not fully understand until I married him. He spent his life next door at the offices of *La Prensa,* glued to a chair and his typewriter, writing opinion pieces for the editorial page of the newspaper, trying to bring about the unity of all Nicaraguans and, ultimately, liberty for all of us. Preoccupied as he was with addressing larger issues, he was oblivious to day-to-day responsibilities and had no vocation for administering the family's finances. There were times when I would suggest that he manage Grandfather Barrios's hacienda, Santa Clara, which I had inherited from Father. "I don't have time" was his invariable answer. Through the 1950s Pedro engaged in his anti-Somoza campaign. He freely intermingled his political activities with our family life. I soon realized that my husband possessed an unusual amount of civic ardor. His training and talents could have allowed him to become a lawyer, an entrepreneur, or a university professor. But he was not interested in these positions. I could not blame him, however, because I was not very interested in wealth or prestige either. Money was never for me more than a means to an end, and with Pedro it became an instrument for crafting greater things! What Pedro wanted was a chance to change things. So the role that attracted him was that of writer and apostle, waging a war against injustice from the trenches of his newspaper. Impatient, fervent, and obstinate, Pedro discovered in journalism his life's calling. But he was not a man to wait half a century to achieve his goals. The day would come when, finding all other paths of action blocked, he would embark on the road to rebellion.

Someone, however, had to run the household, take care of the children, and plan day-to-day affairs, and that role fell to me. Once a month Pedro would entrust to me his wages. Carefully I would calculate our expenses and divide the money into wads of tightly rolled bills, which I administered with rigor. He never questioned a penny I spent, but at the end of each month I would present to him a detailed accounting of our finances in a notebook that I kept. The method was old-fashioned, but it did help me manage our cash judiciously so that we did not disgrace ourselves by having to live on borrowed money.

Accustomed to the austerity of my family, I was able to adapt to a life of frugality. Prudence in the administration of money is a trait that has served me well throughout my life, not only in my role as a spouse and homemaker but also now, when so many depend on me to administer the resources of our country. Government, of course, is not a family, but some of the principles I learned as a child and practiced as an adolescent turned out to be very useful in my adulthood. Order and reasonable planning of one's expenses is one of those principles that serve me well as a leader of state.

Living with my in-laws became a heroic battle. Without indulging in unnecessary negativity, let me just say that Pedro and I had a few problems from the beginning of our marriage because we lived surrounded by people with strong opinions, and not as other couples do, just by ourselves. Naturally I felt crowded and deprived of the right to make my own decisions. But I was not one to let anyone take advantage of me. When I was six months pregnant with our first child, I made it clear to Pedro that I had an imperative need to be the mistress of my own household, no matter how modest. With great care not to insult Pedro's sense of honor, I spoke to him frankly on the subject. I said: "This situation cannot go on. Living with your parents is like living in boarding school, where everything is regimented. We have to have our own home. Please understand, Pedro, you must come with me or I will have to leave without you. I know that with the twelve hundred cordobas a month you earn as managing editor at *La Prensa* we don't have enough money to rent a place of our own, so I would like your permission to speak to Mother about advancing to me part of my inheritance."

To my surprise a conjugal battle did not ensue. Pedro consented to Mother's deeding me a rental house she owned near the *parroquia* of Santo Domingo and the San Miguel market in Managua. With that additional income, we rented a modest home on Candelaria Street, in an old neighborhood where the houses had been built at the turn of the century. This house had checkerboard floors and eighteen-foot ceilings throughout. After we moved in I hung colorful hammocks from the posts in the patios and adorned the corridors with ferns, anthuriums, and birds-of-paradise planted in flowerpots.

The son we had both longed for was born at Managua's General Hospital at 7:30 A.M. on September 24, 1951, eleven hours before his father's twenty-seventh birthday. Don Pedro and Doña Margarita were there. The birth was attended by the Chamorro Cardenal family's chosen obstetrician, Dr. Jacinto Alfaro, and not, as I would have wanted, by Dr. Fernando Vélez Paiz—who had attended to me since I was eleven and in whom I had complete trust.

I was knocked out by the pain and difficulty of the delivery. The postnatal care I received was unsatisfactory, and it took me such a long time to recover from the ravages of childbirth that I was unable to breast-feed. But afterward I emerged with a greater resolve to trust my own instincts. All my other children were brought into the world by the doctor of my choice.

We named the baby Quinto (which means "fifth") Pedro Joaquín de la Merced. He was the fifth Pedro Joaquín Chamorro. We christened him so not because of my husband, who rejected the notion of perpetuating himself through his child, but on account of my father in-law, who asked me to do so. Though I knew it contradicted Pedro's desire to allow our son to have his own identity, I felt I could not refuse the man who had been a friend when I was a lonely, homesick bride in his home.

Soon afterward, in 1952, Pedro's father died. Doña Margarita, Pedro, and his brothers and sisters received equal shares in the newspaper and formed a board of directors. They made all the appointments and policy decisions relating to *La Prensa*. Pedro, who was the oldest and knew the business best, became president of the board in addition to being the managing editor. Pablo Antonio Cuadra, Pedro's cousin, became editorial page manager. At the time the newspaper was a six-page daily, but Pedro swore to make it the best newspaper in the nation. I still have bits and pieces of the letter in which he wrote down his promise. To that end the family erected a new building and bought modern equipment. But this did not mean that Pedro was ready to settle down and become comfortably established in the newspaper business. What he intended was to use the paper to redeem Nicaragua. And so he always maintained an aggressive stance in and outside the newspaper against the Somozas, the oppressors of Nicaragua.

When Pedro Joaquín Jr. was fourteen months old, I learned I was pregnant with our second child. At this time Pedro's attacks against the Somozas and his increasing involvement in civic causes made *La Prensa* the target of political persecution. The Somozas were ordering frequent shutdowns of the paper, which were putting the source of our financial well-being at risk. To cut down on our expenses by saving on rent, I decided to move into the house Mother had given me in Santo Domingo.

Then one day I approached my brothers with an offer to sell them half of Santa Clara. My decision to part with this property took them by surprise. They, of course, wanted to know my reason. I told them quite sincerely that Pedro and I couldn't administer it, so the place was neglected. Selling it would give us the means to be financially independent. To sweeten the proposal I offered to sell it to them on credit and without interest. Everything was agreed upon verbally, without papers or lawyers—the practice of the time. The other half of the farm we kept. We always visited it during Holy Week. Before every vacation, the farmhands would set up a ring where Pedro could engage the young bulls in Santa Clara, much as he had seen done by toreadors as a student in Mexico. On occasion, he would don the complete toreador costume, but most often he went into his makeshift bullring, swirling his cape, simply clad in jeans.

It was on a Friday morning in March 1953, just before Holy Week, when Pedro announced he was going away to Costa Rica with my brother Chale, "to push away the cobwebs," he said, and attend a soccer game as well. This desire to get away was uncharacteristic of my husband. Men like Pedro, with a heightened sense of mission in their lives, never allow themselves the luxury of rest. They feel guilty succumbing to idleness. His father had died three months before, however, and Pedro was under a lot of pressure. So I encouraged him to go, in spite of the numerous physical ailments I suffered as a result of my expectant state and my fears that the baby I was carrying might arrive prematurely.

After Pedro left, so as not to be alone, I decided to spend time with Mother in Rivas. On the same day I arrived, at about eleven o'clock at night, I began to feel unusually strong abdominal cramps. I decided to say nothing to Mother because I did not want to worry her. In those days in Rivas it was the custom for the girls of nice families to have their children at home. To arrange this, Mother would have had to have some prior warning. So instead I resolved to arrange things with the help of Maquín; Raúl was too young, Chale was in Costa Rica with Pedro, and Clarisa was away in boarding school in Managua. I asked Maquín to go fetch the local obstetrician, Dr. Rafael Urtecho. I don't remember why, but Maquín chose to go on foot. An hour passed before he returned with the doctor in tow, after locating him not at home but at the cinema.

By then the labor pains were so strong it was impossible to conceal what was happening from Mother. "Don't worry, Mama, it's just the baby coming a little bit early," I said.

"Oh, Violeta, Pedro is not here."

"It will be okay, Mama. I'll handle everything."

Immediately I called Amalia Carazo, the administrator of Hospital San José, and asked her to prepare a room for me. "The hospital is fully booked," she said. But the child would not wait, so a bed was improvised for me right on the hospital administrator's desk. On Saturday, March 7, 1953, at 1 A.M., among the filing cabinets, typewriters, and wastebaskets, our child was born. She was a tiny baby girl, in apparent good health, though weighing no more than five pounds. We dressed her in clothes borrowed from Chale's baby because the wardrobe I had bought for her at the embroidery shop of Doña Lola Vigil was still being laundered.

After the delivery, I suggested to Mother that we send Pedro a very brief telegram, informative but not alarming, saying: "A girl was born. Violeta fine." We never stopped to consider that Pedro was a journalist trained to pick up on subtle differences. Later we would find out that when Pedro received the wire, he immediately became alarmed because Mother and I had neglected to write at the end of the telegram the usual Barrios sign-off, "Many hugs and kisses."

Pedro concluded from the telegram that I was ill, because of the unemotional character of the message. So he immediately arranged to return to Nicaragua. But in those days flights from San José to Managua were not frequent. When Pedro arrived in Rivas, I was feeling fine. But for the baby the situation had turned critical. She was strangely inanimate; she did not cry; she barely sucked; it was impossible for her to feed directly from my breast, so she had to be fed with a dropper. In three days she had lost two pounds and as a result was having difficulty maintaining her body temperature. At the time hospitals in Rivas didn't have incubators. So Mother and I resorted to wrapping the infant tightly in blankets. But as soon as we uncovered her, she would turn purple. This is the condition in which Pedro found our child.

Sensing my desperation at the deteriorating situation, Dr. Urtecho advised that we send to Managua immediately for a pediatrician. So Pedro departed quickly for the capital to bring to us Dr. Carlos Báez Díaz. Fearful that life was flowing from her, I summoned a priest to baptize our still unnamed child. During the ceremony, which required that we unbutton her dress so the priest could touch her with holy oil, Mother and I kept her warm with the heat of a candle and provided the priest with holy water warmed in a spoon so he could pour it over her head. We named her Claudia Lucía Cayetana.

Shortly after the baptism had concluded, Pedro returned with the pediatrician, Dr. Báez. Like Pedro, he appeared to be in an agitated state.

He examined the baby thoroughly and looked into her mouth, then asked for a pair of scissors and a candle. Using the candle flame to sterilize the scissors, he opened little Claudia's mouth and snipped her tongue free from the overgrown tendon that was restricting its movement. Only then could the poor child, at last, begin to suckle.

After Claudia's birth, Dr. Urtecho advised that I stay in Rivas for a month and a half. Pedro would spend weekdays in the city and arrive on weekends to see us. The result of those ardent reunions was that I became pregnant with our third child.

The prospect of a new addition to the family forced us to move again, this time to the hilly *sierritas* of Casa Colorada, south of Managua, to a Cardenal property, the same house where Pedro and I had honeymooned three years before. A baby girl was born eight months later, on February 5, 1954. We baptized her Cristiana. Unlike the others, this delivery presented no complications. But the baby had what some doctors called an inverted cycle; she slept all day and cried all night.

One night a couple of months later, Pedro arrived home late for dinner. He had a sheepish look on his face and carried in his arms what appeared to be a month's supply of bread. Half suspecting the answer, I jokingly asked, "What kind of hunger must you have, Pedro, that it requires such a meal?"

"It's for the boys," he answered cryptically. "They're preparing an action." In those days that only meant one thing, insurrection. It became known as the April Rebellion, Pedro's first coup attempt against Somoza García. The "boys" were a handful of *guerrilleros* who, like Pedro, had been against Somoza for years. They were joined by a group of ex-military officials, among them Arturo Cruz (a future Sandinista junta member) and his brother-in-law Adolfo Báez Bone, a man who had once been Somoza's personal aide. The weapons came through Costa Rica with a wink and a nod from Don José "Pepe" Figueres, the president of Costa Rica. In previous years, Don Pepe had deposed from the presidency Don Teodoro Picado, Somoza García's good friend, who some people argued had been elected fraudulently. It was with these rebels that Pedro and Emiliano Chamorro had been collaborating. The plan was to ambush Somoza García as he traveled to his sugar plantation by the sea, Montelimar. The insurrection failed because at the last minute Somoza García decided instead to go to the airport to receive a pair of racehorses sent to him as a gift from the Argentinean president, Juan

Domingo Perón. The coconspirators disbanded in a panic, mistakenly thinking the change in route had occurred because they had been betrayed. One of the *guerrilleros* turned himself in; with the information gleaned from his confession, Somoza García, assisted by his son Anastasio, supervised a crackdown. The members of the National Guard, including Báez Bone, who had participated in the conspiracy were hunted down in the countryside and executed, as there was no one to bear witness to the crime. Arturo Cruz, Emiliano, and Pedro were all taken prisoner in the city—in plain view—and so they were jailed.

The day they arrested Pedro we were spending a leisurely Sunday evening in Las Tejitas. We had spent the day with friends, engaged in a game of cards, when we heard the thunder of artillery. Before we could speculate what the target might be, the lights went out and we were immediately surrounded by soldiers of the National Guard. They took Pedro away in his late-model Oldsmobile.

My friends stayed behind with the children, while I, armed with a flashlight, ran toward the road to find a ride into the city. Hours later, I located Pedro in a dark prison cell. He was being tortured, beaten, and questioned without the benefit of legal representation. It was not until three weeks later that we were told the charges against Pedro and the court before which he would be appearing. He was forced to appear before a military tribunal. Accused of being part of a communist plot against the regime of Somoza García, Pedro was sentenced to three years in prison. We never knew what happened to the Oldsmobile. I suppose a lieutenant or captain claimed it as part of his booty.

Pedro's incarceration forced me to return to live under the auspices of my mother-in-law. This time, however, I was accompanied by three children, two of them still in diapers. The support I received from Doña Margarita allowed me to care for Pedro while he was in prison, providing him with daily rations of food and clean clothes. In time I came to have firsthand knowledge of every prison in Managua, where I formed friendships with the wardens, who allowed me to smuggle into Pedro's cell tomato juice, whiskey, and beer—all his little *antojos*—or cravings—because when men are idle they behave like an expectant mother.

After serving two years, Pedro was released in my custody and allowed to return to his mother's home to be with his family and serve one more year under house arrest. Once again, the ardor and passion that overwhelmed us after our separation resulted in another pregnancy. Three months before Pedro was to complete his sentence, another son was born, on March 1, 1956. He was not a pretty sight and had inexplicably dark skin. His excrement left traces of blood on his diapers. Our family doctor concluded the small infant was bleeding to death and advised a quick baptism. In those days, because of Pedro's sentence, we were all subject to the capricious will and macabre moods of our supreme dictator. To attend the church ceremony, Pedro had to obtain a presidential dispensation from Somoza García to leave our house and go to the church a few blocks down the street.

We named the baby Carlos Fernando Fruto Eugenio. "Carlos Fernando" was the Christian name I wanted to give him. "Fruto" was chosen by Pedro in honor of the relative he admired, who died without a son to carry on his name. Father Estanislao tagged on the name "Eugenio" in honor of Pope Pius XII, Eugenio Pacelli, on whose birthday Carlos Fernando was born. At first I opposed such a long name, but it was the only way of accommodating everyone's wishes.

Immediately following our mournful celebration of the sacrament, the pediatrician arrived and inquired whether Pedro and I had been tested for Rh-negative blood incompatibility. We had never heard of such a procedure, but eager to do whatever was necessary, we submitted to the tests. The doctor's suspicions were confirmed. Apparently my blood cells contained antibodies to those of my child. During gestation our blood had become intermingled and my antibodies were now killing Carlos Fernando. Immediately an emergency transfusion was performed on the child.

I will never forget the spectacle. First they pumped Carlos Fernando with new blood and then they hung him upside down, suspended from his ankles like a chicken. When Pedro returned for his next visit, the baby was showing great signs of improvement, though his skin was still an orange color and his gums were a sickly green. Eventually Carlos Fernando recovered.

Pedro completed his sentence on the anniversary of U.S. independence, July 4, 1956. On this day he was given back his liberty, and our life resumed its normal pattern. That meant the resumption of Pedro's political activities. By then his opposition to Somoza had become, as in the teachings of St. Augustine that Pedro was fond of reading, a "moral imperative" he could not ignore.

⩥ ⩥

I tried to divert his attention to other, more joyful issues than his siege against the Somozas, telling him that it was time for us to concentrate on building a home for our children. I reminded him of the small lot his mother had given us on 27 de Mayo Street. However, because it could not accommodate our growing needs, I suggested to Pedro we sell the property and shop elsewhere for land on which to build. He reacted in his usual absentminded way. And even though it was more an act of omission than an affirmative decision, I got his approval.

Shortly thereafter, I found a lot in a new development called Las Palmas. In those days it was not a barrio as it is today, but a cotton field full of snakes, on the outer edges of Managua. I tried to take Pedro to see it, but his thoughts were on rotary printing presses and barrels of ink. Pedro was preoccupied with *La Prensa,* and so he said, "Do whatever amuses you, Violeta." This I interpreted as carte blanche for me to proceed.

I decided, then, to track down the owner of the Las Palmas lot and propose that we swap my smaller but more valuable parcel in the center of the city for his land. The deal was a good one for both us, and with Pedro's tacit cooperation a deed was signed. But it would be several years before we would build our home, because not three months after Pedro was released, Somoza García was killed and Pedro was imprisoned again.

At midnight on September 21, 1956, as we were returning home from a party, a troop of guardsmen armed with machine guns jumped from the shadows and surrounded our car. They said, "Don't move. You are under arrest."

In the penumbra, I could make out the features of the officer in charge of the squad car and to him I directed my question:

"What is all this about?"

"He is under arrest. Don't move, and stay in the car."

I turned to Pedro and told him: "I know you are innocent. I will contact a lawyer for your defense." With those words I opened the car door and ran toward the entrance of our house. The guardsmen did not make a move to stop me. Instead, a handful of troopers climbed into the car and drove Pedro away. I remained at the door in a confused state. Not knowing what else to do, I returned to the party to tell everyone what had happened and to ask if anyone knew what was going on. All over the city, I had noticed, troops were being deployed.

They told me: "Somoza García has been shot in León." He had

announced his intention to seek a fourth presidential term. But after nineteen years of Somoza García in office and twelve coup attempts, thinking of ways to get rid of him was the national pastime. Someone had now come forward ready to trade his life for Somoza's.

I felt no sympathy for the slain Somoza García, because he had killed and betrayed many. But the heirs to his power did not see things this way. Within twenty-four hours Pedro, Emiliano Chamorro, and future Sandinista leaders like Carlos Fonseca Amador and Tomás Borge were rounded up along with other Somoza foes and imprisoned by order of Somoza's son Anastasio, the head of the armed forces. Luis, the elder of the two brothers, assumed the presidency of Nicaragua just as a royal heir ascends the throne.

For me, the ensuing events were torture. First they took Pedro to the cells in El Hormiguero, the notorious police headquarters that stood like a fort in the middle of the city. There he was stripped of all his personal belongings—his clothing, his watch, his cigarettes, his lighter, his money clip—and, most important, his civil rights. Then he was taken to the hill of Tiscapa to the basement jails in the presidential palace, as cold and dank as the Roman catacombs. The first interrogation always took place in the little sewing room under the palace atrium, so named, I am told, because at some point it was the place where the "queen of the land," my relative Doña Salvadora Debayle de Somoza, had her clothes hand sewn. At the beginning, the palace minions would express a mellifluous courtesy toward Pedro. When they were unable to break him, they would beat him, naked, for days and threaten to feed him to the lions they kept in the palace zoo. But no amount of abuse could make Pedro confess what he didn't know and hadn't done. There was no conspiracy. Somoza had been killed by a lone assailant, Rigoberto López Pérez, and Anastasio and Luis refused to see it. The accusations were just an excuse to try to eliminate their opponents. To his last day Anastasio believed Pedro had been part of a communist plot to kill his father and insisted he was generous for having given Pedro his life.

Six months later, they took Pedro to be tried at the Campo de Marte by a military tribunal operating under martial law because the Somoza brothers had declared a state of siege. Confronted with his uniformed captors, Pedro used the strength he had left in his lungs to scream out for the last time, "I am not guilty, and I hold it before this court of mortals and before the eyes of God." But it made no difference at all.

He was condemned to solitary confinement for four years in the cells of the Aviación prison, where it was said Somoza García had had Sandino summarily executed twenty-two years before. I visited him daily to bring him food and clothing, which was slipped into his cell by a friendly guard. In jail, Pedro occupied his time painting watercolors and writing a journal on bits of paper concealed in a thousand places until I could smuggle them out and transcribe them faithfully for him. His chronicles were of a man deprived of liberty, arbitrarily tried, and unfairly condemned to live in isolation. These notes became the basis for *La Estirpe Sangrienta: Los Somozas* (The Bloody Descendancy: The Somozas), published in Mexico City in 1957, and *Diario de un Prisionero* (Diary of a Prisoner), published in Managua in 1961 by the *Revista Conservadora,* a Conservative magazine. Cooperating with Pedro in his writings, I shared in Pedro's suffering and became an integral partner in his political adventures.

On the 420th day of Pedro's imprisonment, I was delivering him his breakfast when one of the guards I had befriended said to me: "Señora, don't leave your husband's side for a second. Tonight they are planning to take him away."

So I stayed and demanded to be told where they were planning to take my husband. After hours of waiting, they told me Pedro was being released to San Carlos, where he would serve parole for five years.

San Carlos was a rustic port on the southeastern shore of Lake Nicaragua, practically on the border with Costa Rica. It offered a golden opportunity for Pedro to try to escape. So I said, "I'm going with you." I thought that if I was with him I could dissuade him from fleeing to Costa Rica, and should that fail, I would join him in his flight.

At first Pedro rejected my suggestion emphatically. But under pressure he acceded to my plans. Hastily, I arranged for the two older children, Pedro Joaquín and Claudia, to stay with my mother in-law and the two younger, Cristiana and Carlos Fernando, to stay with my mother in Rivas.

Once in San Carlos, I became Pedro's shadow. At any moment, I knew, Pedro, aided by Don Pepe Figueres, would rebel against his punishment and flee, which was exactly what Tacho—Anastasio Somoza Debayle—wanted. Tacho had told a good friend of mine that the whole point of sending Pedro to San Carlos was precisely to tempt him into fleeing. My friend recounted that Tacho had said, "Let him try to escape so it can rain bullets upon him." So I was understandably concerned when Pedro, after several months, confessed his escape plans to me. I had brought some money with us, and Pedro's idea was to hire a boatman to take him from San Carlos through the Great Lake, downriver toward Los Chiles in Costa Rica, and from there fly to San José and freedom. Then I would fly with the children to meet him.

But I had sworn when I married Pedro that I would always be by his side, "till death do us part," and I really believed in that. So I said, "Pedro, that won't work. Don't you see—if you escape, Tacho will never let me go. My only alternative will be to seek political asylum with the children. Can you imagine, Pedro, the havoc I would wreak at an embassy with thirty-two soiled diapers daily? There is no other choice but for me to go with you. Afterward we will send for the children."

Having heard the "rain of bullets" story, Pedro, concerned for my safety, still tried to persuade me to stay, setting forth countless objections. But I remained firm in my resolve. "Pedro, I am going. Nothing you can say will dissuade me. You must trust me on this. Women are strong, Pedro, in spite of their fragile appearance." Capitulating to my demands, he said, grumbling, "Women! They are the scourge of men's affairs."

The priest in San Carlos knew we were devout Catholics. So he asked me to read at the liturgical service to be held on Good Friday. In the town, this was considered an honor. But as luck would have it, we had planned our escape for that week because we had hoped that, distracted by the festivities, the town authorities would not notice our absence until we were well beyond their reach. We knew that if I declined the invitation, the priest would certainly be tipped off as to what our plans were. We had no choice but to reveal it all to him through the holy sacrament of penance, or confession. This would obligate him to hold our dangerous secret in silence before all but God.

When the week of our departure finally came, Pedro took me by the arm, and as we walked, we went over our plan. In the three months that we had been in San Carlos, part of our daily routine consisted of walking the short distance that separated our boardinghouse from the boardwalk. There Pedro and I would cast a line into the water and wait until the fish would bite. As the sun began its slow descent, we would enjoy afternoon chats with Capitán Mejía, the father of the Mejía Godoy brothers (who would achieve international acclaim as Sandinista musicians and singers). That afternoon, we did as usual and headed for the wharf, passing the *General Somoza,* the lake steamer that was always docked there. The Somoza name branded on so many things always reminded us who the proprietors of Nicaragua were.

On Good Friday, the streets were crowded with people dressed in colorful attire. Most of the villagers, I recall, were taking part in the procession. We passed the church, where the purple-robed statue of Christ, adorned with garlands of frangipani made by the hands of the faithful women of San Carlos, was ready to bear silent witness to the crucifixion of our Lord. Pedro reminded me then that while I was watching the procession, I had to divert Capitán Mejía's attention so that he could go to the dock and arrange our passage.

"At the appropriate time," he said, "a campesino will stroll by, tip his wide-brim hat to you, and say, "Good evening. The bells are ringing; the service is about to begin." This would be my signal that everything was ready and that I should meet him at the dock.

Every night for the last week our boatman had been on standby as we waited for the right moment to escape. With each passing night Pedro had become increasingly nervous. At 7 P.M. Pedro, agitated, pointed to the unusual brightness of the evening sky. Unfortunately, when we were making our plans, we did not consider the waxing moon, which on that evening was full against a clear sky. This, of course, made the likelihood of detection even greater.

I, on the other hand, felt we had arrived at a point of no return, a situation in which our actions could no longer dictate our fate. "We have to move tonight," I told him. "All we can do now is commend ourselves to God and the Virgin and trust that everything will turn out all right." I explained to my husband that his meticulous attention to every possible contingency was unnecessary. "Relax, Pedro. Everything has been set. We'll be in Los Chiles for our rendezvous before sunrise."

Around eight o'clock, Pedro left for the dock, while I ambled toward the church to observe the procession. Beneath my skirt, rolled up, I wore the pair of denim trousers I would wear in our escape. When I reached the church, Capitán Mejía had saved me a place next to him. After a while, the campesino went by and said the words I was waiting to hear. Calmly, I rose from my chair and said good-bye to Capitán Mejía and left to meet Pedro. Fortunately, the whole village's attention was directed toward the procession, and nobody seemed to notice my departure. It was close to nine o'clock. The streetlights had already been turned off as I walked comfortably in the shadows toward the wharf where Pedro and our boatman would be waiting. But before I had reached my destination I encountered Pedro. "The man is not there," he said. "The plan must be off. We have been betrayed." Just at that moment we saw a guardsman approaching. My heart began to pound with the fear that we had in fact been betrayed. I noticed the guardsman had a girl on his arm and was distractedly caressing her. So, impulsively, I pulled Pedro to me and embraced him passionately. The soldier and his girl went by without even giving us a second glance.

Suddenly, at a distance, barely distinguishable, I saw approaching the silhouette of a canoe with a man on board.

"There he is, Pedro," I said. The man had been waiting for us at another location. Pedro signaled to him. "Careful," the man said as we boarded the small boat. "Don't be afraid," he told us; "we are navigating to a free world." When we were seated on the boat Pedro requested a paddle from the boatman. But the man stubbornly refused and remarked, "If we wish to avoid attracting attention only one of us should paddle." Slowly, he paddled us away from the landing, and we glided like a dark shadow over the still waters. But we could not put out of our minds the powerful boats of the Guardia Nacional that were docked two thousand feet away. If they noticed our absence, with their ninety-horsepower motors those boats could overtake us in minutes.

After a while, the lights of San Carlos got smaller and smaller as the river water engulfed us completely in a darkness that shifted and changed as we passed under the overhanging trees. Suddenly, the boatman lifted his paddle from the water and brought his finger to his lips, signaling us to remain quiet. We were transfixed with fear. I was so terrified at the possibility of getting caught, I barely noticed the playful antics of the garfish we had aroused as we passed through their waters. They jumped all around the boat, emerging, submerging, and reemerging time and time again. Ironically, we could not enjoy this spectacle. As we were passing a bend in the river perilously close to the Nicaraguan garrison situated near its edge, we thought that the splash of the garfish was making us distressingly conspicuous to anyone within hearing distance. Involuntarily, a murmured prayer escaped my lips. Our boatman, whose blurred figure I could barely make out in the darkness, silently lowered the paddle into the water, guiding us gently toward the tall screen of grasses growing along the banks of the river.

"If we hear them coming after us, we jump into the water and fan out into the nearby countryside. Nobody will find us there."

Camouflaged in the brambly growth, we were about to slide overboard when a white beam of light grazed the surface of the water, which forced us to hunker down in the boat. For what seemed to be an interminable period of time the beam swept over the area, but it failed to reveal our position. We waited until the light was turned off and continued our journey.

After a while our paddler announced that we were at the entrance to one of the tributaries of the Río San Juan, along a stretch of land that was the property of the Somozas (they had property all over the country). In the distance we could hear the loud barking of a dog. As a precautionary measure our skipper guided the vessel to the other edge of the river, cutting the water with his oar vigorously to give our boat the necessary speed to escape possible danger. But nothing happened.

The rest of the way we traveled in silence, without further excitement, until we reached a point along the coast where our boatman told us troops of the Guardia Nacional habitually disguised themselves to surprise smugglers trafficking on the border of Costa Rica and Nicaragua. Our boatman guided the canoe with great precaution close to the edge of the opposite side. Up on a hill, we saw a house. Several dugouts like our own were docked at a landing; cattle slept in the pastures; stone washboards lay by the river. Everything was ominously silent. We paddled one or two hundred feet more, and when at last we dared to think we were almost free, another powerful beam of light illuminated the still dark waters.

"Paddle quickly!" the boatman said, then asked, "Do you have a revolver?"

"No," Pedro answered.

The boatman's arms moved with great speed as he broke the water powerfully with his paddle. Pedro joined him in the effort, and with supreme force they put us beyond the light's beam.

"They can't catch us now," he said. "And if they do we will defend ourselves with the paddles."

In all there were five or ten minutes of anguish, during which all of the boatman's energies had been dissipated in his desire to save us. The sun was beginning to rise, and in the distance we could make out a bright cleft in the landscape.

Our boatman pointed calmly to the bright spot and said, "Over there is Los Chiles." At last free of tension, we relaxed and began a conversation. The boatman introduced himself. He told us his family had emigrated from Nicaragua to Costa Rica "for political reasons." He recounted the ways in which the little *comandantes* in the province had taken their land and killed whoever opposed them. He described the lies, the deceit, the exploitation of the poor by people who looked for an opportunity to govern only to enrich themselves—stories that unfortunately were not new to us—which had caused the campesino population to rebel against the Somoza regime. In Pedro they saw a figure who could champion their cause.

The boatman then navigated into a narrow canal about five feet wide, full of tree trunks and thick overgrowth. He smiled and said: "They won't follow us here—their propellers will break."

We went through the canal for a few minutes, until our canoe ran aground in a muddy inlet at a place called Los Robles. There we tied the boat, disembarked, and continued our expedition to Los Chiles on foot.

After an hour we reached Los Chiles. Pedro paid our guide. We bade him a warm good-bye. It had been several hours since we had left San Carlos, and now he was heading back alone. I worried for him and wished him well. Out of gratitude, and to protect him, I gave him the rosary I had been praying with throughout the voyage. Years later when I became president, a man came forward claiming to be the boatman who rowed us to freedom. But I can't be certain anymore. If only he'd had the rosary, I would have known for sure and I'd have thanked him for taking us to freedom that day.

I was hungry and cold, but we could not stop until an hour later, when we saw a lone house atop the windswept moors of a hill. It turned out to be the home of a Costa Rican gendarme. With warm hospitality he and his wife received us into their home and fed us tortillas and empanadas.

Far away we could hear the droning hum of airplane engines. Fortunately we were near the airport, where our plane would be waiting to take us to the capital, San José. But our main concern was how we could travel the distance from the house to the airport in broad daylight without being spotted by the Somocistas who lived in the area. The gendarme was sympathetic to our problem but declined to accompany us. He handed us a pistol and told us, "Walk single file and stay out of plain view." However, Pedro and I marched down the road arm in arm. We figured if we were going to die, we might as well have the warmth of each other's bodies to console us. When we reached the landing strip we did not see the small aircraft that we expected. Instead there was a large Costa Rican commercial airliner. It had been sent by Don Pepe Figueres. Now it sat patiently waiting, parked at the far end of the runway, surrounded by a curious crowd.

We began to run toward it. A uniformed pilot was holding the door open and had lowered a ladder when somebody in the crowd recognized us and began to scream, "They are fugitives, don't take them!" The pilots didn't know for whom they had been sent, nor were they privy to the specifics of their mission. They helped us on board and flew us to San José without asking any questions. We were met by an envoy of Don Pepe, Carlos Andrés Pérez, the future president of Venezuela. Pérez had been living in Costa Rica in exile since 1949, when his boss, leftist president of Venezuela Rómulo Gallego, was deposed in a right-wing military coup. As a result of this Pérez, his chief of staff, had gone into exile to Costa Rica and was working as a journalist at the Costa Rican daily *La República*. He carried with him our safe-conduct passes, courtesy of Don Pepe Figueres. That's how our life in exile began.

When Tacho learned of our escape, fuming with undiluted rage, he ordered that exit visas be denied to our children. Sadly, Pedro and I had to brace ourselves to live without them for a time. Eventually Luis Somoza would prevail over his brother and allow the children to travel with Doña Margarita to Costa Rica.

We also discovered that Pedro's repeated beatings while he was imprisoned had severely affected his health, particularly his back, which needed to be supported at all times with a corset. Deciding that it was time he be examined by an American specialist, we made plans to travel to the United States. Tacho, however, through his contacts in the American embassy, saw to it that we were denied visas.

A year and half later, in August 1958, we learned that I was expecting another baby. "This can't be possible," I argued with the obstetrician. "I have experienced difficulties with almost all of my pregnancies and I do not want more children." Contraceptives existed in those days, but our Catholic faith limited us to observing the rhythms of my menstrual cycles. It was an unreliable method. Five pregnancies in eight years of marriage had proved that so.

The first two years in exile, time flew as I tended to our home, prepared for the birth of my fifth child, and cared for our children, who by then were living with us. Pedro worked now at *La Prensa Libre* and he was writing his book *La Estirpe Sangrienta,* which would be published in Mexico and banned in Nicaraguan bookstores. And he was making plans for a new invasion. All Pedro needed was to breathe the fresh air of liberty for his passion to be rekindled and his patriotism to thrust him on the path toward rebellion.

Don Pepe Figueres, an enemy of dictators, was openly supportive of the growing community of Nicaraguan exiles who lived in Costa Rica. He would often invite us to dine at his coffee hacienda near San José, which he had baptized Rancho La Lucha in honor of our hard-fought struggle for democracy in our continent. There we would meet with Carlos Andrés Pérez and Nicaraguan exiles who, like us, were anti-Somocistas and had participated in other coups—people such as Luis Cardenal, Enrique Lacayo Farfan, Carlos Pasos, Ernesto Solórzano Thompson, Eduardo Chamorro, Reynaldo Tefel, Horacio Aguirre, and Panchito Frixione, and others whose names I don't recall anymore. Later we began to meet at our house in the elegant Barrio Escalante. That is how the idea of the invasion that became known as Olama and Molle-jones began.

It was during this phase of our lives that Castro took power in Cuba, on January 1, 1959. Within days, Pedro was on a plane to Havana with Reynaldo Tefel and Panchito Frixione to enlist Castro's assistance in overthrowing Somoza. But they never got past Ché Guevara. As he met Pedro, El Ché said, without shaking Pedro's hand, "Pedro Joaquín Chamorro, as in the Chamorro-Bryant Treaty." He was referring to General Emiliano Chamorro, Pedro's granduncle, who as a diplomatic envoy of Nicaragua in Washington had signed the agreement that conceded Nicaragua's canal rights to the American government. At the time a canal across the isthmus in Nicaragua had still been under consideration by the Americans. El Ché wrongly interpreted the ratification of this treaty as a sellout to American interests by the Nicaraguan bourgeoisie.

Pedro told El Ché that he was a Chamorro by blood, but that he followed a political line independent of his relatives. "Those issues," he said, "pertain to another generation."

But El Ché regarded Pedro and his compatriots as reactionaries and bourgeois traitors, and turned them away in favor of another group of Nicaraguan *guerrilleros,* who were led by a little-known communist ideologist in our country, Carlos Fonseca Amador, the future founder of the Sandinista movement (FSLN). Understandably, it was their leftist enterprise that received the patronage of the Cubans.

Pedro and his friends returned to Costa Rica from Havana empty-handed and dismayed by Fidel.

This unsuccessful voyage to Cuba was followed three months later by a more productive trip Pedro made to Venezuela to meet with Rómulo Betancourt, that country's newly elected democratic leader.

Perhaps it was the stress of separation, or maybe it was destiny, but during Pedro's absence I went into premature labor. My mother was the first one to tell me that our child, white as a sheet of paper, was stillborn. "She is an angel," the local chaplain pronounced. "We must bless her with the sign of the cross and give her a decent burial." But what should have been a simple matter was bogged down in extraneous formalities. Since we were in exile, finding a crypt for the baby became most difficult. Fortunately, Mother reminded me that my grandfather Manuel Joaquín Barrios had died in Costa Rica and was buried there. With the family's permission, we were allowed to lay the little white coffin next to my grandfather's. In an act of respect, 160 would-be *guerrilleros* escorted my baby to her tomb.

When Pedro returned from Venezuela, he brought with him money to organize the invasion and a small ring for me, which I still preserve. He told me, had the baby survived, she would have been called María Milagros, for it would have been a miracle for her to live. I was not a woman much disposed toward jewelry and other finery, but I understood that through this simple gesture and his words he wanted to recognize my pain and liberate me of any guilt I may have felt for the loss of our child.

The invasion was born in April 1959 on an inhospitable beach in Costa Rica called Punta Llorona (Point of Tears). Had the plotters paid attention to omens, as I do, they would have foreseen that a place with this sad name was the wrong location to begin the invasion. Furthermore, Punta Llorona was a sandy finger bordered by tall coconut palms. The hot tropical evenings make it possible for all types of insects to breed in the woodland. There were no sources of food or fresh water. Nevertheless, it was on this inhospitable tract of land that one hundred Nicaraguan patriots, led by Pedro, met for a month and half to plan and train for the day they could arm themselves and reenter Nicaragua as part of a revolutionary force.

For an entire month, as he planned the invasion, Pedro's only communication with us was through a clandestine radio set up in the campsite. The children were told that their father had to stay at a meeting at a yellow house down the street from where we lived in Barrio Escalante. But I don't think any of them believed us. They knew there was a hidden truth, because they could see my tears and could associate them with Pedro's absences. Our daughters, Claudia and Cristiana, remember this as a difficult time. They missed their father terribly.

In retrospect, perhaps it was cruel to indulge in subterfuge by not telling the children what was actually happening, but Pedro and I had agreed that there was no point in making them participants in our misfortune, though inevitably they were. Together we tried to make up for the disruptions in their lives by enjoying each day we had as a family to the fullest. Life with Pedro taught me that matrimonial bonding doesn't occur simply by being together in the great moments of one's life but that love grows and is nourished by constant acts of kindness in our day-to-day affairs.

I suppose that is why, during our periods of collective living—when Pedro was home with us—our existence assumed an intense and accelerated quality, as we tried to surround our children with warmth and love, giving in to their every whim to make up for the attention they were sorely lacking on other occasions.

On May 31, 1959, the invaders landed in an improvised airfield in a prairie in the Nicaraguan province of Boaco that has always been known as Mollejones. The entire force consisted of one hundred soldiers, but the plane, piloted by an ex-guardsman, could not hold more than sixty-five men at a time. As a result the plan was to make the drop-off in two trips. The first contingent, led by Pedro, was to be met by a group of three hundred rebel campesinos, but when they landed there were only three lone men and their donkey. Without ground support or means of communication, Pedro and his men realized that their only hope of surviving the attacks from the local militia (which had apparently been alerted to the invasion) was to try to flee into the mountains of Chontales.

As the plane returned for its second drop-off, the pilot was unable to find the landing strip because it had already been destroyed by the *guardias*. The pilot was forced to set down elsewhere, but to his misfortune and that of the thirty-five men on board, he made a crash landing in a swamp in Boaco near a place called Olama. While the *guerrilleros* were trying to rescue the plane with a team of oxen they were attacked from the air by an air force squadron. Some of them were gunned down. The pilot and copilot fled toward Costa Rica with three Costa Rican members of the expedition. All five were captured and killed by the *guardias*. The other revolutionaries fled deeper into the mud lands, where they were surrounded and captured by the *guardias*. It was embarrassingly clear that my husband's attack was doomed from the very start.

After a seven-day march, Pedro's contingent rested in the hacienda Fruta de Pan. The following morning they were bombarded by air force planes from the Guardia Nacional and surrounded by troops that demanded their full surrender. Under the force of heavy artillery, they capitulated, except for a loyal core of fifteen men, among them Pedro, Luis Cardenal, and Eduardo Chamorro. Dodging enemy fire, they withdrew into the mountains to fight a guerrilla war that was disappointingly short. Rumors quickly circulated that they had all been killed in an ambush.

The young idealists had expected that, simultaneously with the invasion, there would be an internal uprising and a general strike organized by the Nicaraguan Opposition Union (UNO). But a series of misfortunes derailed their enterprise. Word of what was termed a gigantic expedition had leaked out, and unbeknownst to Pedro, a crackdown had been under way in Nicaragua, preventing Pedro's followers from building grassroots support for the invasion.

I remember thinking how ironic it was that while patriotic Nicaraguans lay dying, the Somoza brothers held banquets in their villas. Pedro wrote a letter to me on June 10, 1959:

Now I am in God's hands. He is great and powerful. He makes miracles happen. But if he decides my time has come, to the other life I will carry in my soul not the anguish of death but the memory of you and the good life that we had.

Forgive me all the sufferings that I have brought upon you. Forgive my roughness, my lack of effusiveness, but I have loved you always and it pains me to leave you and to leave my children . . . but . . . what can I do?

Love: The day before yesterday during a merciless bombardment, the Virgin saved my life. I have faith that we walk hand in hand, but if she decides to call me to her side, forgive me and remember me. Tell our children that the fatherland is them and other children like them, and for them we must suffer and sometimes even die.

I didn't receive that letter until five months and two days after he was captured. But on the morning of June 11 I awoke gripped by morbid apprehension, terrified that Pedro's war against the Somozas had finally killed him. However, on the fourteenth I received a wire from Managua notifying me that Pedro and others had been arrested in Chontales, in a place called San Pedro del Lóvago. Muddy and defeated, they were marched through the streets of Managua.

In a few hours I packed my things and the children's, and we returned to Nicaragua. I told them we were going back to be with their father. But to their surprise, after the hugs and kisses at Doña Margarita's house, their father never materialized. Cristiana, in particular, was very aware of this. We were sitting at lunch, at the long table that sat the entire family, when she asked me where her father was. Though I did not believe in embittering their lives by sharing with them my sadness, I felt compelled to give her an explanation and to try to make all of them understand their father's plight. I also wanted them to know that a father like theirs was a blessing and someone to be proud of. So after lunch I sat them all down and told them their father had been captured while trying to unseat Somoza and I tried to explain to them his motives. "Your father," I said, "rebelled against the Somoza dictatorship and as a result he is now in prison. He did this because he loves his country and saw it as his duty to prove to the world that we are not yet an enslaved nation and that in the breast of our people there beats a noble and patriotic heart."

We stayed at my mother-in-law's Baroque home next to *La Prensa*. She would tend to the children while I visited Pedro. For several days I was not allowed to see him. When I did, he was lying on a cot, still clad in the uniform he had worn when he swam through the rivers in Chontales, covered with the mud of the mountains. Thin and unshaven, he looked at me with a strange brilliance in his eyes. Between deep sighs he said, "Last night I dreamt I had died. It happened in Banadí, where fifteen of us were resting . . . precisely in the spot where I should have died, because, Violeta, now I know what it is like to feel shame. We have failed, Violeta, and our defeat is not just ours but the whole nation's." And so it was that we learned, through the most painful of lessons, that an insurrection without civic support is madness and that a civic movement lacking in military support cannot succeed either.

For the children as well it was a cruel and painful lesson. Usually I refused the children's offer to accompany me to visit their father in jail. I did not want them to see him wrapped in the degrading conditions of his imprisonment. But no matter how hard we tried we couldn't entirely protect them from the repercussions of Pedro's political activities. The failure of the invasion at Olama and Mollejones, as the action came to be known because of the two landings, was food for the children of the Somoza supporters, who accosted our children in school, calling their father a wicked traitor and a coward. By then, the two oldest, Pedro Joaquín and Claudia Lucía, had begun to read secretly Pedro's private journals. Through his writings they came to know the truth about their father. For the sake of defending Pedro's honor, they quarreled furiously with their classmates. At those times I had to be there to love and console them, but always with a firm hand to guide them away from developing a rancorous heart. I would say to them, "Don't mind those children. What do they know about love for one's country?" Ultimately, our children learned to coexist with the Somocistas with grace. But for Cristiana, who was six and a classmate of Carolina Somoza, it was especially difficult. Before she could understand the implications of her father's politics in her life, she was thrown together with Carolina Somoza. The nuns of the school she attended, I suppose believing they were teaching them both a lesson, insisted that from third grade on they sit with their desks paired together in class. As a result, at an early age, other children would accost her with questions. "Cristiana, how do you get along with the general's daughter?" they would ask. "Do you like her?" Stating her beliefs without offending Carolina, who after all was not to blame for her father's actions, was not easy for Cristiana. But her loyalty to her father was great and she could not remain silent when his honor was attacked. Pedro's letter from Olama and Mollejones moved her deeply. Cristiana believed her father was a man who had a vision of the world that gave greater meaning to life. It was a revelation that has inspired her to seek ways to serve her country.

In December, after Pedro and his companions had been in prison for six months, I took the children to their father's sentencing. He and the others were sentenced to eight years for betraying the fatherland, an absurd accusation for those who had tried to reestablish social and economic justice. It was Luis, the more politically astute of the two Somozas because he understood that the public would perceive the absurdity of the charge, who granted amnesty to all the prisoners except Pedro.

Pedro was released six months later, on the anniversary of Olama and Mollejones, in June 1960. Soon afterward, Pedro and I left for the United States to admit him to a clinic, where his various ailments were attended to.

So at the tender age of nine we sent Pedro Joaquín to Granada as a boarder at Colegio Centro América, where he would spend his time shooting down birds with his slingshot and getting into mischief. Claudia, Cristiana, and Carlos Fernando remained with their Chamorro grandmother until our return six months later. Though they were attended to by solicitous aunts, uncles, and cousins, this was a difficult time for the children. Often when nobody was watching, Cristiana would go to a corner of the house and cry.

After we had been away three months, I returned alone to Nicaragua to visit the children, but the many gifts I brought did little to assuage the sadness they felt when I again departed. In my heart I carried the resolve that when we returned for good, I would do everything in my power to give our children the normal childhood they deserved, including a home of their own.

So we began a new life in a rented house in Barrio San Sebastian, close to the offices of *La Prensa*. Like a campesino Pedro rose early every day. By 5:30 A.M. he was out for a ride on the yellow secondhand Honda motorcycle he bought. He loved to ride through the streets of our capital and watch it come to life as the first carts of fruit were rolled into the market square by the campesino merchants and the sound of cars and motorcycles invaded the peace of a city that had been at rest. He would observe his people and see what the *guardias* were up to. He wanted to have as much firsthand knowledge of our country as possible. Often I would go with him, riding on the back of the motorcycle, hugging him closely. On those occasions we rode all the way out to the *sierritas* in Casa Colorada.

By 7 A.M. he was back for breakfast, to have *café con leche* with bread while reading *Novedades,* the partisan daily newspaper of the Somoza family. At seven thirty he would depart promptly for church to offer a prayer to God and ask for his blessing and protection, then go to his office at *La Prensa.*

At noon he would come home for lunch and relax for a while by doing some reading or taking a small siesta. At two he was back at *La Prensa* to write his editorial for the next day's issue, and stayed until 5 P.M., when the paper was being distributed in the streets by local news-boys. Sometimes he would bring home comic strips for the children from a newsstand on the corner. On other occasions he would come home angry and distracted by some problem he had at the office, which he would share with me. I was the one in whom Pedro deposited all his worries. We maintained a special and delicate balance. Pedro was my university and I was his calm wellspring.

At dinner with the children we would discuss politics, a subject that seemed to interest all of them, though we always took care not to discuss issues that could provoke in them feelings of rancor.

Sometimes, if Pedro wasn't too tired, we would go to the movies at six. He loved mysteries, dramas, and films that, like him, were highly moralistic. But more often than not we would sit on our twin recliners and talk. In our evening conversations he would often describe how our children would be as adults. "Pedro Four-eyes," he said, "will be, as now, impulsive, warmhearted, and mischievous; *la Cayetana gorda,* my chubby Claudia, will be passionate and loyal; Cristiana, *la quirina pretenciosa,* my skinny little rebel, will always want to go beyond the established parame-ters. Shy, introverted Carlos Fernando, my *Fruto-Frutin,* is a thinker." (When he was a teenager he called him Karl Marx.)

It was our happiest time. At last we had the beginning of a life together, which matured and developed further in 1963 when we moved into our own house in the neighborhood of Las Palmas, the place where I still live, accompanied by my parakeets and cloistered among my ferns, begonias, and palms.

Chapter Five

WE MOVED INTO THE HOUSE IN LAS PALMAS
in June 1963. Including the walled-in gardens, the house measures about
seven thousand square feet. It has four bedrooms, ours and the children's,
and rooms for the household staff. Later we built an apartment over the
garage.

To build the house, I had to sell my share of another property I had
inherited jointly with my siblings from Father. The timber to build the
house in Las Palmas was harvested from the ceiba trees in Amayo. The
columns are from an old house in León. I'm not claiming they are
museum quality. But they are special. The flagstones in the corridor of
the stones, as we called our patio, are from the Great Lake. Outside this
covered way is a trellis Pedro and I built, where the grapevine Pedro
brought from his mother's house grows. He tended that grapevine personally, making it yield huge, juicy grapes. It was fascinating for him to
see that it was possible to cultivate them in our warm climate. Our son
Pedro Joaquín didn't like them much because they were seedy. But we
always believed it was the seeds that made them sweet.

The furniture for the house came later. Some of it, like the chairs in
the dining room, we inherited from Doña Margarita. Other things, like
my grandfather Manuel Joaquín Barrios's desk, I brought back from my
mother's house; I shined it up and put it in Pedro's office. The brass beds
in our room are from my mother, and so are the carved mahogany
wardrobes. The rest we bought secondhand when there was money to
spare.

It was in this house, in the corridor of stones, that Pedro began to
hold court every Sunday. In attendance were important political figures,

distinguished visitors, colleagues, and friends, who gave these meetings a rich diversity of opinion. The topic of discussions varied. Anyone was fair game, even Pedro. In due time our home became a political salon, to which the children yearned to gain entry. I remember Carlos Fernando, a child of seven, and his friends sneaking into these meetings. Pedro, who was always interested in hearing the opinions of the young, would encourage them to participate actively in the debates. Inevitably, the discussions veered in the direction of the Somoza brothers and how to prevent them from perpetuating their dictatorship in succeeding generations. These meetings often served as the inspiration for Pedro's editorials in *La Prensa*.

The newspaper that the Chamorro Cardenal family had inherited from their father had become, under Pedro's guidance, the forum for Nicaragua's political battles and a platform for civic and moral causes.

There was no debate in Nicaragua for which *La Prensa* was not the preferred vehicle of expression. And so Pedro had baptized the newspaper "the Republic of Letters." The agonizing state of our republic was always the subject of Pedro's editorials. He held the Somoza family personally responsible for the misery that existed in our country. He predicted only two viable alternatives to the Somozas, communism and socialist democracy. The first he rejected as being nothing more than the "enslavement of free people." The second he believed to be the Christian solution to our country's problems.

Pedro's work at *La Prensa* established his reputation as a dedicated and passionate journalist. As a result of this work he was asked by the Universidad Nacional Autónoma (UNAN) to teach a course in journalism. At UNAN Pedro discovered that Nicaragua's youth were against the Somozas and in favor of social reforms that tended toward Marxism. Through his lectures and editorials, Pedro hoped he could influence the youth of Nicaragua to return to the political center, arguing that "there can be no worse employer than a communist state that restricts the salaries of the working class." He cautioned against reacting negatively to our dark past by going to radical extremes. "Extremes," he said, "prevent the creation of a representative democracy." Instead, he invited them to join CIVES, a student organization Pedro had recently founded to bring about change in a positive way.

Pedro called Fidel's Cuba "Russia's Cuba" and lashed out weekly in his editorials against the "international brotherhood of socialism," which forbids patriotism and creates state monopolies through confiscations. "In my opinion," he would say to his readers, "a communist system in Nicaragua will not help to redistribute wealth. It will only serve to spread misery throughout the country. But better job training, better incentives for the workers will increase productivity, and as a result the whole country will be wealthier."

With a new understanding that through education he could begin to bring about change, in September 1963 Pedro launched Nicaragua's first National Literacy Campaign with the slogan "He who does not know how to read might as well be blind." From that day and for a whole year, every issue of *La Prensa* carried the reading lesson for the day. In an editorial titled "The Educated Person's Moral Duty," Pedro encouraged those who knew how to read to teach those who didn't.

The literacy campaign was so widely publicized by radio stations and civic organizations that the Ministry for Public Education and universities throughout the country decided to adopt the plan. The success of this effort was so great that after a year, Luis Somoza decided to shut down the campaign.

Frustrated, Pedro wrote in *La Prensa* that Luis Somoza was incubating a communist insurrection by denying the people of our country their most basic rights. "The Somoza government," he said, "allows extravagant luxury to coexist with misery and makes a mockery of democracy."

By then the Somoza family had been in control of Nicaragua for twenty-seven years, including the brief periods in which they had relinquished the presidency but not the command of the army and so, in effect, had continuously ruled. Currently occupying the throne was Luis, the oldest of the three legitimate Somoza children. The others were Anastasio and Lillian, who was married to Guillermo Sevilla Sacasa, Nicaragua's diplomatic envoy to Washington.

Luis was nearly thirty-four years old when he came to power in September 1956. By the 1960s he had accomplished almost nothing for Nicaragua. We were still one of the less developed nations of Central America. But it is estimated that Luis had more than doubled the fortune he and his siblings had inherited from their father. It is believed that at the time of Somoza García's death, the family was worth about $20 million, most of which was made during World War II by confiscating property from German nationals living in Nicaragua. Luis, who had been sent to Louisiana to study business so he could learn to manage the family fortune, had devised creative ways of increasing the family's wealth. Through intimidation he made advantageous purchases of land at prices below market value. He increased the value of the family's personal holdings by modernizing the infrastructure through public works projects in areas in which they owned land. He augmented the family's liquidity by skimming commissions from entrepreneurs who needed approval for their projects, and if the venture looked really promising, he would demand a share of the new business and thus increase the size and diversity of the family's portfolio.

After John Fitzgerald Kennedy was elected president of the United States, in a meeting of the Central American presidents he publicly snubbed Luis. To appease the new president of their greatest ally, Luis eventually decided to resign his post to a handpicked candidate and thus maintain a semblance of democracy that satisfied Kennedy. "After all," he told his children, "one must always remember that to stay in control of the car one must sometimes relinquish the wheel and resort to being a backseat driver." That is how in May of 1963 René Schick came to be president of Nicaragua, while Luis assumed a less visible role as minister of land reform.

The task of breathing heavily on Schick was left to Anastasio, the younger brother and head of the armed forces. He was the neighborhood bully, while Luis played the role of civilized statesman. At the time of Somoza García's assassination, it was Anastasio who oversaw Pedro's torture and impeded the children's exit to Costa Rica, while Luis subsequently allowed our children to join us in exile. Then, during the Olama and Mollejones invasion, it was Anastasio who orchestrated the pursuit of the rebel forces, and Luis who extended to all but Pedro a presidential pardon. In reality, Luis and Anastasio operated in synchrony by playing their own version of the good cop–bad cop game.

But long before Luis left office he came to be in Kennedy's good graces as a result of the Bay of Pigs fiasco, the invasion of Cuba conceived during the last days of the Eisenhower presidency and launched in April 1961 under John F. Kennedy. The plan was to invade Cuba using the Atlantic coast of Nicaragua as a jump-off point. Kennedy's decision to abort the mission at the last hour resulted in the capture of eight thousand Cubans. But for the Somoza brothers the Bay of Pigs invasion was a golden opportunity to prove they were enemies of communism and therefore vital to the stability of Central America. For all of us who opposed the Somozas, 1961 was a serious disappointment. Protected by the United States, where they had numerous friends and admirers in important places, and sustained by Nicaragua's armed forces, the Somozas were invulnerable.

Nineteen sixty-one was also the year that an armed rebel movement against Somocismo was born, the Sandinista National Liberation Front (FSLN), formed under the leadership of Carlos Fonseca Amador and Tomás Borge. Fonseca Amador was the illegitimate son of Fausto Amador, an administrator of the Somoza family's wealth. As poor boys growing up in a small town in the north of Nicaragua called Matagalpa, Fonseca Amador and Borge had been childhood friends. Together they had participated in student revolts and on more than one occasion had been jailed. Like Pedro's, their consuming passion was to topple the Somozas from power. Unlike Pedro, they were communists and wanted to install a revolutionary government. Before 1961 they were a small guerrilla operation that would gather on Nicaragua's northern frontier with Honduras and from there make incursions into the mountainous territory. From time to time they were captured. We would hear about them when they were deported to Guatemala or Honduras. But these were sporadic occurrences no one paid much attention to.

After Kennedy was assassinated on November 22, 1963, and Lyndon Johnson was sworn into office, Anastasio Somoza, who was still army chief though Luis had stepped down, was called upon once more to cooperate by sending troops in support of another invasion. This time the United States was invading the Dominican Republic to install in power the ultraright political leader Dr. Reid Cabral. Somoza, of course, complied and in doing so further cemented the Somozas' relationship with the United States.

Several years later, at the venerable age of ninety-six, Emiliano Chamorro died. Pedro felt he had passed away unrecognized for his personal talents and misunderstood for his ambitions. In his defense Pedro wrote an editorial that he titled "Emiliano Chamorro, the Humble Man's General." He readily admitted that his "granduncle" Emiliano made some political errors, but insisted that he stood above many in his honesty and courage. "In war," he said, "Emiliano was the first man on the battlefield and the last to surrender."

Tired of having Anastasio breathing down his neck, toward the end of 1966 Schick began to plot against his benefactors. He planned to escape to Mexico to denounce the Somoza regime. It was a gamble that, unfortunately, met with some bad luck. Hours before his departure he was stricken with a heart attack. The Somozas, who had been informed of his plans, immediately seized control of the situation and isolated Schick from everyone, including his family. It is said he died in captivity in 1966, under the care of an army physician and a military nurse. To replace him Luis appointed his loyal friend Lorenzo Guerrero. Less than a year later, Anastasio Somoza Debayle announced his candidacy in the 1967 presidential elections.

At that juncture, the only politically organized challenge to Somoza was Fernando Agüero Rocha, the Conservative Party nominee. After Olama and Mollejones Pedro had become convinced that through "blood and bullets you cannot pacify Nicaragua," so he decided to throw his support behind Agüero and focus on defeating Tacho Somoza through civic means.

From the very start I had my reservations about Agüero. Nevertheless, when Pedro asked me to attend a large political rally in Managua on January 22, 1967, I said, "I'll do it for you, Pedro." The rally was to be a protest of passive resistance, in which twenty thousand people would perform a Gandhi-style sit-in. Agüero, who was a talented orator, excited the crowd by declaring that Tacho had corrupted the purity of the electoral process by purchasing votes and by using government resources to advance his candidacy. He proclaimed that under such conditions Nicaragua's elections could never be fair. He capped his speech by announcing that he was boycotting the elections until international observers could supervise the electoral process. He urged all of his followers to march in protest to the hill of Tiscapa, to the headquarters of the Guardia Nacional and the presidential palace.

The throng responded dramatically. Agüero's mellifluous speech moved the entire throng to action. They had marched several blocks up Avenida Roosevelt when they ran into the Guardia Nacional. Pedro and I were in the midst of this crowd. Sensing that a massacre was about to occur, Pedro tried to appeal to the people to remain calm. He said, "Against such a force the only choice is to maintain a civic stance." They might have listened to him, but just then a shot was fired and the lieutenant in charge fell dead. A riot ensued. I lost sight of Pedro. Later I learned that as Tacho's Sherman tanks surrounded them, Agüero,

Pedro, and scores of demonstrators took refuge in the nearby Gran Hotel. For twenty-four hours we remained sequestered as diplomats negotiated for the removal of the tanks. Tacho promised to extend amnesty to us all. Nevertheless, two days later Pedro was arrested at home. He was accused of being a terrorist leader and sentenced to forty-five days in prison.

I remember that when they came to take him away, Carlos Fernando, who was then only eleven years old, opened the door to the officials of the Guardia Nacional. Claudia, Cristiana, Carlos, and I watched as they presented Pedro with a warrant for his arrest. Pedro didn't argue. Impassively he said to the guard, "All right. I'll go. But first let me remove my watch and allow me to give to my wife these house keys." For the children it became clear that in our country a life in politics implies great risk and that at all times one must be prepared to accept the consequences of one's actions with dignity and grace.

A few days later we learned that on the morning of the march, Edén Pastora, René Schick's bodyguard, had been arrested near Tipitapa. Police reports claim that he was transporting arms in his automobile. He was imprisoned, tortured till he bled, then forced to lick his own blood from the floor. In time Pastora's hatred of Anastasio Somoza Debayle became so great he became a *guerrillero* in the Sandinista army. He was the future Comandante Zero.

Try as we did not to influence the children, so that they could develop their own personalities, Pedro's repeated acts of courage made him a hero in their eyes. The day would come when they would emulate his patriotism and uphold his egalitarian ideals. I also think our children suspected, as I did, that their father would not be with them for long, and so they strove to accompany him as much as possible, partaking in the political meetings in our home or joining him at political rallies and participating in his life at *La Prensa*. Inadvertently, the children and I, by sharing in Pedro's life, came to have a life of our own in politics.

A month after the Gran Hotel incident, Agüero, instead of boycotting the elections as he had indicated in his speech, participated in them without ever saying a word about the events that had occurred at his political rally. His supporters saw this as an act of cowardice and treachery and openly accused him of selling out to Somoza. On February 5, 1967, Anastasio Somoza Debayle was elected to his first term as president of Nicaragua. Two months before Tacho was to ascend the throne, Luis Somoza died suddenly of a massive coronary. He was forty-four years old.

By then the clandestine operations Carlos Fonseca Amador was performing in the mountains of Nicaragua had turned him into a legend. Studious and cerebral, he had become, over Borge, the recognized leader of the guerrilla group. In 1968, leaving Borge in charge of their military operations, he traveled to Costa Rica. Alerted by Tacho, the Costa Rican authorities, who were looking for him because he had held up a bank there, captured him while he was walking on the streets of San José and imprisoned him. Hearing of his arrest, Pedro, who was always looking for ways to unite the opposition, went to San José to visit him in jail. I remember that Pedro, who knew that Fonseca Amador liked to read, bought a stack of books for him. Later he would tell me that when he was allowed in to see him he found a bitter and brooding man. Fonseca Amador was a radical who despised the bourgeoisie. Far from being grateful for Pedro's visit, he rudely rejected Pedro's gift and called him a despicable bourgeois. After that visit my husband was quite clear about the harshness of the leader of the FSLN. He never again made overtures to him.

At the time, Anastasio Somoza Debayle had three sons—Anastasio III (Tachito); Julio, who would also become a military man; and Roberto, who was just a child. There were also two shy and quiet girls—Carolina, who was Cristiana's classmate, and Carla. Thus the succession was assured and the foundations laid for the cross fire between Chamorros and Somozas to continue into the next century.

During his school vacations our son Pedro Joaquín had been working at *La Prensa* as a photographer. When he was not away at school, his joy was hunting and fishing with the Barrios clan. Every chance he got, he was off to Rivas. His favorite uncle was my brother Raúl. The two were very much alike: charismatic, with *don de gente,* winning ways.

Carlos Fernando, who was five years younger than Pedro Joaquín, grew up as a solitary child. He was an introverted boy who spent all his time reading or in the company of adults, listening to our political discourses. His favorite playground was *La Prensa,* where Pedro would send him on errands or give him odd jobs like cleaning the lead bars of the linotype. As he got older, the importance of his sporadic duties increased. First he worked in the delivery department. Then, by the time he was in high school, he was doing occasional reports for the sports pages of the newspaper. During his years at Colegio Centro América, Carlos Fernando had participated in school-sponsored trips with a Jesuit priest by the name of Eduardo Cuadra, to visit the poor barrios to do social work. In time, exposure to the inequities of Nicaragua's society resulted in a political restlessness that turned our son toward Marxism.

With the girls Pedro proved to be a doting father. He allowed them great independence, never set curfews for them or imposed restrictions on their choice of friends. But the trust he placed in them was never betrayed. Throughout those teenage years they proved to have their own moral compass and so conducted themselves with great honor.

Claudia, from her earliest years, wanted to be a painter. She spent every penny of her pocket money on art supplies, paper, and watercolor sets. She had a talent for drawing and was a great colorist. But most of all she was a great recorder of what she saw. When I look at her framed pictures of scenes in Managua before the earthquake I feel as if I have history on my walls. In her own way Claudia was as much a journalist as the other children. She was a storyteller, only in pictures. I think it was because of Claudia that Pedro began Arte-Expo, the art gallery at *La Prensa* that Claudia helped him run. It was through Arte-Expo that Claudia came to know the sorry state of the struggling artists of Nicaragua.

Cristiana by then had also decided to be a journalist and work eventually at *La Prensa*.

I am sure Pedro was thinking of our children when he refused to give quarter in his own war against Tacho Somoza. Pedro maintained as active an opposition against the third Somoza as he did against the first two. By then *La Prensa* was a prosperous newspaper. In addition to the paper's fifteen pages of news, Pablo Antonio Cuadra, who had become executive editor, began editing a weekly supplement called *La Prensa Literaria,* which showcased the work of Nicaraguan poets, writers, and artists. With the paper making money, the Chamorro Cardenal family decided to invest a small sum, $15,000, on an island in the Great Lake that Doña Margarita called El Poponjoche because of the enormous tree that grew at the center. Every weekend we were together—Anita (Pedro's sister) and Carlos Holmann, Jaime and Hilda Chamorro, Xavier and Sonia Chamorro. For ourselves we built a wood cabin with rustic windows and a porch from which to hang our hammocks. For the caretaker, Santos Martínez, we built a much more comfortable brick house. It was so nice that our son Pedro Joaquín wanted the caretaker's quarters. But Pedro thought the caretaker deserved the better place. Soon afterward, Pedro got a good deal to purchase the hull of an old schooner that was in a reasonably good state. With great enthusiasm he equipped it with a twelve-horsepower motor and took us on unbelievably slow rides on the lake. Pedro Joaquín loved to go fishing on the *Santa Libertad,* as he called it. He spent hours fiddling with the motor to make the old schooner go. But for my husband this rustic setting became the new location for his political soirees.

The family outings to El Poponjoche stopped when Pedro Joaquín graduated, in 1969, and left for Canada to study at McGill University. The following year Claudia Lucía graduated and went to New York to attend the College of New Rochelle.

Twelve months later, Cristiana followed her. That was the year Claudia contracted hepatitis B. She flew back to Nicaragua for her recovery, leaving Cristiana without a companion. Wary of leaving Cristiana alone in New York, we decided to send her to Canada to enroll at a junior college where she could be close to her brother.

It was on December 1, 1971, two months after graduating from high school, that Carlos Fernando left for Montreal. He wanted to study law, which required he stay in Nicaragua. Pedro tried to persuade him to go elsewhere to get a better education, but all Carlos Fernando agreed to was to go away for a short period of time to study English.

In Nicaragua Claudia had many friends and acquaintances, but toward the end of the summer of 1972 it was becoming obvious to us that she was becoming serious about José Bárcenas. What had begun as a friendship had turned into romance. When the time came to go back to school she informed us that she had enrolled in Universidad Centro Americana and was going to stay in Nicaragua and study law. After a time, Claudia officially informed us of the deepening of her sentiments for José.

As 1972 ended, both Pedro and I were at a stage of our lives when the love and energy we had poured into our various projects were beginning to bear fruit. For Pedro this meant he had succeeded in making *La Prensa* the best newspaper in Nicaragua and that he was becoming a significant political figure. For me it meant recognizing that our family was united and strong in spite of our life of action and struggle and the separations we had endured. Adversity had fortified our character.

By now, Somoza had stepped down from the presidency. A year earlier, the triumvirate of Fernando Agüero, Roberto Martínez, and Alfonso Lovo Cordero had taken office. However, Somoza had taken the post of chief of the Guardia Nacional and supreme commander of the armed forces. Thus his power was intact while he went about the business of campaigning for his reelection. The only opposition against Somoza that had not been coopted by the triumvirate was the FSLN— which continued its decade-old guerrilla war against Somoza—and, of course, there was Pedro.

Then the earthquake hit.

On December 22, the day before the quake, I was sitting at my dresser preparing for a Christmas party, but not in the mood for a party at all. Carlos Fernando had departed to study English at McGill. With Pedro Joaquín he was spending the holidays in Canada. Cristiana was home for a short vacation. Claudia was talking about marriage. The prospect of our children's absence from our lives had put me in a melancholic state of mind. This is how Pedro found me when he came home to tell me about Carlos Santos Berroterran's prediction.

That afternoon, Pedro said, he was busy preparing the day's edition and in a rush to meet the two thirty copy deadline when Carlos Santos Berroterran asked him to hold the issue because there was an important piece of news he should include. This was impossible because it would have disrupted the delivery of the paper, which had to be ready by 4 P.M. to be in the hands of the legions of delivery boys by five o'clock. However, he read the article and in an alarmed state brought it home for me to see.

The article warned that the citizens of Managua should take precautions against an earthquake that would come perhaps that day or the next, but certainly very shortly. Berroterran went on to explain his theory, which I will summarize: In his investigations of weather patterns in our country he had determined a link between droughts in Nicaragua and seismological occurrences. He cited an example from 1930–31. He went on to say the magnitude of the drought we had been experiencing led him to believe there would be tremors throughout the coming year and perhaps even an earthquake of equal or greater force than that of 1931.

It was Pedro's nature to be skeptical, and mine to be intuitive. I reasoned with him that though it was logical to give credence to the man's theory, given the studies he had conducted on the matter, this simply couldn't be so. And without another word I finished dressing.

We departed for the party after Cristiana had left with her date to go to another celebration, in a house in Los Robles. As we drove through the streets of Managua I noticed that the oppressive heat had given way to a cool breeze that rustled the leaves on the trees. Later the keepers of the National Zoo would report that on that evening the animals were going wild in their cages. But to us mortals, on the eve of the great quake everything looked calm. It was impossible to believe that a sinister force was about to change our lives forever.

As midnight drew near we were still at the party. At our table we were laughing at the latest Somoza joke. It was one in which the dictator arrives in heaven and St. Peter gives him a tour of the place. He shows him into a room full of what appear to be clocks.

Somoza asks St. Peter, "What's that?"

"Oh! This is where we keep track of all the mistakes the leaders of the nations of the world make. Each clock represents a country. Each time the hands move on a particular clock, the president of that country has committed another fault."

Somoza looked around but couldn't see Nicaragua anywhere. So he asked St. Peter, "Where is Nicaragua?"

"We keep that one in the mess hall," he responded. "We use it as a fan."

I was laughing so hard I had tears in my eyes. Just then, Pedro broke in with his own story. He said, "Tomorrow in *La Prensa* you will read a report about the effects the exceptional drought we've been having has had on the earth's crust."

Pedro's words were lost in the revelry of the moment. Around us the music was playing loud. People were dancing and laughing. The women glittered in their sequined party dresses. On that evening, no one would listen to stories about an earthquake.

As we drove home everything looked normal. The food vendors were out on the sidewalks. Christmas lights illuminated the stores along

Avenida Roosevelt. Everywhere holiday parties were in full swing. We returned to a quiet house. The night watchman was sleeping while on duty. Claudia was out dancing with José, and Cristiana was still in Los Robles. Finding everything in order, Pedro and I decided to go to bed.

As always, after putting on his pajamas Pedro enjoyed watching me as I went through my nightly ritual. First I would take off my watch and rings, then I would wash my face and brush my teeth; afterward I would comb my hair, which in those days was down to my shoulders. Then at last I would put on my pajamas. It was 12:15 A.M. when I turned off the lights. I was about to get under the covers when I remembered I had not gone to the bathroom. I was washing my hands when I heard our two German shepherds howling. I turned to Pedro and said, "It must be the parties in the neighborhood that have them so excited." But Pedro had already fallen asleep. So without delay I climbed back into bed. I don't know for how long the room had been silent, but I think it was seconds after I closed my eyes that I was jolted awake by the first shock. The bottles in the room were flying from the dresser tops. My first instinct was to burrow deeper into my covers until it had all passed. But then a second tremor came and I heard the deafening roar of buildings coming down in a gigantic rush of concrete and steel. Pedro, who had also been startled from his sleep, said, "Violeta, get moving! We have to get out of here!" We were groping our way out of the house, sidestepping the overturned furniture, when we encountered the maids.

Outside, everything was an eerie silence. The quake had cut off the electricity, the water, and the telephone lines. One by one our neighbors began to appear—Xavier, Pedro's brother, who lived a block away; Julio Vivas, who was a TV commentator; Alfredo and Lucía Marín, who lived across the street. All of us gathered in front of our house and hugged one another.

We were sitting on the curb of the sidewalk when a woman, her face bathed in tears, drove up to the house. It took me several seconds to recognize her because I was blinded by the headlights of her car. It was Rosario Murillo, Pedro's secretary of thirteen years. She lived nearby in Barrio San Antonio with her mother and young son. She needed help, she said, to pull the body of her dead son from the rubble. Pedro and his brother in-law Carlos Holmann (Anita's husband) left immediately with her. The next day, Pedro would recount to me how they had pulled the dead boy out, how they had rescued another who was caught under a fallen beam, how they had helped save a woman trapped in a fire. "It was one emergency rescue after another, desperate people needing help everywhere we turned."

From our home I could see great plumes of smoke in the sky. The sound of explosions could be heard. It seemed that the quake was setting off fires all over the city. I thought of Claudia and Cristiana and prayed that they would return. Cristiana came home first. She pulled up in a car with her date and told me how in Los Robles the garden had been flooded with the water from the pool. At first they had thought it was a tremor. But then a neighbor came in looking for help. He said his house was on fire and his son was trapped in a second-floor bedroom. "The fires," she said, "are all over the city." She was still relating it all to me when Claudia and José arrived from the center of town. Their impressions were even worse. Claudia said, "Everything is destroyed, Mamá. There *is no* city. People are trapped under fallen buildings and fires have broken out in the destroyed marketplace. The flames are devouring Managua." As she spoke, her face was covered in tears. I said, "What a catastrophe this is. We are one catastrophe on top of another," thinking of the political mess we lived in. And now this!

Night turned into day as I sat with our children in the car, unable to sleep, looking out at the starry sky and wondering why Mother Earth had betrayed us.

Pedro returned at dawn from his evening of mercy. With a handful of twigs we lit a fire and I made him some coffee. Then, riding a motorbike, we ventured out to confront our new reality. The city was leveled. Bodies lay everywhere. Those who were alive had the expression of sleepwalkers as they passed with the bodies of their relatives swaddled like infants in rags.

The places where people had once shopped, laughed, and loved were no more. I gazed at the charred remains of Teatro González, then I glanced in the direction of the Gran Hotel. All that remained of its elegant colonial porticoes was a burnt-out skeleton. Yet from where I stood I could see that Somoza's bunker on the hill of Tiscapa was unharmed. Then we made our way north, toward Lake Managua and to the enormous Plaza de la República. It was a scene of death and decay. Pedro pointed to the calm waters of the lake and said, "Look, Violeta, how brilliant the water is today. It's like a deceptive mirror of illusions."

Situated on one edge of the plaza was Managua's cathedral, built to inspire awe and thoughts of transcendence. The once-mighty pillared structure had virtually collapsed. Chunks of concrete dangled from the fragmented walls. Only the massive piers at each end survived, and the tower with the clock that now recorded the exact hour of the quake, 12:20 A.M. Daylight shone through the broken roof, illuminating the altar. Across the street the imposing edifice of the Palacio Nacional, home of Somoza's rubber-stamp congress, was untouched. Why, I wondered, would God preserve this building and Somoza's bunker as well but not spare us the cathedral and the homes of so many innocent victims? I could not imagine then how the quake would lead, a few years later, to the end of Somoza.

At *La Prensa* the earthquake had partially destroyed all the buildings. Pedro recounted to me how ghostly the place seemed. The only sign that there had ever been people there was the concrete markers in the parking lot reserving spaces for Pedro Joaquín Chamorro Cardenal, Pablo Antonio Cuadra, Xavier Chamorro Cardenal, Rosario Murillo, Danilo Aguirre, Octavio Escobar, Luis Rocha . . . In single file, like tombstones, were the names of the people who collaborated in the day-to-day publication of *La Prensa.* For months to come it would be impossible to operate from our headquarters. But in a few days' time, Pedro arranged for *La Prensa* to be published in León on the presses of *El Centroamericano.*

The third night after the earthquake was Christmas, but no one celebrated. I suggested we go stay at my mother's in Rivas, but Pedro wouldn't hear of it. Instead he helped me sweep the broken glass that covered the floor of the corridor of stones. And hunkering around a fire we cooked the day's meal, a dehydrated mixture that swelled when we put it in the pan.

President Nixon sent aid and, with it, the marines. They came to help Tacho "keep the peace," we were told. A state of emergency was declared, a curfew was imposed, our civil rights were suspended, and a military tribunal was invoked in case the people got restless. Tacho said it was to control the looting that was taking place at dark. But a great part of the looting was done by Somoza's very own soldiers.

Each day was a challenge in survival. The city was completely uninhabitable. The hulks of the destroyed city reminded me of Pompeii after the fire and lava. In Managua after the cataclysm people either left or they became more rooted to the land. We stayed. But every day you could observe standing in the streets, in an eerie double file, the interminable lines of people waiting to be evacuated, clutching under their arms small bundles, all that remained of their possessions. Some had a loaf of bread or a few bananas, which they did not hesitate to offer us. The power lines were down. The water mains were broken. There was no marketplace, no food. Every day, from Rivas, Mother would send us our meals and gallons of water, which we would share with our neighbors. Within the layers of the earth the tectonic adjustments continued. For weeks we slept under a mango tree in the back patio and awoke with every tremor to hear the leaves of the mango tree rustling. So began our new life among the ruins.

Pedro labored, and on March 1, 1973, *La Prensa* was reborn. Prefab warehouses were built on a lot four kilometers north of Managua, where the newspaper is located now. From the debris of the old buildings Pedro transferred the rotary presses to this new location.

Claudia and José married that year. None of the other children were home. No one could think of having a party as we mourned the loss of the city. Never again would we see sidewalks, tree-lined avenues with shops, or parks and plazas.

Because of the shortage of housing the newlyweds moved in with us. We built them an apartment above the garage so they could have the privacy and independence we had sorely lacked in our first year of marriage. In time we came to call it, jokingly, the dovecote, because it sat high and was reserved strictly for lovebirds.

In June 1973 Carlos Fernando returned to Nicaragua to enroll at Universidad Centro Americana, with the full intention of studying law. But after one semester he became disillusioned with the quality of the education and informed us of his intention to go abroad to study economics.

Soon afterward Claudia gave birth to Violeta Margarita, our first grandchild. The child, with her dark hair and thick eyebrows, looked like Claudia and Cristiana. Though Claudia and her husband were still living with us, I can't say I had too much time to spend with her, as there was some reconstruction of the house to oversee.

As the self-appointed head of the Emergency Reconstruction Committee, Somoza pushed aside the triumvirate and became solely responsible for the hundreds of millions of dollars in international relief aid that was flowing into the country. When Agüero protested, Tacho had him replaced by another, more pliable Conservative, Dr. Edmundo Paguaga.

Pedro and I called 1973 the year of the committees. There were committees for everything—committees to request millions of dollars in aid, committees for social welfare, committees for hope. . . . And all of these committees answered to one person, Somoza, who headed the Emergency Reconstruction Committee.

The experts Somoza brought to redesign our city produced many dazzling maps that showed plans to construct new shopping centers, new hospitals, new schools. Some recommended organizing the city in a linear fashion, as our Indian forefathers had, along a single trade route. Others believed in a multicentered city like a constellation of stars, all independent from one another. But as the experts spun the golden thread of our dreams into an urban fantasia, Somoza was fast at work appropriating building materials for use on personal ventures. He built shantytowns (touted as great reconstruction projects) on lands that he had bought and that he now sold to the government at inflated prices; he built new roads out of paving materials manufactured by his cement company. For him the earthquake had, in his own words, produced a "revolution of opportunities." The only perceivable action Somoza ever took on behalf of the victims was to evacuate 250,000 homeless citizens to other parts of the country. Afterward he built a fence around the remains of our destroyed city.

These events were all chronicled in the pages of *La Prensa*. Though the newspaper suffered censorship from time to time, we were able to slip things through. When we did, a period of total shutdown often followed. When the Nicaraguan people became aware of Somoza's blatant misuse of public funds, they began to oppose the regime actively and openly. Somoza blamed Pedro for his unpopularity. He accused him of covertly working with Jesuit priests, students, and the FSLN to bring about an insurrection. From that time onward he called Pedro a communist.

The way Somoza ran the recovery program after the quake and his misuse of the international aid funds for his own personal enrichment would be the cause of his collapse. Even those who had traditionally supported the dictator out of fear, economic interests, or pure servility were appalled by his rapacity.

One by one, members of the private sector who had supported him began to abandon him. Under the leadership of the heads of various chambers of commerce, an umbrella organization named the Superior Council for Private Initiative (COSIP) began to gain strength. The council, through two development programs to assist small farmers and business cooperatives, had grassroots connections. In March 1974 COSIP organized a meeting from which emerged a statement accusing Somoza of corruption in the use of the earthquake funds. This was the beginning of a civic front against Somoza.

Also acting against Somoza on a separate but parallel track was what became known as the "popular church of Nicaragua." Composed of radical priests such as Fathers Uriel Molina and Fernando and Ernesto Cardenal, the popular church acted as a recruiting agency for the FSLN among the sons and daughters of the Catholic elite. They maintained that the Sandinista guerrilla movement was the only earthly salvation for Nicaragua.

Halfway through 1974, Pedro Joaquín and Cristiana returned from Canada. Pedro Joaquín worked for a few months with his father before starting an MBA program at the reputable Central American Institute for Business Administration (INCAE). He also began dating Marta Lucía Urcuyo, the fifteen-year-old daughter of my cousin Martita Torres and Henry Urcuyo, of Rivas.

Cristiana, who had completed junior college, enrolled at UCA in the psychology department. The burden of paying college tuition for two children had depleted our savings. We thought that Carlos Fernando should have preference over Cristiana. Luckily, Cristiana is not worse off for our decision. That was the time Cristiana began to date Antonio Lacayo, whom she would eventually marry. He was a distant "nephew" of Pedro's on the Cardenal side who had been studying to become a Jesuit priest.

Though he was far away, Carlos Fernando always had Nicaragua on his mind. He would write to his father thoughtful letters regarding Nicaragua's social dilemma. On one occasion he sent him a paper on the evils of the multinational companies. It was so good that Pedro decided to publish it under the title "Meditations from a Student Abroad." When Carlos Fernando found out, he was very upset because Pedro had not asked him for his permission.

One day shortly after Pedro Joaquín's return, he intercepted an anonymous threat to his father. By accident our son happened to pick up the phone at the same time as Pedro. He overheard a man say, "Kiss your life good-bye, Pedro, because today is the last day of your existence." Without hesitating, Pedro responded, "You know where to find me, you quivering coward," and he hung up the phone. Pedro Joaquín confronted his father about the call.

He said, "Papá, that man sounds as if he is determined. What are you going to do about it?"

Pedro looked at Pedro Joaquín for a minute and answered, "There's nothing we can do, son," and went back to his writing.

Pedro Joaquín didn't sleep all night. The following morning he was up early in order to accompany his father to the newspaper. At *La Prensa* Pedro Joaquín sounded the alert. For months afterward, our son, armed with a pistol, would not leave his father's side. Eventually, Pedro convinced him it was useless to run around scared. "If someone wants to kill you," he said, "he will find you. You can't let fear get in the way of your goals."

Pedro continued his attacks on Somoza. On this particular occasion he was denouncing the unconstitutionality of Somoza's reelection campaign. Pedro and twenty-seven prominent businessmen representing nine political parties and a group of labor organizations moved to boycott the elections. They declared, "There is no one to vote for."

Tacho immediately had them all arrested. Their sentence was to have all their civil rights suspended. But in a country under martial law there are no civil rights to suspend.

In August, President Richard M. Nixon, who had treated Somoza very kindly, resigned under the pall of the Watergate scandal. For the next two years his successor, Gerald Ford, distanced himself from Nicaragua.

In September, Somoza won the elections. In November, he was inaugurated president of Nicaragua. Under the new laws of the constitution he was to serve seven years.

By December, Pedro and the twenty-seven arrested leaders had succeeded in creating a political coalition called the Democratic Union for Liberation (UDEL). The movement was begun to bring about an orderly transformation of the economic, political, and social structures of the country. As a centrist movement it was rejected by the extreme right and left.

I know it was Pedro's secret dream to have Pedro Joaquín join the UDEL. But he wanted our son to choose his own path. Pedro Joaquín, however, was not ready to commit to a life in politics. He did accompany his father to the inaugural ceremony of the UDEL in Masaya. Rallies were forbidden under martial law, so this was just a celebration in a private house with people waving a lot of party banners. Pedro appealed to the people to join in a national movement for peace, "the crowning achievement in the pursuit of truth, justice, liberty, and unity."

When he was not at *La Prensa,* Pedro was at the UDEL. He pinned all his hopes on this movement.

A week later the FSLN performed its first military operation in the urban quarter. A contingent of thirteen revolutionaries attacked the home of a trusted minister of Somoza and took hostage a gathering of prominent Nicaraguan citizens, including high-ranking Somoza loyalists like Guillermo Sevilla Sacasa, Somoza's brother in-law. The American ambassador, Turner Shelton, was one guest who narrowly escaped the assault.

This was a significant breakthrough, because it showed Somoza weakened for the first time. Somoza responded by tightening censorship on *La Prensa.* The move was designed to give the dictator maximum flexibility, allowing him to apply all measures indiscriminately and at his convenience without a voice to report the atrocities.

For a time, Somoza's tactic helped him maintain the appearance that he was in control. But whenever a story didn't pass the approval of the censorship, Pedro would put in its place a really ludicrous story about UFOs or an irrelevant photo of a movie star like Ava Gardner. People came to understand what was going on. Furthermore, Pedro was not one to be silenced. If he couldn't publish his articles in *La Prensa,* he would give interviews to foreign correspondents, urging them to publish news about Nicaragua, or he would speak his mind at the Sunday meetings with the UDEL, calling for an end to the feudal system. He also spoke at international forums, declaring there was a war going on in our country between the Sandinista National Liberation Front and the National Guard that was leaving thousands of innocent people dead. Finally, he would assail Somoza and his cronies directly by dispatching to them private letters in which he labeled them a Mafia gang dedicated to their own personal enrichment. Pedro never lacked for ways to attack the regime.

His friends began to caution him that he was becoming too personal and that his war against Somoza was endangering his life.

At the beginning of 1975, Pedro began a diary. His first entry went like this:

JANUARY 13, 1975

. . . Today I was told of a plan Tacho has in mind for me. I am to be kidnapped and taken aboard an air force plane, hands and feet bound, then dropped at sea so that I may drown. My body will be left for the sharks to feed upon so that no trace of the violent crime remains.

I said to the man politely, "Couldn't you intercede on my behalf and suggest something less savage?"

Pedro admitted in his diary that he had responded sardonically to the informer's revelation to suppress any spontaneous reaction of fear.

In Nicaragua many benevolent people loved Pedro, but unfortunately there were also treacherous and evil people who hated him and wished to see him destroyed because of his political views. To reside in Nicaragua was to live with the constant specter of death looming over us. We fully expected his death to come, not at the end of a long and painful illness endured within the confines of a hospital room, but by assassination. This was something we discussed regularly, even in the presence of our children. Pedro was a man who had given himself to a cause and who would not back down, no matter what the consequences. And so we, his family, were forced to lived with apprehension, dreading the realization of our worst fears.

I suppose that's why, when I kissed him farewell every morning or when we parted because he was going far away on some perilous mission, I did not bid him good-bye as other spouses do, casually expecting to see him for dinner, never thinking that, perhaps, for some tragic reason, he might not return. Instead, I kissed him possessed by the ever-present sensation that every farewell was quite possibly a final parting, maybe the last time in my life I'd see him alive. I would prepare myself for the possibility that our next encounter might well be the final chapter of our life together. And so, when Pedro was alive, his absence, no matter how brief, always created an eerie tension around the house.

The mere sound of a ringing phone at an uncommon hour would cause me to become paralyzed with a fear that almost prevented me from lifting the receiver to discover the reason for the call.

The unbearable burden of living with these feelings of premonition, however, did not make me a morose, inanimate individual reduced to a state of passivity. And our knowledge of Pedro's jeopardy actually brought our family a heightened awareness that allowed us to savor fully all of our experiences as the pain and the joy of our many sacrifices became inextricably woven together.

After the alarm of the first threat, Pedro received all other threats in a light manner, refusing to hire a bodyguard, carry a weapon, or vary his route of travel. He would always say, "Every man must be master of his own fate, the captain of his soul." At first I thought this was typical Latin male bravado, or machismo. Later I came to understand that he meant a person must not allow others to control him through fear and intimidation. And so he engaged the dark forces of oppression with a "calm conscience and peace of mind."

This is how he said it in a letter to Tacho:

January 18, 1975
Before I receive the repressive blow that will surely end my life I want to clarify several points about the current state of our nation. . . .
. . . I want to make everyone see the naked truth of our untenable position and the urgency there is in attempting to save this country by reminding you in the most calm and peaceful manner that Nicaragua also belongs to us. So if you could, please leave us in peace so that others may come to rescue Nicaragua for future generations.
And by the way, I await the blow you have assigned for me to receive with a calm conscience and peace of mind.

In the fall of 1975, Pedro and I traveled to São Paulo, Brazil, to the annual congress of the Inter-American Press Society (SIP), where Pedro was to be an honored speaker. His talk was based on a series of articles about human rights abuses in Nicaragua that, because of press censorship, he had been unable to publish in *La Prensa*. Pedro's articles exposed the slaughter of entire families living in the rural areas of Nicaragua. It was a part of the country Tacho had designated as "guerrilla territory," and his army had been given a free hand in eradicating what he called the "cancer that was eating up Nicaragua." Pedro's presentation to the SIP was widely applauded and transmitted throughout the world by the media. As a result of this Pedro received an invitation to speak in December before the Human Rights Commission in Washington, days after the wedding of our son Pedro Joaquín was to take place.

A few months before, Pedro Joaquín and Marta Lucía had become engaged. Because Pedro Joaquín was my oldest son I gave him the engagement ring Doña Margarita had given to me. It was a beautiful two-carat diamond in an antique setting that had been passed down for several generations. The couple was to be married on December 20 in Rivas.

When the day of the wedding came I was surprised to see what a great formal affair it had become. There were people everywhere inside and outside the church. Not everyone was an invited guest. There were many simple folks who had come to the Church of San Francisco to see the betrothal of the daughter of Don Henry Urcuyo to the son of Pedro Joaquín Chamorro Cardenal. The bride, seventeen years old, wore a beautiful white satin-and-lace gown.

Pedro had a great time. He loved parties, and this wedding reception was a thunderous celebration. He remembered it for a long time. Marta Lucía and Pedro flew the next day to the historic city of Antigua, Guatemala. But their honeymoon was really spent with us and the rest of our children, celebrating Pedro's and my twenty-fifth anniversary.

While they were in Guatemala we were supposed to have flown to Washington, where Pedro was to present his paper on human rights abuses in Nicaragua. Somoza, alerted to the fact, arranged to have him detained at the airport long enough to make Pedro's appearance in Washington impossible. The incident, however, came to the attention of the Human Rights Commission. Pedro's cousin Father Fernando Cardenal traveled to Washington and gave the presentation in Pedro's place.

Pedro and I left with Cristiana, Carlos Fernando, Claudia, and her husband, José, a few days later to join up with Pedro Joaquín and Marta Lucía and begin a cruise to celebrate our anniversary. We went to the Bahamas, Jamaica's Montego Bay, and Haiti, where we toasted the unity of the family. Pedro was extremely emotional that day. Behind his steely character Pedro hid a great tenderness for those he loved. Unfortunately there was never enough time for him to express his emotions. He was always occupied with his politics. That was the last time we traveled together.

Upon our return the newlyweds moved into Pedro Joaquín's bedroom. He still had another semester at INCAE to complete, so we gladly gave him our financial support. When Claudia finished her own home a few months later, the dovecote became available for Pedro and Marta Lucía.

In spite of her young age, Marta Lucía was from the very beginning an exceptional wife. The eldest of three children, she was unusually mature. Pedro and I found our new daughter-in-law to be intelligent and, like so many Rivenses, full of the personal charm which made her acceptance into our family quite easy. Pedro developed with Marta Lucía a special rapport. As a sign of respect he called her Doña Marta Lucía. She responded to his affection by fussing over him and preparing the gourmet dishes she was learning in her cooking classes. His favorite was raisin cake. To this day, when Marta Lucía makes this dessert we all think, sadly, of Pedro.

That same year, after graduating from UCA, Cristiana announced she was going abroad for a year to study on a scholarship she had secured. Pedro and I were completely taken aback. She had been steadily dating Antonio Lacayo, with whom we had developed great intellectual rapport, often discussing into the night the ideas and concerns of the people of his generation. At the time, Pedro and I, who believed in the old way of doing things—the daughter married at a young age to a trustworthy man who would care for her, build a home, and so forth—did not understand her. We felt that if she loved Antonio, Cristiana should marry him without further delay. She was then twenty-one and, we considered, ripe for marriage. After all, Claudia, who was twenty-two, was pregnant with her second child, Fadrique Damian. Now I realize Cristiana is part of a generation of women who have broken with traditional behavior and have contributed to the transformation of our society. Today women demand relationships on their own terms. They have their own identity and agenda. But at that time in a country like Nicaragua, always ten steps behind the rest of the world, these concerns were rare.

Having experienced a love that could not wait, Pedro and I could only interpret Cristiana's actions as lack of interest. We concluded that

Cristiana and Antonio did not love each other. In our minds a great love was an opportunity to be seized immediately. I remember Pedro advising Antonio, "That girl, Antonio, doesn't understand gentle ways. You have to take her by the hair and make her see." It might have been shyness or something else, but Antonio did let her go and waited devotedly for her return, dropping in from time to time to talk to Pedro.

Pedro Joaquín graduated from INCAE in June 1976. Marta Lucía was then five months pregnant with our granddaughter Valentina. Soon they would have to move out of the dovecote. At *La Prensa* Pedro put Pedro Joaquín in charge of advertising sales, where he was such a great success that Pedro became worried our son would never apply himself to his writing. I suppose in his heart, though he wouldn't admit it, he wanted Quinto Pedro Joaquín to follow in the footsteps of his journalist ancestors. He told him, "I don't want you to be happy with being a salesman. Someday you're going to have to write."

As 1976 progressed the country seemed to be moving away from civic movements like the UDEL and toward more radical solutions. That year Somoza's army killed Carlos Fonseca Amador. In the aftermath of the assassination some Sandinistas decided to extend their guerrilla war into Managua. They became known as the proletarians. Others, under the leadership of Borge, stayed in the mountains. As the proletarians' efforts at radicalizing the masses in favor of an armed struggle met with success, a great vacuum was felt among the parties of the civic opposition that offered a democratic alternative to Somoza.

This became clear at a political meeting in Managua for the UDEL, in a poor barrio called Open Tres where some of the most destitute people lived. The meeting had a poor attendance. Pedro was disappointed and depressed. I remember that day Pedro Joaquín told him, "Papá, you have given too much of yourself to this struggle. The people of Nicaragua do not deserve the sacrifices you make." Pedro began to cry. Our son hugged him repentantly. "I'm sorry," he said. "Forget what I've just said." But Pedro Joaquín silently remained convinced his father would die for a hopeless cause.

The following year, however, the UDEL, in association with the church, student, and labor organizations, demanded that Somoza restore civil liberties. Archbishop Obando y Bravo began to urge all Christian followers to assume an activist role in resolving social conflict. He said, "Inequity damages justice and impedes peace."

Imperceptibly, the country was changing, slipping out of Somoza's control.

Almost paralleling the words of the archbishop, President Jimmy Carter gave a speech at the University of Notre Dame rationalizing the need for a human rights agenda. He described a global change in which a socially passive world was activating. He said the colonialism of the 1940s was collapsing. Because of this speech, Pedro in *La Prensa* dubbed him "the missionary president" and predicted that his presidency would have a profound effect in Nicaragua.

When Cristiana returned in June, a year after she had left, she still wouldn't accept Antonio's proposal of marriage. She was teaching history at UCA and was too preoccupied with her work to think of marriage.

That summer Tacho suffered a heart attack and was taken to Miami. In his absence, two important things happened: the UDEL published a document in which it defined a five-point program for democratizing Nicaragua, which included amnesty for all political prisoners, an end to martial law, political freedom, and the elimination of press censorship. Soon afterward, Los Doce made their debut into Nicaragua's political scene.

Although I did not know it at the time, Los Doce (the Twelve) had been created six months before by Sergio Ramírez, at the behest of Daniel and Humberto Ortega. Put together as the possible head of a provisional government in the event of a successful Sandinista insurrection, the group in the meantime was to act as an ambassador for the Sandinista Front, portraying them as pluralists and proponents of democracy. Some of the members of Los Doce were honestly misled by Daniel and Humberto Ortega. Others understood quite well that the front had communist ideas and were in fact communists themselves.

Los Doce had gone into self-imposed exile to Costa Rica earlier that year. After that, the group fanned out throughout the continent, visiting leaders in Latin America, persuading them that the Sandinista Front was not a Marxist terrorist organization. They visited José López Portillo of Mexico and assured him that if the Sandinistas won they would install a pluralistic government.

Pedro became intrigued with Los Doce because they were the boldest opposition to spring from the private sector. He sent Edmundo Jarquín, who was a protégé of the UDEL, to meet with Los Doce in Mexico. But nothing came of the meeting.

Sometime later the group decided to come forward as the sponsors of a Sandinista-led government.

In August Carlos Fernando came home with a degree in economics. He began to work for a technological institute headed by Edmundo Jarquín that did economic studies. Though we were not aware of it, it was then that he began to get involved with Sandinismo.

A month later, *La Prensa* reported a story about the dictator's oldest son and heir apparent, Anastasio Somoza Portocarrero (Tachito), who had recently returned from abroad to join the ranks of the Guardia Nacional. As a man who wielded considerable influence, Tachito ("el chigüin," the Brat, as he was also known) had some value in the eyes of a Spanish manufacturer of agricultural equipment and had been chosen to represent the firm. With the blessing of his father he was pushing through government a $100 million package in which Nicaragua agreed to buy on credit jeeps, tractors, and cars from the Spanish manufacturer. Afterward, it is said the younger Somoza boasted he had pocketed in a single deal $10 million. Pedro pointed out that the future looked promising indeed for the newest Somoza. And so he prepared to do battle with Anastasio III. Pedro had become an obstacle in the Somozas' path. It would not be long before he would receive the first threats.

On October 21, 1977, Los Doce produced a document that was published in *La Prensa* under the title "A Strange Manifesto." Essentially, what they demanded was Somoza's departure and numerous reforms. They ended their document by calling the nation to unify behind the FSLN in an armed struggle. The manifesto was signed by Sergio Ramírez, a thirty-four-year-old man who had been living in Europe for most of his life; Carlos Tunnerman, a former rector of the national university, UNAN; Ricardo Coronel Kautz, a wealthy farmer, son of a well-known writer; Emilio Baltodano, an industrialist and father of two leading Sandinistas; three priests—the Cardenal brothers, Fernando and Ernesto, who advocated in their respective communities a combination of Marxism and Christianity, and Miguel d'Escoto; two lawyers, Ernesto Castillo and Joaquín Cuadra Chamorro (the father of Joaquín Cuadra Lacayo, then chief of the internal front of the Sandinista rebel army); Dr.

Carlos Gutiérrez; and other veteran opponents of the regime, such as Reynaldo Tefel and Arturo Cruz.

This is the situation Somoza returned to when he came back to Nicaragua in the fall of 1977 after recovering from his heart attack. Immediately Somoza tried Los Doce in absentia and issued an order for their arrest.

Two months later Pedro was arrested. This time he was accused of libel by the majority leader of the House of Representatives, Cornelio Hueck. Pedro had written to him making a number of critical observations regarding his conduct as a public official. Now a court had ruled that *La Prensa* and Pedro were to be fined twenty-five thousand and seventy-five thousand cordobas, respectively. But it was nothing more than a scheme to keep Pedro from traveling outside the country.

It was at this time that Pedro, because of his achievements as a defender of freedom of speech, and because of the human rights violations articles he had written, received the Maria Moors Cabot Award from the Columbia University School of Journalism. This is one of the most important prizes awarded in the United States for Latin American journalism. The dean of the School of Journalism said, "If there is in this entire hemisphere someone who is more consistent in his opposition, someone more deserving of this prize than Pedro Joaquín Chamorro, we have not been able to find him. Chamorro, in his battle against corruption in his country, has known how to replace the power of the sword with the power of the written word."

Pedro and I traveled to New York City to accept the award in June 1978. After I snipped one unruly hair that stood out on his sideburn with a little pair of scissors we bought on Fifth Avenue, Pedro looked impeccable as he received his prize. I looked at him in his dark blue suit and felt proud of what he had become. Through his craft as a writer and journalist, he was a potent weapon against Somoza's tyranny.

Antonio persevered with Cristiana, and on December 21, 1977, they were engaged. Pedro and I concluded that he knew Cristiana better than we did. We were extremely happy that day. It seems what our independent daughter wanted was room and time to grow so that the man she married would accept her not as an adjunct to his life, which is how she saw Claudia and me, but as an equal partner with personal dreams as important to the marriage as his. Pedro's joy at Cristiana's wedding announcement was such that he went to his treasured grapevine and cut bunches of grapes. He placed them in little baskets all around the house. He thought of them as the appetizers of the celebration. For Pedro the grapes, which hung together in tight clusters, were a symbol of unity, the seeds a symbol of renewal. He lovingly tended to them. They were the best present he could think of giving to anyone.

As we prepared for the wedding of Cristiana and Antonio, our lives were moving securely in a direction that held considerable promise and joy. Claudia was pregnant, and Marta Lucía had just given birth to the sixth Pedro Joaquín Chamorro. It was to be our first big wedding. But we were to have little to say on the arrangements. Cristiana wanted it done her way. She chose to be married in the house in San Juan del Sur, where she had spent many vacations as a child. And she and Antonio extended to their friends an informal invitation to share in a day of fun in the country.

Pedro didn't mind the simplicity of the celebration. Cristiana's folksiness was very much Pedro's style. His only request to her was that instead of flower girls the wedding procession be led by a child dressed as an angel carrying a cardboard Star of David, as we had done in our wedding and as is the custom in the towns and provinces of Nicaragua. Everything was scheduled for February 5, 1978, Cristiana's birthday.

Around this time Pedro and I talked again about his death. He was then fifty-one years old. I remember he said to me, with a tone of finality, "You will witness my burial. What will you do when they kill me? Promise me you won't cry. It will be very soon . . . and what a farewell it will be! People will go marching through the streets carrying my body on their shoulders. Others will emerge from their balconies to throw flowers in my path. Spectators will hang from the trees to get a better view. The fires lit by the angry crowds will turn the skies red and yellow and spark a political consciousness in the hearts of people such as you have never seen. Everything will be different after that day."

I tried to jolt him out of his black mood by making a joke. "But, Pedro, the houses in Managua don't have balconies!" I said. My husband, I noticed, was more serious than on other occasions. He refused to be humored. Instead he went on, "Violeta, I think it is time we discuss the enormous responsibilities you will inherit."

At that instant, sitting in my recliner with a little stool in front of me to rest my feet, facing the interior courtyard that over the years has become my private jungle, I realized it would be best to move into the intimacy of our bedroom, away from the children and the rest of the household. Gently I guided Pedro to a chair while I, with my head against the brass posts of the bed that had once been my parents', listened as he described to me the written threats and anonymous phone calls he had been receiving.

At the time, *La Prensa,* always a bulwark against corruption, had begun a campaign against Plasmaferisis, a scandalous enterprise that bought the blood of the poor and destitute in our country and exported it to the United States. In most countries such practices were forbidden, but in Nicaragua the international investors involved in this enterprise operated unimpeded, in full view of the public. Through a series of articles that Pedro titled the "Vampire Chronicles," *La Prensa* revealed that Plasmaferisis had come to our country to sink its teeth into the bony flesh of our compatriots with the protection and blessing of the Somoza family, the so-called champions of free enterprise in Nicaragua.

Pedro's friends once again cautioned him that rumors were circulating in Managua of a plot to kill him. They warned him that the Plasmaferisis articles were a greater and more direct challenge to the dictator than anything he had ventured to do before, for it was widely known that Anastasio Somoza was a silent partner in the enterprise.

Predictably, the paper's stories did not stop. Pedro called the reporters who worked for the "daily of the dynasty," *Novedades,* "dumb tools of Somocismo and traitors to human rights, pluralism, and the common good." He uncovered a "piñata," as he called it (a grab bag), among Somoza's friends, who had deeded to themselves land in the agricultural sector. In a front-page story he reported the results of a U.S. congressional investigation that proved that a U.S. tire company had bribed officials of the Somoza regime, Juan José Martínez López and Daniel Tapia Mercado, into purchasing a huge shipment of tires at elevated prices. The two men denied having received any money. So *La Prensa* asked, Who then was the beneficiary? The obvious implication was that it had been the Somoza family. In what would be his last editorial, Pedro wrote that the Somoza family had a monopoly over the resources of our country. They had cattle lands, a distillery, a sugar mill, an airline, a cement company, a slaughterhouse, a meat-exporting company, and so forth, all of which operated with loans financed through the bank they controlled, Banco Nacional, whose debt had been frozen at $30 million. He asked, "Is it not our supreme jefe who is the beneficiary of everything in our country?"

The threats continued, but Pedro ignored them, utterly disregarded them. But I, the practical Violeta, bought a plot in the cemetery. I knew there was nothing I could say or do to change his ways. I asked José, Claudia's husband, to help me find a place where we could lay his body when they killed him.

Then on January 4 Pedro published an article about a lieutenant from Somoza's *guardia* who had deserted his post and fled to Costa Rica on December 31. The man, José Antonio Robles Siles, gave declarations in which he described the antiguerrilla troop he had belonged to, which acted as a death squad in the northern mountains of Nicaragua. He said that after six months in this troop he preferred going into exile to continuing to kill campesinos indiscriminately.

The very next day came a statement from the offices of the U.S. Agency for International Development, defining their position on human rights, which was against torture and denounced the disappearances of political opponents.

Soon after that Cristiana and I left for Miami to prepare her trousseau and purchase the housewares and linens she would need to begin a home with Antonio. That Friday morning in January, when Pedro and I parted —unbeknownst to us, for the last time—there was a certain element of fatality as we hugged. I uttered an unaccustomed warning, a whispered and barely audible "Take care of yourself, Pedro."

As I traveled with Cristiana, I said nothing about my fears. At the time, my premonition was not fully developed.

That night Pedro entertained some of his friends in the library of our home and, as was his custom, reveled in his analysis of the latest developments in the dramatic political climate of Nicaragua. In the previous week there had been news from the mountains. The *guardia* was demanding that farmers boycott the guerrillas and refuse them food and water. Pressured from both the left and the right, the campesinos were abandoning all they had, their *ranchitos,* their cows, their wheat fields. There were also reports of disappearances among the campesinos. Archbishop Obando y Bravo, who was coordinating a committee in preparation for the opposition's national dialogue with Somoza, had announced they would demand of Somoza, as preconditions for a dialogue, an immediate investigation of the disappearances and of the corruption reported in the government; suspension of the censorship that regulated all radio broadcasts; amnesty for Los Doce; and the release of prisoners who had not been charged with a crime. Carter's human rights policy was putting enough pressure on the dictator that he was being forced to consider these demands. This was something that could never have happened before, and Pedro was extremely hopeful that it might help to bring about the change we desired. Simultaneously, the students of UNAN were on strike. They were protesting the reelection of Mariano Fiallos as rector. They had taken over the university and were demanding that Moisés Hassan be named vice rector of the university. That morning there had also been in *La Prensa* a communiqué from the FSLN denouncing the national dialogue as a "lie being perpetrated against the people." "It is being proposed at the very instant in which the dictatorship is wounded and about to sigh its last breath," the communiqué said.

Pedro had been worried by the tone of the FSLN's communiqués. In his last editorial he had condemned the FSLN's indiscriminate use of the term "bourgeoisie" as a pejorative. He argued that the artisans, the farmers, the shop owners, almost all hardworking people in Nicaragua, are in fact bourgeoisie. He said, "These attacks against the bourgeoisie are becoming a decadent part of our national lexicon that gives no credit to the contribution these people make to the country and to democracy.

"It was all demagoguery," Pedro said, "on the part of people who are not *obreros* [workers] or campesinos, but bourgeois themselves who like to pose as proletarians." To his friends, he said, "It's all an interesting contradiction, isn't it?" Then he cut short their meeting to attend his mother's birthday celebration. So much of what he said that evening was so prophetic. When he bade his friends farewell, he said, "My mother celebrates her seventy-eighth year of life today. By the time all of you are that age it will be the next century and you will speak of Somoza as we now speak of Zelaya, like a long-ago, dark period in our history."

The next day, that fateful morning of January 10, because of his mother's celebration, Pedro awoke later than usual. He bathed, dressed, and breakfasted rapidly, in a hurry to get to *La Prensa*. The day's journey awaited him. He bade farewell to Pedro Joaquín's wife. "Adios, Doña

Marta Lucía," he said. He asked her about her daughter, Valentina, and seeing her in her playpen nearby, he told the child, "Give me a kiss." The little girl planted a kiss on his cheek. Then he glanced toward the arbor. He said to Marta Lucía, "I think it has yielded its last grapes." Pedro looked at it for a second more; he opened the door to the garage and then, in the two-door Saab we had recently purchased, he drove off to *La Prensa*.

Stubbornly, he chose to go to *La Prensa* by the same expedient route he had taken for years.

Pedro never detected the presence of the two vehicles that tailed him. One of them, a green Toyota, bumped him from behind. As Pedro slowed his Saab, I am sure he had no idea of what was to come. I am told he did not make any move to protect himself.

With a sudden maneuver, the other vehicle intercepted Pedro, forcing him onto the sidewalk and into a collision with a lamppost. The assassins got out of their cars. One of them unveiled his shotgun and fired point-blank at Pedro. I don't know how many shots met their target; it was of no interest to me to count them. But in our library, which also served as Pedro's office, I have created in his honor a museum where I have placed in a glass case the clothing, perforated with bullet holes, that he wore that day. Preserved intact are the traces of blood, sweat, and dust of that atrocious incident.

I suppose it was there, in the fabric of his clothing, that the warmth of his last breath was lost, because when they took him to the hospital, Pedro was already dead. But on January 10, 1978, at 8:30 A.M., as he died at the wheel of his car, Pedro carried enough oxygen in his breath to ignite a revolution that would bring the end of the dictatorship.

Ten minutes later someone interrupted an editorial meeting at *La Prensa* to tell Pedro Joaquín that his father had been hurt in a car accident. When Pedro Joaquín arrived at the scene of the crime, there was a great crowd of people. The ambulance was just leaving. He didn't see Pedro's body. But when Pedro Joaquín saw the Saab smashed against the lamppost, the shattered window, the amount of blood, he felt a horrible emotion, sensing that the worst had happened. His fears were confirmed when he looked into the sad faces of the crowd. He knew someone had finally killed Pedro. He asked them if they knew where the ambulance had taken his father. "To the Hospital Oriental," someone answered. Pedro Joaquín got into his car and began to drive. For a moment he was confused. Uncertain whether he was driving east or west, he stopped his car by the lagoon in Tiscapa. After a moment he came back to his senses and drove west toward the hospital. He was the first family member to arrive. Again he noticed the stricken look on the faces of those who approached him. His sadness became greater. A hospital technician then came up to him and asked if he could identify Pedro's body. They took him into a room. Spread before him was the lifeless figure of Pedro. His body, riddled with holes, smelled of gunpowder and smoke. Our worst fears and forebodings suddenly crystallized in one poignant moment.

Later that morning, shopping in Jordan Marsh in Miami for the plain white peasant blouse and skirt Cristiana wanted for her wedding day, without knowing the tragedy that was unfolding, I found myself growing impatient. "Come on, Cristiana," I chastised. "Make up your mind so we can go home." I did not tell her that since our departure that morning I had been disturbed by a growing sense of foreboding. I remember that I was resting on a step in a display area where they had mannequins, waiting for Cristiana to emerge from a dressing room where she was trying on a skirt, when I saw Jaime, Pedro's brother, heading toward me.

I knew he and his wife were in Miami visiting an allergist with their son, so I wasn't alarmed at first. But the soothing voice with which he told me, "Violeta, Pedro has been in an accident," immediately alarmed me. I knew the calmness of his voice belied the true urgency of his words. Suddenly, the happiness I felt for the upcoming celebration evaporated. Without saying more, I went in search of Cristiana and announced, "They've killed your father." Jaime, who had followed behind me, immediately corrected me. This time, however, his voice was trembling as he said, "No, Violeta, he's not dead. It's just an accident." But I knew the truth. I was barely able to control my growing desperation. We paid for the skirt and returned to our hotel room. I greeted a friend, Henry Lópes Ona, who was waiting to take us to the airport, by asking, "They've killed Pedro, haven't they?" Henry nodded his head sadly.

Just then the phone rang. It was a call from Managua. They wanted to discuss with me Pedro's embalming. In the hospital room where Pedro's body lay, his mother and sisters were discussing which clothes to put on Pedro. But for me it had to be the dark suit he had worn when he received the Maria Moors Cabot Award at Columbia University. I cannot remember Pedro looking more handsome and dignified than he did then. I wanted him to look equally distinguished at his own funeral.

We packed our bags in minutes and followed Henry out to his car. At the airport were two ex-members of the Olama and Mollejones expedition—Horacio Aguirre, the owner of *Diario de Las Américas* in Miami, accompanied by his wife, Helen, and Eduardo Chamorro, one of the eleven captured with Pedro in San Pedro del Lóvago. Our friends helped us get seats on a Pan Am flight to Managua that was filled to capacity. All this time Cristiana wept and moaned, blaming herself for not having been there to see her father a last time.

At the airport, as Cristiana and I struggled to return to Managua, I admit that for a moment I questioned Pedro's quest—because I loved him more than any of his causes, and his assassination had blown our life apart.

Meanwhile, in Nicaragua, just as Pedro had predicted, his funeral was becoming a political event of great dimensions. Telegrams of sorrow were pouring into *La Prensa* from all parts of Nicaragua as news of Pedro's death was transmitted in a flash bulletin by Radio Mundial. The reaction of most people was total disbelief. Then came pain, the tears, the flowers. Everyone wanted information regarding Pedro's burial. Long lines formed at the bus stops as people from the provinces struggled to come to town to participate in his burial.

In Managua, Pedro's body was being marched through the city. Though there were no balconies, the people climbed on telephone poles and coconut trees so they could see his coffin go by.

When Cristiana and I arrived in Managua, my sister Clarisa and her children were there to receive us. I didn't see Pedro until much later. Pedro Joaquín, Claudia, and Carlos Fernando were with Pedro when his body arrived in our home on the shoulders of our friends. All through the night we kept vigil over him. There were mourners everywhere. Interminable lines of people streamed in through the doors of our home to shake my hand. Inside the house and out in the park across the street, I could hear people screaming in pain, some in anger. Party flags of all colors were waving everywhere. "Get rid of all these flags" was the first thing I said to the crowds. "The Nicaraguan flag should stand alone." Then one of my guests said: "There are so many people out in the park, Violeta. Perhaps we should hold the wake out there?" But I could not consent to laying him in an open casket in the vast open air of the park at Las Palmas. I worried that the Somocistas might try to do something to his body. But some people protested, "Pedro is not only yours. He belongs to the people."

All through the house I could hear the weeping growing louder, working itself into a powerful crescendo that was beginning to resonate beyond the walls of our home. It was as if our private lament was somehow finding its way into the streets of the city and blending with the sobs of women and men who, with fists extended, demanded justice. And without any of us intending it, I could feel our voices compounding into one tremendous echo against the Somoza regime. In everybody's mind there was no doubt that Somoza had killed Pedro.

To tell you the truth, I don't know how I arrived at a state of lucidity and serenity sufficient to carry me through the proceedings. I didn't know what to do. Pedro and I, in our countless conversations regarding the final scenario of his death, never anticipated the conflict that now arose between my personal desire to give him a simple and private burial and the wish of the masses of people to mourn their catastrophic loss, their need to share in our bereavement.

I understood then that the killers hadn't just killed Pedro. They had silenced the voice of an entire nation. Repeatedly I told myself, "Pedro has died for the people. I cannot deny them their wish to bid him a final farewell."

From our home in Las Palmas we carried Pedro's body to *La Prensa*. The poor, the rich, students, labor unionists, nuns, and priests, they all came. Some of them would sprinkle holy water on him and utter a last prayer as they blessed themselves; others tore off pieces of the black muslin cloth that covered his coffin.

But when it was over, I gathered the Chamorro clan together and told them, "We will transport him in a delivery truck and take him to the church at Las Palmas. There, behind closed doors, we will hold our private wake." In the church I felt as if Pedro and I were sharing a solemn farewell surrounded by a wall of silence no one could penetrate. His death was an intimate experience to which I opened myself without reserve, offering no resistance to the pain. For I knew from the other deaths in my life that the torment would not last forever. Long ago I had come to accept that death and birth have their time. They are forces we cannot control.

Within hours of Pedro's assassination, the investigations conducted in haste by Somoza's minions brought the speedy apprehension of the perpetrators. But those who had pulled the trigger were not the intellectual authors of the crime. The trail led to a Cuban American entrepreneur by the name of Pedro Ramos, who had fled the country. He was the owner of Plasmaferisis, the blood plasma exporting company in Managua that had been the subject of Pedro's exposé in *La Prensa.* The implication was that Pedro's editorials were the motive for his assassination.

But that only implicated Somoza, whose network of political forces and business interests, which Pedro had attacked in *La Prensa,* was the more likely cause. Pointing us in that direction were the obvious advantages to the Somozas of Pedro's elimination.

Outside the church, ten thousand people were waiting to accompany us to the cemetery. I stood on the steps and spoke to them. I said, "Let us stop the clamoring and have peace. Let us sing the hymn of the republic." With that, we began our march through the crowded streets of Managua in a mournful procession that led up to the cemetery gates. Cristiana and I walked ahead, holding the Nicaraguan flag. Behind us, guarding Pedro's coffin, were Pedro Joaquín, Claudia, Carlos Fernando, and the rest of the family. We laid him to rest under the shade of the oaks in a plot that, in accordance with our last conversation about his death, I had purchased just weeks earlier. Standing by his graveside surrounded by my children, I could not imagine why I had instructed the gravedigger to excavate a hole so deep that for all practical purposes it had become a well. I suppose I felt that if we buried Pedro under three meters of clay and pumice the earth would protect him, cradle him, just as I carried the thought of him so deep within my body that his death seemed almost a dream to me.

After the gravedigger lowered the coffin into the ground he offered me the Nicaraguan flag that had led the procession. "No," I said, "put it on top of him so that he can take it with him." Pedro's sea of admirers then gathered around his grave. Throwing sprays made of the jasmine and oleander flowers that grow wild in our country, they wept and cried, "Death to Somoza!"

I imagine that on the hill of Tiscapa, for decades the seat of government in our country, the tyrant could hear the calls, and with the chilling breezes of January he must have felt fear.

Throughout the procession, the National Guard was under strict orders to maintain a safe distance from the multitude of people. They were to refrain from reacting to any provocation. But the lieutenants did not have enough foresight to place the soldiers that guarded us far enough to escape hearing the antigovernment slogans that Pedro's friends and admirers were shouting. That evening fifty thousand angry people poured into the streets, burning buses and trucks and attacking the banks and factories that were the property of the Somozas. It was a tumultuous scene that heralded the bloody demise of the dictator's ruthless dynasty, as Pedro had often called it.

The nation was inflamed. And I, who had never before spoken in public, found myself before a microphone denouncing the Somozas: "We live in a dictatorship so vast and encompassing," I said, "that even the smallest insect must have the tyrant's permission to fly."

When news of Pedro's murder reached the Department of State in Washington, for the first time in the history of Nicaragua a red alert message was sent to the White House. Pedro's death had finally jolted the world to attention.

Speaking to the media on that day, sitting in a corner of my house, I never had the slightest notion what was to come. Three forces were swiftly converging: Pedro's death, the unification of the entrepreneurial middle and upper classes against Somoza, and the militant actions of the Sandinistas.

But as we reached that crossroads in our history I was absorbed by grief. I wanted to die. Life without Pedro had ceased to have meaning for me. I hadn't yet realized what role I was to play. "What am I going to do without him?" I said, leaning on the shoulder of Pablo Antonio Cuadra, Pedro's cousin, who was blind with pain.

"*Be him,*" he said.

I thought he was making reference to *La Prensa*. The paper was Pedro. Clearly there would be a void at *La Prensa* no one could fill. How could I, a simple housewife?

But Pablo's words, "*Be him,*" took on greater meaning when I stopped to consider Pedro's many other roles. He had been so much more than a newspaper editor. He was a multifaceted individual who had fought the

Somozas on many fronts. It was nearly impossible for anyone to replicate Pedro. But I thought, Perhaps, unified, we can fulfill the expectations created by Pedro's crusade. Pedro can live through our actions if, together, we can embark on a road to liberty and justice. Several days later Pablo Antonio wrote an editorial entitled, in boldface type, BE HIM.

Chapter Six

IN THE FIRST DAYS OF MY WIDOWHOOD, MY grief was unabating. I retreated into a loneliness from which I refused to emerge, rejecting the company and sympathy of my own children, feeling oddly detached from all those who could acknowledge the painful reality of Pedro's death. In fact, I survived by surrounding myself with a wall of denial that shielded me from the true heartache of the tragedy.

Aware of the limits of my endurance, I refused to ponder the economic difficulties that surely lay ahead as my children and I attempted to go on with our lives. These issues, I reasoned, would force themselves back into my conscious mind later. But for now I kept them at bay.

What I could not keep from my thoughts, however, was the memory of Pedro's pain at not having realized his great objective. In the past year he had reiterated his commitment to liberate Nicaragua. Yet he wondered if God would give him time to fulfill the promise he had made so long ago. Now pounding at my heart was the realization that Pedro's project had been stopped, his efforts halted by the treacherous hands of those paid assassins. What futility I felt when I contemplated Pedro's life as a sacrifice to an unfinished and perhaps hopeless cause. So much was left unfinished at his death.

I lamented that I could not die in his place, return to him the years that had been stolen. I realized then that the anguish I felt would never dissipate unless I could find some purpose in his death. If the blood he shed could somehow inspire the thousands who had marched beside his coffin to rise against Somoza, then Pedro's death would not be in vain. I understood that the tribulations of my life with Pedro had prepared me for this difficult moment. The pain we had both felt had fueled us into action.

Like his father before him, my son Pedro Joaquín became involved in the editorial aspects of the newspaper. Each day that passed without justice and retribution for Pedro's killing he recorded in an insert on the front page of our newspaper. Four hundred and eighty-five days had passed when Somoza, on the brink of disaster, shut down the paper. Forty-nine days later, after a pitched battle, the Somoza dictatorship ended. Indeed, anti-Somoza sentiment had reached critical mass as a result of the assassination: 534 days after Pedro was killed, Somoza fell.

The day after Pedro's death, the UDEL canceled its participation in the national dialogue. They said, "There is no point in discussing anything with a regime that uses repression as a way of sustaining its power." The announcement was signed by Pedro's friend Rafael Córdoba Rivas, who had assumed the leadership of the movement.

International news services echoed this condemnation, calling Pedro's murder "a cowardly and brutal slaying." Journalists the world over were horrified. The Federation of Latin American Journalists (FEPAL) held Somoza directly responsible for the death of his most tenacious opponent and asked that he be publicly repudiated.

The day after the assassination, Silvio Vega, the conspirator who drove the car and contracted the assassins, confessed. He said a man by the name of Silvio Peña had paid him $3000 to kill an enemy of "the chief." "After this you'll be made a lieutenant," Peña had said. "If they catch you, deny everything. Cornelio Hueck and Fausto Zelaya will send you twenty or thirty lawyers, who will come to your defense." Vega claimed that when he found out Pedro Joaquín Chamorro was the target he wanted to back out, but Peña wouldn't let him. Peña threatened to kill Vega's family if he didn't go through with the plan. For a whole week they had Pedro under surveillance. Their intention was to kill him at the first opportunity. But each time Vega botched it. So instead, he contracted professional killers, Domingo Acevedo and Harold Cedeño. They were the ones who pulled the trigger, for the sum of ten thousand cordobas. During his confession Vega pleaded for protection and broke into tears. He said, "I killed the one who was our only protector, the guardian of the poor."

That same afternoon, Silvio Peña was apprehended about an hour's drive west of Managua, in Chinandega, the city of the cotton growers. He confessed he had arranged Pedro's assassination. But the intellectual authors of the crime, he insisted, were a group of Somoza loyalists. He fingered Cornelio Hueck, the man who had sued Pedro for libel; Pedro Ramos, the Cuban from Plasmaferisis; Fausto Zelaya, who managed the housing projects that were one of Somoza's profiteering schemes after the earthquake; and Somoza's own son Tachito, Anastasio III. At one time or another all had come under attack from Pedro. But they denied any connection to the crime.

When asked how much he had received in payment, Peña said, "Five hundred thousand." "Cordobas?" he was asked. "No, the real big ones. . . ."

If the amount was correct, it undoubtedly meant some powerful people were involved. But I didn't believe for a minute that under Somoza the truth could be found.

In *La Prensa,* the children wrote their eulogies.

First, Carlos Fernando:

We have lost a father and a friend, a person of integrity, who excelled as a family man and as a public figure. . . .

. . . There is a lot I could say about his life—talk, for instance, about the path of rectitude he followed until his death, about the impact he had in our country. But the people have spoken with far more eloquence than I by pouring into the streets en masse, expressing their outrage for his murder and solidarity for his cause.

. . . Who will do justice for this crime, I ask? Not Somoza, who lacks a modicum of credibility. Not Somoza, who kills or has others kill for him. Justice can come only from the people.

Then Claudia:

Father, there are no words to describe you as a parent, as a man, as my best friend. . . . The pain I feel for your death is great, but greater is my pride in you. . . .

Father . . . one day you told me you'd die for us. For years these words have been silent in my heart. Now your words have found my voice and I speak so that all can hear:

". . . Our children are the fatherland, for them we must suffer and sometimes even die."

. . . Father, today for you the earth and sky will tremble. . . .

. . . No one can stop us.

Father, you were chosen by the Lord. . . . Now that you are in his glory, watch over us.

A week had passed since Pedro's demise when Rafael Córdoba Rivas read Pedro's last will and testament. It was a last good-bye in which he restated the aims and goals of his life. What little he possessed he bequeathed to me. There wasn't much in terms of material wealth. He named me "sole executor and friendly arbiter" of his will, "so she may carry out her duties unencumbered."

"To each one of the children, Quinto Pedro Joaquín de la Merced, Claudia Lucía Cayetana, Cristiana María, and Carlos Fernando Frutos Eugenio, all four with the name Chamorro Barrios," he said in the will, "I leave one thousand cordobas." In those days that was about $300. He could have given them more. But I think he was trying to tell them he held little regard for money. Pedro's real legacy was the numerous books and diaries in which he shared his thoughts and experiences.

After the reading I held a press conference. I told reporters that on the previous evening, while watching TV, I had seen Pedro's body for the first time. He was shown on his back in the morgue, his arms and torso bloody. He looked as if he had been unnailed from a cross. I mean no blasphemy, but he reminded me of the figure of Christ after the crucifixion. His blood had flowed darkly. I told everyone that Somoza knew that he could not wash his hands of this.

Encouraging me to continue with Pedro's mission were my family, Pedro's friends, and his political allies. Among them was Carlos Andrés Pérez, the president of Venezuela.

Like most people's, Carlos Andrés's immediate reaction to Pedro's assassination was incredulity—particularly because he had recently met with Tacho, who had assured him that he had no interest in hurting Pedro. Instead, Tacho had cynically argued that Pedro's continued existence and that of *La Prensa* helped him. He said, "Pedro is living proof that freedom exists in our country." Carlos Andrés had planned to meet with Pedro after we went to the SIP meetings, but because of a tight schedule the appointed rendezvous did not take place. Now Pedro was dead, and Carlos Andrés regretted not having seen his old friend one last time. In Carlos Andrés's mind there was no doubt Somoza was the culprit. Disturbed by Tacho's lack of morals, he dispatched a letter to President Carter, asking him to participate in a joint action against Somoza.

On the ninth day after Pedro's death, we attended a commemorative mass in Barrio Rigüero, celebrated by Padre Uriel Molina. He said, "What appears before our eyes to be a defeat can become our salvation and our triumph." Drawing subtle parallels from the book of Samuel, he spoke of the Philistine invasion of Israel and of the need for the people under the leadership of Saul to become a unified front against the common enemy. In the months to come, this call to unity would become our national mantra. After the mass all of us marched in a quiet procession to lay a wreath in the cemetery before Pedro's tomb.

That afternoon, the Superior Council for Private Initiative (COSIP) called for an end to Somoza's farce of justice. "This brutal crime," they declared, "has brought to the surface the moral decadence and lack of personal guarantees we, as Nicaraguans, are forced to live with."

After the Democratic Union for Liberation (UDEL) pulled out of the national dialogue, the private sector and the church also withdrew. In a public statement, issued by Archbishop Obando y Bravo, they said it was too late to sit down and talk with Somoza about reforms. They called for an end to Somoza's regime.

At the Universidad Nacional Autónoma, the strike that had begun the day before Pedro was killed continued. Now it had turned into a bloody riot, in which two hundred were injured and ten killed.

That same day, COSIP fired off a series of communiqués calling the entire nation to a general strike. First the shops in the *centro comercial* closed, then the auto dealerships, the hardware stores, and the supermarkets, followed by the largest industrial complex in the country, the Nicaragua Sugar Estates. From the first week of the strike the streets of the capital were deserted. There was little or no commercial activity.

For the first time in the country's history you could see there was unity in our opposition. The people had made up their mind. They wanted Somoza out. It was the beginning of the civic revolution Pedro always thought possible.

That week, Claudia, Cristiana, and I appeared before a district judge, directly accusing Somoza of Pedro's death. Afterward the clamor for

Somoza's resignation could be heard. It became a condition for ending the strike.

Twenty-one days after the assassination, Venezuela announced a boycott on Nicaragua: "No more petroleum." Nicaragua at the time was entirely dependent on Venezuela's oil.

Then, almost simultaneously, the United States said that until it saw progress in the human rights situation in Nicaragua, it was suspending military aid.

At last realizing that he had his back up against the wall, Somoza began calling his friends in Washington to intercede for him. There were many congressmen who came to his aid: George Hansen, Republican from Idaho; Charles Wilson, from Texas; John Murphy, Democrat from New York, an ex-classmate of Somoza's. The two had first met at La Salle Military Academy, then later they attended West Point together. Murphy was the chairman of the Merchant Marine and Fisheries Committee, which had under its jurisdiction an important piece of legislation (relating to the Panama Canal) that President Carter was trying to push through Congress. Resolving the United States's differences over the canal with the Panamanians had been a primary objective of Carter's administration. Now Murphy was threatening to sink this initiative unless Carter let up on Somoza.

As American aid to Somoza teetered in the balance, thousands of marchers rallied in the streets of León and Granada chanting, "Down with Somoza," and "The people united will never be defeated!" In Matagalpa ten persons died in a confrontation with the *guardia*. In Managua the campesino mothers of the *desaparecidos,* the "disappeared"—men and women who had been arrested without account, tortured, and perhaps executed—took control of the offices of the United Nations. They demanded that Carter send a human rights mission to Nicaragua to investigate the disappearances, while throughout the nation the strike continued.

February 1 marked the second week of the strike. *La Prensa* reported that the entire financial system was shut down and that 75 percent of Nicaragua's commercial activity had come to a halt, racking up millions of dollars in losses per day. Meanwhile, Somoza continued to assert that he had U.S. support and was not going to resign. It was at this point that the Federation of Latin American Journalists, with a membership of sixty thousand newsmen, began an aid fund for the strike. Money began to flow in from everywhere.

One day, at the offices of *La Prensa,* I received a call from Pedro's brother Jaime, who was then in Costa Rica. He told me there was a $100,000 check, sent to me by Carlos Andrés Pérez, deposited in my name in a bank in Costa Rica. He wanted instructions on what to do. I did not know if the money was for me or for some other purpose. Carlos Andrés had said nothing. So I instructed Jaime to hold off until I could find out the purpose of these funds.

A few days passed, during which I kept my silence. Then one night Claudia came into my room. She asked me, "Is it true that Carlos Andrés has sent you $100,000?" "Yes, it's true," I said, surprised that she even knew about it. "What about it?"

"We would like you to lend some of it for the cause."

"Who is we?" I asked.

"Los Doce. They will pay you back."

"Claudia, I don't know why I have been given this money. Let me think about it." Later, on the phone with Carlos Andrés, I learned that the money was for me. "Do with it as you please," he said. "I know Pedro wasn't rich. You are a widow with four children. I know you need this money. It's my gift to you. Please accept it."

I remembered the time in Costa Rica when I had given him our old refrigerator, and I thought gratefully, This is payment with interest.

"I'll visit you soon," I said, "to thank you in person."

To Los Doce I decided to lend $50,000. I figured I could afford it. I received enough income from *La Prensa* to survive on. Besides, this was just a loan. Between us there was only our word. After all, Los Doce were people I could trust: Joaquín Cuadra Chamorro and the Cardenal brothers, Fernando and Ernesto, were Pedro's relatives; Reynaldo Tefel had been a member of the Olama and Mollejones expedition; while the others—Emilio Baltodano, Carlos Tunnermann, Ricardo Coronel Kautz, Ernesto Castillo, Arturo Cruz, and Dr. Carlos Gutiérrez—were all men Pedro and I related to socially. Miguel d'Escoto I knew to be from a Somocista family, but he was also an activist priest, which seemed to balance the equation.

So that morning, I simply called Jaime and told him to allow Ernesto Castillo's wife, Rosa, to withdraw the agreed amount. I wish now that

Jaime had made a copy of the check he gave to Rosa, because to this day I've never seen a penny back. The money doesn't matter. It's the feeling I have of being deceived that bothers me. Few people know this, but I helped to finance the revolution against Somoza.

A mere thirty days had passed since we had lost Pedro when we gathered together to celebrate Cristiana's twenty-fifth birthday, the day she was supposed to have been married. On the spur of the moment, she and Antonio decided to go ahead with their plans to marry. That night somebody found a judge, who performed a civil wedding at Claudia's house. A Catholic ceremony was scheduled for the following weekend at our house in Las Palmas.

Xavier Chamorro, something of a schemer, immediately requested that he be the one to take Pedro's place and give Cristiana away. Within the Chamorro clan and the UDEL, there was a certain amount of expectation as to who would be the anointed heir to wear Pedro's political mantle. Nobody in our immediate family imagined that this action of Xavier's would be construed as the least bit symbolic.

The next day, happy to fulfill my duty as a mother, I buried my grief and submerged myself in the details of preparing for Cristiana's wedding. There was no time now to arrange for a trunkful of linens and housewares. The house in Las Palmas had to be cleaned, the food had to be prepared, the flowers ordered. Claudia took it upon herself to sew a blouse for Cristiana to wear with the skirt we had purchased in Miami. Cristiana and I argued over whether she should wear a slip under the gossamer wedding skirt, a request to which she finally acceded. She would not give in, though, on her decision not to take her husband's name. This was an unprecedented act in Nicaragua, where women traditionally used *de* after their Christian, or first name, indicating their husband's dominion. "I do not belong to anyone," she said. "Cristiana Chamorro Barrios is who I am. I can't give this up to be Mrs. Lacayo or de Lacayo." Antonio said, "Let her do as she likes."

As we went about our quiet family celebration in the dusty, red-tiled village of Monimbo, a revolt was simmering. It began with the protest of marchers every evening after curfew, which escalated, in a matter of days, into burning tires and throwing bombs. The local *comandante* and his troops, following strict orders not to engage the demonstrators, kept their distance.

When the day for Cristiana's wedding arrived, the ceremony was short and simple. Cristiana wore fresh flowers in her hair and sandals. Following Pedro's wishes, his niece Erica Holmann, Anita's daughter, carried the Star of David we bought at the marketplace in Rivas. Xavier's presence by Cristiana's side was understood to be an honor, and some people inferred that Xavier, the deputy director of *La Prensa,* now succeeded Pedro in some way. Though I was surprised by this reaction I failed to give it any importance. Between the weeping and the laughter I had no time for divisive thoughts. Happy to be with my family, I led us all to rejoice in what was still to come while privately I wept for what could no longer be.

The newlyweds left for South America on their honeymoon that afternoon. Afterward they moved into the house in Las Palmas. Pedro Joaquín, Marta Lucía, Valentina, and Sexto Pedro Joaquín were still living in the dovecote, so Cristiana and Antonio moved into her old room, right next to mine.

By the end of February, the unrest in Masaya had begun to spread to other cities—Managua, León, Estelí, Matagalpa, and so on. All over the country a new groundswell of support for the young rebels *(los muchachos)* could be felt among the population.

Carlos Andrés, who had been in constant communication with Jimmy Carter, told me he felt the United States had to intervene to push Somoza out. I don't know if it was due to Murphy's threats to derail the Panama Canal treaty, but Carter was against a military action. "The United States," he said, "cannot intervene in deposing the government of any country, no matter how worthy the cause." Carlos Andrés was furious. My view, on the other hand, was that Nicaragua must never put in jeopardy its sovereignty, which is what foreign interventions generally do. Somoza's fall would come as the result of internal pressure, provided the United States stayed out. But I did want to see that the temporary suspension of U.S. military aid became permanent.

The opportunity to promote this idea came several days later in the form of an invitation to me to speak at the annual convention in Cancún, Mexico, of the Inter-American Press Society (SIP), the news organization where Pedro had presented his paper on human rights abuses in

Nicaragua. A few days before my departure, more bloodshed occurred. In the church of San Sebastian in Monimbo, a group of two thousand women and children attending a commemorative mass in Pedro's honor were attacked with tear gas by the National Guard. That evening, which also happened to be the anniversary of Augusto César Sandino's death, primitive bombs were made by the villagers and detonated all over the city. The rebellion was crushed by General Reynaldo Pérez Vega and a platoon from Somoza's army. The siege, though short-lived, became a symbol of heroic resistance and the model for the Sandinistas' future guerrilla campaigns throughout the country.

With a greater resolve to see an end to this killing, I departed on February 28 to Cancún. Everywhere I went I was followed by reporters who wanted me to speak about Pedro, "the martyr of civil liberties." This natural sympathy for Pedro, coupled with the bold actions of the popular masses, had turned Nicaragua into a breaking story. I remember that Pedro Joaquín and Marta Lucía, my companions on this trip, insisted on sneaking me through back entrances in order to shield me from the reporters. But in my passionate drive against Somoza I was beyond exhaustion. I insisted on giving as many interviews as possible. I wanted everyone to know that the Somozas had shown no will to discover the truth about the crime.

In Cancún I read the speech I had written with Pedro Joaquín's help. Though I initially struggled with my oratory, the words now came easily: "My friends, as we stand here today in the sunlight of this beautiful city . . . freedom of the press remains captive in the brutal hands of the Somoza dictatorship. . . . *La Prensa,* the largest circulating newspaper in the nation, is under daily censorship . . . and all independent radio and TV stations are subject to Somoza's black code . . . an arbitrary set of rules that controls the media." The dictator could literally close us at his will. When I finished, I sat down to thunderous applause.

Charged with the emotion generated by my first speech, I spoke a few days later before a gathering at New York's Freedom House and opposed the notion that the Somoza dictatorship and the National Guard were agents of stability in our country. I said, "This assertion runs contrary to the desires of the majority of Nicaraguans, who want Somoza out. If an armed revolt ensues, it will be because of Somoza's refusal to leave power."

My speeches to the press must have had some effect on President

Carter because at that point, at Carter's behest, the American ambassa-dor, Mauricio Solaun, stepped in to end the hostilities between the strikers and Somoza. He paid a visit to Somoza and extracted from him a promise to resign from politics at the end of his term and to commence a series of liberating measures that would restore civil liber-ties, lift the state of emergency, and remove press censorship against *La Prensa*. With those concessions, the strike ended.

But the opposition did not dissipate. Young professionals and entre-preneurs, the middle ground of the opposition, who deplored Sandi-nismo but had a social conscience, banded together behind Alfonso Robelo to form a new political party, the Nicaraguan Democratic Movement (MDN), in February 1978. Simultaneously, Alfonso an-nounced his resignation from the leadership of COSIP, sold his shares in his business enterprise, and packed his family off to Miami, while declar-ing himself from that moment on a full-time politician. Many of the original founders of the MDN—Ernesto Leal, Fernando Guzmán, Pablo Vigil, Carlos Hurtado—later became cabinet members in my administration.

Somoza kept his promise to Solaun, which was to lift the state of emergency and censorship of *La Prensa*. Immediately our newspaper reported that paramilitary troops were keeping Monimbo in a virtual state of siege; that in Estelí a massacre had occurred when the entire city had taken to the streets in protest after army troops had shot a twelve-year-old boy; that in León as well as in Matagalpa, people had been killed when they tried to set up burning barricades to protest against the regime. The headline of our cover story read, "All over the country people have lost their fear of Somoza and are calling for an end to his rule."

At the same time, in Washington, I attended a ceremony honoring Pedro given by a prodemocracy group called the World Organization for Democratic Freedom. While there I met with Senator Edward Ken-nedy and other influential members of the U.S. Congress. I also met with the undersecretary of state for inter-American affairs, Terence Tod-man. To each of them I reported the latest events, emphasizing the bloodshed that would take place in Nicaragua if Somoza stayed. I told them, "People are not afraid of Somoza anymore. They will stop at nothing to push him out."

I wanted to undermine the effect of Somoza's core-group supporters.

They persisted in arguing that Somoza was a deterrent to communism and that Carter's suspension of military aid to Somoza indicated a leftist tendency in the American president. "Quite to the contrary," I argued, "the unrest in my country is a reaction to Somoza's own unyielding desire to hold on to power. It cannot be blamed on Marxists. Ours is a classless struggle for national liberation, undertaken by an overwhelming majority of the population. *Obreros* and campesinos have united with other sectors of society to push Somoza out. Until he leaves, Nicaragua will continue to be mired in blood and tears." I was not an orator, but I spoke passionately. I felt deeply that prolongation of Somoza's rule was pushing us all to the brink of desperation. A few days later I was to learn how true this was.

Upon my return, in the beginning of 1979, I learned that Reynaldo Pérez Vega, the general who had repressed the Monimbo rebellion, had been assassinated. The blood-soaked body of the general was found in the house of a well-known lawyer, Nora Astorga Jenkins. It was wrapped in the black-and-red banner of the Sandinista Front.

Nora Astorga had worked for five years as the legal counsel for our old friend Enrique Pereira. Enrique, who had the sharp instincts of a shark, held Nora in high regard and assured us there was no possibility she could have any connection with the gory crime. Everyone was befuddled.

A week passed. Then one morning at our offices in *La Prensa* we received a letter from Nora Astorga Jenkins proudly declaring herself a Sandinista militant and claiming full responsibility for, as she put it, "executing Somoza's henchman." Under orders from her superiors in the front, she seduced Pérez Vega, leading him into her home and into an ambush, where he was repeatedly stabbed in the neck with an ice pick.

The decision to print the controversial letter in *La Prensa* fell to the newspaper's editorial board, which at the time was controlled by people who were secret members of the Sandinista movement, like my son Carlos Fernando, Danilo Aguirre, Eduardo Holmann, Xavier Chamorro, and Edmundo Jarquín. They had a secret strategy to tilt the day's news in favor of Sandinista objectives. The other editorial board members, Pedro Joaquín, Pablo Antonio Cuadra, and Horacio Ruiz, who were not Sandinistas, often sympathized with their positions, though not always unanimously. In this instance, however, the determination to publish Nora's letter was undisputed. And so, it appeared in that day's issue along with a photo of the machine-gun-toting corporate lawyer dressed in military fatigues. The news became an immediate sensation in Managua. It was the story of an ordinary person driven to extremes of behavior by a desire to expel Somoza. People compared Nora to Judith, the biblical heroine who had to kill King Holofernes in order to liberate the people of Israel. The event brought greater social acceptance of terrorist acts and contributed to the radicalization of the moderate opposition.

Some weeks later, on March 28, Carlos Andrés met with President Carter in Caracas. Aware of the recent developments, he told Carter, "Nicaragua is on a violent path to rebellion. If nothing is done to intervene, it could become a replay of Cuba under Batista." In response Carter outlined a series of multilateral diplomatic channels the United States could explore. Carlos Andrés, a forceful and dynamic man who liked taking matters into his own hands, had no faith in or patience for multilateral talks. He decided then and there to aid the Sandinistas in his own way.

He professed not to be concerned with the Sandinistas' politics. Several times he said to me, "They are the enemies of my enemy; as such they are deserving of my assistance." To succeed against the tyrant we had to form a unified front and forget about our disagreements. But the Sandinistas were *guerrilleros,* living outside the law, with no conception of how to behave in a civil society. Though we did not understand it at the time, an alliance with the Sandinistas was dangerous. In those days we were too obsessed to reason. Besides, in our minds and in the context of our struggle, Pedro, not Marx, was the spearhead of our revolution.

This emotion was expressed in an event hosted by the Democratic Union for Liberation (UDEL) in Granada. A statue of Pedro was unveiled, and distinguished leaders of all the different parties took turns speaking. "Greater than any monument we can unveil is the memory of Pedro. . . . We carry it in our hearts like an emblem as we move against the dynastic dictatorship of the Somozas." In Monimbo and in Estelí the battle cry was "Pedro Joaquín Chamorro lives!"

Standing at the microphone, I stared for a while at the whiteness of Pedro's monument, so real it was as if his flesh had been cast in stone. Then, finding my voice, I said, "The gift we have received from the tragedy of Pedro's death is national unity. His martyrdom, though devastatingly painful to me and my children, is the medium through which Pedro's ideals are becoming realized."

For Carlos Fernando, Pedro's murder was a turning point. For years he had been collaborating with various Christian revolutionary movements doing sociopolitical work. When Pedro was killed, Carlos Fernando began to lead a double life. By day he was a reporter at *La Prensa;* by night he was out doing political work, developing mass support for the FSLN's armed struggle. He would not share any of this with me. Sometimes he disappeared for days into the poor barrios. As a mother I sensed his deepening commitment to the revolutionary cause and I worried about his safety. If he fell into the hands of Somoza's *guardias*—he, the son of Pedro Joaquín Chamorro—what would happen? I honestly didn't know. All I could do was, through *La Prensa* and my campaigns abroad, to work toward finding a resolution to the conflict as soon as possible.

After Pedro's death, everyone at *La Prensa* would ask, "What does Violeta think?" As president of the board I didn't have the constant influence of Xavier, who had elbowed his way into being the director of the newspaper, over the protest of Carlos Holmann and Jaime. But as the widow of Pedro, who had dedicated his life to *La Prensa,* I had a position of preeminence that allowed me to act as roving ambassador for the newspaper.

In mid-June President Carter traveled to Panama to sign the official transfer documents that concluded the treaty in which Panama and the United States agreed to declare the canal a permanent neutral zone. The crucial waterway had been for the last decade a subject that had sullied Panamanian–U.S. relations. Now the two countries were to be allies in managing the canal for the benefit of both. In Latin America this was hailed as a significant advance in U.S.–Latin American relations. Carter took the opportunity to discuss with the leaders of Venezuela, Costa Rica, Colombia, Mexico, and Jamaica the human rights situation in Latin America. The issue on everyone's mind was Nicaragua and how to encourage freedom and democracy in our country.

Until then Panama's head, General Omar Torrijos, had been Somoza's friend. Now, perhaps as a result of the treaty and a desire to be held in good standing with his new democratic friend Jimmy Carter, Torrijos decided to try to influence Somoza. Through Luis Pallais, the dictator's cousin, Torrijos sent word to Somoza to democratize or perish. He set the upcoming elections in Panama as an example and suggested to

Somoza that he do the same. Word of this secret meeting leaked out and became a topic of discussion in the political and social circles of the capital. Humiliated, Somoza became enraged with Torrijos.

It was at this juncture that I departed to visit Carlos Andrés in Venezuela to thank him personally for the money he had sent me. As he had done many times before, Carlos Andrés offered us his unconditional friendship and support.

On June 19, several days after Somoza had received the message to step down from Torrijos, he announced a new series of liberalization measures. They included amnesty for all political prisoners and the return of Los Doce from exile.

At the time, I was on my way back to Nicaragua. En route, I stopped in Costa Rica to meet with Rodrigo Carazo Odio, the newly elected president of our neighboring republic. He met with me at the airport. He said that, short of intervening directly and breaching its position of neutrality, Costa Rica would help our cause. At the time Costa Rica was already acting as a safe haven for Los Doce and leaders of the Sandinista movement such as Humberto Ortega. In time Costa Rica would become a land bridge in the flow of arms to the Sandinista *guerrilleros* operating in the north of that country.

About this time, Somoza's liberalization measures began to appease the opposition. Talk was circulating about a negotiation with the private sector. This must have unsettled the Sandinistas. They wanted an armed revolt that would give them total victory and full control of the country. Soon afterward, through Los Doce, Sandinistas Daniel and Humberto Ortega proposed a tactical alliance with the bourgeoisie. By denying their Marxist views, this segment of the Sandinistas, which became known as *terceristas,* moved to attract a pluralist following and form a broad opposition front in favor of the armed struggle. Privately, two other segments of the Sandinistas disagreed with this position, which caused, for a time, a rift within the rebel movement.

On July 5, Los Doce returned to Nicaragua to put this new plan into action. On the morning of their arrival thousands of spectators lined the road to the airport to receive them. Cristiana and I watched from the offices of *La Prensa* as they went riding by on the back of a pickup truck.

Their first stop was in Monimbo, to lay a wreath in the place where the Monimbo massacre—which had happened in Pedro's name—had begun. In the crowd as an observer was Carlos Fernando. He had been skeptical of the effect a group of wise men like Los Doce could have in helping to bring about a revolution, but he came back impressed with the massive popular support these men seemed to have garnered.

Inciting the people to heights of euphoria, Los Doce lauded the heroic way in which Pedro had lived his life. Later that afternoon Cristiana and I welcomed them to Pedro's house; together we marched to the cemetery to lay flowers before Pedro's tomb. To honor Pedro was a good tactical move for Los Doce. In doing so they were associating themselves with the symbolic figure of my martyred husband. Since I felt certain this would further our cause, I cooperated and pledged them my support and that of *La Prensa*.

In the days that followed, *La Prensa* publicized Los Doce's every move. Much to Somoza's annoyance, they wasted no time moving throughout the country advocating an armed rebellion. It was a matter of weeks before they had brought into their new movement the Broad Opposition Front (FAO), the UDEL, the MDN, and two labor federations.

President Carter interpreted news of these unrestrained activities as a sure sign that the dictator was coming to his senses. To further encourage him he wrote Somoza a letter on June 30, 1978, congratulating him for allowing Los Doce to return and encouraging him to go forward with his plans to offer amnesty to all political prisoners, reform the electoral system, and ratify the American Convention on Human Rights.

For most of us it appeared as if Carter was trying to make amends with Somoza. I felt at the time the honesty of President Carter's policy on human rights had come into question. (Today I think it might have been an innocent gesture on his part.) So immediately I dispatched a letter to him urging him to consider Pedro's assassination, directly traceable to the Somoza family, as part of the human rights problem in Nicaragua. I asked him to make good on his promise to punish human rights abuses. In my letter I said, "Mr. President, the Nicaraguan people are still waiting and hoping that you will demonstrate a more consistent approach in the implementation of your human rights policy."

Toward the end of July Somoza traveled to the island of Orchilla, off the coast of Venezuela, to meet privately with Carlos Andrés. In this meeting Somoza revealed to Carlos Andrés the contents of Carter's congratulatory letter. He implied that he had come to an understanding with the American president. Carlos Andrés would later recount to me that he had told Somoza repression could take him only so far. Sooner or later his dictatorship would end, with or without American support.

Carlos Andrés's commitment was almost as great as mine. In my desire to bring our cause to the forefront of any discussion I wasted no opportunity, no matter how personal or poignant, to point out the nefarious presence of the Somozas in Nicaragua. To all the journalists who came to my house, I spoke of my twenty-seven years with Pedro. "As we battled the Somozas, there were years that overflowed with suffering and anguish, always fleeing, always in danger. I don't wish my hardships on anyone. At the same time our passage together was so full of passion because of the ardor of Pedro's ideals that I would not trade places with any woman." Then I took them into Pedro's office, now a museum where Pedro's struggle, waged for more than thirty years, is depicted. The photographs, letters, and mementos of our life hang like relics on the walls. I have the striped garments he wore during his imprisonment, the paintings he produced in solitary confinement, the spinal corset he wore after his release because of his beaten vertebrae, the bloody clothes from the day of his murder, the empty shells from the tear-gas bombs thrown by the *guardias* at the crowds as they carried his casket to the cemetery. To each journalist I repeated the same thing: "Pedro died not just for the sake of the poor, but for the freedom of all Nicaragua."

On August 21 the Broad Opposition Front (FAO) released a sixteen-point plan calling for Somoza's departure. It was published in its entirety in *La Prensa*. Chief among the demands was a call to create a national unity government that would succeed Somoza and complete the transference of command of the National Guard to officers unrelated to Somoza. The FAO also announced a second general strike for September. I was brimming with optimism at the prospect of a peaceful transference of power. Then from the Sandinista camp came a bold military strike.

On August 22, 1978, two truckloads of revolutionaries disguised as National Guardsmen disembarked at the Palacio Nacional. They captured twelve hundred hostages, including Somoza's congress. Among the hostages was a reporter from *La Prensa,* Manuel Eugarrios. Through the intervention of Archbishop Obando y Bravo, the Sandinistas' chosen mediator, Manuel smuggled out several rolls of film as well as an FSLN manifesto. The pictures portrayed the youth and courage of the insurgents. Risking another shutdown, we featured the photos and manifesto on the front page of that day's issue of *La Prensa*.

The photos elevated the participants in the expedition to a level of media stardom that was unprecedented in Nicaragua. One in particular, Edén Pastora, René Schick's former bodyguard, became the celebrated Comandante Zero. There was also a woman, Dora María Téllez, who would gain fame as the military leader of the rebel army in León.

The palace siege lasted forty-eight hours, from August 22 to 24. It netted a half million dollars in government funds from Somoza and the release of fifty political prisoners, chief among them Tomás Borge. The palace raiders and the liberated prisoners flew to freedom in Panama, where they were received like heroes by General Omar Torrijos. Afterward some of the group left for Cuba for military training. Others went to Costa Rica. Pastora left to meet with Carlos Andrés in Venezuela, where a plan was hatched. In the first days of September, Pastora, or Zero, as he became known, returned to Costa Rica to start a southern attack front supplied by arms shipments from Venezuela.

The day after the palace siege ended, FAO summoned the nation to a second general strike. Within a week, the strike succeeded in paralyzing the entire nation.

Rumor had it that this time the strike was not an act of mere civic resistance but part of a larger military action planned in coordination with the Sandinistas. It was rumored that Alfonso Robelo, leader of the MDN and a member of the FAO, had met with Humberto Ortega on several occasions in Costa Rica and had forged a secret alliance between the MDN civic movement and the FSLN.

The fact is that two weeks after the strike began, the FSLN in collaboration with members of the bourgeoisie launched simultaneous attacks against several cities—Managua, Masaya, León, Chinandega, Estelí, Diriamba, Jinotepe, and Rivas—as well as a frontal attack from Costa Rica. It became known as the September Offensive. When the Sandinistas were overpowered, their retreat was protected by members of the bourgeoisie. Being less experienced, many were injured or captured.

One group whose story I'm familiar with was that of Alfredo César, Bernardo Chamorro, Carlos Schutze, Pierre Peñalba, and Alejandro Carrión. Some were members of COSIP, others of the MDN. All of them were professionals with jobs in the private sector, children of the bourgeoisie. However, incensed by Pedro's assassination, they had been secretly collaborating with the faction of the FSLN to which Humberto and Daniel belonged. Their orders were to provide cover for an FSLN commando that on September 9 was going to attack a military post south of Managua. When they arrived to take their positions, the group was caught in the cross fire between the *guardias* and the *guerrilleros.* They defended themselves with the carbines they carried. But they were ill prepared to confront such a situation. Almost immediately, Bernardo Chamorro and Carlos Schutze were seriously injured in their extremities. So, as the fighting continued, the group took refuge in a Catholic boys' school nearby. There they spent the evening. In the morning they tried to escape. But only Schutze and Chamorro, who left with their injuries bandaged and concealed under priests' robes, met with success. The other three waited until dark before leaving on foot in three separate directions. César and Carrión had the misfortune to be captured, and were tortured for twelve days by Somoza's *guardias.* The beatings they received were so great that when their families were finally allowed to visit them, they were black-and-blue from the neck down. César in particular had the traumatizing experience of having a friend die, after a brutal thrashing, while handcuffed to his wrist.

Claudia and José had also been collaborating with the *guerrilleros* by allowing their home to be used as a safe haven by Sandinista field commanders. To avoid their meeting a similar fate at Somoza's hands, I urged them to take flight to Costa Rica with their five-year-old daughter, Violeta Margarita, and their two-month-old son, Fadrique. I thought about the way life seems to repeat itself at times. Claudia and José's departure for that neighboring country was a replay of Pedro's and my life in exile.

On September 13, 1978, 180 *guerrilleros* led by Comandante Zero invaded Nicaragua on its southern front. After forty-eight hours of fighting, the invaders fled into Costa Rican territory with the Nicaraguan air force in pursuit, attacking with bombs and machine-gun artillery. In the cross-border incident a Costa Rican schoolteacher was killed. President Rodrigo Carazo Odio, in retaliation, broke diplomatic relations with Nicaragua and called upon the OAS for sanctions against Nicaragua.

Aware that Somoza would not fall to a military defeat, the FAO met with U.S. ambassador Solaun to propose that a delegation of friendly countries visit Nicaragua and persuade Somoza to cease fire and pursue a peaceful solution to the situation.

The September Offensive was a military failure but a diplomatic success, in that it mobilized the U.S. government into action. The Carter administration realized that if the United States did nothing, Nicaragua would polarize into two opposing camps—Somozas and Sandinistas. And so, rather than choosing between a dictator they could not support and a communist movement they would not endorse, State Department officials took a conciliatory tack, arranging multilateral mediation talks on behalf of the OAS.

On September 21 the OAS foreign ministers passed a resolution calling for mediation. Two weeks later the Interamerican Commission on Human Rights visited Nicaragua. When they arrived Somoza was still busy carrying out minor "cleaning operations," flushing out the remaining insurgency forces. The indiscriminate practice of capturing or killing anyone suspected of being a rebel was duly recorded by the observers. In just two weeks the commission declared Nicaragua to be in gross violation of human rights. It cited the killing of children, the bombing of civilian territory, the torture of political prisoners, and mass executions.

William P. Bowdler, the U.S. representative to the mediation team, concluded that the only way to avert war was for Somoza to leave. At this point, Carter stepped up the pressure. He persuaded the International Monetary Fund to suspend a $20 million line of credit for Nicaragua. His expectation was that this would influence other international creditors to do the same, thereby leaving Nicaragua in a state of virtual illiquidity.

Somoza proposed a plebiscite. Whoever emerged as the strongest would cogovern with him until 1981. But the United States proposed instead a referendum on Somoza, in which he would step down if he lost. Somoza rejected the plan and the mediation talks broke down.

Carter's advisers wanted to prevent Somoza's swift removal because they felt certain that after his departure a power vacuum would be left that would facilitate the ascent of the Sandinista leadership. In Washington it was no secret that the Sandinistas were unabashed admirers of Fidel Castro and that they were deeply indebted to him for the assistance they had received.

Unsure of what to do, the Americans refused to make any public displays against Somoza.

On his part, the dictator was doing everything possible, short of resigning, to reestablish American faith. Early in December he declared a general amnesty and freed the political prisoners in his jails. The released prisoners flew to Costa Rica, where they immediately began training for an invasion. Among those freed was Alfredo César, the Pellas executive who had been captured during the September uprising.

Alfredo's involvement with the Sandinistas had surprised many of us. Since he was a protégé of the Pellases—the richest family in Nicaragua after the Somozas—his interests, everyone believed, lay in forging a career as one of their top executives. In addition, his starched and primped appearance was not what one would normally associate with the image of a *guerrillero*. As it turned out, his future was not as a soldier in the trenches but as a cabalist in the upper echelons of power. It was this aspect of his personality that most interested the Sandinistas. After his release, they recruited him to work full-time as a strategist for the future Sandinista government.

United States–sponsored talks to resolve the crisis, which had been renewed, broke down again on January 13, when both sides declared an impasse. All hopes for a civic solution died, and the only course of action left to the people was armed struggle.

A month later, pressured by Senators Edward Kennedy and Alan Cranston and New York City mayor Ed Koch, Carter permanently suspended military assistance, canceled economic aid and credit, and recalled a large portion of American embassy personnel and Peace Corps members, including the U.S. ambassador, Mauricio Solaun, who was replaced by Lawrence Pezzullo. This was perceived as a hardening of relations between Somoza and Washington.

Fourteen months after Pedro's homicide, it was becoming increasingly clear that though Washington was still unwilling to give Somoza the final nudge, they were pushing him to the brink of disaster. But Carter's thoughts were not on Nicaragua but on Iran.

On the weekend of April 7, 1979, between two and three hundred *guerrilleros* came down from their mountain enclave and took over the city of Estelí. The revolutionaries simultaneously staged lightning raids on various smaller towns in northern Nicaragua—Ocotal, El Sauce, Condega. These were followed by rebel attacks on the more populous western cities of León and Chinandega. After a few days of fighting, the *guardias* reclaimed the cities by bringing their Sherman tanks and air power to bear on the rebellion. The savagery with which the Guardia Nacional repelled the insurgents, killing in the process many innocent victims, turned the civilian population completely against Somoza and further damaged his image outside Nicaragua.

I was in Houston at the time, undergoing a general checkup, accompanied by Claudia, when I received the news.

In late April news leaked out that the MDN's Alfonso Robelo and the UDEL's Rafael Córdoba Rivas were engaged in discussions with Moisés Hassan, the leader of the FSLN's National Patriotic Front (FPN), regarding the commencement of a third national strike. At once Robelo and Córdoba Rivas were jailed.

As of May the Sandinista army was on the march. Attacking from all sides—north, south, east, and west—they forced Somoza's troops to disperse. Then in one swoop they moved to cut Somoza's army off from its supply center, Managua.

Somoza's army fell within sixty days. *La Prensa,* until its closing in early June, faithfully recorded the events of each day, tolling the dictator's downfall with every headline.

May 7: STUDENTS RISE AGAINST THE REGIME

May 8: COMANDANTE ZERO VOWS VICTORY

May 12: 42 CONGRESSMEN WRITE LETTER TO CARTER AGAINST SOMOZA

May 14: 11 BODIES IN THE MORGUE—Entire family massacred in Jiloa for alleged nexus with the FSLN
ROBELO AND CÓRDOBA RIVAS SET FREE

May 15: COMBAT IN MASAYA—FSLN is on the march

May 16: EXTERMINATION CONTINUES—Somoza bombs civilians

May 19: HONDURAS MOBILIZES TROOPS ON NORTHERN FRONT—They will intervene in favor of the dictator

May 20: FSLN FORCES LEAVE JINOTEGA CUT OFF

May 21: MEXICO BREAKS RELATIONS WITH SOMOZA—López Portillo denounces horrendous genocide

   JINOTEGA, A LIBERATED ZONE

May 23: COLOMBIA PROPOSES A COLLECTIVE BREAK IN DIPLOMATIC RELATIONS WITH NICARAGUA

On May 27, I boarded a TACA airlines flight to Costa Rica to visit my children in exile, Claudia and José, and my two grandchildren Violeta Margarita and baby Fadrique. Pedro Joaquín, Cristiana, and Carlos Fernando remained in Managua.

Once in Costa Rica I started a diary, into which I poured my angst and anger:

MAY 27, 1979   *San José, Costa Rica*

I have arrived in Costa Rica. Claudia is pregnant and alone with my two grandchildren. José has gone off to war to fight against the tyrant and beast, Anastasio Somoza Debayle. . . . He is not the only one. At this very moment it is said there are thousands of young armed men and women fighting against the dictator in our southern front.

   I have decided to stay with Claudia until the last moment. I recall quite well the loneliness of my own life in exile, and I thought, as mothers do, that she needed me. We will wait out the war together. Hopefully it will not be much longer.

In the next days, *La Prensa* urged citizens to join the national mobilization that was in full swing against Somoza. Then, after *La Prensa* reported news of important military action against him, on June 1, Somoza reimposed censorship and shut down the newspaper.

From my diary:

WEDNESDAY, JUNE 6, 1979   *San José, Costa Rica*

I awoke thinking about Somoza's fall. . . . How much longer will this killing last?

   In the days since they shut down *La Prensa* the fighting has continued to escalate. . . . I am told Managua has fallen into a deep silence. No buses or automobiles circulate on the street; all commercial activity has ceased.

In church I pray for my children, for the young of Nicaragua who are dying. When I return, hours later, I am greeted by a smiling Claudia. José, her husband, has been in touch with her. Thank God, he is alive. For a moment this alleviates my sadness. But my concerns are larger than my own family. I grieve for the whole country.

Somoza is bombing civilian neighborhoods. He has cut off water and electricity to Managuans. He wants to flush out *los muchachos* from their hiding places as if they were rabbits in their holes.

JUNE 9, 1979 *San José, Costa Rica*

Managua is under siege. Trained *guerrilleros* and a ragtag army of citizens occupy the buildings surrounding the command posts. They cut doorways in the common walls of the buildings, moving from one to another as if through a corridor, without exposing themselves to gunfire. Barricades cut off access to the streets. The major arteries into the city are blocked off.

The *guardias* try to isolate the *guerrilleros.* Becats, bulletproof patrol jeeps equipped with a mounted machine gun, tour the perimeter of the fighting zone, taking aim at the barricades. But they are unable to penetrate into the core of the action. A convoy of Sherman tanks breaks through the barricades. At once the tanks are encircled by scores of civilians who crawl onto them and like ants devour them, ripping them apart piece by piece and setting them on fire.

Unable to kill the insurgents on the ground, Somoza reverts to air attacks, indiscriminately bombing the civilian population as well. Waving a white flag, the feeble, the aged, and the young abandon their homes.

SUNDAY, JUNE 10, 1979 *San José, Costa Rica*

Somoza sent his air force to bomb *La Prensa* today. By land, his *guardias* attacked with tanks. Afterward, with kerosene, they set fire to the place. Fortunately, because of the shutdown there had been no one at the plant.

The beast can now rest happy. It is the fulfillment of his fondest dream. He rules Nicaragua unencumbered by opposing opinions.

The press is camped outside my door. They have heard the news. They all want to interview us. They tell us Somoza has blasted *La Prensa* to bits, that everything is in flames.

Claudia and I are in constant touch with Managua. Calls come in every minute, international calls too. Everyone is saying it is an act of savagery. All night I have been awake thinking about Pedro. How he used to worry about my future as a widow without an income.

In our conversations together Pedro had predicted that *La Prensa*'s campaigns against Somoza would culminate one day in its destruction. But we never imagined how vicious Somoza would become in his final hour. In his indiscriminate search for dissidents Somoza had turned irrational, perhaps even insane. Gagging *La Prensa* had not been enough. He was possessed by a desperate need for vengeance, and so without any apparent remorse he had trained the cannons of his hatred on the newspaper.

Chapter Seven

SOMOZA'S ACT OF VENGEANCE TOWARD *LA Prensa* was not without consequences. At the behest of the foreign ministers from several countries in Latin America—Venezuela, Colombia, Panama, Mexico—a resolution was passed on June 18 by the OAS. For the first time in history, this group recommended the removal of a ruler who claimed to have been legitimately elected. In fact, from this moment on, at the U.S. State Department, Somoza's departure was seen as a certainty.

Shrewd and astute, Somoza did not bother to respond. Instead, he combed the continent looking for military leaders who would support him. But everywhere he turned, Somoza found his path blocked; Nicaragua had become an outlaw nation. As a last measure Somoza attempted to win President Romeo Lucas García of Guatemala to his cause. But the Guatemalan wouldn't lift a finger without U.S. approval. For the first time, Somoza realized he was alone and had no more cards to play.

As this was happening, at Claudia's tiny apartment in San José people came to offer their condolences.

I tried to record the moment for history:

SUNDAY, JUNE 10, CONTINUED

The first visitors begin to arrive. They've come to mourn the loss of the newspaper. I stand by the door receiving them, grieving and listening. Their voices surround me. Their arms embrace me. I feel as if I am under water, submerged in a dark nostalgia. Seventeen months have passed—it is as if Pedro has died all over again. The man who distributes *La Prensa* in San José is at my side. Since my arrival he has been sending me the daily issues of *La Prensa*. He tells me he has some money. He offers it. "It's *La Prensa*'s," he says. "I can give you that, and more, if you need it."

But the whole passage is so unreal. I tell myself it can't end here. *La Prensa* must rise again.

Jaime, in the name of the board, has asked me for the remaining $50,000 Carlos Andrés has sent him. I tell him of course I'll give it to him. It's what Pedro would have done.

Around nine o'clock two men arrive with Reynaldo Tefel. I recognize them as members of Los Doce. Claudia tells me they are Miguel d'Escoto, the Maryknoll priest, and Sergio Ramírez. "They need to speak to you urgently," she says, "and in private." I move around the place talking, helping serve refreshments. The men are with Claudia. They seem to be in a hurry. But there is never a moment alone. They leave without talking.

By the time the last few guests leave it is past midnight. Claudia and I sit at the dining room table. "Somoza's opponents," she tells me, "those in exile here and those fighting in the trenches . . . all want you to be part of the new junta."

My first instinct is to say, "No, it's a huge commitment." But that's not what worries me most. "I really am not a politician," I tell her. "You know that I like to speak my mind, that I am stubborn. It is one thing to help bring down Somoza, another to govern in his wake."

"Please, don't make any hasty decisions," she pleads. "The men will be back tomorrow. You have nothing to lose by listening to them. They're under a lot of pressure from the Americans. They really could use your help."

Since Pedro's death it has been my custom to gather my children together and request their opinion and advice on matters related to *La Prensa* or to Nicaragua, which under the circumstances is impossible to do.

I tell Claudia that in my mind this is the greatest obstacle. I refuse to do anything without her siblings' approval.

Afterward, I lie awake staring at the ceiling. I ask Pedro, my husband, companion, and teacher of thirty years, to instruct me on the right course of action, to give me a sign if he thinks I can be of use to my country.

MONDAY, JUNE 11, 1979   *San José, Costa Rica*

I rise early.

The men come for my reply at 8:30 A.M. To my surprise, Alfonso Robelo is with them. "What are you doing here?" I ask. "Well, I am going to be part of the junta," he responds. In my mind his presence is a good sign. It means these people aren't communists as some people say.

Sergio Ramírez takes the lead in the conversation. "Doña Violeta," he says respectfully, "did Claudia tell you why we're here?" Instead of answering, I ask, "What sort of government are you planning?"

He speaks to me about a five-member provisional governing junta that will assume the leadership of Nicaragua after Somoza leaves. He says, "Our dream is to build a democracy responsive to the people's need, that gives people work, lands to the compesinos, and health services for all. Sergio is one of the five. Alfonso Robelo is another. There are also two *guerrilleros,* Daniel Ortega and Moisés Hassan, who I have heard are avowed Marxists."

"Why me?" I ask. "I don't represent any party and I am not an eloquent person. There are others better qualified than I."

He tells me I am a respected individual and that Pedro's prestige and that of our defunct newspaper can help the revolution.

I want to help them. I believe, as Pedro did, that every attempt at unity is positive. But as part of a government, I feel, I will just be another obstacle.

In addition, I think that if for some reason events do not move as swiftly as expected, I will be indefinitely detained in San José—awaiting the fall of Somoza. Who would protect my children then?

As if guessing my thoughts, Sergio tells me, "Somoza's fall is imminent. Bowdler, Carter's special envoy, is standing by to hear the results of our discussion so he can return to Washington to make plans for Somoza's exit."

Nobody wants to see Somoza go more than Violeta Chamorro, the widow of the martyr of civil liberties. But there is also the question of commitment. *La Prensa* is in ashes. I need time to rebuild it. How can

I do this if I am part of an insurrection movement? Again sensing my hesitation, Sergio says, "It's only for a couple of years, or however long it takes to prepare for free and fair elections."

Still unwilling to commit, I promise him I'll give the matter some thought. I worry about repercussions on the rest of my family. My mother, three of my children and their families, Pedro's sisters and brothers are all within striking distance of the dictator. Surely, they too will be put at risk by my decision!

Getting up to leave, Sergio says, "You have until tomorrow to decide."

As I bid him farewell I ask, "Do you think this junta is a bit to the left?"

"I can't deny that Daniel and Moisés are communists," he answered earnestly. "But you and Robelo are democrats, and I am a social democrat. I will act as a bridge between you."

Thus I was lulled into believing that we had a chance to build a free and democratic government dedicated to carrying out social reforms while maintaining a place for private enterprise. And so I believed that the new government would defend Nicaraguans of all creeds. I agreed to join.

I entrusted myself to God and Pedro and told the junta representatives, "I accept, pending, of course, the approval of my children. I will call them this very day."

"Be careful what you say because Somoza monitors all the calls," Sergio told me.

"Don't worry. After all these years, I know how to deal with these situations."

After they left, I called Managua. I cryptically explained the situation to my children. I asked them to think about it overnight and I told them that I would call them the next day.

That night I didn't sleep again, thinking about the offer I had received. I thought if I could help pull up Somocismo from its roots to replace it with democracy—not communism, as Somoza liked to say—I would be doing a good thing.

At home the children gathered together to decipher my message. When they spoke to me the following morning, Pedro Joaquín, Cristiana, and Antonio told me in unison, "We support your decision."

"What about Carlos Fernando?" I asked.

"He's helping the country in his own way," they said.

I knew this meant that Carlos Fernando, whose involvement with Sandinismo had grown out of a natural affinity for their ideals, had joined the military action. In fact, at the very moment in which I was weighing my decision whether to join the junta, he was under fire in a barrio outside Managua called Open Tres. Later he would tell me that news of my involvement came to him while underground by way of an announcement on the clandestine Radio Sandino.

The battles in León, Chinandega, Matagalpa, Estelí, and Managua, the children told me, had entered into another bloody phase. Each morning, by the shores of the lake, Somoza's *guardias* executed dozens of boys who had been arrested for suspected revolutionary activities. The people of Managua were vacating the city in fear. Tens of thousands of refugees were reported to be in the Red Cross centers and in churches throughout the country. At the American embassy an evacuation of the families of diplomats was under way. I thought of Carlos Fernando and wondered what would happen in the event that he was captured. Would his being the son of Pedro Joaquín Chamorro help or hinder him?

To Pedro Joaquín and Cristiana I said, "I hope everything my friends tell me about the honesty and dignity of this movement is true, so that we can work toward a new beginning and let our people live in liberty. It is all I desire."

JUNE 14, 1979   *San José, Costa Rica*

Today we hear that as the battle is raging in Matagalpa, León, Estelí, Masaya, Rivas, and Managua, an Israeli ship carrying badly needed arms and ammunition to Somoza, within sight of Bluefields, has been ordered back to home port. Somoza has an insurmountable problem resupplying his troops. Meanwhile a deluge of men and equipment is flowing directly into Nicaragua. I've placed my faith in God. Somoza cannot win this war.

JUNE 15, 1979   *San José, Costa Rica*

Our offices are in a beautiful house that belongs to a Costa Rican family; they left it to us so we can use it. We call it the Garage; as in a mechanic's shop, we are always at work here, day and night planning the future of Nicaragua. There are a lot of decisions to be made, a lot of obstacles to overcome. All of this reminds me of when Pedro was planning Olama y Mollejones.

A lot of people from the FSLN come here, as well as civilians. But some of our friends are having second thoughts about the composition of the junta. They worry about the presence of Daniel and Moisés, who are supposed to be Marxists.

One day a special envoy from the United States appeared here. There was talk of an arrangement. I told Sergio, Alfonso, Reynaldo, and Miguel that in Pedro's day we referred to such arrangements as pacts or interventions; I was categorical in my rejection of this plan, because Pedro was always on my mind and I felt that if he had been there in my place he would have said the same. Everything had to be the result of a purely Nicaraguan effort.

My disapproval is qualified as "female obstinacy," which causes me great pain and even some tears too. But my motivations are entirely of a nationalistic sort.

The pressure is so great, the temptation to quit is enormous. But I feel that these sacrifices are all for my country and I am willing to go with my colleagues to wherever this may lead us, even to combat, if need be.

In these last few days journalists from all over the world have begun to concentrate in San José. The eyes of the world are upon us. By "us" I mean Sergio, Alfonso, Daniel, and me. Moisés is in Managua doing battle.

The newsmen can't understand how a country as small as ours, with a population of only 2.5 million people, has dared to confront a dictatorship like Somoza's.

JUNE 16, 1979   *San José, Costa Rica*

My participation in the junta is now a certainty. At a news conference this day we announced the formation of a Junta for National Reconstruction.

The Andean Pact nations—Venezuela, Bolivia, Ecuador, Colombia, and Peru—who had hoped in days past to negotiate a cease-fire and persuade Somoza to resign, have instead announced they are recognizing the Sandinistas as a legitimate army, recognized under international law. The way has been paved for our junta to be recognized as a lawful body of government.

That's how we, the junta, began—as friends. Sometimes the meetings were in my home. Breakfasts, luncheons, everything at my expense. Alfredo César had by then risen in the ranks of the opposition, and so he was chosen to be the secretary of our junta. He proclaimed himself a moderate and an adherent of Alfonso. I was unsure of his motives.

A few days later, at a dark and dreary restaurant on the outskirts of San José, I met for the first time with Daniel and Humberto Ortega. Tomás Borge, whom I remembered from his days at *La Prensa,* was also there. They were all sitting together clad in black leather jackets buttoned up to their necks and wearing dark glasses. The purpose of the meeting was for us to become acquainted, but they looked so intimidating in their inscrutable outfits, apparently standard issue for political dissenters, that they gave me the chills.

I looked around and saw Rosario Murillo, Pedro's former secretary. La Chayo, the nickname we all called her, was relegated to a corner table with a group of women I didn't know. When I went to her table to greet her she was strangely deferential. She called me Doña Violeta. I was embarrassed. When I invited her to join us she demurred. I was left as the lone woman at a table of angry-looking men. Something about our little group didn't feel quite right. So I told the men, "I hope we will always be able to work amicably."

After that encounter I wrote in my diary:

MONDAY, JUNE 18, 1979   *San José, Costa Rica*

I pray to the Lord and Pedro to help me go forward with this plan. I have undertaken an enormous responsibility with a group of people I don't really know. Clearly the Ortegas, Los Doce, and now our junta are all in the same league. The more I see of my colleagues, the more I wonder who they are. Thus far, I have received assurances from my fellow junta members that civilian power will rest in the hands of the junta and prevail over the military, which under our command will become a depoliticized force, and that indeed there will be elections shortly after our triumph so that the people can elect new rulers.

But in the past few days I have begun to question whether they are really interested in developing this kind of society. Why do they want me in this position? The possibility that they are using me to legitimize their actions and not to realize Pedro's dream (democracy), gives me great unease. I must however, put my personal fears aside because "each day that passes without unity is a lost day."

In view of our history together, I wish I could remember more of that first encounter with the Ortegas. They seemed to me like caricatures then. But I recall that at first glance I began to feel uncomfortable with them and with the idea of representing them. By then I understood that my participation in the junta was giving credence to the decency and purity of what was clearly now a Sandinista movement.

A day later, at our offices, people from all walks of life began to present themselves as volunteers. For many of these people, Pedro had been a mentor. Now they wanted to express their appreciation by working for his cause. Some were of great caliber and were selected to form a kitchen cabinet. Had we stayed together, Nicaragua would have had a good chance. But divisive feelings were already evident. Sergio, Daniel, and Miguel d'Escoto (who was appointed foreign minister) were communicating with secret looks or by whispering among themselves. In our discussions they used a military tone that offended me. Under the surface calm, I began to suspect these men were like the French revolutionaries, radicals who once in power would wheel out the guillotine and yell, "Off with their heads!" I remarked on this to Arturo Cruz, a member of the kitchen cabinet. "Arturo, what do you think of these guys? What's all this talk about the bourgeoisie?" Patting my hand, he responded as if calming a hysterical child. "They are just *muchachos*. Give them time. Everything will work out fine. You'll see."

By mid-June a new American strategy was evident. U.S. ambassador to Nicaragua Lawrence Pezzullo moved quickly to ask for Somoza's resignation. He told him there were no solutions without his departure. In Somoza's place the Americans wanted a government that would unify the country, and a reformed National Guard under a new leadership. Having secured Pezzullo's word that there would be an orderly transition and a new life for him in the United States, Somoza agreed to go. Without being able to resupply his troops, he had no choice but to accept this offer. It was only a matter of time before the Sandinistas, who received regular shipments of arms, would prevail.

JUNE 23, 1979 *San José, Costa Rica*

Miguel d'Escoto, who has been given a seat as part of the Panamanian delegation at the OAS meetings, informed us that the American proposal of a peacekeeping force was crushed in a vote by the OAS members. They have called for the immediate replacement of Somoza and the installation of a democratic government in Nicaragua and the holding of free elections as soon as possible.

JUNE 27, 1979 *San José, Costa Rica*

Everything with these people is done at the witching hour. Today I was awoken at midnight for an urgent meeting. . . . The Americans have proposed creating an alternative governing structure, an Executive Committee, they call it, that will have the support of the National Guard and after Somoza's departure will negotiate with us a cease-fire. They also propose we broaden the junta. We (in the junta) are meeting in Panama with the new president, Aristides Arroyo, and with Carlos Andrés Pérez and General Omar Torrijos.

On the plane I see Chayo Murillo. As Daniel's translator she is always discreetly by his side. We are the only two women on the plane. But again I find she keeps a strange distance from me.

We land on an island off the coast of Panama called Contadora. Carlos Andrés is already there when we arrive. I greet him with the warmth our family has always felt for him. But I don't neglect to tell him that I am upset at him. He is the one who always tells me I have a role to play. And now I am in this fix.

We spend the day at the beach. Have lunch together. We discuss the Americans' proposal. None of us is happy with this latest effort to intervene. We all lean in the direction of rejecting this plan.

Later we fly to Panama city to meet with the American special envoy, Mr. William P. Bowdler.

Bowdler tells us he has spoken to Somoza and presented the plan to him. We tell him we are the true government of national unity.

JUNE 30, 1979   *San José, Costa Rica*

Those who are in the moderate opposition in Nicaragua are feeling left out. The moment to get on board has passed them by. Behind closed doors, Adolfo Calero and company have been meeting with Pezzullo, who now assures us that opposition leaders within Nicaragua want the preservation of the National Guard. They view us as supported by the FSLN forces and Panama and Costa Rica. They want the National Guard to act as a buffer between us and exclusive power.

A week ago the FSLN forces that have held Managua retreated to Masaya, twenty-eight kilometers away. After seventeen days of being pummeled by Somoza's *guardia,* their troops were exhausted. Constant air attacks had decimated their ranks and demoralized the civilian population that acted as an adjunct force in the operation.

The top field commander of the internal front, Joaquín Cuadra Lacayo, led the contingent. They were in the last quarter of the trip when Somoza's surveillance planes detected the massive exodus. An air force squadron opened fire on the group. The unarmed civilians ran for cover while the *guerrilleros,* dodging enemy fire, fought back.

Thirty-six hours later the survivors of the raid reached Masaya. Without delay, they moved to take control of the city. By evening Masaya was theirs.

The morning after, we receive the news. We are told that in the exchange of gunfire, Moisés Hassan, our colleague, has been injured. A rocket has entered his left side. Fortunately, he is now in stable condition.

JULY 1, 1979   *San José, Costa Rica*

In the past three days twenty cities and towns have capitulated to the Sandinistas. In the southeast they control Diriamba and Jinotepe; in the north, Jinotega, Estelí, Matagalpa, Boaco, and so forth. In the west, Chinandega, Chichigalpa, and León.

Somoza's back is broken. His military might is history. Today, in the *Washington Post,* I read that Somoza has told Pezzullo, "O.K., I'm ready, just tell me when." It seems that for days Somoza has walked with his resignation in his pocket, waiting for Pezzullo to give him the go-ahead. Soon we will return to Nicaragua. I am happy—but worried about the role I will play. Things are not as Sergio Ramírez has painted them. The junta had been designed to appear broad-based, but moderate elements like myself and Alfonso are irrelevant. Daniel, Humberto, and Tomás, whom I mistrust as radicals, are the ones in control.

Don Pepe Figueres has publicly said he fears Somoza will be replaced by a Marxist government. He singles out Edén Pastora as a moderate and democratic element within the FSLN.

As my photograph in a friendly embrace with my junta colleagues circles the globe, I come to the conclusion I must resign.

I call Sergio Ramírez and tell him, "I want out. This is as far as I go."

After he leaves, others come. They meet with me to try to persuade me. "Be reasonable, Violeta," they say. "You have to rethink this. We need you," and so forth. But I refuse. They leave for a short while, then return pleading. The phone rings. It's Carlos Andrés, calling from Venezuela. What a coincidence, I think.

"Listen, Violeta, I'm told you want to resign. I urge you to—"

I cut him off. In spite of our friendship I tell him, "I'm sorry, my friend. No one, not even you, tells me what to do." I am very stubborn, and the more people press me, the more unreasonable I become. Almost in tears, I hang up. Turning to the men, I say, closing the door on them, "Please go."

JULY 2, 1979   *San José, Costa Rica*

I was naive to think they would let me go. In the last couple of days a procession of presidents and diplomatic envoys has passed through my door. They tell me, "The United States already thinks the junta is dominated by leftist guerrillas. If you go it will be an indication that indeed there is no place for moderates in the junta. Our fear is that they will try to sustain Somoza in power or intervene militarily. The revolution needs you, Nicaragua needs you," and so on. Slowly they begin to erode my resistance. They make me doubt my better instincts. So often with Pedro it was like this. On the brink of greatness, victory disintegrated.

In the end, in spite of my disappointment and fears, I decide to stay with the junta. I feel that as a good citizen, as a woman who loves her country, I must.

JULY 7, 1979   *San José, Costa Rica*

My colleagues tell me that when the attack on León began, the FSLN forces surrounded police headquarters. Two hundred of Somoza's *guardias* were trapped inside without the possibility of receiving any reinforcement. All available troops had been sent to the south to prevent Comandante Zero and his army of five thousand from taking Rivas.

If the Sandinista army keeps advancing, the Americans won't be able to insist that we broaden the junta.

JULY 9, 1979   *San José, Costa Rica*

We continue to work on plans for the future government of Nicaragua. It is agreed that any honest *guardia* should be allowed to be part of the new Nicaragua.

The United States persists in offering its assistance. We tell them our past history with them is too bitter to forget. We are glad to have their friendship but we want to be left alone. This is an authentically Nicaraguan effort.

Bowdler was working to shape our junta into a larger, more moderate, pro-U.S. body of government. Because we were resisting his efforts— such a junta would be too cumbersome—he put Somoza's departure on hold. Though Somoza was now anxious to go, he had become a pawn in the negotiations between the junta and the United States.

I was the reason the mediators were unable to broaden the junta. Again Sergio and the others called on Carlos Andrés to persuade me. With a reprehensible tone Carlos Andrés said to me, "You have to be more flexible, Violeta. The success or failure of these negotiations is on your shoulders." I resented the pressure. It was all Sergio's and Bowdler's doing, I knew. "No more of this," I said to Carlos Andrés. "These people cannot be trusted. They operate under a cloak of secrecy, making important decisions that exclude me."

At that point, I didn't want to hurt the revolution, but I felt I should no longer be a part of it.

JULY 10, 1979 *San José, Costa Rica*

It is 8:30 P.M. I have just received a courtesy call from William Bowdler. Sergio Ramírez accompanied him. Nothing much is said. So I am still wondering what the real reason was for this call.

Around 9 P.M. Sergio returns, alone. "The Americans," he tells me, "insist on broadening the composition of the junta. If we don't accept, they are saying they will seek alternative approaches." One can only imagine he means a military intervention. Sergio tells me they have proposed seven men—Adolfo Calero, Ernesto Fernández, Emilio Alvarez, Ismael Reyes, Mariano Fiallos, and two others whose names I can't remember. Theoretically they are all good people. But who can govern with twelve? The idea strikes me as ridiculous. But Sergio persists. He tells me, "We are going to have to do what the Americans want. We must obey the Yanqui or we are not going to get anywhere." This surprises me from him because I know he and the others are anti-Yanqui. Perhaps because I am not a politician and I understand little about power, I can't see my way through to accepting this premise.

Though a broader political representation is more in keeping with Pedro's pluralistic frame of mind, I feel compelled to reject the mediators' proposal. My fear is that this new demand will derail our imminent victory.

"If you wish to acquiesce," I tell Sergio, "you are free to do it. But count me out!" So once again I offer to resign. I mean no harm by disagreeing, but I don't wish to be an obstacle to peace. I tell him I don't see the wisdom in negotiating anything away. With little ammunition left in his arsenal, Somoza has practically lost the war. For weeks now we have been hearing that he is bleeding the public treasury dry, that he is squeezing every dollar out of his various holdings. All these are signs of his impending surrender.

JULY 12, 1979 *San José, Costa Rica*

Somoza agonizes. He has been abandoned by everyone. All seventeen Latin America countries, members of the OAS, have voted against him. All we have to do now is wait. It won't be long before his regime collapses.

Sergio comes to the Garage. He tells us, "We have a meeting with

Bowdler. Something very important is going to happen." This upsets me. I tell him I remain opposed to these interferences, which they call "mediation." We are on a straight path to victory. It's no time to fold.

Nevertheless, all four of us, plus Tomás Borge, Humberto, Miguel, and Comandante Zero, leave for Punta Arenas, to a Costa Rican beach resort, as guests of Rodrigo Carazo Odio. When we arrive at the beautiful house, which sits directly facing the sea, waiting for us at the door are Carlos Andrés Pérez and Doña Estrella (Carazo Odio's wife) and a delegate sent by General Omar Torrijos.

Bowdler is inside the house with Carazo Odio and the U.S. ambassador to Costa Rica. He tells us that Colonel Federico Mejía, whom we will soon meet, has been chosen to occupy the posts of National Guard director and chief of staff. With this new appointment in place, Bowdler assures us, Somoza's departure will be arranged. The plan he states is for Somoza to resign before the Nicaraguan congress. Then it will appoint Francisco (Chico) Urcuyo Maliano (a well-known doctor from Rivas whose attachment to the Somozas is unconditional) as provisional president. After Urcuyo is appointed, Urcuyo will transfer all powers to Archbishop Miguel Obando, and he will transfer power to the junta. We will call for an immediate cease-fire. Mejía will then cede one of his posts to Comandante Zero. After that, discussions for an amalgamation of forces can begin.

The Americans argue that it is in the interest of stability that the guard remain. But the disadvantages of this to the revolution are clear. If the National Guard is dissolved, it will be a complete military victory. The revolution will have a 100 percent chance of eradicating Somocismo; if not, we will have a compromised government that will effect only modest reforms.

Bowdler strongly recommends that Bernardino Larios, an official from Somoza's guard who defected in months past in protest, be appointed minister of defense, not Humberto Ortega as some have suggested.

After some wrangling, we accept this plan and the appointment of Larios. It is agreed as well that those men of the National Guard who lay down their arms will be incorporated into the new Nicaraguan army. But many of my colleagues are thinking there is little chance this will ever come to pass, because one of Somoza's dim-witted generals will make a clumsy last-minute grab for power and release us from having to comply.

We await the arrival of the new general, Mejía. But he does not come.

After the Americans leave, we sit down to lunch with the Carazos, Carlos Andrés, Torrijos, and Don Pepe Figueres.

As the Sandinista forces push toward Managua, Rodrigo Carazo Odio is advising us to return to our homeland. He suggests we secure a piece of liberated territory for ourselves and proclaim a new government, then request international recognition.

Our relations with our Costa Rican host have been rapidly deteriorating. His support for us is eroding. Frequent border crossings in the fighting zone on our southern front have inflicted many civilian casualties in Costa Rica. Carazo Odio is under pressure from his countrymen to expel us.

But the main topic of discussion is the plan of government. The question is, Will we preserve a mixed economy and respect private property? The answer to these queries is yes, but with certain unspecified transformations in key sectors of the economy. Then they ask, How much time will pass before the junta calls the nation to elections? Until then they had implied this would happen as soon as things settled, six months, a year, maybe two. But now, to my surprise, Tomás Borge and Daniel were circumventing the issue.

However, determined to win the support of these noteworthy Latin American leaders, both men agree to elections and a policy that is respectful of human rights. However, Carlos Andrés, unsatisfied with their mere word, pushes the Sandinistas to have the junta commit to all this in a letter to the OAS.

As we leave we discover there are TV cameras waiting outside to interview us. Someone has alerted them to our meeting. All of us smile happily and declare ourselves cautiously optimistic. Except, later, the car I am traveling in develops a flat tire. Being as superstitious as I am, I wonder if it is a bad omen.

JULY 13, 1979   *San José, Costa Rica*

With both sides citing irreconcilable differences, the negotiations with Bowdler have come to an end.

JULY 15, 1979 *San José, Costa Rica*

This morning, the names of our cabinet members were released to the press. Tomás Borge has been appointed interior minister with full command over the police and national security. Many of the other appointments went to members of Los Doce: Emilio Baltodano receives a lifetime appointment as controller of the republic. Arturo Cruz is going to the presidency of the Central Bank. Joaquín Cuadra Chamorro (Comandante Joaquín Cuadra Lacayo's father) is finance minister; Carlos Tunnermann is education secretary; Miguel d'Escoto is foreign minister; Alejandro Cardenal (Alfonso's brother-in-law) is minister of tourism; Noel Rivas is minister of industry, and my cousin Mache Torres is minister of agriculture.

JULY 16, 1979 *San José, Costa Rica*

Sergio comes at midnight to inform me that we are flying to León to declare it a "liberated zone." "If possible," he says, "we will leave this very day. Plans are under way for us to depart this morning, if possible, with the cabinet."

JULY 17, 1979 *San José, Costa Rica*

News reports this morning indicate that in the early hours of the day, Somoza left his bunker, presented his resignation, and took a short helicopter ride to Las Mercedes airport. At 5:10 A.M. he boarded a Learjet, accompanied by his half brother José Somoza and his son Anastasio III. Hours later he touched down at Homestead Air Force Base in Florida.

In a radio address Urcuyo informed the public that the Somoza era had ended and the time had come for all the democratic forces to participate in a national dialogue. Strangely, Urcuyo said nothing about the transference of power.

Around 10 A.M. we are already at the airport awaiting our departure for Nicaragua. Carazo Odio appears to tell us that an urgent message has arrived from Bowdler in Nicaragua. It seems Francisco (Chico Beto), in his crazy desire to be always loyal to his master, has decided to install himself in Somoza's bunker and keep control of the army. The amount of blood that is being spilled is appalling.

Somoza's intentions are becoming evident. He never intended that

Urcuyo transfer powers to the junta. Somoza figures that with him gone, Urcuyo can persuade the Pentagon to renew military aid to the Guardia. Urcuyo can then stay in power until it is safe for Somoza to return, at which time Somoza will rule again.

We return to the Garage to await Pezzullo's final word about Chico Beto Urcuyo. The decision has already been made for us to fly to Rivas, Masaya, León, or any other place in Nicaragua. Daniel, Tomás, and other *comandantes* have already left for León.

Pezzullo was now learning firsthand that Urcuyo was willing to deliver the presidency to a "pluralist and democratic junta" but never to a "communist" one.

JULY 17, CONTINUED

We await a fax transmission from Bowdler. He is confident that he can persuade Urcuyo to fulfill the agreement! But it is clear that whatever understanding existed between Bowdler, Pezzullo, Somoza, and that infamous Urcuyo, the latter two apparently have a separate, very different agenda between themselves.

Somoza knew he could not allow his supporters to think he had abandoned them. The anger that would swell inside the hearts of his loyalists could even put his own life at risk. He understood that he needed time to put himself out of harm's way, not just from the threat of the Sandinistas but also from the wrath of his own supporters. They were the real victims of his deceit, along with the Americans, who were totally bamboozled into believing he really intended to leave Urcuyo in power only provisionally.

In the end it was not one of Somoza's dim-witted generals who made a last grab for power and by so doing handed the Sandinistas a military victory, but Somoza himself. He predicted the Americans would not protest such an alternative and continue the war against the Sandinistas. But he was completely wrong. Once Urcuyo failed to comply with the agreement, the Americans lost the power to influence the events that followed.

With Carazo Odio pressuring us to leave immediately, we made the decision that afternoon to fly secretly into León and declare it a liberated city. Once there, we were to establish a provisional government while the insurgent forces marched into Managua for a last confrontation with the remainder of Somoza's army.

So on that evening we, the junta members, boarded two small Piper airplanes to Nicaragua. My traveling companions—Alfonso, Alfredo César, and my son-in-law José Bárcenas—and I boarded one plane. Sergio, Ernesto Cardenal, René Núñez, and Juan Ignacio Gutiérrez boarded the other plane. I wasn't afraid. I had placed my faith in God and so I was ready to confront whatever came. But I did have some concern that Somoza's killer planes would detect us and shoot us down.

It was the second great adventure of my life. The first was when I escaped with Pedro to Costa Rica, down the Río San Juan. This time, however, I was flying home to a liberated Nicaragua.

We journeyed for two hours, flying low over the Pacific about ten kilometers from the coast to avoid detection by radar. It was a full moon and I wondered if this was a good thing. The others fell asleep but I couldn't. Through the open window I could see the sea and feel the wind. At times I was very cold. After a while I began to see the little lights of houses. The others awoke as we passed Somoza's sugar plantation, Montelimar. Everyone became animated and started to point to each landmark as we passed, until we reached Poneloya, a seaside resort outside León.

A short while later, around 2 A.M. on July 18, the pilot guided us down onto the middle of what looked like a cattle field. But I was told it was Aeropuerto Godoy, situated between León and Chinandega. The landing was incredible because the runway, which was very short, was lit by bluish-purplish lamps, and as we were touching down one of the pilots was screaming to the other, "Brake! Brake!"

Our departure had been so harried that each of us carried only the bare essentials: a change of clothing, pajamas, a toothbrush, and a roll of toilet paper.

We were driven to a handsome house on the outskirts of León. We were told that the owner, a wealthy Leonese, had graciously lent it to us. At that time I had no way of knowing this was not true. After all, the private sector was fully participating in the insurrection, and so this action did not appear strange to me. By then it was 3 A.M. So each one of us took a room. José Bárcenas and I shared one of the children's bedrooms.

When we awakened a few hours later we sat down to have coffee and eat *gallopinto*. Everyone was so attentive I marveled at the owner's sense of hospitality.

A while later columns of *guerrilleros* began to arrive. I figure there must have been eight hundred or more men, women, and children coming across the hills and valleys in single file from the north. Some of them, wearing olive-green uniforms, were heavily armed with machine guns and M15 rifles; others were wounded or ill. Our colleague Dr. Gutiérrez attended to them. Then he vaccinated all of us. The vaccines gave me a strong allergic reaction, which required that I be injected with antihistamines.

I noticed a group of *guerrilleros* walking about the house taking measure of the place. They said the beautiful house we were in belonged to a Somocista. With this rationale, the rebel troopers kicked open the wardrobes and helped themselves to the owner's trousers, his guayabera shirts, his shoes. I had never seen such disrespect for private property. The maids, scared and confused, began to sob. I tried to console them, to tell them, "Everything will be all right. No one will harm you." But I was scared myself.

Sometime in the afternoon Daniel Ortega appeared, and we were transported to León. In a ceremony conducted on the grounds of the venerable campus of the Universidad Nacional Autónoma, surrounded by foreign correspondents and the jubilant faces of the humble peasants and children cheering and applauding us as if we were liberators, we baptized it "first of the liberated cities."

Afterward we attended the funeral of a group of young *guerrilleros* who had lost their lives fighting in the early hours of the morning. In nearby Chichigalpa we attended a mass for them. Outside the church, in the crowded plaza, people were fainting in the heat, though there was intense emotion and joy registered on their faces.

Immediately following the ceremony we went in a caravan to Chinandega, which had just been liberated. But we never made it past the Cosigüina volcano, because we were caught in a cross fire between *guerrilleros* and the last vestiges of Somoza's army. We returned to the house somewhat shaken by the experience.

• • • •

On the morning of the nineteenth I awoke to the voice of a radio commentator who was announcing that the city of Granada had fallen after a few hours of fighting; in Masaya army troops had surrendered. From across the country Sandinista forces were marching toward Managua for the final encounter, even as Somoza's army was disbanding, fleeing. "At the airport it is complete chaos," the commentator said. "Air force planes are taking off by the dozen, loaded with deserters of the *Guardia Nacional* and their families." Heedless to the directions of the traffic controllers, a C-47 and a DC-6 almost collided. Riding buses and taxis, *guardias* and mercenaries were filing into the airport, desperate to leave the country. By midmorning there were no more planes. The desperate soldiers then tried to hijack an English fuel cargo plane. They climbed onto the wings of the plane. Shaking them loose with a series of moves, the plane took off. The men then turned to a Red Cross plane. Throwing all the cargo out, an entire troop climbed on board and took off. The stories went on and on. It was all too fabulous to be believed.

All the while, Urcuyo was busy appointing a new cabinet as though he planned to remain in office. He suggested that the Sandinistas surrender and lay down their arms. Pezzullo, who was ordered back to the States, kept insisting as he was leaving, "This was not the plan."

A direct threat to Somoza, who must have been busy tanning himself on the beaches of Florida, was necessary to convince Chico Beto to step down. Somoza was warned that he might be extradited and sent to face the judgment of the new revolutionary government. Thus, at the end of that day, on July 18, 1979, Urcuyo became a short chapter in Nicaraguan history.

That same night, Urcuyo and his band of supporters fled the country. The people of Managua, I am told, saw him off with a shower of bullets and didn't allow him to take with him even his personal luggage.

When the Sandinista forces converged upon Managua for the last battle, they found the enemy troops had abandoned their trenches and that Urcuyo had departed. In light of this, it was decided that we should leave for Managua to take hold of the reins of government. That evening a plane was sent for Moisés Hassan to join us, so that the junta could make its triumphant entry into Managua as a complete governing body.

I realized that in the drama that was now unfolding, a new chapter was beginning in my life. I didn't know then what direction it would take or how long it would last, but I decided I would forge ahead and attempt to realize the ideals Pedro had fought for until his death.

Chapter Eight

UP UNTIL THE MOMENT WE MARCHED INTO THE Plaza de la República in Managua (now Plaza de la Revolución) on July 20, 1979, I had been impelled by the need to see Pedro's dream fulfilled. I expected that this would somehow mitigate the pain of his tragic end and the conclusion of our life together. But as I stood atop the immense fire engine that transported us—Daniel, Moisés, Alfonso, Sergio, and I —I felt both confused and depressed.

I did not immediately comprehend why on that triumphant day there was anything other than happiness in my heart. I thought, Here at last is a reality that surpasses my greatest fantasies. I stood at the threshold of a new nation, liberated from oppression by a series of selfless acts of heroism. The fruits of our human and political sacrifice were evident in the glowing faces of the people who came to receive us like conquering heroes.

I responded to those cheering crowds with a befuddled smile that masked the sadness I felt as I heard Alfonso proclaim, "Long live the revolution." In my ears this sounded frighteningly monarchical.

The crowds were so thick our vehicle was forced to a stop before the shattered grandeur of the Managua cathedral. Its crumbling state was a reminder to me of the earthquake Somoza had used for his personal gain. Slowly we made our way toward the steps of the Palacio Nacional, where the *comandantes,* the Ortega brothers (Daniel and Humberto), Tomás Borge, Victor Tirado, Jaime Wheelock, Luis Carrión Cruz, Edén Pastora, and others were already taking their bows.

Once inside the palace, I shed tears of joy and collapsed into the arms of my daughter Claudia, whose exile in Costa Rica had finally ended.

As I hugged her, the happiness I felt at seeing Pedro's dream fulfilled was tinged with sadness. I wished he could be with us savoring this moment. But I understood that without the sacrifice of his life, none of it would have been possible.

Afterward the victory speeches began. Humberto Ortega's message was that every day, at every hour, every Nicaraguan had to remain on alert against the "enemy within" so that we could consolidate the revolution, strengthen it, and make it greater under the leadership of the FSLN. Daniel went into a long and inflammatory diatribe in which he railed against imperialism, which the FSLN had at last defeated. Then he intimated that there was no need for elections. "The people have voted," he said, "with their presence here today." Tomás Borge said to expect clemency from the FSLN. He said, "The revolution was implacable in combat, but it will be generous in victory." He added, however, that society had to be reeducated because the vices of the old society persisted among the population. And so a new war was beginning, a war against backwardness, against poverty, against ignorance, against immorality. "This war will be longer," he said, "and more arduous than the previous war."

This gave me pause to think. Why, instead of simply asking of our people a more positive attitude so that we could reconstruct the nation for the good of all of us, did he frame issues in terms of war; and why was there no mention of the non-Sandinista sectors of our society? We heard only of the FSLN. As well, I thought it strange that they did not allow Comandante Zero to speak, though he had waged a tough battle on the southern front against Somoza's elite-force general Commander Bravo. Nevertheless, I noticed that whenever Zero appeared the crowds went wild. Clearly the *comandantes* were jockeying for power among themselves while struggling to establish the FSLN as the vanguard of the revolution. I was quite sure then there could be no unity of our coalition government.

That afternoon we went to the Camino Real Hotel to begin our first day as the Junta of National Reconstruction. When we arrived the place became a mob scene, with diplomats and journalists crawling over us to interview us and shake our hands. It was easy to see people were happy now that Somoza was gone. There was liberty in the air. So, in spite of what I thought would be our inexorable path toward disbandment, our mismatched junta behaved at the onset with enthusiasm and camaraderie. Sergio Ramírez, who I now realize was manipulating the situation to the benefit of the Sandinistas, led the session in which we issued our first decrees. The first one abolished Somoza's constitution, the National Assembly, and other organs that were deemed to be corrupt expressions of Somoza's power. In its place were established a temporary set of laws that would protect and guarantee for all human rights, liberty, and equality, and respect for private property. The second decree forbade idolatry: no images of the Somoza family would be allowed in the country, and everything that had the Somoza name would be rebaptized with that of a fallen Sandinista hero. The third decree expropriated the Somoza family's $500 million empire and the properties of military and government officials who had participated, in the past forty-five years, in the looting of the national coffers.

When these decrees were announced that same evening, there was unanimous support for them. No one imagined then that the Sandinistas would take advantage of the situation to declare an intermittent state of emergency that would severely limit freedom, or that they would not be satisfied with Somoza's wealth but would go much further and eventually control the greater portion of the nation's economy. Nor could anyone envision an idolatry so great for the heroes of the FSLN and for Marxist theoreticians that Lenin's own portrait and that of Carlos Fonseca Amador would be permanently affixed to the facade of Nicaragua's crumbling cathedral, as if they were gods.

The morning after our first day of government, Alfredo César went in search of suitable headquarters for the junta. Among the half dozen buildings he suggested, we ruled out Somoza's military bunker on the hill of Tiscapa. It was renamed El Chipote after the hill in northern Nicaragua where Sandino had operated, and it became, perhaps symbolically, the Sandinista military's official headquarters. We felt this was an inappropriate setting for our civilian junta.

We also ruled out the ivory tower that was the former headquarters of the Banco de América. Because it was patronized by the ruling class and controlled by the wealthy Pellas family, it too, we felt, was inappropriate for a revolutionary junta.

As well we thought it unsuitable for us to occupy the ornamented brown-and-beige Art Deco edifice of the old Banco Nacional, because it was established in 1914 during the presidency of Adolfo Díaz (when Emiliano Chamorro was diplomatic envoy in Washington) with part of the proceeds from the Chamorro-Bryan Treaty, in which Nicaragua ceded its rights to the United States to build an interoceanic canal through the Río San Juan. The treaty, while basically ratifying an agreement negotiated long before Emiliano, was widely misinterpreted as a degrading example of subservience to American imperialism.

The only possibility that remained was across the street from these two buildings—the modern, reinforced-concrete structure of the Central Bank of Nicaragua. The rest of the landscape consisted of hopeless overgrown lots, the ruins of our destroyed city, which Somoza never bothered to rebuild after the earthquake of 1972. So it was decided that we would set up offices in this "lesser symbol of the tyranny of the previous sociopolitical order."

That same afternoon we took possession of the Central Bank and called it the House of Government. I remember we entered the House of Government through the rear court, previously reserved for VIP visitors. I could see that the pavement was beginning to give way to the weeds and that some of the windows were broken. But I was astonished when we pushed open the great armored doors and stepped into the inner sanctum of the organization that had defined economic policy in our country. Under the tutelage of Roberto Incer, it was a formidable institution that contributed to whatever development there was in the country. But after Somoza's looting, all that remained was an abandoned shell. As we continued our way down a long hallway, we reached a sad cavernous atrium, partially illuminated by the sunbeams that filtered in through the slits of a broken window blind. Farther down, through a vestibule that led to the private offices, we passed the portraits of the three Somoza presidents, Anastasio, Luis, and Tacho. I felt a rush of relief to know there would be no successor to the dynasty. Directly before us were the offices and meeting rooms of Somoza's financial wizards. The carpet had been torn off and the furniture was broken. Not one chair remained on which we could sit. Among these pathetic remains we established residence and began a disorderly session in which everyone seemed to speak at once.

People wanted us to decide everything. We moved freely, ruling on what I considered housekeeping issues as well as matters of economic policy.

They spoke of the need to protect the safety of savings. "If we control the system," they said, "we can see to it that it functions more efficiently and responsibly without the profiteering and corruption of private enterprise." The implication was that by eliminating the "greed factor" of the private sector they would help rehabilitate the country's economy at a much faster pace, since credit would be extended only to projects identified as being of "high national priority."

Besides confiscating the accounts of the Somocistas, they indicated we needed to extend this action to areas they had subjectively determined to be of "national interest."

I had previously been guaranteed that we would respect free enterprise, except for certain minor structural changes, which until then were never explicitly articulated to me. What they were talking of doing now was creating a state monopoly, which I felt smacked of communism and promised to create a greater bureaucracy and more corruption. But to my surprise no one objected. "This was all in the Plan of Government," they said.

Conspicuously ignored was the issue of the six thousand ex-members of the National Guard who were imprisoned or had sought political asylum at foreign embassies. Similarly, no one seemed to be concerned with the countless Nicaraguan refugees who had camped on the Costa Rican border and were anxious to reenter the country. Also unanswered were the pleas of the homeless and hungry who were awaiting the distribution of emergency humanitarian aid.

I went home that day feeling things were not going to work out between us. The Sandinistas' path and my own were clearly different. We were there to serve, I thought, and not be served by the revolution. While they seemed to care only about assuming control, I wanted to champion more altruistic ideals.

Carlos Fernando, who knew for certain what the rest of us could only guess at—that the true direction of the revolution was communism—understood that the seeds of conflict had already been sown. Sooner or later the Sandinistas and I would clash. He told me I should resign immediately. "This is much too complicated for you," he said, and from that day on he began to actively campaign among the *comandantes* to give me a graceful exit. I resigned a total of six times after the revolutionary victory. But it took nine months for them to finally let me go. This brief chapter in my life I endured like a painful and cumbersome pregnancy, except that in my case, at the end of my term I gave birth to a democracy that was stillborn.

After the constitution, the court system, and the congress were abolished by national decree, revolutionary justice took the form of a People's Court that was organized by Nora Astorga, the Sandinista heroine of Pérez Vega fame. While she declared that in Nicaragua there would be total freedom and respect for human rights, she also declared that "revealing state secrets or issuing verbal or written expressions intended to harm the people's interests" were crimes punishable by law that could result in three- to five-year sentences. Aiding and abetting a Somocista carried a maximum penalty of ten years.

Archbishop Miguel Obando took issue with these rulings because he felt that in their ambiguity they offered little promise of justice. But he was most opposed to them because they curtailed freedom of expression. So he and six bishops composed a pastoral letter in which they urged the government to revoke these orders. The letter was also openly critical of the new Sandinista Defense Committees (CDS), a neighborhood watch organization. As an extension of the committees that prepared the people of the barrios in the rebellion against Somoza, they proclaimed the CDS to be a grassroots movement that came from the bottom up and as such was the democratic expression of "popular power." They predicted, rightly so, that it would serve the revolution under the leadership of the FSLN.

For a little more than a week, the CDS leaders had been organizing the people to do day-and-night vigilance and to keep in a notebook a record of every car or stranger that came to their neighborhood. At the onset this task was undertaken with great enthusiasm by most people because they were told that the revolution would make them prosperous. The Sandinistas recognized that self-interest motivates most people. Hence, it was promised that many rewards would await those who cooperated with the revolution. To further stoke the flames of the people's revolutionary zeal, a measure of power was extended to the CDS leaders by giving them the right to apprehend and expropriate "suspicious-looking elements."

Though after the revolutionary victory the Sandinistas had promised that never again would there exist in Nicaragua immorality, corruption, influence peddling, and blackmail, the CDS organizations they established became the breeding ground for all these corrupt practices.

Soon neighbors were pitted one against the other in their ambition to be the chief denouncer of their neighborhood, with the expectation that they would gain from others' misfortune. And so in their pastoral letter the bishops noted with alarm that the power the CDS had been given had turned the groups into the "feared informants of the revolution."

Within my own family I saw a microcosm of the national fracture. Pedro Joaquín, who returned to *La Prensa* to begin its reconstruction, became completely anti-Sandinista. Claudia, who had been enraged by her father's assassination, was strictly in the Sandinista camp. She felt strongly that we should all support the revolution. In the months to come she would also become my unofficial personal assistant and personal adviser, traveling with me to all official functions. Cristiana, who had left her position at UCA, wrote for *La Prensa.* Her sensibilities reflected the general mood of the populace. While not a communist, she felt that as a patriot she needed to help rebuild Nicaragua in a way that was more idealistic and egalitarian. For a while she gave the Sandinista leadership the benefit of the doubt. Not so Antonio, her husband. As a businessman he was wary of those who proposed radical transformations of society or, worse, of the economy.

Carlos Fernando, the most radical of my children, never returned to *La Prensa* after July 19. He went on to pursue a variety of projects. He was Ernesto Cardenal's deputy in the Ministry of Culture, and as an FSLN militant he was involved in party affairs that included the creation of an FSLN newspaper that would replace Somoza's *Novedades.* As I recall, there was some argument over the name the daily would have. *Patria Libre* (Free Fatherland) was the first of many suggestions. But the name that ultimately prevailed was *Barricada,* in memory of the barricades that had been erected by the people in the barrios to protect themselves from *guardia* attacks. The Sandinistas felt the newspaper, so named, would be an eloquent symbol of the armed struggle that had swept our new government into power. In time, as the official voice of the government, it came to represent an obstruction to free speech and a barricade against independent thinking.

During the first month of the revolution a plane arrived from Cuba carrying a delegation of doctors and medical supplies. In the days that followed I learned, although it was not publicly known, that along with the doctors came one hundred Cuban military and security advisers, to advise us on all aspects of foreign and domestic policy. They wasted no time also in instructing the Sandinista nine-man National Directorate on how to seize and maintain power.

Soon afterward Cubana de Aviación carried Alfonso Robelo and Moisés Hassan to Cuba. Previously, Humberto Ortega, Bayardo Arce, Edén Pastora, and twenty other *comandantes* had departed to attend the twenty-sixth anniversary celebration of the Cuban revolution. In Havana, twenty thousand people attended their welcoming reception in the Plaza of the Revolution.

Taking a page from Tomás Borge's speech, Alfonso lauded the FSLN and its preeminence in Nicaragua's political arena. His speech so pleased the Sandinistas that it was picked up by *Barricada*. He said that the FSLN was in the forefront of the Nicaraguan revolution and, like Borge, he said that the task of reconstructing Nicaragua would be a harder war than the one that had just ended. But he assured his audience that in this process the Cuban people occupied a preferential place. He said, "Cuba and Nicaragua will be, as always, part of the same brotherhood. Cuba and Nicaragua united will conquer."

Castro gave a long speech in which he declared the Nicaraguan revolution to be a "double victory" because we had triumphed over Somoza and over 150 years of foreign dominance and intervention in our country. He congratulated his "Nicaraguan revolutionary comrades" for their "strategic brilliance," which permitted them to circumvent the possibility of an American intervention in the final days of the insurrection. He said that the Sandinistas showed "considerable talent" in keeping the Americans at bay by making a few concessions, which in the end they did not even have to honor because "a certain Chico Urcuyo, who is soon to be forgotten, tried to take over the government. . . . So in less than seventy-two hours the Guardia Nacional was disarmed." He went on to imply that the Americans had shown a suspicious interest in saving Somoza's army. "Strange," he said, "that when Somoza's men massacred *los muchachos Sandinistas,* the Americans were unmoved. It is evident that in advocating a mixed army of Sandinista combatants and members of the National Guard, the Americans were laying the foundations for opposition to the Sandinista movement."

In this way Castro assured himself that the Sandinistas would forever disdain American influence, though I don't think he needed to exert himself in that regard. It was obvious that comrade to comrade spoke the same language.

After the speech the delegation presented Castro with a Galil rifle used by Somoza's *guardia* in the insurrection, which they said had been provided by Israel, the "bastion of [American] imperialism in the Middle East."

After reading this news, I thought, We are in way over our heads.

Soon afterward daily flights from Cuba came to Nicaragua. They brought doctors, teachers, and even more advisers. As well, they took back with them groups of Nicaraguan students to receive "revolutionary training."

Indeed, a new Central Committee comprising Comandantes Tomás Borge, Luis Carrión Cruz, and Humberto Ortega was in control of all military matters. Comandante Joaquín Cuadra Lacayo, who commanded the internal insurrection, was named chief of staff under Ortega.

Curiously, the best known of all Sandinistas, Comandante Zero (who unlike the other Sandinista leaders was not a communist), received no command post. He was relegated to be Tomás Borge's deputy at the Ministry of the Interior.

Meanwhile, Luis Carrión Cruz announced from Central Committee headquarters that in Miami a counterrevolutionary force was in the making with Tachito (Anastasio III) as its head. Rumor had it that he would attack with the famous Commander Bravo from the north with a contingent of seven thousand men. Carrión promised, before a core of foreign journalists, that if these authors of Somoza's genocide ever tried to set foot in Nicaragua, they would fight until the last man was dead.

But in fact at that moment the big threat came from the Sandinistas' own ranks, the Sandinista Milpas, a contingent of campesinos who had fought under the fallen leader Germán Pomares. Now his men declared that the FSLN National Directorate was a bunch of "city people who hadn't done much fighting." They refused to lay down their guns and instead retreated to the mountains of Quilalí.

On July 28 the Carter administration put aside whatever doubts it might have had about the new leadership and, in a spirit of generous cooperation, sent Ambassador Pezzullo to Managua with several million dollars' worth of food and supplies for the Red Cross.

Tomás Borge met Pezzullo at the airport. In their brief interview Pezzullo informed Borge that the administration was also requesting from Congress approval of an $8–10 million emergency aid package for Nicaragua. Borge, one of the most radical Sandinistas, unsmilingly expressed the new government's willingness to work with people of different ideologies for the reconstruction of the country.

To Pezzullo, Borge's words were a revelation. He concluded that Nicaragua's pressing economic conditions had forced the Sandinistas to take a pragmatic approach to government. Indeed they had—but not by subscribing to pluralism as they had originally promised, but by maneuvering, intriguing, plotting, and betraying all of us.

By pretending to be something less than Marxists, the Sandinistas could enjoy America's largesse while buying time until they were economically and militarily strong enough to be an independent and totally radical power.

Alfonso left Cuba for Venezuela that same day to take the first steps in resolving Nicaragua's economic crisis. He revealed that the situation in Nicaragua was critical. There was a shortage of food and petroleum. "In the coming days," he said, "Nicaragua will need $150 million to solve its balance-of-payment problems. In time, to reconstruct the nation we will need $2.5 billion in foreign aid." He hastened to add that "Nicaragua was not interested in receiving any assistance that would in any way inhibit the full exercise of its sovereignty. . . . It would be a betrayal of the ideals of the people of Nicaragua."

In my opinion Alfonso was beginning to sound holier than the pope. To my surprise, years later I would read in one of the many books that have been written about Nicaragua that on that trip Alfonso talked privately with President Luis Herrera Campíns and conveyed to him his distress.

More vociferous in their complaints was the COSIP organization, now rebaptized the Superior Council for the Private Sector (COSEP) under the leadership of Enrique Dreyfus. He complained publicly that things were not being done according to the Plan of Government, which called for a mixed economy and the establishment of a democratic government. Dreyfus expressed concern that the foundations were being laid for one-party rule, which in view of the private sector's participation in overthrowing Somoza was unfair. He said, "We have earned the right to give our opinions. Somoza's ouster was the result of our united effort."

At a rally Daniel Ortega characterized it as a mistake to think that the Sandinista Front was only a military organization. "It was, is, and will continue to be," he said, "a political organization. . . . And we have the right to say we don't like this or that. And so, we are going to make some changes." He added that "victory over Somoza was the exclusive work of the FSLN." He proclaimed, "We were the spearheads of the revolution and will continue to be so until our program of government is complete."

Now that the Sandinistas were the victors, they wanted to vanquish all those who had aided them on the road to achieving power and deny us the right to participate in a meaningful way in the decisions that affected our country. While there is no question that our civic movement alone could never have deposed Somoza, I felt the Sandinistas were wrong to appropriate for themselves the victory we had achieved together.

In the beginning of August, however, when Alfonso returned to Nicaragua, he did not hesitate to announce that by "state canon" the financial system was going to be nationalized and that all foreign exports would now be commercialized under a new entity, the Ministry of Foreign Commerce. He said that the private sector had to forget about profit sharing and understand that "it is our patriotic duty to place our technical and professional capabilities at the service of the revolution."

The next day Alfonso and Arturo Cruz paid a visit to one of the businessmen who had been affected by the decree, Tono Baltodano, the general manager of his family's coffee export firm. They told him, "Your business has been nationalized, and if you want to help prevent the Sandinistas from radicalizing the government, you should come work with us." They wanted him to establish ENCAFE, the foreign trade entity that would export all of the nation's coffee crop.

It was a stunning proposal. At the same moment that they were putting him out of business, they were inviting him to exploit his contacts for the benefit of the revolution. He promised to think about it.

Tono's family had supported the insurrection. They were anti-Somocistas to the core. His younger sister Milena was Tomás Borge's trusted assistant. His uncle Emilio was a member of Los Doce and now comptroller general of the republic. His cousins were all in the Sandinista high command. So he knew that the Sandinistas were radicals. They had confiscated his older sister's personal accounts and taken her home simply because she was married to a nephew of Guillermo Sevilla Sacasa, Somoza's brother-in-law, though these individuals had never committed any crime. It was evident there was a great amount of class hatred. On a rational level Tono doubted anything could be done to dissuade the Sandinistas from the course they had set. But on an emotional level he felt he had to try. The following morning he called Alfonso and accepted.

Tono's reaction was typically patriotic. In the private sector there were many who, forgoing personal gain, put their lives on hold to work for the reconstruction of the country—men like my cousin Maché Torres, minister of agriculture; Noel Rivas Gasteozoro, minister of industry; and Dr. César Amador, minister of health. The list is long. Unfortunately, their efforts and sacrifices were wasted because the Sandinistas were single-minded in their mission to break the system because it was based on free enterprise and was an obstacle to their absolute dominance over the populace.

Aid from the United States and Venezuela was followed by assistance from Mexico, Panama, and Costa Rica, who all helped with money and other forms of assistance. The Sandinistas cannot rightfully claim that they had to resort to their con games because they were short on support from the private sector or from the Western democracies. But it is indicative of where the Sandinistas' sympathies lay from the start that in the pages of *Barricada* it was the good deeds of the FSLN militants and the Cuban Mission that were exalted most. Evidently, Cuba alone had the gratitude and the ear of the Sandinista Central Directorate.

Pezzullo's July flight of mercy was followed thirteen days later, on August 5, by a second gesture of friendliness from the Americans. On a forty-eight-hour visit, Edward Zorinsky, an important member of the Senate Foreign Relations Committee, flew to Managua to assure Borge of the United States's good intentions toward the new government. The Carter administration, after failing to prevent the Sandinistas from coming to power, had given him instructions to go to great lengths to express sympathy for the revolution. (In an interview that Secretary of

State Cyrus Vance gave to the U.S. press, he said that the success of Nicaraguan-American relations now hinged on the United States's ability to communicate to the new leadership of Nicaragua that they would not try to destabilize them; only then could Americans expect to exert influence.)

On the eve of Zorinsky's arrival Tomás Borge declared that the Americans would gain the sympathy of all of Nicaragua if they returned Somoza to be judged and condemned to thirty years in prison.

Zorinsky was met at the airport by Borge, who immediately went on the offensive. In a play of words he said that the Sandinistas were well aware that the revolution had many friends and enemies and that today "they wanted to be friendlier with their friends and less unfriendly with their enemies."

The senator experienced a moment's hesitation but nevertheless moved unequivocally to embrace the revolution. Verbalizing the Carter administration's new approach, with d'Escoto acting as an interpreter, Zorinsky asked Borge to bear no grudge against his country. He then distanced himself from the mistakes of previous American administrations and declared that he was part of a "new generation of Americans" that at last was on the right side of the issues, and that they wanted to contribute to making Nicaragua each day a little better; upon returning to the United States he would recommend approval of economic assistance to Nicaragua.

Borge responded, in an apparent non sequitur, "Let me be crystal clear. The United States and Nicaragua can be excellent friends or excellent enemies."

That was Borge's style, always making direct or veiled threats. In the aftermath of the revolution it was Borge people most feared.

Zorinsky's visit was followed by that of Rodrigo Carazo Odio, who came dressed in a safari suit. The entire junta met him at the airport. We were accompanied by Miguel d'Escoto. Our delegation reviewed the troops that had come to honor Carazo, led by Tomás Borge, Humberto Ortega, and Luis Carrión.

In his welcoming remarks Sergio Ramírez made it clear that it was the Nicaraguan people who had won the war, as if we had little to be grateful for to others. But he added that the struggle would have been much longer and tougher had it not been for the loyal support of the neighboring republic of Costa Rica.

In fact, the struggle would have failed had it not been for Costa Rica. It provided a sanctuary for the Sandinista forces. Had those forces been forced to fight Somoza's army without having the recourse to flee into Costa Rican territory, they would have been annihilated after a short while.

In all, it was not the kind of reception I had expected for Carazo. Perhaps his remarks about liberty, justice, and peace did not sit well with our belligerent revolutionaries, who were champing at the bit to exercise what was already becoming their military might in Central America. But I think that there was as well a certain amount of resentment toward Carazo because near the end of our exile it was clear he had had enough of our revolutionary activities. I understand totally. Carazo incurred a great deal of political loss for allowing his country to be overrun by revolutionaries.

On August 18, when General Omar Torrijos came to Nicaragua to pay us a courtesy call, the celebration was much greater. Tomás Borge met him at the airport with a full military display. Borge, an occasional writer and poet, was melodramatic in his welcoming speech. He hailed Torrijos as the "captain of the hearts of the Panamanian people and the man who placed himself at the forefront of our struggle. But more important, Torrijos is the man who shed tears when he learned of the death of Germán Pomares." Torrijos wept again, this time in full view of the thousands who had gathered to honor him. He said that to assist the revolution had been a duty and an honor, and that never in his life had he felt such emotion as the one that overtook him when he landed in Aeropuerto Sandino. Afterward there was a march in the Plaza de la Revolución in his honor, where it was announced that Humberto Ortega had been appointed army chief. I wondered, knowing as the Sandinistas did that Torrijos didn't like Humberto, why they had chosen that day to make such an announcement. I could only conclude that it was a deliberate gesture, intended to express their power and independence.

About six years later I read that at the time of this effusive speech, Torrijos was already displeased with the Sandinistas because they had failed to place Edén Pastora in a position of influence. The fact is that an agreement regarding military cooperation that was supposed to be signed during that visit never came to pass.

Pomares's name had been popping up in several speeches in the weeks before Torrijos's visit. Pomares, a cotton picker from Chinandega turned revolutionary, had become a cult figure among the *campesinado*. So while visiting the region, Ortega exalted Pomares to try to mend fences with the campesinos, who were angry at the FSLN's agricultural policies.

The original intention was that after the revolution we would extend title of Somoza's properties to the campesinos. Now, however, the Sandinistas had decided to consolidate the lion's share of these properties under the Institute of Agrarian Reform, run by Comandante Jaime Wheelock, and to offer only ten thousand titles to campesinos who would work the land as part of a system of state-run cooperatives. Ortega had first tried to rationalize the situation by saying that it was necessary because there wasn't enough working capital for the campesinos to operate independently. He said that though the banking system had been nationalized for them so that the private sector could no longer take away their land if they defaulted on a loan, Somoza had taken all the cash and now there was no money for loans. No matter how he talked around the issue, the idea did not sit well with the Nicaraguan campesinos, who cherished their independence and liked planting their corn patch and selling their corn without interference from anyone.

I felt we had exchanged one form of injustice for another, perhaps greater. Now the people would be exploited by the state and the party instead of by Somoza or the bourgeoisie.

Shortly after Torrijos's visit, on August 21, Carlos Andrés came on an official visit. I was among the junta members who went out to receive him. Comandante Zero, Cap's favorite *guerrillero,* and Dora María Téllez presented to him the Nicaraguan flag Zero and Dora María had rescued from Somoza's congress on the day that they stormed the palace.

Carlos Andrés's first visit in the "free Nicaragua" was celebrated as a day of victory. He had been a tenacious opponent of Somoza, and I felt he well deserved all the honors. Cap, as he is widely known, had been a friend not just to our family but to our country.

I did not have the opportunity to discuss with him on that occasion my growing discomfort with the FSLN. But I know that for a long time he had hoped the *comandantes* could be guided away from Marxism.

Then, on August 22, I was told that the FSLN directorate had decided that our national military force would be called the Sandinista People's Army (EPS) and that it would be under the control of the FSLN in the person of army chief Humberto Ortega and not, as agreed in Costa Rica, under the defense minister, Bernardino Larios, who was supposed to oversee our land, sea, and air military forces. Because he was not a Sandinista, Larios was being ignored. As part of the junta I was asked to sign the official ruling. Now, with their guns, I felt, the Sandinistas had empowered themselves to a degree that they were the only ones who could be heard in Nicaragua.

In his acceptance speech at a mass rally, Ortega said the EPS would defend the sovereignty of Nicaragua and act as the military arm of the party while defending the advances of the revolution. He spoke also of the need to establish solidarity with an international brotherhood of revolutionaries because in Sandino's struggle as well as in our own revolution, we had received the support of Mexican, Central American, and South American rebels. Luis Carrión was appointed the number two man in the army, and Tomás Borge was appointed an adjunct.

This arrangement was not to last because of the old rivalries between the Ortegas and Tomás, which were renewed soon after the revolutionary victory. So after a brief period, Borge left the EPS to oversee the establishment of the Ministry of Interior, which became an independent power center for Tomás that housed a secret police and, at a later time, had its own combat force.

The EPS announcement incensed many moderate Nicaraguans, who railed against me for signing the decrees. "How can you let them have the army?" they asked.

But how could I explain that I was told after the fact by a kid from Tomás Borge's office to sign the paper? It was not a question of my letting them do anything. The Nicaraguan bourgeoisie had not yet awakened to the fact that the Sandinistas could flex their military muscles at will. They still thought of the Sandinistas as sons and daughters of our friends, children we could influence or order around. They had helped us bring down Somoza, and now they expected that the Sandinistas would simply step aside and let the anti-Somoza establishment rule. But the Sandinistas had no plans to cede control.

I was now painfully aware of this. Unfortunately, I chose not to decry any of these maneuvers. At the time I thought the Sandinistas were misguided, but I failed to ascribe any evil to them. So I told Enrique to give them a chance: *los muchachos* are not bad. Like Carter and Carlos Andrés and perhaps Alfonso, I felt this way too, though we had never discussed it—if we put a good face on the situation it might in fact improve. Furthermore, I felt my presence as a moderate, along with that of others like me, could still serve to temper the behavior of the radical elements in the government.

The next day there appeared a notice in *Barricada* announcing the reorganization of the Sandinista National Directorate. It was an intricate network of executive committees and acting committees comprising an endless permutation of the same nine characters: Humberto and Daniel Ortega, Victor Tirado, Tomás Borge, Henry Ruiz, Luis Carrión, Bayardo Arce, Carlos Núñez, and Jaime Wheelock. My impression was that by weaving this complex web of power they were trying to prevent the formation of tactical alliances. In spite of this, however, in the end no one could avoid recognizing that Humberto and Daniel, who were united by blood, had become the true centers of power because Humberto controlled the army and Daniel controlled the executive, much as the two Somoza brothers had.

On August 24, 168 industries and 159 private residences were confiscated. The Sandinistas claimed they belonged to Somocistas. But who could be certain? It was evident that communism was an ideology that had strong roots in the Sandinistas. They were deeply opposed to capitalism, and so they harbored great hostility for private enterprise. They meant to do away with it completely.

In the barrios the bakers, the shoemakers, and others were all being told that if they wanted to have access to raw material they would have to cooperate with their CDS. If they could prove they had complied with their revolutionary duties, and only then, they could have access to a trade union cooperative that would furnish them with the necessary raw material. Their products would then be purchased by this same cooperative at an established price. They could keep whatever they needed for their own private consumption.

In the countryside, the small farmers were being forced to join collectives. They were constantly called to political meetings. If they didn't attend they had difficulties getting loans for fertilizer and seed. They were further hampered by the imposition of price controls. Those who resisted complying with the new edicts lost their land or went to jail.

The Miskito Indians, who lived on the Caribbean coast, had it even worse. They governed themselves independently through a Council of Elders and followed their own traditions. At the time of the insurrection a platoon of Miskitos had joined the Sandinistas in combat, believing that in exchange they would receive complete autonomy. Now the Sandinistas were attempting to organize them through the CDS leaders. Sandinista troops rounded up a group of "subversives" and would have carried them off to jail if the local people had not intervened to set them free.

Two months after the much celebrated Sandinista victory, all over Nicaragua the people in whose name the revolution had been fought were being alienated by Sandinista policies. Campesinos, small merchants, and Miskitos began to quietly slip across the border into neighboring Honduras. Once in exile, these separate groups eventually organized.

As this was happening, an unrelated event served to bring out into the open the ambiguous nature of the Carter administration with respect to the Sandinista leadership. In the first week in September, with the SALT II arms control treaty still pending approval in the U.S. Senate, news stories about the existence of a brigade of Soviet troops in Cuba swept across the country, forcing Carter, on September 7, to go on television to qualify as "unacceptable" the current levels of Soviet troops in Cuba. And so, he promised to expand American military presence in the Caribbean and increase economic assistance to some key countries in the region. Military aid to El Salvador would be expanded to combat the rise in Marxist guerrilla activity that country was experiencing since the advent of the Sandinista revolution. For Nicaragua, Carter said he was requesting a $75 million economic aid package, 60 percent of which was to be funneled to the private sector. The Sandinistas were enraged. They said the United States was strengthening the private sector at the expense of the revolution.

Perhaps not coincidentally, on September 15—Independence Day—in honor of Pham Van Dong, the head of state of the Vietnamese people, a massive demonstration was held in the Plaza de la Revolución. Scores of little children marched, dressed in the olive uniforms of the FSLN army and red bandanas, and bearing rifles on their shoulders. When the Sandinistas intoned their new anthem they called for the elimination of "the Yankee enemies of humanity." They also expressed to Pham Van

Dong the revolution's profound respect and admiration for the revolution in Vietnam, "a shining example of anti-imperialism."

This display of affection for Vietnam, a country with which the United States shared a sad and bloody past, did not stop the pragmatic Daniel from flying a week later in the company of the moderate Alfonso to the United States on his first official visit to the White House to discuss the $75 million economic aid package. Ortega told President Carter, "We want your aid, but unconditionally."

The suggestion was unreasonable. Traditionally, U.S. aid is reserved for governments viewed as allies, which the Sandinistas were clearly not. However, it is a testament to the Carter administration's willingness to bend over backward in accommodating the Sandinistas that Carter promised Ortega to go forward with his plans to request approval of the aid package. In return, Carter simply asked Ortega not to hold the United States's past diplomatic blunders against his administration, and he besought him to refrain from publicly attacking the United States. In addition, he warned Ortega not to succumb to the temptation of getting involved in aiding the Farabundo Martí Liberation Movement (FMLN) in El Salvador. Ortega gave assurances this was not about to happen. Later we would learn that the FSLN was from the start helping the FMLN.

Afterward they flew to New York to attend the U.N. General Assembly. To everyone's surprise, Ortega denounced the United States as the big lone imperialist that through the CIA was training a counterrevolutionary force in Miami for an imminent invasion of our country.

At the time, Ortega must have known this was not true. The anti-Sandinistas in Miami were nothing more than a nostalgic and disorganized group of exiles. Each week they met to discuss the latest news out of Managua. They were not united in their background or beliefs.

At the General Assembly Ortega attempted to subvert U.S. interests throughout the world. Repeating parts of a speech he had given in Cuba some weeks earlier, he loudly defended liberation movements across the globe. He declared support for the PLO and the Puerto Rican people's struggle for self-determination. He denounced Yankee imperialism and then very adroitly asked for help in consolidating the revolution.

It was a tactic against the United States that Nicaragua would learn to master over the years. The charges became progressively more outra-

geous, the denunciations progressively hyperbolic. The goal was to isolate and humiliate the United States and create the impression that world
opinion was united in condemnation of American imperialism.

The aggressive-rhetoric strategy was used by the Sandinistas against
any political ideas or demands the Sandinistas did not like, which were
dismissed as bourgeois or Yankee imperialist notions. In time the ani-
mosity directed at the bourgeoisie and the United States was such that it
appeared their former allies in the insurrection were as odious to the
Sandinistas as any Somocista had ever been.

Eight weeks after the revolutionary victory, my son Pedro Joaquín
cofounded the Social Democratic Party. He told me that he didn't
like my participation in the junta; he felt the revolution was a
complete disaster. These people, he said, "have no sense of loyalty.
They are confrontational. They are turning against the people who
helped them." So he decided to actively oppose the Sandinistas. Predictably, the Sandinistas denounced the new party as a threat to the
revolution.

At the end of September, a confidential memo written by the Sandinista National Directorate was leaked. The true intentions of the Sandinistas were unmasked. The "Seventy-two-Hour Document," as this
memo became known, was a kind of revolutionary charter, in which
the leaders of the FSLN outlined their plan for assuming total control of
Nicaragua. They spoke of sabotaging the junta government, crippling
the private sector, eradicating from government all moderate elements,
neutralizing the church, completely militarizing Nicaragua, and aiding
the burgeoning guerrilla movements in Central America. The language
they used was one of resentment and belligerence. They said, "The
disloyal bourgeoisie, obsessed with continuing to keep our country subjugated under the economic dependence of imperialism, must be isolated via an appropriate political tactic. We must hit them, not attacking
them as a class, but individually through their most distinguished and
influential figures. By giving them political and economic blows we will
reduce their capacity to strike back against the revolution."

One of their first blows was against Comandante Bravo. As the elite
commander of Somoza's troops on the Costa Rican frontier, Bravo had
kept Comandante Zero at bay, making it impossible to penetrate into
Rivas and seize territory for a provisional government. In the past
months, rumors had come to the Sandinistas that Bravo was touring

Central America as an unofficial ambassador for Somoza, trying to convince governments to accept the former guardsmen into their troops. The rationale was that if the units were kept intact they could be mobilized against the Sandinistas later.

So, on October 10, in Honduras, while he was on a tryst with an ex-lover (who was now, unbeknownst to Bravo, his archenemy Comandante Zero's lover), at a hotel in Tegucigalpa, the unsuspecting Bravo was ambushed and killed. They tortured Bravo, slowly protracting his death by burning him, tearing off his genitals, and slowly ripping the flesh off his face.

When the photograph of Bravo's body with its bare skull was unofficially circulated in Managua, Borge was in an obviously celebratory mood. He said, "Somoza's henchman is now six feet under." All that I had thought was left behind—acts of corruption, torture, and murder on the part of our leaders—I could see was having a new beginning in the Sandinista directorship. My urgency to leave was great. But once again my resignation was not accepted.

While this was happening, Marta Lucía and Pedro Joaquín had their third child, Sergio Antonio, named for his godfather, Tono (José Antonio) Baltodano. Cristiana was the godmother. At the baptism, Cristiana, who had not yet had any children, was holding the baby awkwardly. It's a miracle she didn't drop him! Of all my grandchildren, Sergio is the one who has the Barrios family's *don de gente*. He could be a politician someday.

The Sandinistas, who rejected my resignation, offered all kinds of solutions to my problems. My discomfort, however, could not be easily put to rest. In the months to come I would attempt to depart amicably four more times.

The next time was on October 3, after the Permanent Commission on Human Rights, following leads about unjustified detentions, disappearances, and executions at unofficial detention centers, discovered the existence of common graves near the city of Granada. When the graves were found, the Interior Ministry stonewalled the investigation. Mass graves were also uncovered in León, Masaya, and other cities. The Sandinistas had promised they would treat with clemency all who surrendered—"The revolution will be generous in victory." Now, the long arm of revolutionary vengeance had apparently seen to it that they were secretly murdered.

Gradually I began to realize that the Sandinistas were revolutionaries who had come to power after years of living outside the rule of law and that they had grown accustomed to executing their opponents. *Ajusticiamientos,* they used to call the murders, implying that there was a measure of justice in their act.

At the end of October the Sandinistas began actively to sabotage the private sector. Companies that were targeted were first weakened by a newly organized Sandinista labor organization, the Sandinista Workers Cooperative (CST). The CST instigated strikes and labor disputes which automatically made the company subject to intervention by the government.

The agricultural sector was also treated to the same kind of harassment from a similar group, the Agricultural Laborers Union (ATC). In a short period the Sandinistas confiscated more than 1 million acres of land, organizing it into cooperatives under the Institute of Agrarian Reform, headed by Jaime Wheelock. In addition, small growers and cattle farmers were forced to join collectives and subjected to price controls and other regulations that curtailed their independence.

Alienated farmers and ranchers crossed the border to Honduras and joined the Milpas.

Then, on November 9, Alfonso Robelo announced the creation of an economic planning commission that would be jointly composed of members of government and the private sector. He said it was necessary "so that our move toward socialism is gradual and without hasty measures that can affect production."

But the private sector did not agree to cooperate. On November 14, COSEP addressed the junta and the FSLN in a document that repeated in stronger terms many of the complaints made in July. Alfonso Robelo then made it quite clear that the move toward collective enterprise was unstoppable. "The fiesta is over," he said. "It's time to recognize the revolution is socialist and that eventually all production assets will be in state hands."

In one swift move the Sandinistas had abandoned all democratic pretenses and were gathering all the strands of power into one clenched fist. It was clear from then on that under their direction every sector of the

My family (standing left to right): Carlos José, me, Ricardo; seated, my mother Amalia, with Manuel Joaquín (Maquín) on her lap.

My father, Carlos Barrios Sacasa, not long before he died at the the age of fifty.

Pedro with his parents, Pedro Joaquín Chamorro Zelaya and Margarita Cardenal.

A view from the porch of the house in Amayo.

The galleries that surround the Plaza Central viewed from the corner of my house in Rivas, as they appear today.

My wedding day.

In "Las Sierras" de Managua on my honeymoon.

With Pedro Joaquín the day before the escape in San Carlos.

The family back in Managua after the invasion of Olama and Mollejones. This photo was taken so Pedro could have a reminder of the children while he was in prison. Sitting from left to right: Claudia Lucía Cayetana, me, and Carlos Fernando. Standing left to right: Quinto Pedro Joaquín and Cristiana.

Pedro Joaquín Chamorro (front row, second from left) with some men of the Olama y Mollejones invasion.

Front page of *La Prensa* showing Pedro's bullet-riddled body.

Anastasio Somoza Debayle (Tacho II), at a campaign rally during one of the elections for president of Nicaragua that he couldn't lose.

Pedro's body carried on the shoulders of the people. The headline reads, "These people can't be killed."

Mourners pay their respects at Pedro's funeral.

AP/Wide World Photo

President Daniel Ortega flanked by Interior Minister Tomás Borge (left) and Defense Minister Humberto Ortega (right).

I was part of the delegation with Jacinto Suarez (left) and Daniel Ortega (right), visiting the Pope in March 1980. Daniel looks uncomfortable wearing a jacket and tie instead of military fatigues.

Rosalyn and Jimmy Carter visiting me at *La Prensa* while it was shut down.

Holding a copy of a censored edition of *La Prensa*, just after the Sandinistas allowed us to publish again.

Daniel Ortega handing me the presidential sash at my inauguration.
(left) With my good friend, Carlos Andrés Pérez, President of Venezuela, and Vice-President Virgilio Godoy at a breakfast at the Venezuelan Embassy the day before the inauguration.

My official visit to the White House, where I presented President Bush with a rifle from a demobilized Contra. Standing left to right: National Security Advisor Brent Scowcroft, Secretary of State James Baker, translator, Cristiana, President Bush, myself, Senator Jesse Helms, Enrique Dreyfus, Nicaragua's Foreign Minister, and Ernesto Palazio, Nicaragua's ambassador to the United States.

I was thrilled to greet Pope John Paul II on Nicaraguan soil when he visited in February 1996.

With my children, from left to right: Pedro Joaquín, Claudia Lucía, me, Cristiana, and Carlos Fernando in April 1990.

With some of my grandchildren. Back row, from left to right: Sexto Pedro Joaquín, Sergio Antonio, Fadrique Damian; seated, middle row: Cristiana María, Violeta Margarita, me, Valentina; front row, seated: Marcos Tolentino, Antonio Ignacio, María Andrea.

government and the economy would serve the interests of the Sandinista party.

Notwithstanding evidence to the contrary, the FSLN directorate continued to promulgate the official line that the revolution had been created for all of us. It had freed Nicaragua from oppression to make it pluralistic and nonaligned.

The veracity of the Sandinistas' statements was hotly debated in the pages of *La Prensa* by my son Pedro Joaquín. Their reaction to Pedro Joaquín's articles demonstrated that the Sandinistas did not welcome any criticism.

At the end of the month came a purge of the moderate elements in the government. First, Bernardino Larios was fired as defense minister and Humberto Ortega was appointed in his place. Then the Ministries of Industry, Commerce, and Agriculture were yoked under one entity, the Ministry of Central Planning, which came under the firm hand of Moscow-educated Comandante Henry Ruiz, the most orthodox Marxist of the revolution. Moderates like my cousin Maché Torres, who headed the Ministry of Agriculture, were pushed out of key positions.

Alfonso and I were kept as window dressing while Humberto Ortega built the Sandinista People's Army into the most powerful and disciplined force in Central America and Daniel consolidated his bureaucratic power, casting aside all moderates. We were props for the Sandinistas, to be used to promote the notion that the revolution was not merely a communist takeover of Nicaragua. They claimed that "if Pedro, the martyr of civil liberties, were alive today he would be unfailingly on the side of the revolution."

To benefit further from my husband's prestige, they offered to name boulevards, parks, schools, and museums after Pedro. When asked for approval of these plans to honor him, I referred them to my children. I did not like flattery and I felt a distinct discomfort with what I was beginning to feel was the exploitation of Pedro's name. Nevertheless I let my children decide. Invariably they chose to accept the honors, and I did not stand in the way.

One of these lavish displays of affection was staged in Monimbo on a Sunday in January 1980, on the second anniversary of Pedro's assassination, a mere six months after we had come to power. I arrived with

Sonia Chamorro, Xavier's wife, at 10 A.M. The whole town came out for me, the people chanting, "Pedro Joaquín Chamorro lives!" The members of the junta who rode with me that day, I am sure, noted the jubilant smiles that the mere mention of Pedro's name brought to the faces of these people.

The ideological divide created by the revolution was everywhere evident. It affected everybody's life. The country was in a state of total agitation. The puritanical social norms we had inherited from our Spanish ancestors, which required a minimum level of comportment between the sexes, were being radically overturned. The revolutionary boys, like Fidel, let their hair and beards grow. They wore military garb at all times and addressed one another as *compañero,* or "comrade," as in the Soviet Union. The girls also rebelled against the ladylike image that had been imposed upon them by their mothers. They too donned army fatigues and combat boots. I suppose they saw it as a symbol of their equality with the men. Unfortunately many excellent family values were thrown overboard as well.

There was, for example, an open disdain for all things feminine and moral. Marriage was regarded as a trite symbol of a woman's enslavement, which precluded her participation in the "revolutionary new world." Commitment between two people was now made by having the young couple simply walk under an arch formed by the crossing of bayonets. This type of wedding came to be known as *por las armas,* under the bayonets. Needless to say, many of these arrangements did not last, and many fatherless children abound in Nicaragua today.

Meanwhile, confiscation, subsidies, and price controls were destroying the economy. There were food shortages and ration cards.

Anita, my friend and companion who does my household shopping, would rise at dawn to purchase a few emaciated chickens and a stack of tortillas for our dinner. She would pay what I considered to be an exorbitant price. From time to time on the radio we would hear about products that were rumored to become scarce, and off she'd go to buy what she could, not really thinking whether we needed it, but just in case. It was mass hysteria, and the black market people exploited it to perfection.

Simultaneously, the value of our currency began to drop at such a speed that instead of the government issuing new bills, the currency was simply stamped each day with its new value. The running joke was that to go shopping you needed a wheelbarrow to carry the money but a handbag to bring back your purchases. Certainly, from one moment to the other, people could not predict what the value of goods would be. Everything began to be marked in dollars. What an irony for those who denounced American imperialism! But the last straw came when gasoline was rationed. The lines of automobiles extended north and south for days on end as people desperately waited to turn in their coupons for the badly needed petrol. This was the state of things when the taxi drivers in Managua declared a general strike against the government, only to be swiftly coerced back to work by the force of the Sandinistas' firearms.

At the end of January 1980, the $75 million aid package was approved by the U.S. Congress. Many legislators were dubious, but ultimately they resolved in its favor because they felt it would help strengthen the private sector, the church, and the press against the Sandinistas. Again the Sandinistas declared that U.S. support was going to the "traitorous bourgeoisie."

Then in February, at a Nicaraguan Democratic Movement (MDN) political rally, Alfonso, for the first time, openly proclaimed to thousands of his supporters, "We live in a free Nicaragua and no one has the right to tell us what to do or think. If you have a complaint, make it known. If you want to join a political party, you have the right to do so." The Sandinista mobs were sent to break up the rally, screaming, "People's power is Sandinista power," and setting fire to the MDN flag.

La Prensa noted that the Sandinistas were intolerant of other people's views, and of law and civil liberties. At first, the Sandinistas did not openly turn on us. Concerned that by attacking the newspaper of Pedro Joaquín Chamorro they would suffer a bad image abroad, the Sandinistas tried to buy us out. Through the auspices of Xavier Chamorro they proposed a deal to purchase the family's stock in *La Prensa*. The family declined to sell. But problems began to arise between Xavier and the board of directors. Xavier had developed a revolutionary zeal that was at odds with the beliefs of the board of directors. Under his administration, *La Prensa* was becoming a partisan daily that praised the revolution.

Meanwhile, in our own family the political choices my children made were cutting to the very heart of our family relations. Except for Pedro

Joaquín, my children were in favor of the revolutionary process. Claudia, who was then pregnant with her third child, was working at the Foreign Ministry. In the absence of Pedro the Sandinistas had become her political mentors. Cristiana was at *La Prensa,* uncomfortable with the tensions there and trying to maintain a neutral position in a situation that was becoming deeply polarized. Carlos Fernando had become the director of *Barricada,* which required that, in addition to managing the newspaper, he make sure all the journalists were toeing the political line of the party—a position that would pit him against his older brother, Pedro Joaquín, at *La Prensa.* During this period in his life he was blinded by Sandinismo. He was in an ideological straitjacket that brought him on occasion almost to blows with his older brother, who wanted democratic pluralism for Nicaragua.

In the interest of harmony, I declared all political discussions off-limits in my home. This enabled us, in spite of our differences, to remain reasonably close throughout those difficult times. Years later, when I was elected president of Nicaragua, after the country had been polarized by years of political extremism, I remembered the lessons I had learned in those days of family strife. Tolerance, reconciliation, and the right tactical approach are the three premises on which to build peace.

In March the National Literacy Campaign was launched under the guidance of the Cubans. They designed the texts and sent more than a thousand literacy teachers *(brigadistas)* to assist the sixty thousand high school students; these *brigadistas* fanned out throughout the countryside to live with and teach campesino families. The young teachers were instructed not just to teach reading and writing but to raise political awareness among the people.

The sort of thing illiterate Nicaraguans learned in the campaign was that the Sandinistas were at the forefront of the revolution. "The FSLN," they were told, "led the people of Nicaragua to liberation." They were also taught in the most simplistic terms about the advantages of land reform, nationalization, and "people's power." The effort was clearly a move to teach the campesinos Marxism and consecrate the Sandinista leadership in power.

Archbishop Miguel Obando in his Sunday homilies denounced the literacy campaigns. He said that the parallel goal of the campaign was political and social indoctrination.

The Sandinistas responded to his criticism by arguing that "there is no teaching method that is not political" and that their method awakened the campesinos to their history and their political and social reality.

When my junta colleagues talked about joining the literacy campaign or going off into the mountains to help harvest the coffee, I thought they were hypocritical. The instinct to do good comes naturally to a person. These massive campaigns, I was certain, would be the end of us.

Notwithstanding, my decision to counter the Sandinistas openly was not something that came easily. It was a slow, painful process of recognition of betrayal that was heightened every time a new edict was published that I, a member of the ruling junta, had not been made aware of. My jurisdiction was strictly confined to public relations matters.

Predictably, I was always asked to be part of diplomatic delegations. I was present at the inauguration of the president of Ecuador, Jaime Roldos, and at the ceremony in which the canal rights were returned to the Panamanian people. And, of course, no one was better suited as an emissary to Pope John Paul II than a faithful apostle of the Roman Catholic church like myself. When the men of the junta came to ask me to accompany them to see the pope, I said, "All right," and asked Claudia to go with me.

I arrived in Rome for the papal visit ahead of the others, not knowing what arrangements they had made for their lodgings. Daniel Ortega arrived with Rosario Murillo, La Chayo. I knew she spoke several languages, and so I thought she was there as a translator. But I was told she had traveled as Daniel's wife. I had never heard of a marriage taking place between them!

By then I was so unhappy with my junta colleagues that I distanced myself from their group. "Let them do their sightseeing and their shopping," I remarked to Claudia, who accompanied me. "I don't have to consort with them until tomorrow." On the morning of our audience with the pope, I dressed as Vatican etiquette required, in a black dress with long sleeves, and waited in the lobby for my colleagues to come down. I'm very punctual, so when I noticed the time for our audience was nearing and the delegation was still nowhere in sight, I got nervous. I said to Claudia, "Go find out what's holding them up." Claudia came back with the news that no one dressed in a military uniform was allowed into the Vatican Palace; at that very moment the delegation was scrambling to find a suitable outfit for Daniel. A short time later they came down. Daniel was in a blue suit. I don't know where it came from.

❯❯   ❯❯

Maybe they borrowed it from a hotel employee, but the collar in his shirt was open and wouldn't close. His tie was draped untidily around his neck. His discomfort with the social norms of civilized society was so obvious that I said nothing to him about his slovenly appearance. We left the hotel in separate cars and headed for the Vatican.

In the Vatican we were led to the luxurious papal apartments. In the official *stanze,* surrounded by Raphael's paintings, we waited for the pope to appear. When I saw the pope I nearly fainted. There is a softness and grace in the pope's presence that immediately transported me to a more spiritual realm, one that made me feel closer to God. Here was a man who I felt could never misuse his authority.

I don't know what feelings His Holiness may have harbored in his heart for the Sandinistas who had disavowed Catholicism. I don't know if because of his own bad experiences with communism in Poland he thought the Sandinistas good or evil—but he treated us all equally well. As he walked through the room the pope blessed each of us in turn, and for every one of us he had a kind phrase. To the delight of our delegation, he spoke to us in perfect Spanish.

The fact that men and women of all nationalities and religions flock to meet the pope demonstrates, I think, that he is more than just a man. People feel a need to move away from greed and toward greater spirituality. So, for many of us, he is a leader whose teachings rise above the fray between nations, races, social classes, ideologies. For me the experience was transformative. As I looked at His Holiness, who is so beautiful, I thought of all that I had suffered and I offered it as penance to God for all my imperfections. But I don't think the experience changed Daniel one iota.

We returned to Managua a few days later. Sadly, the Sandinistas, encouraged by their leaders in their efforts to destroy Robelo as an opponent, continued their campaign of hate.

I tried to deny the truth of what was happening. I had been fighting for so long I thought I lacked the strength to embark on another crusade. I tried to assuage my growing anxiety by going for short trips in the countryside. I talk to people with great ease, so I was able to speak with farmers, shopkeepers, and mothers. Like Pedro on his morning jaunts touring the city, I wanted to know the reality of my people. I asked them what they wanted from our government. Their answer was invariably simple: "We want peace, freedom, and work." Nobody said they wanted nationalization, collective farms, military might. I marveled at how their humble demands stood in stark contrast to the complicated ideology spewed by the Sandinistas. I concluded that the FSLN was out of touch with our countrymen. They seemed to want, not a better Nicaragua, but a communist one.

I spent sleepless nights agonizing over the right course of action. For years I had been suffering vertebrae problems. Now the tension, the disillusionment, the emptiness I was feeling were producing an unnatural fatigue that gave me a pinched nerve and impaired my mobility. One Sunday in March I fell at home and broke my right foot. Forced to amble about in a cast on crutches, I found the burden of my position unbearable. Each day, with great difficulty, I would climb the stone stairs of the House of Government and think of all the things that ailed me, not just physically but spiritually as well. The time came when I could think only of quitting.

The conflict between the Sandinistas and the non-Marxists and moderates finally blew up on Friday, April 11. The Sandinistas announced that they were barring from participation in the Council of State political parties that they considered no longer politically viable, including the Communist Party of Nicaragua. In essence they were eliminating parties that were critical of the Sandinista directorate.

"These seats," Sergio Ramírez announced, "will be filled by the new Sandinista labor organizations." They also revealed their intention to add three more seats to the Council of State. Now that the Sandinistas were in power they wanted to assure themselves a legislative majority.

The non-Marxists argued that, as stated in the Plan of Government, only those who had taken part in the insurrection had a right to a seat; so these new organizations had not earned the right to participate. They also opposed expansion because parliamentary equality was part of the original plan.

On April 12, my cousin Maché Torres had his hacienda in Rivas seized by campesinos. When I tried to intervene on his behalf, pointing out to the Sandinista leadership that this was a man who could never be accused of being a Somocista, they told me the people had their own will.

Over the next couple of days, in a display of power, the Sandinistas staged massive demonstrations in Managua and in León, screaming,

"Free fatherland or death! The people united will never be defeated! People's power!" and so forth. It was an intimidating spectacle.

When the time came to vote on the proposal to expand the Council of State, Alfonso and I voted against expansion. Sergio and Moisés voted in favor, resulting in a 2–2 tie. Only four of us voted because Daniel was traveling in Africa. Out of nowhere three Sandinista leaders turned up to tilt the vote 5–2. Their action was not just irregular but contemptible.

At last, realizing that as a junta member I was powerless in influencing the turn of events, I decided to resign. This time I would not take no for an answer. At whatever personal cost, I would go. I had wanted to make our revolution the democratic realization of our goals, but I had failed. The hopes of the Nicaraguan people had been betrayed, and there was nothing I could do in the junta to change things.

Diplomatically citing my lame foot and my advancing age, I asked to be excused from my post, without ever mentioning the word "resign." I was concerned about the consequences of my leaving for our negotiations for U.S. aid. I also wanted to avoid an argument with Claudia and Carlos Fernando. Pedro Joaquín, who was becoming a political leader, wanted me to take a confrontational stance. But as it was, my oft-spoken disillusionment with the Sandinista leadership had increased the tension among us. There was also the potential threat to *La Prensa*. So I did not want to speak against them, but I could no longer stand with them.

Several days later I received a call from Alfonso Robelo making known to me that the other members of the junta had decided to accept my decision to retire. It was April 19, 1980, and I was overjoyed with happiness. At last I had been relieved from the burden of the last nine months.

Alfonso came by with Moisés around 11 A.M. In a moment alone with Alfonso, I asked him if he was all right. I knew things weren't going well for him. The others in the junta said he was committing political suicide by going against the Sandinistas. But he made no comment. To Moisés I said nothing because I believed him to be a super-Sandinista. "The rest of the junta and Sandinista National Directorate," he told me, "will come to pay you a visit tomorrow."

I recall it was a Sunday when news of my departure was printed in *Barricada*. The Sandinista National Directorate came first, then the junta, then the top brass of the military, followed by the cabinet members and the representatives of the mass organizations—the Sandinista Children's Committee and on and on. Pretty soon we were spilling into the hallways and patios of the house. People kept on coming by the dozens. So we opened the front door and let them take over the park across the street. There were placards and banners hailing me as *"Violeta patria"* (patriotic Violeta). Notoriously absent from this crowd of well-wishers was Alfonso. I kept asking his whereabouts. But all I got was evasive remarks. Someone came and told me we should start without Alfonso. I refused. He had been my only friend on the junta.

A little past noon Alfonso appeared. The *comandantes* immediately began addressing the masses. They thanked me for my participation in the junta and invited me to continue "collaborating in the revolutionary effort." A man who represented the Agricultural Laborers Union (ATC) said the most heroic and noble example of resistance was Pedro Joaquín Chamorro: "It was his blood that unleashed the fury of the rebel movement . . . and when we were up in arms in the coffee plantations it was the moral integrity of comrade Violeta . . . that sustained us." Then I received a bouquet of flowers from an old and frail lady, a member of the mighty Association of Women in Combat.

Lodged between Borge and Arce, I smiled outwardly at their Sandinista flattery, though I knew none of it was heartfelt. I thanked them for their kindness and pledged to the people of Nicaragua, "I will remain in the service of the people, ready and willing to work for the construction of the idealistic Nicaragua Pedro dreamed of."

The whole event brought memories of Pedro's wake. I thought, First it was Pedro being carried out of here to be buried. Next it will be me.

Chapter Nine

THE DAY AFTER THE SANDINISTAS BADE ME AN an emotional farewell they moved in on *La Prensa*. Encouraged by Sandinista party bosses, labor leaders at the paper went on strike, ostensibly to protest the firing of Xavier Chamorro as director of *La Prensa*.

For some time now, a serious conflict had existed between Xavier and the board of directors over the direction of the newspaper. Xavier had with great acumen perceived that as an opposition publication under a totalitarian regime, *La Prensa* had no future. So he had striven to ingratiate himself with the new powers by turning *La Prensa* into a partisan daily, always unequivocally on the side of the revolution. My son Pedro Joaquín and the board of directors opposed this policy. Cristiana was ambivalent. She felt the newspaper should be nonaligned, without being passionately opposed as Pedro Joaquín certainly was. I believed the Sandinistas, left unchecked, were a threat to freedom and justice and that *La Prensa* was our last hope of countering them. I reminded Cristiana that we couldn't allow these issues to divide us. I said, "Family comes first, politics and other things later." Eventually she came around to seeing things our way.

As this was going on, Alfonso resigned on May 22. In a letter addressed to his colleagues in the junta he charged that the revolution was "deviating from its main objective, the achievement of democracy." He ended his letter saying he trusted God would place the Sandinistas on a path that led to peace, justice, and liberty. Later he would admit that after nine months of working without rest to forge a better Nicaragua, what had finally pushed him to resign was the Sandinistas' arrogance in assigning to themselves a parliamentary majority in the soon-to-be-convened Council of State. Back in exile in San José, the Sandinistas had given their word that there would be equal representation in the Council of State. Now that they had an army, this meant nothing.

The next day, in solidarity with Alfonso, seventeen members of the MDN vacated their government posts, denouncing the Sandinistas. None did so more explicitly than Tono Baltodano. He revealed that while managing ENCAFE he had been infiltrated by Tomás Borge's informers; that after he had negotiated an advantageous coffee contract with East Germany, Tomás Borge, with no apparent authority, renegotiated the contract into a coffee-for-arms deal, forgoing $24 million in urgently needed foreign exchange earnings. Tono said to Alfonso, "Now that they've got the army under control, these guys want to take over the economy!" In his letter of resignation he declared, "We are going in the direction of economic and political totalitarianism . . . and there is an obvious intent on the part of the Sandinista leaders to turn our country into a communist satellite." When Tono tried to read his letter on national TV, the Sandinistas literally pulled him off the air.

Dissenting opinion was burgeoning into a large problem for the revolution.

At the same time, Arturo Cruz resigned the presidency of the Banco Central. He said his decision was entirely personal and not political. He said he wanted to return to Washington, to his family, and to his old job as an officer of the Inter-American Development Bank.

On April 26 the strike at *La Prensa* ended. Having failed in his bid for control of the paper, Xavier, encouraged by members of the Sandinista directorate, decided to start his own partisan daily. To the strikers he said, "Together we can create a newspaper that will be truly revolutionary, objective, and accurate. It will be the true *Prensa*."

Danilo Aguirre, our news editor, joined forces with Xavier. He said that at *La Prensa* we were "obsessed with pluralism" and with the opinions of an "insignificant minority."

The younger brother Pedro had loved so much had allowed himself to be seduced into betraying *La Prensa,* the newspaper his brother had labored to build into the greatest daily in the nation and whose independence and objectivity Pedro had defended with his life.

Xavier's defection was almost the death of *La Prensa*. On the day he left, Xavier took with him 75 percent of *La Prensa*'s employees. In some key departments we lost all of the staff. Those who remained—Jaime, Pedro Joaquín, Horacio Ruiz, and Mario Alfaro—had to hire and train new personnel. It would take us a month to return to our readers.

Alfonso had hoped that the departure of the moderates from the government would bring the Sandinistas back to the center. But publicly the Sandinistas declared that no one was going to push them aside. They went to great lengths to discredit Alfonso as a leader.

They isolated Alfonso from the private sector by inviting the COSEP leadership to sit down at the negotiating table with them. The COSEP leaders knew that the Sandinistas were anxious to appear conciliatory with the private sector because they had already been warned by Pezzullo that the $75 million U.S. aid package, still pending approval in the U.S. Senate, was at risk. The moment was at hand for the COSEP leaders to try to gain some concessions from the Sandinistas. They pressed for a return to economic freedom, for parliamentary equality in the Council of State, for a decentralization of power, and for an end to press censorship. They pushed hard for the Sandinistas to set a date for elections. Finally, they requested that two moderates be elected to the junta.

The Sandinistas said that Arturo Cruz had already been asked to be part of the junta and they claimed Arturo had accepted as long as the second moderate was someone of equally good reputation. The other issues the Sandinistas would not consider.

The next day the COSEP leadership announced they were going forward with their plans to boycott the Council of State. They knew that the Council of State had been touted by the Sandinistas as the true expression of "people's power, a genuine example of democracy in Nicaragua." If COSEP did not participate, all of the non-Marxist political parties might follow suit. With the Sandinistas alone at the Council of State, in the eyes of the world pluralism would be considered dead in Nicaragua and support for the nascent revolution might falter.

But after complicated negotiations the COSEP leaders agreed to take part in the Council of State in exchange for a feeble promise from the Sandinistas that they would announce a schedule for elections on July 19, the anniversary of the revolution.

On May 4, when the Council of State was inaugurated, Comandante

Bayardo Arce was elected president. In turn, Arce nominated to be vice presidents of the council Dora María Téllez and COSEP leader José Francisco Cardenal.

Cardenal objected that no one had asked for his consent on this nomination. He accused the COSEP leadership of allowing themselves to be coopted by the Sandinistas. Six days later, José Francisco Cardenal and his wife left Nicaragua; ostensibly, he was going as one of three COSEP delegates to a Central American business conference in Costa Rica. While there, he announced he was resigning from his post as one of the heads of the Council of State and going into exile.

Not long afterward, José Francisco Cardenal flew to Miami. He was received by a throng of anti-Sandinistas exiled there. The feeling was that in him they had found a leader. After his arrival, a group of them coalesced into the Nicaraguan Democratic Union (UDN).

Meanwhile, ex–National Guards who now called themselves the Fifteenth of September Legion had united under the directorship of Enrique Bermúdez. With the support of a few Cuban exiles, they had begun training small groups of men in the Florida Everglades and in Guatemala.

On May 18, the Sandinistas, anxious to show the Americans that the revolution was not moving to the extreme left, announced the official appointment of Arturo Cruz and Rafael Córdoba Rivas to the junta. I know Arturo was unwilling at first to take the post. But under pressure from the archbishop and his own brother, he understood that because of his participation in Los Doce he was a founding member of the revolution. And so he had a moral duty to stay and fight as long as there was hope for democracy.

Arturo described himself as a patriot and a pragmatist and invoked images of Pedro by declaring himself his follower. "Like Pedro," he said, "I am committed to building a better, fairer, and more egalitarian Nicaragua."

Córdoba Rivas, who as the president of the UDEL brought to the position impeccable credentials as a defender of democracy, also invoked my dead husband as a guide.

But I knew that these men would be used, as Alfonso and I had been, to put a false face on a revolutionary dictatorship every bit as despotic as Somoza's. Instead of one tyrant we now had nine, the nine members of the Sandinista directorate.

. . .

La Prensa returned to its readers on May 26, 1980, with me as president of the board and director, and Pedro Joaquín as editor. Cristiana stayed on as a reporter for a while. But she missed her former colleagues and was uncomfortable with the new situation. Two months later she left *La Prensa* and accepted a job at the Council of State.

With the two Sandinista point men, Xavier and Danilo Aguirre, gone from the newspaper, we announced the birth of a new era, that of Sandisomocismo. In one of his first editorials, titled "The Narcissistic State and Democracy," my son Pedro Joaquín lambasted the Sandinistas for their monolithic control of the government. He reasoned that a state that is the only employer, the only political party, the only source of power becomes narcissistic because it promotes servility on the part of those who are bonded to it by need.

Enraged, the Sandinistas began to attack the newspaper seriously. Daniel Ortega accused *La Prensa* of harboring counterrevolutionary sentiments and fomenting hatred among the population. From his new position on *El Nuevo Diario,* our ex-editor, Danilo Aguirre, predicted that we would be out of business in a matter of months.

In due course, the Sandinistas cut our access to foreign exchange and thus deprived us of the imported raw material we needed. President Carter came to our rescue; he arranged for *La Prensa* to receive regular shipments of newsprint.

When the Sandinistas realized that their economic pressure had failed, they leveled the loaded gun of press censorship against us. There were times when two thirds of our edition had to be published carrying the black strips of the censors cutting across the text of our articles.

In addition, pressure was being put on *La Prensa* by the Sandinistas who harassed our reporters. At a rally on May 28 in the Plaza de la Revolución, one of our summer interns sat in a small park jotting notes. A group of sinister-looking men began reading over her shoulder. She explained she was a reporter for *La Prensa.* "These are just notes for my article," she said.

One man said in an incriminating tone, "She was taking pictures."

"I didn't know it was a crime," she said and bolted from the bench.

An hour later, she was sitting in the press booth waiting for the beginning of the rally when two men escorted her from her seat. At a secluded spot behind the cathedral, they questioned her.

"What is your name?" "Where do you live?" "How many brothers and sisters do you have?" Impertinent questions.

One man accused, "She was canvassing the place. I saw her making a map."

The men grabbed her arms. Though she had done nothing, these men were ready to make her disappear, as others had, without explanation.

She told them that she had relatives in power, and gave the name of a new member of the junta.

"You of all people," they admonished, "should know we have to watch over our revolutionary leaders."

She returned to her rally shaken.

That was one of the first instances in which the rights of one of our journalists to observe and report freely had been threatened. Had our intern not been able to cite her revolutionary pedigree, I am certain something worse would have happened.

On June 6, the U.S. Congress approved an aid package for Nicaragua. The aid package included a clause that required Carter to report to Congress every three months on the Nicaraguan situation. If at any time evidence was found that human rights were being violated or that Nicaragua was interfering in the affairs of other nations, the administration had to suspend the aid. And so Carter sent a mission to Nicaragua to hold high-level talks with the various sectors in the country and to try to get the Sandinistas to commit to elections. Congressman Jim Wright, a Democrat from Texas, headed the delegation.

Two things happened that did not favorably impress the congressmen. First, Alfonso Robelo was attacked in Chinandega while inaugurating the headquarters of the MDN. After a speech in which Robelo denounced "proletarian dictatorships, as they are an exploitation of man against man," a mob of Sandinista sympathizers, identified as members of the Sandinista labor union (CST), was sent to attack him.

Then the Farabundo Martí Liberation Movement announced that a final offensive was under way in nearby El Salvador. As in Nicaragua, the insurrection was to begin with a national strike that was supposed to paralyze the entire country.

Rumors abounded that in this effort the Sandinistas were giving the Salvadoran guerrillas their full assistance. In time we would come to know, by way of the diary of an FMLN guerrilla, that the Sandinistas had begun aiding their Salvadoran counterparts practically from the very first day they came to power. Nobody wanted to believe it, but it was revealed in their speeches. The Sandinistas saw it as a moral duty to help other insurrectionary movements, even if it meant risking the aid that was so badly needed for the people whose interests they claimed to represent.

Cristiana, meanwhile, at the Council of State, was becoming disillusioned with the undemocratic ways of the revolution. She observed firsthand that the council was a useless legislative body.

On the morning of July 18, the eve of the first anniversary of the revolution, Managua awoke to the clamor of Sandinista televisions and radios replaying underground radio broadcasts from the final days of the revolution. You could hear the voice of Zero during the palace siege, or tapes from Radio Reloj, in Costa Rica, as they questioned the *comandantes* on the advances of the insurrection. I even heard myself speaking on the day I had accepted a role in the junta, and later, the voice of the commentators on the day that Somoza went into exile and vanished from Nicaragua.

I thought, This country is our common heritage. It binds us together regardless of our political allegiances because all of us at one time or another suffered for it, sometimes even died for it, like Sandino, or Rigoberto López Pérez, or Adolfo Báez Bone, or my husband, Pedro, and people from the FSLN. Everybody has a martyr in their family; and so we are in certain ways obliged, for the sake of those fifty thousand heroes who have died, to defend our liberty. So alone, at home that day, I discharged my own salute "for a free Nicaragua."

The rest of the day I observed as the brigades from the Sandinista Propaganda Committee festooned the city with the red-and-black flags of the Sandinista party, put up posters of their fallen heroes, and rejoiced in their day of victory.

That evening the Sandinista *comandantes* threw a gala anniversary affair at the once-posh Nejapa Country Club, where the aristocracy had played golf on an eighteen-hole course reputed to be one of the best in Central America.

With the pomp and circumstance of five-star generals they circulated among the celebrity crowd of international revolutionaries and socialists. Among them were Felipe González, the prime minister of Spain; Maurice Bishop, who had recently seized power on the island of Grenada; Nobel laureate Gabriel García Márquez, a parlor Marxist with ties to Cuba's dictator; Hortensia Allende, the widow of slain Chilean Marxist president Salvador Allende; and the Salvadoran *guerrillero* Juan Chacón, commander of the FMLN movement.

Also attending was my old friend Carlos Andrés Pérez. We had planned for him to stay with me, but when he arrived at my house, Cap said, "I'm here to have lunch, but I cannot stay."

Noticing my look of surprise, he hurried to explain. "They want me to stay in a protocol house with the others, because of security reasons. You know."

By then, the Sandinistas believed it was an insult to the revolution for an honored foreign dignitary like Cap to stay at the home of one who had had the perfidy to abandon the revolution. But not wanting to put my friend in a difficult position, I said nothing.

He told me that the Andean countries viewed the first year of the revolution as a success. There had been scattered acts of vengeance, but no real bloodbath had followed Somoza's fall. Then there was the massive national campaign to stamp out illiteracy. The drive, near its six-month end, was a most impressive accomplishment. "The possibility is still alive," he said, "that after this period of rebuilding, Nicaragua will become another liberal democracy like Costa Rica or Venezuela."

I did not dare tell my friend that I felt this view was naive. The Sandinistas were Marxist-Leninists. The day was near in which they would establish in Nicaragua a systematic totalitarianism that would make the most atrocious acts of the dictator Somoza pale by comparison.

It was noontime the next day when the entourage arrived at the newly built Plaza 19 de Julio. It was not a real plaza in the traditional sense, a square surrounded by civic buildings, but an enormous spread of asphalt bisected by a highway that circles Managua. On one side the Sandinistas had built a huge stage and equipped it with a potent sound system.

Hundreds of thousands of Nicaraguans were already assembled when the *comandantes* filed into the plaza in a convoy of Mercedes-Benz limos. For security reasons each *comandante* had to have three limos. They had heard it was that way in Cuba. The rationale was that any potential assassin would not know which of the three automobiles to strike. This ludicrous notion, it is said, was carried a step further by Tomás Borge, who appropriated for himself three of the most magnificent houses in Ciudad Jardín, then connected them with tunnels so that no one could know which house he was sleeping in on any particular night.

To me, such preoccupation with security indicated that even in the early days of their power, the *comandantes* did not delude themselves. In spite of the public demonstrations of support, they must have known they were hugely unpopular.

At the anniversary celebration, there was an impressive display of military might. In just one year the Sandinistas had doubled the size of the army. Humberto Ortega beamed as he reviewed the troops. Platoon after platoon marched by and saluted him, doing in perfect synchrony the goose step they had been rehearsing for months in the open fields in Managua.

Afterward, several heads of state made brief remarks. Carlos Andrés described himself as an unrepentant proponent of democracy. He said something I will never forget, that "only free men can make a nation free." For these words he was politely applauded. I don't imagine his remarks were well taken.

The greatest emotion was reserved for Castro. For thirty-five minutes he held his audience captive. His stocky figure embraced the lectern as he cocked his head to one side while playing with his graying beard. He began by recalling one of the most embarrassing episodes in U.S. history, the Bay of Pigs fiasco. He said he could never forget that the invasion had been launched from Nicaraguan soil and that Luis Somoza had asked the invaders to "bring him back at least one hair from Castro's beard." "Today"—he smiled broadly—"I offer my whole beard to the people of Nicaragua."

The man is an amazing orator. He spoke with the ease of one who sits chatting in his living room with a trusted friend, at intervals pausing to interact with his audience. He praised the heroic struggle of the people of Nicaragua in the war of liberation. He said that ours was a country of deeply committed revolutionaries, very much like his own Cuba. In fact, he felt as if he were back on his island. Visibly moved, he recalled the twenty-year struggle waged by the FSLN since the days of Sandino. He called on all the nations of the world to come to Nicaragua's aid. He chided the Americans for their lack of generosity. "The United States," he said, "the richest country in the world, has lamentably contributed to this country a paltry $60 million."

In the pipeline was $60 million more, but this, conveniently, he did not mention. In fact, in past days, Moisés Hassan had downplayed the importance of U.S. aid. He declared that in relative terms Cuba had been most generous.

I wondered how the American delegation felt about this. I also thought that our leaders were degrading our country by turning us into a nation of beggars.

Castro continued. He assured his audience that he had not come to Central America to set the continent on fire. "The people of a nation," he said, "are like volcanoes; they explode on their own."

After Castro, Daniel Ortega spoke. In passing, Ortega addressed the issue of elections. He said, "We are committed to holding elections, but not the kind of elections known in Nicaragua in the past. These will be elections that are consistent with the aims of the revolution" and that confirm Sandinista power.

Most likely the Sandinistas would use a system like one they had already employed for municipal elections. A town meeting was held, and those in attendance were given the opportunity to vote yes or no on a slate presented by the leadership. Elaborating on the subject of elections, Tomás Borge had been clear that if elections were held, their main purpose would be to put a judicial stamp on Sandinista rule.

There could be no doubt that the Sandinistas, in spite of their early promises of democracy, were going to hold on to power for life, if possible. They had the means to do it. They controlled the state security forces, the army, the people's militia, the police.

As the ceremony ended with the singing of the Sandinista anthem, I noticed that the U.S. delegation quietly walked out and drove straight to the airport. Donal McHenry, one of the members of the delegation, gave an interview to a reporter from *La Prensa* before departing. When asked what he thought of Castro's suggestion that the United States had not been generous enough with aid to Nicaragua, McHenry said that issue concerned only Nicaragua and the United States. He wished Nicaragua all the best.

Several days after the anniversary celebration, at a press conference held in the Hotel Intercontinental, Jorge Salazar, speaking for COSEP, revealed the contents of a secret agreement in which the FSLN promised to announce on the first anniversary of the revolution a date on which to hold elections. "This has not happened. . . . It is an issue that worries all of us. We feel we are being kept from participating in a process that we all worked hard to achieve."

Jorge was related to Alfonso Robelo by marriage. Both men were married to Cardenal sisters, the siblings of Julio Cardenal, a member of the top brass in the Sandinista army, and of Toño Cardenal, a leader in the FMLN movement. Surrounded by the enthusiasm of his relatives, Jorge had tolerated the Sandinistas. Though he opposed their Marxism, he believed them when they told him that if the private sector did its part in helping to reactivate the economy, it could have the political pluralism it wanted.

So Jorge had told his colleagues he felt they could trust the FSLN leaders to set a date for elections at the upcoming anniversary celebration of the revolution, on July 19. As a result, COSEP joined the Council of State and, as Jorge had promised, contributed to Nicaragua's economic reactivation by planting two hundred thousand acres of cotton, cultivating coffee, raising cattle, and reopening factories. Now the Sandinistas no longer felt compelled to keep their promise to COSEP. Jorge intimated that the private sector could not work in a climate of insecurity.

On that same day Yasser Arafat arrived in Nicaragua, via Cuba. To the horror of many of us, the head of the PLO terrorist organization was received with great honors. He spent three days in our country in private meetings with the Sandinista leadership. It was obvious from his words at a farewell reception given in his honor by the Arab community in Nicaragua that an understanding had been reached. Arafat assured the Sandinistas that their enemies were his enemies, because, as he put it, "the cause of liberty knows no boundaries." Pitting the Palestinians and Nicaragua against U.S. interests, he said, "We are together in the trenches doing battle against imperialism, against Zionism. We know that your arms are outstretched to receive us, though it brings great pressure upon you. That is the glory of being a revolutionary, taking activist positions without caring about the consequences or the loss that one might incur."

That year, Nicaragua's representatives at the United Nations became part of a radical contingent of diplomats, most notably those from China and the Soviet–Eastern bloc countries, who together with the Arab bloc labored to forward the PLO's cause.

On July 25, Jorge traveled to Miami to meet with the exiles who were anxious to fight the Sandinistas. He discovered that anti-Sandinista conspiracies were hatching right and left, not just in Miami but throughout Central America. There was the UDN, led by Cardenal; the Fifteenth of September Legion, led by Bermúdez; there were the Milpas, former Sandinistas fighting on our northern border with Honduras; there were Comandante Zero's former companions, who were trying to put together a southern front; there was the Salvadoran government, which was experiencing a strong communist insurgency sponsored by the Sandinistas.

It was this last group with whom Jorge Salazar decided to join forces. He told them he was going back to Managua to form an internal front against the Sandinistas.

Upon his return, Salazar contacted an army officer of his acquaintance who had in weeks past told him of a group of disaffected army officers who wanted to launch a coup. Salazar met several times with the supposed conspirators. One of them, a member of the high command, was a trusted friend, a *guerrillero* whose life Jorge had once saved. Placing his trust in this friend, Jorge went forward with his plans. Several members of COSEP suspected Jorge was involved in a covert operation and wanted to participate in it. But Jorge refused. He did not want to endanger their lives.

In August the Sandinistas celebrated the end of the literacy campaign. At the ceremony, Humberto said, "Demands for elections are part of a counterrevolutionary threat. . . . The FSLN directorate are the guardians of the people's interest." As such, they had decided there would be no elections until 1985 and no political campaigning until 1984. "And even then," he said, "those elected will be expected to continue the FSLN's program of government."

On September 17, 1980, twenty-four years to the month after Anastasio Somoza García was killed, his son Anastasio Somoza Debayle, then living in Paraguay, was blown to pieces by a high-powered rocket. Somoza's body was so utterly destroyed that his mistress, Dinorah Sampson, identified him by a ring on his finger. The Sandinistas denied any involvement. They leaked rumors that Somoza was having an affair with Alfredo Stroessner's lover, implying that Stroessner in a jealous rage had Somoza killed. Seven members of an Argentine guerrilla movement were identified as the killers. A link between the Argentinean rebels and the Sandinistas existed. The implication was that the Sandinistas had contracted the murder. Arturo Cruz and Rafael Córdoba Rivas denied that there was any Nicaraguan government involvement. But there was no such denial coming from the Sandinista directorate. In fact, in the hours after the news was released throughout the world, the Sandinistas were frantic with joy.

But then on November 4, 1980, Ronald Reagan was elected president of the United States. For the Sandinistas, Reagan's election was not good news.

Chapter Ten

FOUR DAYS AFTER RONALD REAGAN WAS ELECTED elected president, the Sandinistas violently disbanded an MDN mass meeting in Nandaime, organized by Alfonso Robelo. The Sandinistas would claim afterward that Alfonso lacked a permit from the Ministry of Interior for the rally and that they could not be held responsible for the reaction of the Sandinista youth organizations, which had been duly provoked by Alfonso's anti-Sandinista rhetoric.

Alfonso has always maintained that the political meeting was planned in full compliance with Sandinista law and with the knowledge of Tomás Borge. Alfonso believes that Sandinistas deliberately and maliciously set him up for the attack.

News reports of the event and other acts of violence against the MDN were not published in *La Prensa*. The censors—citing articles 511 and 512 of the Nicaraguan Bill of Rights, which decreed that "it was forbidden to publish any reports regarding strikes, political rallies, armed rebellions or uprisings, etc."—did not allow it.

Three days later, however, on November 11, we were able to print a document issued by the COSEP leaders, as it did not fall in any of the above categories. COSEP leaders urged the junta to return to the "abandoned" Plan of Government, which called for unity and political pluralism.

They said that the junta had become the "government of one party." In truth, the FSLN controlled all the powers of government—the army, the executive, the legislature, and the judiciary. And so they had ordered the elections postponed until 1985, thereby assuring they could stay in power indefinitely.

The COSEP document further stated that the FSLN, with their unlawful seizure of land and businesses, price controls, and political manipulation of the labor force, had created an unfavorable climate for economic development, and one in which social development could not effectively take place. "In view of this," the COSEP leaders concluded, "we believe the FSLN is leading the country into political and economic chaos." The document was signed by the five member organizations.

At 3 P.M. that afternoon, COSEP, along with all the non-Sandinista organizations, walked out of the Council of State in protest after a representative from the MDN was denied the chance to respond to Tomás Borge's assertions that it was the MDN that had provoked the events in Nandaime.

Just as the *comandantes* had promised in their speeches in the plaza, their "anti-communist enemies" would be subjugated. The once-admired "revolutionary boys" had become despotic men, straight out of our tyrannical past.

On January 20, 1981, Ronald Reagan took office. One of the first acts of his administration was to release evidence showing that Cuba was deeply involved in the Nicaraguan government and that, with the Soviet Union and Vietnam, the Nicaraguans had been supplying arms to the FMLN guerrilla movement. The Nicaraguans, Reagan concluded, meant to undermine U.S. interests in the region by arming insurrectionists who were trying to overthrow pro-American governments.

On February 19, 1981, the Sandinista *comandantes* ordered the arrest of dozens of Miskito leaders for protesting Sandinista policies on the Miskito Coast of Nicaragua. In weeks past the Miskitos had demonstrated against Cuban teachers who taught atheism and Marxism to their children. Their protests continued when the government tried to establish logging operations in their homeland, along the Coco River in the north of Nicaragua. For two weeks the Miskito leaders were jailed and forced to promise that they would refrain from further demonstrations.

On March 4, Sandinistas announced the reorganization of the junta. Arturo Cruz was appointed ambassador to Washington, and Moisés Hassan was sent to the Council of State. Daniel was appointed coordinator of the new triumvirate government, which included, besides himself, Sergio Ramírez and Rafael Córdoba Rivas.

Now it was official. Daniel controlled the junta. He was the de facto president of Nicaragua.

Sandinista pressure on *La Prensa* continued. One day in March, Borge warned us that mobs might come to attack the newspaper. In days past, one of our delivery boys had been injured by a car in what appeared to be a deliberate hit-and-run accident. The Sandinistas meant business. There was no point in risking anyone's life. So we canceled the day's issue.

Two weeks later, Ronald Reagan suspended aid to Nicaragua.

Predictably, the Sandinistas responded by denouncing American imperialism. For a while world opinion was in their favor. In time the whole world was alerted to the fact that the Sandinistas were playing a game of the meek and the powerful, on the one hand portraying themselves as the weak, innocent victims of Yankee economic aggression, on the other training a two-hundred-thousand-member militia force that was ready to fight alongside the forty thousand soldiers enlisted in the Sandinista People's Army. It was the biggest military force in the region and a constant threat there.

The neighboring countries were understandably concerned: Costa Rica because it had no army; Honduras because it was anticommunist, a supporter of the counterrevolutionary cause; El Salvador because it was threatened by a revolutionary movement with strong links to the Sandinistas; and Guatemala because, once El Salvador fell to the communists, it could expect to be the next target. Everyone's fear was that the Nicaraguan revolution was metastasizing in the isthmus. The perception was that a domino effect could occur in the region.

On March 9, Reagan signed a secret finding authorizing covert aid to the Nicaraguan resistance movements. Stopping the Sandinistas became the centerpiece of Ronald Reagan's foreign policy for the region. However, as a result of the military strengthening of the Nicaraguan opposition in exile, the Sandinistas tightened their grip on *La Prensa,* COSEP, the church, Alfonso Robelo—all of us who opposed them from within.

All through 1981, tensions in our country spun out of control. As the Sandinistas made a despotic grab for power, we became submerged in violence. *Las turbas divinas* (Daniel's "divine mobs") now operated as an unofficial phalanx of the Sandinista Mass Organization Committees under the guidance of the secret police. *Turba* attacks became a common occurrence that could escalate into the burning of a citizen's home or place of work and, on occasion, even death. In justification of these animalistic acts of oppression, the Sandinistas repeated that it was all for the defense of the revolution.

At *La Prensa* I had no choice but to embark on another torturous journey as the voice of opposition. Armed with the moral authority Pedro's martyrdom had conferred upon us, we launched a media campaign against the Sandinistas. We spoke the truth about them. Through our articles we brought to light that a communist clique had taken control of our country and that the Sandinistas were more involved in maintaining their own power than in rebuilding the nation.

We hoped that the pressure we were exerting would force the Sandinistas back to the center, but instead they became more radicalized and more repressive.

My opposition fanned their hatred and inclined them to greater acts of intimidation. Publicly they called me a bloodsucker, a spy, and stated that "in this juncture of our history we have to be either for the revolution and the people or against them." I became the lead story in all their television programs and dailies. They vilified me before the whole nation. As a final measure they unleashed the divine mobs against us. The mobs were like a pack of angry dogs, writing insults on the walls of our homes, physically attacking our editor, and terrorizing our journalists with anonymous death threats.

Even my aging mother-in-law, Doña Margarita, was not spared. This woman, whose personal sacrifices on behalf of her country were well documented, was called a traitor to the fatherland, *vendepatria*.

To what greater depths could the Sandinistas sink? Even in Somoza's time I had never seen the people of my country behave in such a way. But things would indeed get worse. The attacks and threats continued. Eventually I had to put up an eight-foot fence around my home.

The brute force of their repression was not aimed at us alone. In the first week in July, a series of decrees was issued that gave the Ministry of Media and Communications a free hand in determining what was suitable for publication. Under the new edict all of the media underwent rigid censorship. The Sandinistas said that producing stories that were "detrimental to the revolution" was not allowed. The slightest dissent was considered treason and provoked an avalanche of violent responses. Radio shows were regularly kicked off the air and periodically shut down.

I was stupefied by the Sandinistas' claims that their platform of government was the embodiment of Pedro's political ideals. This was a falsehood I could not allow to go unchecked. I would not permit these people to tarnish the image of one who had led his life guided by noble principles. I rejected the notion that their totalitarianism bore any resemblance to Pedro's civic rectitude.

Commenting on the decrees, I said I believed the concept of freedom of speech carried within itself the understanding that it was unrestricted. And if for some reason the need arose for controls, I understood fairness required they be applied equally to all the media organizations and individuals and not just to a select few. I pointed out that the media had an educational role to play, often serving to inform the government where its weaknesses and failures lay so that it could better serve the people.

The Sandinistas responded on July 10 by shutting down *La Prensa*. In the following three months, *La Prensa* was closed five times for "publishing lies," among them reports concerning the souring relations between the church and Sandinista leaders.

In his Sunday homilies, Archbishop Miguel Obando, referring to the Sandinistas by their code name "the great danger," coyly implied that the FSLN was "fundamentally evil."

One day a small but violent group belonging to the divine mobs attacked the archbishop. Throwing stones and screaming revolutionary slogans, they entered the church where the archbishop had just completed mass and lunged toward the Catholic leader. A human wall formed around the archbishop to protect him. The mobs then proceeded to destroy the archbishop's automobile, slashing the tires and breaking all the windows.

In the following day's homily, the archbishop asked, "Are these the acts of those who are trying to forge a new man?"

Similar attacks were launched against other representatives of the Catholic church. What the Sandinistas failed to see was that by engaging in these lowly acts of repression they were turning us all into martyrs and sullying the revolution. Eventually, people would begin to question and reject Sandinismo.

On the second anniversary of the revolution, Daniel Ortega announced a new set of decrees. One of them extended government authority to confiscate the property of those who had been out of the country for more than six months. The decrees were not submitted to the Council of State, nor were they discussed with political parties. Daniel simply asked the crowd in the plaza, "Do you agree with these decrees?" Of course they did.

So much for the Sandinistas' often-stated respect for democracy and political pluralism, for freedom of speech and for religion. In Nicaragua there could only be one form of respect: respect for the Sandinistas.

It was into this unhappy scenario that my next two grandchildren were born. Claudia and Marta Lucía had babies nine days apart. Claudia had a boy, Marcos Tolentino, who grew to look astonishingly like Pedro, my husband. Marta Lucía had a girl, María Andrea, who is a frail, light-haired creature with a powerful voice. In time and with training she could be a great singer.

In the first week of August, Thomas Enders, the U.S. assistant secretary of state for Latin American affairs, traveled to Nicaragua to talk seriously with Daniel Ortega about stopping aid to the Salvadoran guerrillas. In exchange Enders offered to renew American aid to Nicaragua. But Ortega said, "No. Nicaragua chooses its own friends."

Enders warned Ortega that relations between the United States and Nicaragua were close to a complete halt. This would not bode well for Nicaragua. Enders proposed to Ortega that he think things through. He promised to wait until September for his formal reply.

In the months that followed, however, the Sandinistas continued to export their revolution. Soon the Americans received reports that a contingent of Cuban troops had passed through Nicaragua on their way to aiding the guerrillas in El Salvador.

On October 9, before a gathering of officials in the Sandinista army, Humberto Ortega declared that the FSLN's doctrine was unequivocally Marxist-Leninist.

This was the first time that such an admission had been made. Soon all the news agencies in the country were quoting the sensational remarks. It was interpreted that Humberto Ortega's remarks had the deliberate intent of drawing a clear line in Nicaraguan society. From then on one was either with the Sandinistas or against them.

The COSEP leaders dispatched a letter to Daniel Ortega requesting an explanation and accusing the Sandinistas of mismanaging the economy.

The following day the Americans tried to block the approval of a $33.3 million Inter-American Development Bank loan for Nicaragua that was essentially destined for the private sector.

At *La Prensa* we protested U.S. interference in Nicaragua's economic affairs. As patriots we were against withholding economic assistance as a form of leverage on the government, because it is the economy and our people that suffer. We urged our leaders to reflect on their actions and follow a mature policy of nonalignment.

On October 21, 1981, the leaders of COSEP were jailed by the Sandinistas. At the crack of dawn, without being told the charges against them, Enrique Dreyfus, Benjamín Lanzas, Gilberto Cuadra, and Enrique Bolaños were taken from their homes. Some of them would remain in prison for months.

Recently, the government had declared a state of economic and social emergency, which made all strikes illegal, and warned that all actions that resulted in the endangering of foreign aid would be punishable by law. Tomás Borge accused the COSEP leaders of violating this ruling.

The arrests were an example to all Nicaraguans that the Sandinistas were prepared to play hardball.

A U.S. Department of State spokesman deplored the action. He accused the government of Nicaragua of intimidating the democratic opposition and thereby disrespecting political pluralism.

The government of Costa Rica said it held the Sandinistas accountable for the fate of the COSEP leaders and promised to see to it that they were freed.

In the court of world opinion, the Sandinistas were losing support. However, believing that they could count on the Soviet Union and its allies to keep them afloat, the Sandinistas remained unrepentant.

On October 31, Nicaragua formally replied to Enders's August proposal. They called the offer "sterile and unrealistic" because it expected of them actions that went against the character of the revolution. Solidarity with other revolutionary movements was part of the consolidation process. They offered, however, to remain open to further dialogue.

Notwithstanding, the CIA had already prepared another plan, which involved increasing aid to the growing Contra movement. Two months earlier, under the leadership of Enrique Bermúdez and José Francisco Cardenal, the Fifteenth of September Legion and the Nicaraguan Democratic Union (UDN) had signed an agreement formalizing their alliance. The new name for the organization was the Nicaraguan Democratic Force (FDN).

On November 1, CIA director William Casey met with the Argentineans (who had been giving modest aid to the exiles) and arranged for them to coordinate and train the Contras. The United States would provide the money and the weapons. One cannot say that, prior to U.S. involvement, there truly existed a Contra force.

When news of the U.S. decision broke, Arturo Cruz was summoned to Nicaragua for an emergency meeting with Miguel d'Escoto, who drafted a letter to Thomas Enders categorically denying U.S. assertions that Cuban military troops were present on Nicaraguan soil.

At the same time, prominent leaders of the FSLN moved to establish a dialogue with a sampling of Nicaraguan opposition leaders. Archbishop Miguel Obando y Bravo cautioned against being "manipulated."

The Sandinistas' dialogue initiatives were all empty gestures. The Sandinistas had belatedly understood that the Americans intended to use force in the absence of diplomacy, and they were now trying to reestablish negotiations with the Americans.

American intentions were made clear by the comments of Alexander Haig, the U.S. secretary of state, to the press. He said that the United States was studying military options against Cuba and Nicaragua. He said that the two countries that were supporting the insurrection in El Salvador would be strangled.

News reports indicated that tensions in El Salvador had risen. The revolutionaries were systematically destroying the means of production in their efforts to weaken the government and block the upcoming elections.

On November 8, the anniversary of the death of Carlos Fonseca Amador, one of the founders of the FSLN, Humberto Ortega declared that if an invasion or internal uprising occurred, anyone who "unintentionally aided or willingly participated" in the unrest would be found by the wayside, hanging from the trees and lampposts of the roads of our country.

Copies of his speech were distributed by the COSEP leaders. His words so alarmed Catholic leaders that they called the faithful to a week of prayer for peace.

When I recently asked the new army chief, General Joaquín Cuadra Lacayo, what he thought of these comments, he said, "Those were different times; things were very tense. There was a siege mentality. We felt we had to prepare to defend ourselves from an American aggression." In fact, at great cost the Sandinistas were maintaining a huge contingent of men in the Pacific—where there were no Contras.

On November 15, we were visited by an official delegation from the Inter-American Press Society (SIP), who came to Nicaragua as observers. Pedro Joaquín, Cristiana, and I received them at *La Prensa.* We gave them copies of all the laws and decrees the Sandinistas had put in effect that limited freedom of the press. They also visited Archbishop Miguel Obando y Bravo, who related to them the aggressions that officials of the church had suffered at the hands of FSLN hacks.

SIP members also talked with the permanent Commission on Human Rights, who informed them of the mass graves that had been discovered and of attacks on opposition parties.

Afterward they visited with my son Carlos Fernando at *Barricada,* who assured them that the laws governing the media did not have the intent of limiting freedom of expression but rather meant to guarantee that that freedom be exercised with a measure of responsibility. He explained that we were going through a very difficult transition and that a negative attitude from the press could have grave consequences.

During the repartee, Jaime Chamorro suggested that the Sandinistas in their approach to government were engaging in "Nazilike" behavior. It was a challenge to Carlos Fernando, who was trying to rationalize the Sandinistas' authoritarian rule. Carlos Fernando grew extremely agitated and broke off the conversation. In front of the SIP delegation he scolded his uncle and said it was impossible to carry on a dialogue in such a manner.

Arturo Cruz, a man who possesses great humility, resigned from his post as Sandinista ambassador in Washington. Prior to his resignation, Arturo had lamented the Sandinistas' lack of statesmanship. He said they needed to learn to make the transition from being soldiers to being political leaders who could tolerate opposition. Otherwise, he predicted, the Sandinistas would be thrown out of power.

Notwithstanding these declarations, after resigning Arturo persisted in characterizing the Sandinistas as pluralists and men of honor.

I've never understood why Arturo, who is a good, decent man, was so unwilling to break publicly with the Sandinistas. Perhaps he feared for his son, who was then an official at the Foreign Ministry.

Less than two weeks after Haig hinted at the possibility of a blockade, or perhaps even invasion, of Cuba and Nicaragua, Humberto Ortega traveled to Moscow to meet with his Soviet counterpart, Marshal Ustinov. In diplomatic circles it was commented that he was negotiating a generous arms deal with the Soviets.

Information about a Nicaraguan-Soviet alliance reached Carlos Andrés Pérez. In a television interview he rejected the notion of another communist regime in Latin America. He said this would be a "catastrophic thing." Then he expressed concern for the increased levels of militarism in the area, which now threatened the stability of democracy in Costa Rica and Honduras. He qualified the latter country as the epicenter of the conflicts in El Salvador, Guatemala, and Honduras. He urged his "Sandinista friends" to bury their "anti-Yankismo" and agree to hold multilateral talks—with the United States and the four Central American nations—that could bring peace to the region.

On December 1, 1981, a year into his first presidential term, Ronald Reagan finally authorized $19 million to arm the one thousand Contras stationed in training camps in Honduras.

Liberating Nicaragua, however, was not on the administration's mind. Contrary to the prevailing notion, Reagan didn't want to topple the Sandinistas or invade Cuba. The primary U.S. concern was saving El Salvador, and had the Sandinistas agreed to stay out of El Salvador, the Contra war would never have happened.

In early 1982, the Sandinistas continued their attacks on the Miskito Indians who lived on Nicaragua's Caribbean coast. When the church came to the defense of the Miskitos, the Sandinistas turned on the church. The reaction among the Catholics in Nicaragua was mixed. Most of us believed the confrontation the Sandinistas were creating between politics and religion was a grave error. After all, the church was only doing what it had done for hundreds of years: protect those who were truly destitute, like the Miskito Indians.

The Sandinistas, however, made no headway in swaying to their cause the vast majority of campesinos living in the rural areas of Nicaragua. The rural people were certain the Sandinistas were robbing them through their cooperatives and their price fixing. Now the Sandinistas were heaping abuse upon respected church leaders like Archbishop Miguel Obando y Bravo.

By the spring of 1982, the Contra ranks operating out of Honduras had swelled to two thousand with the influx of new campesino recruits and were poised to do battle with the Sandinistas. For the past year the Contras had been staging periodic forays into Nicaraguan territory, blowing up bridges, ambushing Sandinista People's Army military patrols, attacking Sandinista farm cooperatives, and capturing and killing Sandinista officials. As the number of available combatants increased and their logistical planning improved, they embarked on more ambitious adventures, attacking the nation's oil supplies, bombing airports and ports.

The way the Nicaraguan drama was unfolding, it was obvious we were heading in the direction of economic chaos and violence. For the Americans, what had begun as a relatively simple arms-interdiction operation was mushrooming into a full-scale assault on the Sandinista government.

As this was happening, Edén Pastora, Comandante Zero, who had been missing for six months, resurfaced in Costa Rica and declared himself ready to do battle against his former comrades. Pastora's charm and innate leadership abilities had a unifying effect on the exiled anti-Sandinistas living in Costa Rica.

After Zero's defection, it was noticed that most of those who had fought with him on the southern front had left the government and fled to Costa Rica to join a new southern front. Among them was Alfredo César. After marrying my son-in-law Antonio Lacayo's younger sister Silvia, Alfredo took a leave from the presidency of the Central Bank of Nicaragua, presumably to go on his honeymoon. He never returned.

Some weeks later, Antonio received a call from Alfredo asking him to go to his house and pack all his belongings. He said the Sandinistas wanted him dead. And so he was running off to join the opposition, which by then had been organized by Zero and Alfonso Robelo into the Democratic Revolutionary Alliance (ARDE). Rumor had it that the ARDE had strong CIA backing.

In fact, the new rebels appeared to be well funded. In just a few months they acquired a fleet of cars, leased a dozen houses in the best neighborhoods in Costa Rica, and boasted of having so much military equipment at their disposal they could arm the whole nation if they so desired.

In three years' time, Alfredo, always the able politico, would reappear at the forefront of a Contra directorate.

Alfredo has often said that from the very start, there existed resentment between the rebels in the north (FDN) and the rebels in the south (ARDE). Recriminations abounded between those who had been with Somoza and those who had been with the Sandinistas.

Alfonso's involvement with ARDE resulted in the government's taking temporary control of GRACSA, a cottonseed-oil manufacturing concern managed by Antonio. It was the Sandinistas' mistaken belief that Alfonso had a controlling share of the company. In fact, GRACSA's two major stockholders were both foreigners. Antonio had irrefutable evidence of this, which the Sandinistas refused to believe. The issue was still unresolved when Alfredo César went into exile. Antonio's new family connection to the now counterrevolutionary Alfredo only complicated matters for Antonio. The Sandinistas suspected Antonio of having ties with the resistance; and so they expelled my son-in-law at gunpoint from the company he managed and in which he, too, was a minority shareholder, forbidding him ever to set foot on the premises again.

Antonio, resolute and full of fire, hired the best lawyers in the country and prepared to fight it out with the Sandinistas in court. It would be a long-drawn-out battle, one that Antonio had complete faith he would win.

Faced with the same kind of aggression from the Sandinistas, other members of the private sector either gave up and left the country or fought the Sandinistas in the political arena, where the former were sure to lose.

"Why did you choose to stay and fight?" I asked Antonio several years later.

"Because I knew the Sandinistas wouldn't last forever," he said. He had the certainty that Nicaragua would change.

I think, as well, Cristiana's feelings contributed to his decision. She couldn't leave Nicaragua; it's part of her identity, her reason for living. At the time this was happening, they were expecting their first child and shopping for a home.

They settled on a beautiful property called La Guadalupana, built by Antonio's grandfather in the Spanish neobaroque style. It sits on a hill south of Managua, where it commands a magnificent view of the city.

Cristiana, who had left her job at the Council of State, spent the next six months of her pregnancy decorating, and organizing Pedro's personal papers.

As the ambitions and confidence of the Contra rebels grew, CIA officials reconsidered the goals and intentions of the paramilitary movement. No longer were they satisfied with merely interdicting arms. They had a greater, more ambitious idea, "a crusade for democracy." To congressional leaders, the covert program was beginning to sound very much like war.

The FSLN responded to the Pastora threat by accusing him of selling out to the CIA and allowing himself to be used by "Yankee imperialism." The Sandinistas feared that Pastora's defection would cause desertions in the ranks of the army.

To be sure, the Contra threat, though lacking a real chance to topple the Sandinistas from power, had some adverse effects on our society. Greatest of all was the invasion paranoia it created. The government decreed that as the menace of war existed, a more encompassing state of emergency needed to be put into effect. The new restrictions choked civil liberties: they banned freedom of speech, the right to assembly, the right to privacy, and the right to travel freely, and they suspended all constitutional guarantees.

Thus began another downward spiral into repression.

As the months went by, it became impossible to ignore that we were all living in extreme danger. In spite of this I remained determined to fight the Sandinistas at every turn, having resolved long ago that no Marxist was going to run me out of my country.

One night at home, before going to bed, I noticed that Pedro's old Saab, which I keep in the carport, had a light on. I opened the garden gate and noticed that someone was inside the car.

In situations of danger, I react instinctively—instead of closing the door, I confronted the stranger. "What are you doing here, you thief, you assassin?"

I was certain the man had been sent to harm me, but I had caught him in the act before he could make his move.

The man got out of the car and began to walk toward me. He implored me to calm down. *"Dialóguemos"* (Let's have a dialogue), he said. What a ridiculous idea. Only in a country where reason has been perverted does a delinquent break into one's house and ask to have an exchange of ideas.

At that moment I noticed there was another man, who stood on the wall that surrounded the house, waiting. I realized I was out there vulnerable and alone. And so I began to scream.

As two maids appeared, with great agility one man jumped over the wall while the other disappeared over the rooftops of the neighboring houses. The two men were later apprehended, though they never confessed their true intentions. I imagine that when the fanfare blew over they were released. Quite probably they were agents of the state.

In January 1983, the foreign ministers of Venezuela, Mexico, Colombia, and the five Central American countries met for the first time on Contadora Island, in Panama, to discuss diplomatic ways of ending the hostilities in Central America. The general consensus was, as Carlos Andrés had suggested, multilateral talks between the warring countries.

Contadora diplomacy did not produce the expected result of bringing peace to Central America. But it did pave the way for subsequent negotiations in 1987 and for the Esquipulas accords, which led to the elections of February 25, 1990.

On March 3, 1983, Pope John Paul II came to Nicaragua. He stood at the top of the stairs of his plane and opened his arms heavenward. He then descended, kneeled down, and put his lips to the ground. I am told he does this every time he visits a country for the first time. He thanked the Lord for allowing him to come to this land of lakes and volcanoes. Standing all in a row were the bishops of Nicaragua in their black cassocks and pink sashes.

The Sandinistas were off to one side, as I recall, looking somewhat uncomfortable. Everyone knew that the pope was a visceral opponent of Marxism. Accompanying the Sandinistas were also the two priests who worked in the government: Miguel d'Escoto, who had abandoned his priest's skirts long ago, wearing a guayabera, and Ernesto Cardenal. As always, Ernesto was dressed in a *cotona* (peasant blouse) and a beret à la Ché Guevara.

His Holiness warned both Sandinista priests to stop using the garb of the church to do their proselytizing. In a photograph that made international headlines, John Paul wagged his finger at Ernesto Cardenal, who knelt meekly before him. Afterward, Ernesto Cardenal complained with indignation that the pope had come to Nicaragua to insult our people.

That afternoon in the plaza, the pope celebrated mass. Speaking in perfect Spanish, he debunked any notion that there could be two churches or two doctrines. "There is only one universal church," he said, "one faith . . . and one God who reigns over everything and lives in all of us."

He said there could be "no alternatives to the church that had been created around the bishops." He admonished, "They are the true representatives of Christ . . . and they alone have been entrusted to carry out Christ's spiritual mission. . . . It is absurd and dangerous to think otherwise."

Wearing red-and-black accents, the divine mobs booed and ridiculed His Holiness. This did not silence the pope. And so they tried to drown his words by clamoring, "Power to the people." As they did so, all five *comandantes* lifted their fists and chanted in unison.

The message was clear: the pope disapproved of the Sandinistas and he supported the nine bishops.

Before departing Nicaragua, the pope had a private meeting with the Sandinista leaders, in which they tried to persuade him that they were the victims of American aggression. They accused the United States of trying to strangle Nicaragua politically and economically. In El Salvador, they said, where the guerrillas had scored many successes, the United States had increased its military presence in preparation for an invasion. On these issues, they asked the Holy Father to intercede on their behalf.

The Sandinistas believed they could manipulate anyone's opinion easily. In fact, they were quite good at this. But the former cardinal from Poland knew how to play the political game well. He told them his tour was essentially of a religious nature and that as such it had a moral objective, which was to promote good over evil.

For his rejection of their cause, they called him the pope of the West, the pope of imperialism.

In the months that followed the pope's visit, Archbishop Obando and the nine bishops denounced a slew of Sandinista human rights violations, especially in northern Nicaragua, where the Contras were active.

Meanwhile, the constant border conflicts between Honduras and Nicaragua, occasioned by the growing presence of Contra forces in Honduras, were threatening to break into a war.

Nicaragua went before the U.N. National Security Council, where it denounced American aggression and asked the U.N. secretary general to intervene in the crisis. The council decided this was an issue to be resolved through the OAS. In the spring of 1983, Honduras proposed a series of multilateral talks that might lead to a diplomatic solution to the military conflict between the two countries. Talks involving other nations would undoubtedly exceed the parameters of the Contra problem and would lead to discussions regarding Nicaragua's support of the Salvadoran guerrillas. This was not an issue on which the Sandinistas were prepared to cede. So they made a counteroffer to initiate bilateral talks directly with Honduras.

A month later, on April 13, 1983, in a second effort to revive multilateral talks, the foreign ministers of the Contadora group and of Mexico met with Daniel Ortega in Nicaragua.

As this was happening, the U.S. House Intelligence Committee in Washington, after reviewing the covert program, voted to cut off covert funding to the six thousand Contras fighting on the Honduran border. They felt the military approach needed to be abandoned in favor of the diplomatic. Reagan declared that the security of the United States's own borders was at stake. He described the Contras as freedom fighters and swore they would fight on.

In May, the U.N. Security Council voted to support the Contadora initiative, which made democratization a condition for any proposal.

I was in Costa Rica then with Cristiana, who gave birth to Cristiana María. She wanted to have the child in Nicaragua, but this was her first, and she was understandably concerned. Because of the Sandinistas, half of the medical community had left Nicaragua.

Cristiana María was born on April 25, 1983. The child was big but did not weigh much. She had Cristiana's delicate features and Antonio's light brown hair. She was a little jaundiced. Though this is often the case with newborns, it alarmed Cristiana a great deal when I told her.

The task of defending Sandinista power proved to be overwhelming. Four days before the third anniversary of the revolution, Humberto Ortega announced that every man over the age of seventeen and under the age of twenty-two had to enlist in the armed forces.

The people of Nicaragua didn't want to go to war with the Contras or (more understandably) with the powerful United States. In days past, the United States had been flexing its military power in a series of maneuvers in the Caribbean and in neighboring Honduras. Nicaragua was ablaze with talk of war. The Sandinistas were certain the United States would invade us. After all, they had done everything in their power to provoke them.

The rhetoric of the *comandantes* reminded me sometimes of children in a schoolyard fight.

After universal conscription was enforced, people of all classes decided to leave Nicaragua for good. They sold their property and went into exile to endure a life of hardship. It was preferable, they said, "to a life without freedom."

The Sandinistas denounced these people as traitors and said, "Anyone who doesn't like Sandinismo can go. We want only true patriots and revolutionaries in this land."

Later, when the number of families leaving Nicaragua began to soar, the Sandinistas tried to clamp down on emigration by creating a mountain of obstacles for would-be travelers. In order to obtain an exit visa, a person had to present proof that he had paid all his utilities, find three witnesses to vouch for his personal data, and then obtain the signature of the head of his neighborhood Sandinista Defense Committee and the Sandinista military authority in the region. When this was not enough to stem the flow of emigrants, as it was in Cuba, they came right out and decreed that doctors and teachers, people whose professions were of national interest, could not leave. But Nicaragua is not an island, and people swore they would escape any way they could through our porous national borders. In less than a week, the panic their announcement brought forced the Sandinistas to back down.

· · ·

For Pedro Joaquín, his wife, Marta Lucía, and their four children, life in Nicaragua had turned intolerable. As the editor of *La Prensa* and a rising political star of the Social Democratic Party, Pedro Joaquín, as well as his family, had to endure a stream of public attacks describing him as a bloodsucker and a bourgeois traitor. On a daily basis they received telephone threats and were subjected to acts of vandalism. Pedro Joaquín and Marta Lucía told me they were concerned for the safety of their children.

I asked my son not to emigrate. Since the death of his father, he had played an important role at *La Prensa.* His own achievements as a defender of free speech were recognized in Norway, where he was awarded the Golden Pen Award.

For a time Pedro Joaquín agreed to stay. But he moved his family to Costa Rica and commuted. The arrangement could not last very long.

The year ended with a string of successes by the Contras that convinced the Sandinistas that the Contras now posed a real challenge to Sandinista power. As the FDN attacked from the north and the ARDE attacked from the south, the Sandinistas were being forced to fight a debilitating war on two fronts. Humberto Ortega went on TV and said the Contras were a "grave risk."

When the Sandinistas saw their survival threatened, they began to discuss the possibility of holding elections.

Amid rumors that the United States was about to establish a military base in Honduras, Daniel promised to schedule elections the following year. He said that if he, the FSLN candidate, lost, the FSLN would "hand over power."

Early in 1984, it was revealed that the CIA had taken part in a clandestine operation to mine a harbor in Nicaragua. All around the world the United States came under intense criticism. Reagan's views were rejected by our Latin American neighbors, who felt the escalation of tensions in the region was putting their fragile democracies in jeopardy and causing a severe economic crisis in Central America. They felt the conflict in Nicaragua had the potential to destabilize the whole region.

In Nicaragua most of us felt, as well, that Reagan's policies were mistaken and needed to be countered by a diplomatic dialogue that could lead to peace.

Lack of support for a military solution tilted the balance in the direction of the twenty-one-point plan set forth by the Contadora group. Though the plan had been formally accepted by Daniel Ortega, he had not implemented it. The United States recast the proposal, distilled it into a four-point treaty, and added some verification amendments to it.

The Contadora group agreed that the United States was best qualified to extract from the Sandinistas the concessions the process required—the implementation of democracy, an end to subversive activities, removal of Soviet and Cuban personnel from Nicaragua, and verifiable reduction of the military to parity with other Central American armed forces. In exchange, the United States would stop support of the Contras and normalize economic relations with the Sandinistas by suspending an embargo that had been in effect for more than a year.

In late June, Nicaraguan and American diplomats met in the Mexican town of Manzanillo to begin bilateral talks over the Contadora document. Representing the Americans was a top senior diplomat, Harry Shlaudeman, while representing Nicaragua was d'Escoto's deputy foreign minister, Victor Hugo Tinoco.

The fact that d'Escoto himself did not dignify the talks with his presence indicates that the Sandinistas did not seriously consider coming to an agreement with the Americans. Shlaudeman agreed. He said there had been no real advancement.

The episode was just a show, used as a propaganda tool to rehabilitate the Sandinistas in the eyes of the international community. Tinoco admitted as much a month later when he publicly rejected major provisions of the draft. The Sandinistas could never agree to severing their Soviet-Cuban connections.

Nor would the Sandinistas permit true democratic elections. As things stood, the Sandinistas had advantages that included control of the press, the police, and the Supreme Electoral Council.

To ensure the elections would be proper, the opposition drafted a series of demands. In essence, what they asked for was a leveling of the playing field. They wanted the lifting of the state of emergency, which restricted individual freedom, and the separation of the Sandinista party from all the powers of state, the military, and the media. The Sandinistas ignored the demands.

Then, on July 19, the fifth anniversary of the revolution, Daniel

Ortega unveiled two stumbling blocks for the opposition: the state of emergency would not be lifted until two weeks prior to the elections, which made it very difficult for the candidate of the opposition to move about and campaign freely. In addition, any mention of the economy was off-limits to the opposition candidate.

In the summer of 1984, the economic situation was probably the Sandinistas' most vulnerable spot. The nation's economic output was at an all-time low as a result of price controls, rises in costs of production, and the serious undermining of property rights by an indiscriminate application of agrarian reform. Nicaragua, once Central America's leader in beef exports, with more head of cattle than people, now didn't have enough meat to feed its own people. Dairy production, which in 1978 had stood at 20.6 million gallons of milk, had dropped to 9 million gallons. The same was happening in coffee, sugar, cotton. With the drop in exports, the country lacked sufficient foreign exchange to import the most basic necessities. Medicine and oil supplies were scarce. Under these circumstances, in a fair game any oppositional candidate could have triumphed over the incumbent Sandinistas. But the Sandinistas did not intend to allow the opposition a victory.

Arturo Cruz, the chosen candidate of the opposition, who represented a coalition known as the Coordinadora Democrática (Democratic Coordinator), gave an interview to *La Prensa*. He said he was honored by the selection, although he believed ninety days to campaign was unrealistic. With the assistance of foreign leaders, he set out to persuade the Sandinistas to postpone the elections for at least three months.

For the Sandinistas, Arturo's candidacy provided the first opportunity to hear the people speak. It was a great shock. In town after town, people celebrated his arrival. They would chant, *"Basta ya, el cambio va!"* Loosely translated this means, "Enough is enough, a change will come!" Or they would intone in perfect rhyme, *"Qué quiere la gente? Que se vaya el frente"* (What do people want? That the front leave.).

For years now, the Sandinistas had been able to read the mood of the nation only through the chorus of approval heard at Sandinista rallies. Like Somoza, they seemed to forget these were not spontaneous demonstrations but a massive mobilization effort staged by their own organization committees. Arturo Cruz's campaign was an embarrassing reality for the Sandinistas to absorb.

At *La Prensa,* the Sandinistas prevented us from chronicling Arturo's campaign efforts. At times their draconian censorship forced us to cancel our entire issue.

Then the Sandinistas said Arturo had failed to register as a candidate before the August deadline and so had automatically disqualified himself. Arturo's ill-fated intention had been to hold his abstention as leverage to incite the Sandinistas into conceding more rights and guarantees for opposition candidates. But his plan backfired. Now he was out of the race.

Unavoidably, Daniel Ortega was elected on November 4. No one believed his presidency was legitimate.

Then, on November 6, Ronald Reagan was reelected to a second term as president of the United States. The scene was set for four more years of confrontation.

Daniel Ortega was forty years old when he received the blue-and-white sash of the presidency of Nicaragua. The day of his inauguration, January 10, 1985, was also the seventh anniversary of Pedro's death and marked almost the sixth year of Sandinista rule. Of all the leaders who had once supported the FSLN, only Fidel Castro was in attendance.

Twelve days later, as Ronald Reagan arrived at his inauguration, a group of demonstrators lifted their posters to him: "Hands off Nicaragua." No one stopped them; no one abused them. That's democracy. In Nicaragua, the Sandinistas did not permit such open opposition.

Though polls showed that Reagan's landslide victory was not a ringing endorsement of his policy in Central America, in his inaugural address Reagan continued to defend his administration's support of the Contra insurgency. He said he wanted his presidency to be remembered as a golden age in which the United States defended free enterprise, the right to self-determination, and freedom. He believed that because of U.S. intervention, liberty was advancing in the world.

After the elections, Reagan began an all-out effort to secure aid for the Contras. In January 1985, Congress tacitly approved $14 million for the anti-Sandinista forces. Ratification of the approval was still pending. When asked if his new goal was to overthrow the Sandinistas, Reagan said he wanted to "change the existing power structure of the communist-totalitarian state." And he added that the Sandinista government had not been legitimately elected by the people.

In Nicaragua, the war continued. In the days following Daniel's inauguration, more Soviet armaments poured into the country, including high-performance helicopters, the kind that appear in the *Rambo* movies. They were like flying armored tanks and proved to be a deadly weapon against the Contras. As the war dragged on, ten thousand lives were lost. On the streets, the sight of young men in wheelchairs, blinded, or missing a limb became pathetically common.

As a result of the fighting, production in our country came to a grinding halt.

Toward the middle of 1985, in an interview given to *La Prensa,* the Independent Liberal Party leader Virgilio Godoy accurately described the effect of the Sandinistas' economic policies. He said they had left the country "prostrate," confined to a wheelchair.

The people's discontent began to manifest itself in widespread defections among the military, in the moral decadence that touched off riots, in the spontaneous uprisings against the draft, and in a pervasive disillusionment that asserted itself in countless acts of political rebellion.

It was at this juncture that I wrote to João Baena Soares, the director of the Organization of American States (OAS), asking him to take an interest in our plight and demand our government make good on its promises to foster political pluralism in our country, as well as establish a mixed economy and maintain a foreign policy of nonalignment. I reminded him that all of this had been stated in the commitment letter that we, the junta, had signed in July 1979 before the OAS.

I went on to say that "the fundamental principles on which the Nicaraguan revolution was based had been betrayed by the party that was now in power, the FSLN," and that as a matter of conscience, I felt compelled to denounce the fraud being perpetrated by the so-called representatives of the people in whom we had deposited our trust. "These men," I said, "have perverted our democratic ideals and corrupted our Christian morals by setting Nicaragua onto the path to Marxism-Leninism." Furthermore, I added, "their abusive, confrontational attitudes" have created serious internal and external conflicts that are "bleeding the country dry."

In search of solutions to our crisis, I suggested to Mr. Soares that the OAS convoke a national dialogue between all the warring factions and thus provide the basis for a national reconciliation.

My action was interpreted by Daniel Ortega as an "invitation for the

Yankees to launch an invasion of our country." He accused me of being an "instrument of the CIA" and part of the economic boycott that was being orchestrated by the capitalists in our country.

Indeed, we had many democratic friends, though we were beholden to no one and acted only in the interest of the nation. *La Prensa* was the first stop on the itinerary of visiting foreign dignitaries. They asked us, "How are you faring? What is *La Prensa*'s situation?"

We were operating in a virtual state of siege and repression. But with support from our international friends, we were encouraged to continue to denounce abuses, to defend the weak, and to demand democracy. In addition, we, as responsible citizens, couldn't simply cross our arms and let things go their own way, though in our commitment to publishing the truth, we faced personal risk at every turn.

The situation of the church was no different. Earlier that year, the sympathy that Pope John Paul II felt for the people of Nicaragua and the admiration he felt for the leadership of our pastor, Archbishop Miguel Obando, was expressed in the archbishop's elevation to the status of cardinal. Upon the cardinal's return, hundreds of thousands gathered at the airport to receive him. They chorused, "Long live our Cardinal Miguel" and "Christianity yes, communism no!" The reception he received was not just an endorsement for the cardinal but a rejection of the Sandinistas. The following Sunday, the Sandinista Ministry of Communication banned the pope's homily and mass from Radio Católica.

On June 12, after a tough battle, the U.S. Congress approved $14 million in humanitarian assistance to the Contras, with the understanding that the Contadora talks would resume. The aim was to force change in Nicaragua by exerting both military and diplomatic pressure. The latter tack, however, failed when Reagan insisted on a face-to-face dialogue between the Sandinistas and the Contras.

When the Sandinistas rejected negotiations, Reagan argued that he had to strengthen the Contras. He was adamant. Central America would not fall to the communists on his watch. He moved to increase financing for the armed rebel movement by requesting Congress to approve $100 million in military and humanitarian assistance.

Meanwhile, the Contras were beset by leadership squabbles. The CIA had recruited Arturo Cruz into the Contra leadership. Arturo got along with Contra leader Alfonso Robelo, but not with Adolfo Calero or with military leader Enrique Bermúdez, a former Somocista. And the National Opposition Union (UNO), as the Contra leadership was now known, turned out to be a complete disaster. Robelo and Arturo were in constant conflict with Bermúdez over the running of the military, complaining that they didn't recognize the civilian leadership.

From June through September, counterrevolutionary forces advanced from Honduras and Costa Rica. A border dispute with Honduras erupted after one exchange in which a Honduran soldier was killed and several wounded by Sandinista mortar. The Hondurans accused Nicaragua of launching an invasion against their country.

In the south, two Costa Rican gendarmes were also wounded, in an exchange of fire between Sandinistas and ARDE. The Costa Ricans blamed the Sandinistas and demanded an apology. The Sandinistas denied any culpability.

Claudia, who had recently been appointed the Sandinista ambassador to Costa Rica, was denied diplomatic recognition until the dispute with Costa Rica was settled.

The year ended with all roads to peace closed. The Sandinistas called for a suspension of the Contadora talks until the American aggression stopped.

On December 14, my son Pedro Joaquín left Nicaragua for good. "There was no point anymore," he said, "in being the editor of a newspaper with eighty percent of its news slashed by the censors." He felt he could be of more help abroad, publishing a four-page weekly insert in the Costa Rican newspaper *La Nación*. It would be called *Nicaragua Hoy*, he said, and "it will tell the truth about the Sandinistas."

On March 3, 1986, *La Prensa* celebrated its sixtieth birthday. An anniversary mass was celebrated by Cardinal Miguel Obando y Bravo. As a Catholic newspaper, we shared with him a great bond and were 100 percent behind all his efforts on behalf of our country. The mass was followed by a barbecue under a huge ceiba tree that Pedro, my husband, had christened the "tree of liberty" because of its powerful and perfect form.

I could not attend the celebration. As a member of the board of directors of SIP, a post to which I had been appointed the previous year, I was required to be at the annual meeting in Bahia, Brazil. But I was present in Managua in heart and spirit. In those days, at *La Prensa* we were like a big family. AT THE SERVICE OF TRUTH AND JUSTICE—these words were inscribed on the masthead of the newspaper, and all of us without exception lived by that rule.

No sooner did I return from Brazil than the Sandinistas attacked Contra base camps in Honduras.

On March 25, Honduras asked the United States for emergency military assistance to repel the Sandinista forces. American military forces in Honduras were given the authority to go into action, and so the Sandinistas withdrew.

It was clear from that action that the Sandinistas retreated only when confronted with force. Without the Reagan administration's strong reaction, they would have overrun the Contra camps. Though I have never believed the solution was to go to war, I don't think the Sandinistas would ever have sat at the negotiating table in the face of a passive response from the Americans. A selective use of military force did play a role in the ultimate achievement of peace.

The Sandinistas' actions effectively killed any hope for resumption of the Contadora talks and handed the Reagan administration a legislative victory.

As the debate in the U.S. Congress over Contra aid continued, the Sandinistas put pressure on leaders of the Nicaraguan opposition to speak out against the bill. Daniel Ortega told visiting congressmen he would sign the Contadora treaty if the United States agreed to drop its demands that the plan include efforts at democratization.

It was about this time that Jaime and I were invited to Washington as the main speakers at a ceremony to honor *La Prensa*. The newspaper was exalted as the "daily of the Nicaraguan people." Jaime gave a speech in which he appeared to argue in favor of aid to the Contras. He said something to the effect that "war was a necessary evil." His comments appeared in the *Washington Post*. Sandinista officials in Managua were furious.

Afterward, Cristiana (who was six months pregnant with her second child) and I traveled to Boston, where I was awarded the Louis Lyons Award for honesty and integrity in my journalistic enterprises and because of my efforts in defense of freedom of expression. In my speech, I gave a brief and accurate account of the restrictions the Sandinistas had imposed upon us in the past seven years. "Last year alone," I told them, we were obliged to cancel an issue eight times because most of the paper was censored. On two additional occasions, the censors punished us by not allowing us to publish. *Turba* attacks harass our agencies and impede the distribution of the newspaper. Because of these aggressions, one third of the agencies have been shut down. By restricting our purchases of newsprint and by denying access to foreign exchange, they have reduced us from being a daily with twenty pages to one that has six. This is the sad state of freedom of expression in my country.

Several months went by. Cristiana and I continued our defense of free speech. Then, on June 15, 1986, at 4 A.M., I received a call from Cristiana. She told me she was having contractions and leaving for the hospital. At 6:30 A.M., Antonio Ignacio Lacayo was born. As with all my other grandchildren, I gave him a thorough examination. This child weighed nine pounds seven ounces—he did not look like a newborn. To this day he is strong and resolute in his ways. In many ways he is like his father, Antonio, and not like my delicate, lithe daughter Cristiana. To me it was astonishing to think he had developed in her body.

Ten days later, on June 25, 1986, President Reagan's $100 million aid package for the Contras was approved.

The day after the vote, Ortega reversed himself on Contadora. He said it was urgent the accord be signed because it was the only instrument for peace in Nicaragua.

Ortega also characterized the aid approval as immoral, and he accused all of us at *La Prensa* of being "an instrument of imperialism." He said the revolution would know how to deal with us. He added that I deserved to have a thirty-year prison sentence and that I was an enemy of the revolution. Ten years earlier, it was Somoza who denounced me; now it was Daniel Ortega. In their opinion, I was a foe of Nicaragua simply because I opposed them.

Then, in a dramatic act of vengeance, Daniel Ortega ordered *La Prensa* indefinitely closed.

That morning, June 26, 1986, when I arrived at the newspaper around 9 A.M. to meet a group of foreign dignitaries and diplomats, I became immediately alarmed when I found the doors to the plant shut. I got out of the car and approached the entrance. Pointing directly at me were a pair of machine guns. It was a Sandinista takeover. For the past year now, Sandinista *turbas* had periodically threatened to burn us down, and on Radio Sandino they said nothing could save us from a stray bullet or from being flayed alive. So, long before that day, I was prepared for whatever might come because I wasn't going to allow anyone to push me out of *La Prensa*. The newspaper was a sacred trust from Pedro and the only voice of opposition in Nicaragua. As such, it had to continue to operate until our country achieved true independence.

"Open the doors," I said to the soldiers. "The owner is here."

They let me in. I walked to my office. Cristiana was there, and Carlos Holmann was sitting down. Military men were questioning him. One of them said to me, "Señora, we need to ask you some questions." As the questioning was going on, there was silence in the room. A man took copious notes on every word I said. They were looking for evidence that we were agents of the CIA. When they were done with their inquisition, I asked to see their notes. I put on my glasses. *"Dios mío,"* I thought. None of what was written were my true words. Three times I tore up their transcript of my interrogation, until they produced an accurate version.

I discovered later that their visit was just a formality. They had decided to shut the paper, and so they did. They ordered us to stop the printing presses, fire the workers, lay off the newsmen, and then they let all of us go home. It was a simple matter for them. But for us it represented an assault on the most valuable jewel of democracy, freedom of the press.

The old dictator of Nicaragua, Anastasio Somoza García, had done the same, forcing my father-in-law into exile forty years earlier. That was the beginning. Since then, *La Prensa* had had to endure more shutdowns, bombings, threats to our directors, press censorship, imprisonment, and defamation—and, of course, the greatest loss of all, the life of my husband, Pedro Joaquín Chamorro Cardenal.

With the Sandinistas, we had thought all that would change. But the oppressive hand of tyranny had come back to silence *La Prensa*.

It was a day of mourning for all of us. After everyone had left, I ordered the blue-and-white flag of our revolution lowered to half staff. I sat in my office thinking, This is not the government we dreamed of. It is not what Pedro died for. The Sandinistas had better not think that I will let it end like this.

Chapter Eleven

I THINK MY FURY WITH DANIEL AND COMPANY began when they took to calling me "an instrument of the CIA and a Somocista." When I first heard those words, it was as if I had been struck a physical blow. I remember that I sat before my typewriter and expressed my outrage in a series of disdainful opinions that appeared in the op-ed section of the *New York Times*.

And so, on the day the Sandinistas shut down *La Prensa,* with Cristiana's support I began a personal crusade against them, geared toward creating international awareness about Nicaragua. I wrote to countless senators in the U.S. Congress. I spoke at every international press forum. I consulted with the leaders of the democratic nations. I said that a "curtain of silence had fallen" over Nicaragua since the Sandinistas had ordered *La Prensa* and other non-Sandinista news media shut down. "For this action," I said, "no explanations were given, no legal process was followed, no chance of a defense was given." It was an assault on freedom of expression that left democracy defenseless. So, each time I asked that "pressure be exerted on the Sandinistas to return to the original Plan of Government, lift the state of emergency, return civil liberties to our people, and reinstate a mixed economy."

When tensions were at their highest with the Sandinistas, Claudia called from Costa Rica. She told me she had decided to marry Edmundo Jarquín, Pedro's former protégé. After a four-year formal separation, Claudia was now divorced from José and had been dating Mundo, as we called him, for almost a year. I like Mundo. He is intelligent and honest. I had no real objections to the match, except that as the Sandinistas' ambassador in Mexico, Mundo had contributed, in my opinion, to creating abroad a false image of the Sandinistas. With Mundo I now had three Sandinistas in the family to contend with.

The wedding was in Mexico. It was a high-powered diplomatic affair, with members of the FSLN directorate in attendance. By then *La Prensa* had been closed almost three months, and tensions with the Sandinistas ran high. Fortunately, as the mother of an adult bride, I wasn't expected to be a hostess. Cristiana and I kept our distance from the directorate, engaging in minimal amounts of conversation.

With the country in an economic crisis, the Sandinistas, politically damaged, too, by the effects of the war, felt vulnerable for the first time. They seemed to show a new interest in peace. Indeed, their revolution had reached a make-or-break point. They had to find a way out of the war or the whole nation was going to rise up in arms. To defeat the Contras at the negotiating table, they said, was the best way.

As the year ended, a chain of seemingly unrelated events turned the wheel of fortune away from military engagement, and the climate became more propitious for peace.

On October 5, an airplane flown by Eugene Hasenfus, an American pilot, was shot out of the air by the Sandinistas while it was flying on a secret mission over Nicaragua. The incident confirmed rumors of a secret arms operation on behalf of the Contras, which resulted in a U.S. congressional investigation.

The investigation revealed that in 1986, a White House aide named Oliver North, in an effort to gain the release of American hostages in Iran, had sold arms to Iran through a private enterprise. After aid to the Contras was cut off, North established a network of private supporters who made business deals, apparently to generate funds for the Contras. Some of the proceeds of the arms sales were secretly diverted to finance the Contras' covert activities. In doing this, Congress charged, Ronald Reagan's administration had subverted the rule of law by trying to engineer the overthrow of a foreign government. The Boland Amendment, named for Senator Boland, its author, specifically forbade that CIA money go toward military activities. As a result of a public uproar, Reagan had to shift his attention from aiding the Contras to defending his administration at hearings that threatened to cripple him politically.

Reagan's political problems opened the way for someone to step in and seize control of diplomacy in Central America. That man was Oscar Arias Sánchez of Costa Rica.

With Reagan under attack, Arias decided that the peace process could be handled by the leaders of the Central American nations. So he proposed his own plan to put an end to the war.

In March 1987, as the question of whether to continue support for an armed struggle was being debated in the U.S. Congress, I was invited to testify. My role, however, as I saw it, was not to play politics between the Democrats and the Republicans but to focus their attention on the silencing of *La Prensa* as an important arm of the opposition. I told them that in my opinion, violence in Nicaragua could end only with the restoration of a system of government that truly represented the will of the people, a state where civil liberties were guaranteed, and that in the current struggle, *La Prensa* had become a weapon of civil resistance neglected by those who opposed the Sandinistas.

Nine months had passed since the day we had been arbitrarily shut down, and no one had come to our defense. Frankly, I was discouraged. The reaction of the free world to this flagrant injustice was indifference. No one seemed to be impressed by the gag on *La Prensa*. I had expected more solidarity from our democratic friends, who now seemed blind to our struggle. So, to the U.S. Congress I explained, "In Nicaragua we are waging a war for liberty, battling against an ideology that comes wrapped in an attractive but false package. Against that kind of proselytizing," I said, "we are now defenseless. So, as you center your discussion around the question of whether to support an armed struggle, don't forget that it is sometimes possible to bring down the temple walls of totalitarianism with just two sentences."

I warned them that the youth of Nicaragua were being indoctrinated while in the Soviet Union, East Germany, and Cuba studying on the scholarships these countries provided. I asked that the United States try to match the communist bloc's efforts. One congressman, Republican Amos Houghton, heeded my call, and persuaded Congress to provide eight scholarships for impoverished Nicaraguans to study in the United States.

That same month, the Arias Plan took shape. It had a commitment to democratization (to which the FSLN had previously objected), and it

called for an immediate cutoff of aid to the Contras and their repatria-
tion. This is what the Sandinistas wanted. Now they had no more
excuses. If they did not sign, they would be exposed as tyrants. Soon
afterward, Arias shut down the Contra operation in Costa Rica and
expelled the contra directors from his country. He gave them the choice
of renouncing their counterrevolutionary activities or going elsewhere.
Pedro Joaquín and several others left for Miami.

However, in my opinion the plan was incomplete because it did not
give the Contras any say in the negotiations. I believed that until the
two warring sides talked, there could be no peace.

In Washington, with a presidential election a year away, there was a
desire to try to calm the furor over aid to the Contras. Nevertheless, an
agreement existed between Reagan and Speaker of the House Jim
Wright not to abandon the Contras. The plan was that, after a cease-fire,
the Contras would be kept intact, and though military aid would be
halted, humanitarian aid would continue until a reconciliation plan with
the opposition was put into effect.

Ortega had no choice but to leap at the chance to sign the Arias Plan.
He was pressured by the economic situation, which continued to decline. Hyperinflation reached levels considered the highest in the world,
over 13,000 percent a year. Lack of local production and investment, lack
of availability of consumer products, and out-of-control government
spending made the national currency worthless.

On the other hand, Daniel Ortega knew that if he didn't sign, he
would have to deal with the Americans, who had a tougher bargain in
mind. They would insist that the Sandinistas sever their military ties with
the Soviet Union.

So, on August 7, 1987, Daniel—in front of the Central American
presidents Vinicio Cerezo of Guatemala, José Napoleón Duarte of El
Salvador, José Azcona de Hoyo of Honduras, and Oscar Arias Sánchez
—signed the peace plan.

Soon afterward, sidestepping the issue of negotiating with the Contras,
the Sandinistas announced a unilateral cease-fire. Then, in compliance
with the treaty, they appointed a National Reconciliation Commission, to be headed by Cardinal Obando, with the purpose of monitoring
the implementation of the agreement.

At this time, it was estimated, there were forty-eight thousand fighters
and refugees in the Contra camps. Thousands more were coming out of

hiding from inside Nicaragua. Without ammunition, there could be a massacre of these troops. The responsibility was enormous for the leaders of the counterrevolution. The decision was made, in September 1987, to seek ways to initiate peace talks with the Sandinistas.

Meanwhile, among the Sandinistas there was a feeling that the danger of war had been removed. They could afford now to take some liberalization measures that could help bring international aid to our beleaguered economy. It was the beginning of our own perestroika. The *comandantes* in charge of the economy began to talk in terms of returning to a mixed economy and eliminating the inefficiencies in the system. It had to be on their terms, however. And so they began to approach successful entrepreneurs whose properties they had taken, to offer them the return of half their properties if the former owners would agree to manage the other half for the government. I don't know of any businessman who accepted the deal.

I too received an interesting offer.

It was eight in the morning of September 19, 1987, when Ortega called me directly to suggest that we meet and discuss the conditions under which he might agree to let us reopen *La Prensa*. Somewhat taken aback by his offer but eager to get the process under way, I asked for just enough time to dress and locate the rest of *La Prensa*'s board of directors —Anita Chamorro Holmann and her husband, Carlos; my daughter Cristiana and her husband, Antonio Lacayo. Missing was Jaime Chamorro, who was not living in Nicaragua at the time.

Ortega arrived two and a half hours later, preceded by a caravan of motorcycles and cars big and small, sirens and horns blaring. With Daniel came the foreign ministers of Nicaragua (Father d'Escoto) and of Costa Rica (Rodrigo Madrigal Nieto), and several other functionaries. He greeted me with a smile and planted a kiss on my cheek as if he were an old family friend. He hardly seemed the man who had waged a guerrilla campaign to discredit and smear me while threatening to send me to jail for thirty years. But I had long since stopped being surprised by his abrupt changes of behavior, which always seemed calculated to suit his needs.

He took momentary leave of me, and with d'Escoto began to examine the photos in my office, the same office where Pedro had always met with friends to discuss the politics of Nicaragua. Every object, every photo has a meaning that I share with my visitors.

For Ortega, the study was not an unfamiliar place. Yet he insisted on carefully examining each and every one of my mementos as if seeing them for the first time. In the days when we were colleagues serving together in the junta for national reconstruction, he would come to my home to discuss affairs of state and would always linger to reminisce with me about my life in politics and the moments I had shared with Pedro, whom he claimed to admire. However, on this occasion I did not want to engage in a sentimental journey with a man who had so disrespected us. I cut him short by pointing out, in jest, that the only novelty in my office since their last visit was the absence of the photographs taken of all of us, back in 1979, on the day they had asked me to join the junta. Wishing to break the ice, I remarked that I had put them in an armoire. "Their presence," I said, "is a constant reminder of days I would just as soon forget."

Nicaraguans indulge in a lot of self-deprecating humor, so after that bit of jousting, the negotiations began on a more relaxed note. Ortega went to the heart of the matter. He said his administration wanted to assure me, in the presence of our mutual friend Madrigal Nieto, that *La Prensa* could reopen with minimal censorship. He said only certain topics regarding the war with the Contras, for reasons of national security, would have to be restricted. He recognized that the limitations the government had placed on *La Prensa* were excessive, irrational, and prejudicial.

He went on to explain that the recent Arias Plan specified that he had ninety days to begin taking steps toward democratization. Reopening *La Prensa* was the first step.

It pleased me to hear that Daniel was willing to call an end to the persecution. But I tried to explain to him that our commitment to the people of Nicaragua was always to be "at the service of truth and justice." Thus I could not agree to resume publication of *La Prensa* unless I was guaranteed complete freedom of expression. And because we didn't want anyone to say we had received preferential treatment, the arrangement would have to include all other media organizations in Nicaragua.

The discussions went on for hours. But in the end he accepted a press without censorship. Having said that, he promised to have Jaime Wheelock drop by to take care of the details. Wheelock arrived around two o'clock in a less accommodating mood. But it was clear that they needed us to reopen. With the world watching, they had to prove that they were liberalizing their regime.

And we were eager to be in circulation once again and wanted very much for the Arias Plan to succeed. So there was a clear urgency to arrive at an agreement that very day. Any delay would work against us. Already the more radical forces of Sandinismo were lining up to oppose liberalization. Fidel Castro preached that freedom of the press was a greater foe than an armed counterrevolution.

So before they could change their minds, we drafted a joint communiqué and entrusted it to Madrigal Nieto so that he, an eyewitness and trusted friend of both parties, could be the one to let the world know that the worst inquisition ever to have hit Nicaragua was at last over.

I expressed my thanks to President Oscar Arias Sánchez for his part in the democratization of our country. And for Ortega, as well, I had some congratulatory remarks because, though he once believed it was necessary to shut us down in order to "restore the national dignity," with this action he had reversed the damage he had done to his countrymen.

La Prensa reopened on October 1, 1987. After sixteen months of enforced silence, our first issue was designed to push the Sandinistas' patience to the limit.

The front page read:

THE PEOPLE TRIUMPH

IN THE NAME OF THE PEOPLE OF NICARAGUA, *LA PRENSA* TODAY WELCOMES THE OPPORTUNITY TO TELL THE SANDINISTA GOVERNMENT THAT NICARAGUA HAS NEVER WANTED, AND DOES NOT WANT, A TOTALITARIAN-STYLE COMMUNIST DICTATORSHIP.

In its first week back in business, our newspaper gave the Sandinistas no quarter. Though they did not close or censor us, once again they restricted our purchases of newsprint and they sent *turbas* to my home. They attacked the poor little newsboys who sold *La Prensa*. They would pummel them with stones and take their copies of *La Prensa* and burn them. One child said, "I was only trying to sell the newspaper that sells the most, so I can bring home more money for my family."

I concluded that little had changed among the Sandinistas. They were only pretending to comply with democratization. In the weeks that followed, several demonstration rallies were suppressed, and opposition leaders imprisoned. But with the lifting of the press censorship, the opposition could not be silenced anymore.

The Sandinistas refused to negotiate with the Contras, and the Reagan administration asked Congress for more aid for the Contras.

That year, Oscar Arias Sánchez received the Nobel Peace Prize for his work in Central America. But another year would pass and many more accords would be signed before conditions in Nicaragua truly began to change. Looking back, I now realize it was a slow process of democratization that depended largely on the efforts of Nicaraguans. It is a process that continues to this day.

Nine months before, in January 1987, while Pedro Joaquín was in Costa Rica publishing *Nicaragua Hoy,* he had been approached by the CIA and asked to join the Contra directorate. It was the CIA's intention to open a new southern front that could replace Pastora's movement, which was then in total disarray and about to collapse.

The CIA wanted Pedro Joaquín, the son and namesake of the martyr of civil liberties, to be the new face of the reformed Contras. Pedro Joaquín agreed to join. Pedro Joaquín was well-intentioned though he was young and politically unprepared for the situation. He didn't immediately grasp that power was controlled by Bermúdez and Calero, who controlled the military.

As the Iran-Contra scandal broke, the trouble between Calero and Arturo Cruz resurfaced. In February 1987 Calero resigned from the directorship of the Contra (he would be reappointed a short time later). He was followed, on March 9, 1987, by Arturo, who felt the whole scandal had besmirched his reputation, particularly since it was revealed he had been receiving a monthly stipend directly from Oliver North. The only difference between Arturo and the other Nicaraguans in the counterrevolution was that they received their money through their party organizations. Alfredo César had Opposition Block of the South (BOS), which was little more than a small band of fighters, Robelo had the MDN, Calero had the FDN, and Zero had ARDE. All of these opposition groups were receiving financing of some kind or other.

After Arturo left, with another bill for more aid pending approval, there was a lot of pressure from Congress on the Contra leadership. In an effort to broaden the base of popular support for the Contras and to project a more pluralist image, a representative from each political faction was given a seat in the directorship. Besides Alfonso Robelo, Adolfo Calero, Enrique Bermúdez, and my son Pedro Joaquín, three new members were brought in. They were Bermúdez's ally, Aristides Sánchez, Alfredo César, and Azucena Ferrey from the Christian Democratic Party, who represented the internal opposition. In addition a seventy-person assembly was formed so that disputes could be settled in a parliamentary fashion.

As the hearings progressed, the integrity of the Contra leadership was called into question. Millions of dollars were supposedly diverted to the Contras; however, the investigations revealed that less than a million was actually delivered. In fact, North's private associates, whom we by now knew to be Richard Secord and an Arab named Hakim, swindled the operation.

Nearly a year later, on February 3, 1988, the U.S. House of Representatives defeated an aid package for the Contras. As a result, the Contras had little choice but to begin seriously considering a cease-fire.

After the House voted down the aid, Daniel Ortega seized the moment. Responding to a previous suggestion from President Arias, he declared at a speech in the Plaza de la Revolución that he was willing to meet with the Contra leadership.

A date was set for talks—February 10. Then they were postponed by the Contra leadership to February 18. In the days that followed, the Sandinistas delayed.

Then, on March 15, Sandinista troops stationed on the Honduran border began an invasion. On March 16, President Reagan called an emergency meeting in Washington. That same day President Azcona of Honduras officially requested the United States to intervene. Reagan sent in the 82nd Airborne. Two American F-5 bombers reportedly bombed Sandinista army positions. Sandinista troops suffered losses and were surrounded by the Honduran army. The Honduran government issued a deadline to Nicaragua to remove its troops; otherwise they would suffer expulsion by force. On March 18, Humberto Ortega called a halt to the offensive.

The Sandinistas had been planning the offensive for five months. They had mobilized thousands of troops, artillery, and aircraft at the

Honduran border. Very adroitly, they had delayed negotiations with the Contras while they moved surreptitiously to demolish Contra bases.

The fighting was expected to endanger the peace talks. The Contra leadership, however, knew there was almost no chance of renewed military aid. The talks finally took place on March 23, 1988. The Contra delegation was composed of Adolfo Calero (who had the proxy votes of Azucena Ferrey and my son Pedro Joaquín), Aristides Sánchez, who was close to Bermúdez, and Alfredo César.

Everyone who followed the talks was certain Alfredo César alone had the capacity to make the deal. His mystique was such that he totally eclipsed Calero, the chosen head of the delegation. Even before the negotiations began, it was with Alfredo—who had once been a Sandinista leader—that the Sandinistas chose to open a private channel of discussion.

On the third day of the negotiations, March 26, Humberto took Alfredo aside on two occasions for private talks that lasted nearly an hour. Afterward, Humberto Ortega put forth a proposal that was not unfavorable to the resistance. It did not require the rebels' surrender and disarmament; it stipulated that they would move into enclaves of at least ten thousand square miles of territory that could ensure their safety, and it offered total amnesty, even for those who were former members of Somoza's *guardia*.

Some members of the delegation, particularly a resistance commander known as Toño, felt the war had to continue at all costs. Alfredo César spoke in favor of the offer, arguing that with a presidential election eight months away, no more aid would be coming.

Alfredo, by his own admission, pulled out all the stops in an effort to get his colleagues to sign. "It was the fiercest fight of my life," he said. Aristides Sánchez, himself a military man, supported Alfredo.

And so a truce was signed that gave the Contra negotiators until May 30—sixty days—to disarm and demobilize their forces. Once this was completed, negotiations for an overall settlement would continue. A new round of talks was set for April 6 in Managua.

During the negotiations the Sandinistas made stricter demands. As the May 30 deadline approached, tensions increased within the resistance leadership. The Contra directors were plagued with doubts soon after the signing, particularly when they tried to envision the reaction of Enrique Bermúdez and the other combatants. A rift formed within the resistance between those who were for peace and those who were not, which made it difficult for Alfredo César to lead the talks to a positive conclusion in the months to come.

The Sandinistas, alerted to the fact that there was division among the Contra negotiators, took back concessions made in the first talks. Eventually the peace negotiations would be suspended for six months.

After the talks were suspended, the Contra directorship slowly fell apart. Peace was ultimately achieved through the efforts of the Central American presidents and the intervention of the new Bush administration in the United States and of Carlos Andrés Pérez, in addition to the courageous effort of the internal civic opposition, who continued to exert pressure on the Sandinistas to make reforms.

In July, Pedro Joaquín left the Contra movement and returned to the business of being a journalist. He continued to live with his wife and children in exile for another year.

Nineteen eighty-nine began with the Sandinistas in an impossible situation. Nicaragua was on the verge of an economic collapse, internationally discredited, while the Soviet Union, the Sandinistas' source of economic support, was declining and the Contras were still an armed force waiting in camps in Honduras. So when, at the beginning of February 1989, Carlos Andrés Pérez was inaugurated president of Venezuela for the second time, Ortega traveled to Caracas for the inauguration, prepared to compromise. Ortega told the Central American presidents in attendance that he would allow internationally supervised elections. Arias then demanded that Ortega shorten his presidential term by moving the elections up from their scheduled date of November 1990 to February 1990. On his part, Carlos Andrés, who no longer trusted the Sandinistas, demanded that Ortega take steps to guarantee the campaign would be a fair contest. With this commitment, a new date was set for Ortega to meet with the four Central American presidents.

They signed an agreement in Tesoro Beach, El Salvador. Ortega promised to hold elections in February 1990. The elections would be monitored by international observers. The campaign would start on August 25, 1989, after Ortega had reformed the electoral and media laws written in the constitution. As they stood, the laws forbade political organizations and mass rallies. Daniel also promised the lifting of the state of emergency, which restricted freedom, and amnesty for all political prisoners. The counterpart of the agreement was that the Contras would voluntarily disarm, demobilize, and repatriate within a period of ninety days. The five presidents agreed to present, within a month, a plan for the demobilization of the Contras.

In April, the Sandinistas unveiled the new electoral and media laws. The laws were so self-serving that the opposition felt the offer was a sham. Nevertheless, I felt we had to seize the moment and challenge the Sandinistas at their game by going to elections.

At this crucial stage of our history, my personal desires and my political activities were pulling me in opposite directions. On the one hand, I wanted to be left alone to indulge in the pleasure of reclassifying all my mementos, the clothing, documents, photographs I keep. On the other hand, I wanted to be of use.

Through my defense of freedom of the press, I had become a well-known figure of opposition. In March of the previous year, the Coordinadora Democrática had elected me Woman of the Year. People were talking about me as a presidential hopeful. Carlos Andrés kept telling me, "Violeta, you have a role to play." So, to a great extent I thought it a duty to comply. At the time, Cristiana, Antonio, and I discussed the idea. Until then my political endeavors had been the by-product of Pedro's. I wasn't convinced I could carry the burden of a presidential campaign alone. I told Cristiana and Antonio that with them by my side, I would do it. But it was one of those things you talk about; until it happens, you never really believe it.

When I discussed the idea with Pedro's mother, Doña Margarita, a woman for whom I have great admiration, love, and respect, she told me, "Do it for Pedro, Violeta." The cardinal also encouraged me to run and gave me his blessing.

In May 1989, I received an award as a Guardian of Democracy. It was given to me by the U.S. Senate majority leader, Robert Byrd. So I traveled with Cristiana to Washington, D.C. On our way back, we stopped for a fortnight in Miami.

Alfredo César and his wife, Silvia Lacayo, invited us to dinner at their town house. By then Alfredo was no longer in the Contra directorate. Seeing that being in the armed opposition no longer held any political promise, he was in negotiations with the Social Democratic Party (PSD). If he succeeded in being appointed to the directorate of the PSD, he was planning to return to Nicaragua in July in time for the campaign scheduled to begin in August. Alfredo's presidential ambitions were common knowledge. So it surprised me when Alfredo told me he regarded me as someone who could unify the various factions because I was above the fray of politics and a symbol of peace. He added, "Doña Violeta, I want to tell you that I am willing to promote you as a presidential candidate. Have you thought who will manage your campaign?"

I had already discussed this with Antonio and Cristiana. So I told them, "In the eventuality that I become a candidate for the presidency, I want Antonio to be my campaign manager." Alfredo looked surprised. I don't know what might have been on his mind. I had my reservations about Alfredo. Fresh on my mind was the controversy over his private talks with the Sandinistas during the peace negotiations, and also my son Pedro Joaquín's experiences with him in the Contras. I had heard there was some element of deceit in the way Alfredo handled himself politically. Because of this, in Nicaragua, people had dubbed him (perhaps unfairly so) Seven Daggers, and they delightedly rattled off each one of his alleged betrayals. Logically, I was unwilling to commit myself to naming him to any position. The element of trust wasn't there. I decided to let Antonio decide.

After a thorough discussion with Alfredo, Antonio and Cristiana's advice was that we appoint Alfredo campaign adviser. They felt that we in the opposition had to be united against the Sandinistas.

Soon after that, two representatives of the Socialist Party of Nicaragua came to visit me at my offices in *La Prensa*. They told me, "Doña Violeta, we want to propose that you be our candidate in the upcoming elections. We want to know if you will accept."

That was the first official request I received. I was beginning to see my candidacy as something that had a real dimension to it.

But the opposition remained fractured, which would favor the Sandinistas. In addition, many of the opposition leaders were dispirited. Some threatened to boycott the elections. They complained of repression and of being obligated to hold back campaign efforts until August, while the Sandinistas were already campaigning. Daniel, making use of his oratorical skills, was going around the country promising a better future now that relations with the United States were going to improve. With his voice full of passion, he wove illusions out of thin air because, in reality, the Sandinistas were so discredited that I doubt the Americans would have renewed foreign aid to Nicaragua as long as they were in control. Well into 1989, the Sandinistas were still confiscating properties, cracking down on opposition rallies, threatening to finish off whole sectors of our society that opposed Sandinismo, while at the same time creating the appearance of change.

Despite the unfairness of the situation, I saw a real opening for democracy. To abstain or withdraw would be cowardly. We had to challenge the Sandinistas at every turn.

Daniel Ortega was well aware that he could not sustain another year of war without the economic support of his Soviet allies, so on August 3, 1989, at the urging of President Arias, Daniel made another attempt to come to terms with the opposition groups. He called us to a national dialogue to settle the differences. At the meeting Daniel made a number of concessions. He pledged to suspend the military draft for five months, stop arrests of political activists, and grant equal television time to opposition parties. In exchange the opposition parties had to call for a disarmament of the Contras.

Many in the opposition, however, remained unconvinced. Most of all, they were unhappy with the scheduling of the elections. They enumerated the difficulties we faced. Our political organizations had been inactive for more than a decade. So we were in a state of political disarray, while our opposition was a finely tuned political machine with the resources of the entire nation at its disposal.

I, on the other hand, felt strongly that even if we lost, we would be achieving a lot of good for the democratization of the country. But I thought that with the right amount of civic ardor and moral determination, we could do it. The people of Nicaragua, I was certain, would not forget who had plunged us into a civil war that lasted a decade, killed so many of our sons and daughters, and lowered the country to a level of such severe economic decay that we might never be able to emerge from it. Under their rule Nicaragua had become, after Haiti, the poorest nation in our hemisphere. Who could thank the Sandinistas for that?

The Sandinistas saw things differently. They were certain that with twenty opposition candidates on the ballot, our anti-Sandinista vote would be hopelessly divided. This meant Daniel could win with as little as 30 percent of the vote.

In their assessment, the Sandinistas made three major miscalculations. The first was to misread totally the level of discontent that existed among the people. The second was to believe that in one year they could turn around the economic debacle that had taken them a decade to create. (Sixty-five percent of the workforce did not have jobs. More than 70 percent of Nicaraguans lived below the poverty level. Inflation stood at 20,000 percent per year. A worker's salary was worth 6 percent of what it had been worth a decade before. Our trade deficit had ballooned and the country was in default. None of these problems would be resolved overnight.) The Sandinistas' third misperception was to underestimate our capacity to coalesce into one strong party.

Then, on August 5, the Central American presidents met again. An agreement was signed by both sides the next day. The five presidents agreed to complete the demobilization of the Contras by December, two months before the elections.

Once the peace was signed, all our attention turned toward defeating the Sandinistas at the ballot boxes. Alfredo César and several others returned to Nicaragua to join the civic opposition. Soon an earnest effort was under way to become a united opposition.

By late August, we had formed a rainbow coalition of parties called the Nicaraguan Opposition Union (UNO). Within our ranks there was a broad range of political ideologies and socioeconomic interests, beginning with every shade of Liberal and Conservative down to the very extreme left, represented by the Communist Party of Nicaragua (which had suffered as much repression as we had simply because it did not accept the Sandinistas' leadership). Socially, moreover, we were a fusion of businessmen, farmers, and proletarians. And though we had agreed on a platform, it had less to do with ideology and more to do with our shared distaste for Sandinismo and our love for human rights and liberty.

There were three candidates for the UNO nomination besides myself. Dr. Emilio Alvarez Montalván was an ophthalmologist by training but a much celebrated politician. Enrique Bolaños was the president of COSEP. (As the leader of this group, Enrique had been persecuted and imprisoned and had had property expropriated. He had also been vilified by the *turbas divinas,* the divine mobs. The other candidate was Virgilio Godoy, an economist, head of the Independent Liberal Party, ex-

minister of labor under the Sandinistas, a politician of the old school
with a lot of mileage. Godoy is a tough negotiator, always unwilling to
cede any ground.

The process by which the candidates were chosen was less than ideal.
There was no time to hold a primary, so all of us were called before a
selection committee. Each of us sat in a tiny waiting room, which was
more like a holding cell, sweating nervously until our name was called.
But I felt, if God wants me to do this, I will be chosen.

When my turn came I was taken before the fourteen leaders of the
parties in the UNO coalition. I felt as if I were before a tribunal. The
tables were arranged in the form of a horseshoe. Around the table the
delegates sat in solemn discussion. They gestured for me to take a seat in
a chair at the center of the group.

The questions they asked me were simple. I answered them succinctly.
They wanted to know what my platform of government would be,
should I be chosen.

I told them quite frankly that I could run a very successful campaign
with two basic ideas. I stated them simply: "I will work for peace and
freedom." To achieve peace I would end mandatory military conscription and aim at reconciling the family—Nicaragua—which had
been polarized for too long. I would give back to the people their right
to choose their leaders through fair and open electoral competitions.
And above all I would give them honesty, honesty, and more honesty,
not just in appearance but in full practice. I would serve my people and
not ask to be served by them.

These were the same issues we had been discussing with the Sandinistas in all our dialogues.

Antonio tells me that after the questioning was over, the delegates
spent the rest of the day in heated debate. It was impossible to reach a
consensus. After two pollings, I had six votes, Virgilio Godoy had four,
and Enrique Bolaños had four. So a method of selection was proposed.
The candidate who won ten votes or more out of the fourteen would
be the candidate. In the third polling, someone floated the idea of voting
on various permutations of a formula that had me paired with Godoy
and Bolaños, in both instances with me as president and one of them as
vice president. Then the formula was reversed. On both pollings the
votes were higher with me as the presidential candidate. But it seems

Enrique didn't want second billing. So Virgilio was the one, and on the evening of September 2, Antonio came to tell me I was the nominee.

If my voice never faltered during the years of brutal confrontation with the Sandinistas, it was because I was always guided by the selfless desire to improve the lot of my countrymen.

My best forum for accomplishing this was still *La Prensa*. Since renewing our journalistic activities without press censorship, we had regained the much honored position of being the principal source of headaches for the government.

But now, driven by the Sandinistas' persecution of me, I had evolved from the publisher of a newspaper, waging a campaign against them from the pages of *La Prensa,* to being a leading political figure in our country.

From the very first public opinion poll, in November 1989, in a runoff against the other candidates, I emerged as the front runner, ahead of Daniel. So it came as no surprise to me when I was chosen to be the candidate for the UNO democratic coalition.

I had to begin my campaign abroad. The UNO's need for international legitimization required me to travel to the United States and Europe to plead for financial aid for Nicaragua.

We had just arrived in London on the morning of November 12 when something happened to convince me that we would win the elections. We learned through the papers and television media that the Berlin Wall had fallen.

It was very early when we received this wonderful news, but not so early that the hotel's bar service was closed. We promptly ordered a bottle of champagne, and I proposed a toast. A wall whose foundations had been laid upon the suppression and abridgment of an entire country's rights had just fallen. We could accomplish a great feat, too. United we could remove the yoke of the FSLN from our necks and transform Nicaragua into our own monument.

Less than a week later, following meetings with British prime minister Margaret Thatcher, German foreign minister Hans-Dietrich Genscher, and Pope John Paul II, I was in Spain to meet with Prime Minister Gonzalez and Foreign Minister Fernández-Ordóñez.

Mr. Gonzalez promised to remain neutral throughout the electoral process. Mr. Ordóñez, who had been given a piece of the Berlin Wall by a friend, presented it to me as a memento before I left.

It is only a small piece of the wall, a bare rock made of sand and cement. Each particle, however, contains such pain, so much lamentation for the past, and an even greater amount of optimism for the future. This little rock holds such significance for me that I sometimes keep it in my pocket as one of my most cherished possessions.

Barely four months after my nomination, on January 2, 1990, Pedro Joaquín, Pablo Antonio Cuadra, and I were lunching together in my private office at home. Pedro Joaquín had returned from exile in Miami. I remember that Pedro Joaquín was remarking on the infectious euphoria he had observed at our rallies. I stood up to close the door when suddenly my legs folded under me. In that fraction of a second before my fall, a thousand images went through my head as I imagined the hospital they would take me to, the stitches I would receive on my forehead if I fell forward over the glass case that was directly in front of me. I also considered the consequences if, instead, I were to fall backward and cause irreparable damage to my ailing back. So I allowed myself to fall on my knees, thinking this the least of all evils. Little did I know my unfortunate decision would almost put an end to my short political career.

Pedro Joaquín and Pablo Antonio rushed to my side as I lay on the floor. There was a buzz in my ear and I couldn't move. I could feel I had injured my kneecap, and I guessed it was shattered into a hundred little pieces. I was screaming in agony, offering no resistance to the suffering, having been convinced long ago that pain is an inevitable part of life and unless we surrender to it, it can become unbearable.

My household staff were all gathering around me, and in a chorus of voices were all murmuring, *"Dios mío, qué barbaridad."* But the pity they felt for me did nothing to alleviate the discomfort I was in. So I asked them to please fetch me some ice so that I could numb my senses. It seemed only a short while afterward that my orthopedist, Dr. Gutiérrez-Quant, arrived. He pronounced the fracture too serious to be attended to in Nicaragua. Consequently, he recommended I fly to the United States, where I could get better care. But the last flight to Houston had already left, and it seemed I had no other option but to wait until the following day.

Carlos Andrés Pérez, always the greatest of friends, upon hearing of my plight immediately sent a Venezuelan military transport plane. Unfortunately, on that particular day, it seems, my luck was running sour, because the pilots in their rush neglected to secure the regulatory permits to fly over Honduras, and we were forced back to Managua.

Meanwhile, my leg was badly bloated. I feared that it would have to be cut off to prevent gangrene from spreading. For sixty years I had led an active life and was used to running to achieve my goals. And now, at a crucial period in our history, I was forced into inaction by a trivial occurrence. Nevertheless, as I looked into the glum faces of my friends and colleagues, I struggled to maintain a semblance of humor. I joked about the great caricatures my new image "as an invalid on crutches" would inspire in the Sandinista journals. But in my heart I was lamenting the terrible misfortune of the UNO to lose the election over something as inconsequential as a broken kneecap.

Finally, I got to Houston. When I awoke after four hours of surgery at St. Luke's Hospital, my kneecap was an intricate assembly of fractured bones that had been pieced together by the talented hands of the surgical team. They said to me, "It's as good as new. You will recover completely. But rehabilitation is going to be very slow, and you will have to have total rest."

I returned to Nicaragua on January 16, 1990. In my absence, Antonio had organized a march to commemorate the eleventh anniversary of Pedro's death. The Sandinistas did not monitor or interfere with this march, but they ridiculed it through all their media channels. They reported that the marchers had been joined by three or four stray cats, but didn't mention that there were ten thousand demonstrators. They also tried to discredit the marchers by characterizing them as a small group of ambitious leaders whose only goal was to revive and give continuity to Somocismo.

But their jokes and their taunting only served to pull us closer to-gether. I remember that after the march our unity was so strong we were like a wall of granite in our opposition to Sandinistas. And their attacks could not dim our enthusiasm. I felt it was only a matter of time before things would begin to change dramatically for all of us.

Back on the campaign trail. My new, immobile condition had been a much discussed topic among our young staff, who were struggling to figure out how to get me out on the campaign trail with my crutches and my wheelchair while all the time striving to keep me immobile. They came up with a plan that had military ingenuity. They procured a four-wheel-drive pickup and equipped it with a canopy to protect me from the sun, pillows to mitigate the blows from the potholes on the road, cold water to quench my thirst, watermelons and oranges to satisfy my hunger. This is how the Violemobile came to be.

In this contraption I toured the country, spoke to the people, felt the warm glow of their affection, and breathed in the air from the barrios, the orchards, and the haciendas. My companions in this new adventure were Cristiana, Antonio, my sister-in-law Elena, my niece Clarisa Barrios, my nephew Carlos Hurtado, and occasionally my son Pedro Joaquín —and a bedpan I had borrowed from St. Luke's.

And so, while I wandered about the countryside in the Violemobile, spreading my party's message of hope from town to town, Daniel Ortega and the FSLN conducted a rather leisurely campaign. Here was a man whose every whim and desire literally lay at his fingertips. With astonishing facility he could extract presents and other gratuities from his socialist friends around the globe. However, the ease with which he obtained whatever he wanted clearly inspired within President Ortega and his Sandinista cronies some dangerous complacency.

None of the FSLN leaders held even the slightest inkling of doubt about the success of their campaign. For them, the presidential seat was secure and defeat was impossible. All that stood in the way of a Sandinista victory was a crippled old woman and a diminutive fourteen-party coalition that was David to the Sandinistas' Goliath. While we ventured through the lakes and rivers of the frontier on tiny boats with outboard motors, Sandinista chieftains traveled in luxury on huge patrol yachts. Expropriated factories, confiscated properties, and stolen businesses were at their disposal.

There was virtually no one to denounce the Sandinistas for their lack of fairness and equity, their squandering of the state's assets for personal gain, or even their illicit use of funds to maintain their control over the country. Nevertheless, it was they who later vilified freethinking Nicaraguan citizens and branded the UNO a piñata because of the huge foreign aid amounts we were supposed to be rolling in. They accused us of submission to Yankee imperialism.

However, of the $4 million donation we were supposed to have received through the U.S. National Endowment for Democracy and the U.S. Agency for International Development, a mere $2 million had come through, of which $800,000 had gone to the purchase of vehicles for our staff, which the Sandinistas kept tied up in customs procedures. The remaining $1.2 million by law had to be split fifty-fifty with the Supreme Electoral Council.

Meanwhile, the Sandinistas could count on contributions from international socialist allies and on the resources of the nation. In cash alone, it was estimated, they had spent $7 million by February. The disparity of resources between our two campaigns was absolutely staggering. In all truthfulness, the only two advantages we held over the Sandinistas for much of that race were the support of *La Prensa* and our own determination. Since the ascent of the Sandinistas, *La Prensa* had lost much of its income, and its free voice had been muffled by Ortega's regime. However, the newspaper still remained the grande dame of Nicaraguan journalism, as bold and sincere as ever. By this time, Cristiana had assumed management of *La Prensa* and made herself responsible for its continued preeminence.

No matter how much propaganda they spewed out, the Sandinista journals could never match *La Prensa* in terms of quality. For the most part, the newspapers attached to the regime concentrated on FSLN publicity, and along with the television networks, they functioned as the primary advertising vehicle for the state. In contrast, *La Prensa* found it increasingly difficult to get advertising contracts: our country had fewer and fewer private companies. With the nationalization of businesses, the government's restriction of prices, and the Sandinista boycott on syndicates, private enterprise in Nicaragua was on the verge of collapse. Obviously, *La Prensa* was desperate to find advertisers, but financial difficulties notwithstanding, it continued to be the finest paper in the country. Essentially, *La Prensa* served as the united voice of opposition to the Sandinistas, the ideological antithesis to the Sandinista organs, *El Nuevo Diario* and *Barricada*.

Just as important as *La Prensa* were the commitment and tenacity of our campaign staff, particularly that of my campaign manager, Antonio Lacayo. With this element factored into the political equation, I surmised that we were dead even with the Sandinistas in that presidential race. Ortega and his minions could suppress our free voice, they could crank out as much propaganda as they wished, they could even condemn us as American pawns. But they could never quash our spirit and our resolve. My campaign leaders were too devoted to our cause for that to occur.

Quite possibly, a greater concern for UNO than the Sandinistas was my health. The pillows placed inside the Violemobile softened the blows from potholes and other road obstacles a bit, but they could not sufficiently lessen the pain to give me true comfort. Every excursion in the Violemobile was a tremendous ordeal.

Whenever we stopped at a certain site, I was rolled out like some traveling circus attraction, and from my wheelchair I addressed the public. The wheelchair felt like a prison. I felt only embarrassment and despair every time I had to face my countrymen in that unwieldy contraption.

However, up on the podium, the instant I picked up the microphone, I was overcome by a peculiar transformation, a metamorphosis if you will. I can truly say that every time I spoke, I felt like a butterfly emerging from its cocoon. When I addressed the public, I shed all the insignificant minutiae of daily life. I felt liberated from that horrible wheelchair. I transcended my physical impediment, reaching out to the Nicaraguan people and attempting to commiserate with their suffering and hardship. On that stage, there was an intangible bond between us that seemed almost magical. It felt wonderful to help the citizens of my country, to pump hope into their hearts. At the same time, however, I feared that if we failed, I would only be making political lies, empty promises to the people for whom I cared so much. I could only describe my state of mind as a certain sublime agitation, a blend of both bliss and terror.

Without digressing into tearful melodrama, I think the reasons behind the exceptional link between the Nicaraguan public and myself stem from the fact that I understood them. Now, I realize it is a common and hackneyed assertion among politicians to say that they understand their constituents, that they know what they want. I did not necessarily know what the people wanted, but I knew what they did not want. They did not want to be preached to, nor did they wish to be chastised. They were tired of the vacuous and vain Sandinista dogma that had been forced down their throats for so long. In essence, they did not want the same old rhetoric they had heard for the past decade.

Consequently, I incorporated these ideas into my oratory. I spoke to the people in clear and direct language, relating to them the goals of my crusade. I spoke to them of Pedro, of my religious faith, of the salvation of our nation, and of what it meant to be a republic. I tried to open myself to them, revealing many of my feelings and idiosyncrasies in the process. I made myself vulnerable. Instead of rejecting my cause as that of a crippled old weakling, many Nicaraguan citizens embraced it and joined the ranks of the opposition.

Fortunately, God gave me enough wisdom and strength of character to hold steady. His divine hand taught me the true implications of what it meant to persevere.

Deep in my heart, I was always certain that the elections would bring about the dramatic political change that our party desired. My certainty was reinforced every time we traveled through our impoverished provinces. One that I particularly recall was Chontales, where the reception was absolutely astonishing. To arrive at one village by noon, the caravan had to depart from Managua before daybreak. We drove on 150 kilometers of dirt roads, crossed donkey trails, and traversed deep canyons. Thankfully, we were able to reach our destination through the miracle of four-wheel drive. As we pulled into the scorched and sweltering hamlet, we were treated like crusading liberators. There, where the sun pounds down mercilessly upon the earth, we were greeted with cheers, praise, and hundreds of expectant smiles.

From that moment, I sensed the unhappiness of the people toward what they perceived as the communist takeover of Nicaragua. In me they saw the eternal companion of Pedro Joaquín Chamorro, their martyr to civil liberties. I was the woman who had raised the standard of civic and moral resistance against the Sandinistas. All their hopes for change rested in me. The memory of these rallies was the best painkiller to ease my ailing back and knee.

Meanwhile, cracks were beginning to appear in the Sandinista campaign. As is the case with the majority of politicians who have enjoyed the spoils of power far too long, the directors of the FSLN had lost touch with their public. Once the proud orchestrators of a popular revolution, they were now reviled by many. The Sandinistas had liberated Nicaragua from the clutches of an obsessive despot, but in the process of reconstructing the country, they had become estranged from the very people on whose support they depended.

Still, many FSLN chieftains could not conceive of losing the election. They believed the people would appreciate their redistribution of private lands, their extensive literacy campaigns, and their national health program. Poverty, inflation, and unemployment—all of Nicaragua's social ills—the Sandinistas blamed on the diabolical machinations of the Reagan administration, the Contras, church officials, the leaders of the UNO, and, of course, myself. After a while, the fierce invective of President Ortega and his associates became monotonously boring. The Nicaraguan people were starving and destitute, but they were by no means idiots. They saw easily through the regime's transparent facade. Through their cursory and superficial attempts at brainwashing, the Sandinista leaders inadvertently revealed another one of their fatal flaws —the inability to assume responsibility for their own failure.

Chapter Twelve

AS THE CAMPAIGN SWUNG INTO ITS LAST FOUR weeks, the obstacles we faced seemed infinite. The perception was that the Sandinistas had outsmarted and outspent us. They had certainly outspent us. Theirs was rumored to be a $20 million campaign advised by a top American public relations team. Had it not been for the people's determination to rid themselves of Sandinismo, I don't think I would ever have won. In the end it was the people of Nicaragua who outsmarted the Sandinistas.

For most of December and January we subsisted on private donations. As a result of our own private fund-raising efforts we had $170,000 in cash. In addition, while on the campaign trail we benefited from occasional donations in kind, such as free gasoline for our vehicles or free meals from the local farmers. At the time, the people of Nicaragua had gone through a decade of hardships and they didn't have a lot to spare, particularly on a candidate who had little chance of defeating a government that was supported by a powerful army and that had at its command the resources of the entire nation.

One of the most useful private contributions was a five-hundred-dollar sound system my son Pedro Joaquín brought in from Miami, which we used in the campaign trail to amplify my voice so the people could hear my speeches.

The difference in resources between the two campaigns, as I've said before, was vast. So it is ridiculous to suggest, as some books do, that foreign assistance leveled the playing field. At all times the Sandinistas had the upper hand. The legions of foreign journalists who covered the campaign described our efforts as being so weak they were "almost invisible."

Add to that the constant intimidation we suffered throughout the six months of the campaign—*turbas* armed with stones and machetes broke up our rallies, ambushed our cars, and savaged our homes under the observant and passive eye of the Sandinista police. After my own life was threatened, my son-in-law Antonio made a formal complaint to the presidents of Central America. He said that in that climate of insecurity, it would be impossible for the people to vote freely on February 25. The presidents sent a letter to Daniel warning him that he was not keeping his end of the bargain, and sent more observers.

The Sandinistas' physical aggression was complemented by a campaign of verbal intimidation aimed at discrediting me as a candidate. In all his speeches, Daniel persisted in calling me the candidate of the Somocista *guardias,* the candidate of Yankee imperialism, the candidate of the counterrevolution, and so forth. He also intimated that the vote was not secret and that the Sandinistas would know who had voted against them.

We had no means of defense. The news bulletin *Habla UNO* that was supposed to be broadcast through the state-owned radio show every Sunday of the campaign was censored. The only voice left to us was *La Prensa,* which doesn't reach more than one quarter of the reading public of Nicaragua. We knew this was enough to create opposition, but we wondered if it was enough to win an election.

It's understandable that most people expected the Sandinistas to be the sure winners. No one was more fooled than the American press. Four weeks before the elections, *Newsweek* magazine declared that "Violeta Chamorro and her party had been unable to make any significant gains against the Sandinista political machinery." *Newsweek* predicted an overwhelming Sandinista victory.

Even the *New York Times* was deceived by the splendid mirage created by the FSLN's Mass Organization Committees. Just before the elections they released the results of a poll that predicted a 2–1 win for Daniel Ortega. This opinion echoed throughout the world: the *Economist,* the BBC, and the *International Herald Tribune* were all stating similar odds against us.

These forecasts were refuted by *La Prensa,* which predicted 46 percent of the vote for me and 26 percent for Ortega, with 28 percent undecided.

When on February 25 the Sandinista pollsters asked for whom they would vote, the people of Nicaragua did not lie but they did not tell the truth. Thus they helped to create an illusion that the Sandinistas would win 75 percent of the vote. It was fortunate for us that this was so, because the Sandinistas would never have risked their power if they had thought they would lose.

The Sandinistas' perception was further enhanced by the size of the crowds that attended their political meetings and by their reliance on the one hundred thousand votes of the Sandinista army, police, and paramilitary organizations. Certain that they could mobilize a contingent of fanatic supporters, they could not imagine their defeat.

With meticulously trimmed sideburns and mustache, sporting a populist plaid shirt, Ray-Ban sunglasses, and cowboy boots outfitted with spurs (like the gamecocks with razors strapped to their talons), Daniel Ortega would make his appearances. His arrival was always heralded by the Klaxon of his Gallomobile, which would let out a sonorous *kikiriki* before he descended into the crowd of admirers.

By contrast, I was a peripheral figure, a señora dressed in white, struggling to speak from the depths of her wheelchair with the words and ideas appropriate to a simple housewife and mother. In the macho culture of my country, few people believed that I, a woman and an invalid, would have the strength, energy, and will to last through a punishing campaign.

But though I lacked the style of the professional politician, I could see in the wide-eyed faces of the handfuls of families—men, women, and children—who would come to hear me speak, and hug me in their warm embrace, that there were enough Nicaraguans who simply wanted peace and a chance to dig our country out of its ruins and put it back on the road to recovery to give us a victory. So I tried to unite the opposition by reaching out to all Nicaraguans.

The elections took place on the last Sunday of February 1990. When the official vote count was in, I learned *La Prensa* had indeed been wrong. My victory margin was only fifteen points, not the twenty points *La Prensa* had predicted.

But even before we could celebrate, our victory was in jeopardy. At 3 P.M. on February 25, President Carter asked Antonio to go to the building where the Supreme Electoral Council was located. Antonio was accompanied by Cristiana and my nephew Carlos Hurtado. Carter, Elliot Richardson, and Mariano Fiallos, the president of the Supreme

Electoral Council, said, "It's evident that the ink being used in some of the voting precincts is so thin it can be washed off with water. This could raise questions about the honesty of the electoral process." The observers had decided that if either of us wanted to nullify the elections and call for a new vote, it would be so.

In fact, the first person to cast doubt on the trustworthiness of the elections had been Virgilio Godoy, my running mate. At eight that morning he was already denouncing the elections as fraudulent. Lending no importance to his declarations, I said, "Fraud or no fraud, we are going to win." My concern was that our people would be discouraged from going to the voting precincts to cast their vote.

Carter told Antonio that Bayardo Arce, Daniel Ortega's campaign manager, was outside, waiting to know our answer. Antonio said he wanted to notify me immediately. But Carter said no. "If one of you decides, speaking on behalf of your candidate, that this thing needs to be canceled, we cancel it now."

Antonio shared my belief that we could win no matter what the Sandinistas did. So his decision was that we go forward with the elections. He feared that the Sandinistas had tampered with the ink deliberately so they could have an excuse to invalidate the elections.

Fortunately, at the same moment Bayardo Arce, also feeling victory was theirs, came in to say he wanted to allow the voting to proceed.

When I was informed of the situation I felt lucky to have a campaign manager who didn't flinch. It was a tough call for Antonio. In less than a minute he had to decide our fate. Three hours later, after making their own fast count, the FSLN knew that things weren't going their way.

At 8 P.M. a preliminary scrutiny of the vote count in Barrio Monseñor Lezcano, a middle-class suburb of Managua, revealed that I had a 2–1 lead over Ortega. We were also winning in Batahola Sur, which was a neighborhood of Sandinista military families. In the proletarian region of San Judas, Ortega was ahead, but by a small margin. I prevailed, however, even in the city of Masaya, which was a bastion of Sandinismo. Las Segovias, the northern province where Sandino did battle against the U.S. Marines in the 1930s, was also overwhelmingly in my favor. But it was when we carried Estelí, in the northern region, where the Sandinista army had had its bloodiest encounters with the Contras, that I knew for certain that what people wanted and had voted for was peace.

On the day of the election the Sandinistas had cut our telephone wires. So the source of most of our information was the international observers, foreign correspondents, and members of the diplomatic corps who were in continuous communication with our campaign directors.

By the time the first fifty thousand ballots were counted, a stunning pattern of victory for Violeta Chamorro had begun to emerge. What I had predicted was happening. What had seemed impossible had become a staggering reality for the FSLN to absorb. Just hours before, their only concern had been by what margin they would defeat me. Never did they doubt that they would win. Even the soldiers, who they had expected would vote unanimously for the FSLN, in the end cast thousands of votes for Violeta. Before the Sandinistas was irrefutable evidence that people had repudiated their totalitarian rule. There was only silence from the Supreme Electoral Council.

Aware that I was winning the election, President Carter apparently had been trying to get in touch with Daniel Ortega. Daniel and the other members of the Sandinista directorate were huddled behind closed doors trying to decide what their next course of action should be. But time had run out. Thousands of international observers and journalists who had come to witness their victory were anxiously lined up waiting for them to concede defeat. In effect, what the Sandinistas had achieved by indulging in their own delusions and relentless boasting was to summon the world as spectators to their own hanging. And now they had no choice but to proceed to tie the noose around their own necks.

I was advised that the circumstances warranted that I immediately assume the posture of a responsible and conscientious president-elect by calling my people to order. I assured them that I was already well aware of the risks of our victory. We were the new leaders of Nicaragua and had been constitutionally elected. But it was uncertain the army would afford such recognition. We would have to act prudently.

So from the start, we resisted every urge to embrace or dissolve into tears of joy. Instead we determined to apply ourselves rigorously to the task of managing a potentially explosive situation. Yet in my heart I felt this was also a golden opportunity to reject the long-held tradition in our country that called for the winners to banish the losers from the political scene and, if possible, send them into exile. I decided then to set a new trend and open the doors of Nicaraguan political life to everyone.

I gathered my children and their spouses together—Pedro Joaquín, Marta Lucía, Cristiana, Antonio—and I told them not to fear, there would be no splendid fiesta. Instead we would pray, thank the Lord for having gotten us so far, and, more important, ask for his light in the days that were to come.

Then we went out to address our young troop of campaign aides, who were gathered outside my room.

Clarisa Barrios, the niece who had been loyally by my side in all my trips in the Violemobile, came up to hug me. I thanked her and all the other young volunteers who had accompanied me on my treks to the farthest corners of the land and who had protected me from the stones that had been hurled at us by the violent mobs of Sandinista supporters.

"We are going to govern," I said. "Nicaragua will soon be a republic, and I want all of you to be a part of my presidency."

But my warmest and most poignant emotions I reserved for Cristiana and Antonio. Following Pedro's death and the shutdown of *La Prensa* and throughout the elections, they had become trusted and competent allies in the treacherous world of politics and power. They had combatted with me the intrigues and betrayals of some of the members of the UNO coalition. But most of all they shared with me an unspoken commitment to confront, as a team, the challenge of going against the tide of Nicaraguan history. Instead of overpowering the losers we would opt for reconciliation and pluralism. Instead of destroying those we defeated to govern only for ourselves, we would embrace all people in Nicaragua.

This had been the recurrent theme of my campaign, and it was what people had voted for. For me there was never any other way to rule Nicaragua. After all, I had two Sandinista children and I couldn't very well take a position that excluded them from participating in the rebirth of their country. I couldn't say, "Nicaragua is only for me and my supporters."

It was past midnight when Carter arrived in my home. I received him in my office, the room that held so many memories for me, the little study where Pedro had spent so much time talking with his political allies and where I had received Daniel to accept his apologies for closing

La Prensa. There, Carter briefed me on his talks with Ortega. He told me he had been with him at his campaign headquarters. He said Daniel was holed up with the members of the Sandinista National Directorate and had asked for more time before he could give assurances that he could "accept this defeat."

Then Carter addressed me as Madam President, which I recall sounded very odd to me because in my mind I was simply Violeta. And he told me he had impressed upon Ortega the importance of accepting the results of a democratic process that indicated the people's choice had been Violeta Chamorro. Carter and his wife, Rosalyn, I later learned, had sat with Ortega, sharing with him their own painful experience of electoral defeat. They told him that he didn't have the power of the presidency anymore but he could still find significant ways to contribute to his country. But Ortega had demurred. He had asked for more time to manage what he termed a "problematic situation that was spiraling out of his control." All that Ortega asked was that I abstain from making any statements and that our people cancel any plans for a celebration so as not to unduly provoke the ire of his followers.

The vice president, Virgilio Godoy, felt differently. He wanted to have a press conference and denounce what he felt was a ploy by the Sandinistas to alter the results of the final tabulation.

Carter looked at me and then asked what my desires were. My knowledge of the Sandinistas' perfidy gave me cause to consider Godoy's fears. But I reasoned that the international observers, who were not merely symbolic figures, would take steps to see the results were not tampered with. On the other hand, I felt we ran a greater danger in detonating the Sandinistas' fury. It could bring down upon us a civil war. After reflecting for a few moments I told Carter I was willing to wait. Perhaps it wasn't such an unreasonable request.

Then the ex-president, who in my view with his mediation was regaining the respect of all Nicaraguans, departed for Sandinista campaign headquarters to communicate my decision to Ortega.

Consequently I went on the air, not to claim my victory but to ask those who had voted for me to please remain at home and desist from expressing any joy but to save their exuberance instead for the hard work we had ahead of us. I spoke to them about the importance of not losing sight of our objective, which was not to celebrate a quick victory, but rather to forge a democratic national agenda in an environment of stability. I told them, "Peace is a process that we must now all work to achieve."

The rest of the evening, surrounded by friends and supporters at home, passed like a long and tedious vigil at the end of which might be a new dawn for Nicaragua. Sometime after midnight I gathered everyone together and we prayed. Then we sang the hymn of our republic, a song that had been until now replaced by the hymn of the Sandinistas.

The hours that followed were full of tension and anxiety. Jimmy Carter rushed from one camp to the other trying to mediate a peaceful transition.

But at Sandinista headquarters there existed no such resolve. I'm told defeat enraged Daniel Ortega. He called in the American public relations team he had hired to advise him, which had conducted extensive polling on his behalf. When he demanded an explanation for their inaccurate polls, the story goes, they told him the people of Nicaragua had lied. Then he called the more radical FSLN leaders and told them that they should refuse to cede the reins of government. Others were promising to sabotage our first days in government and to boycott all our legislative actions. The exceptions were those who argued for calm and a peaceful transference of power. It was these civic-minded Sandinistas that Carter's diplomacy depended on.

Desirée, my son Carlos Fernando's future wife, did not know that the Sandinistas had lost. She was counting votes at a barrio the Sandinistas had happened to win. She assumed this was the case throughout the country. Around 5 A.M. Desirée went to *Barricada* to meet up with Carlos Fernando. She saw my son's languid face, and because defeat was so far from her mind, without asking any questions simply concluded that the much-feared gringo invasion was coming. It wasn't until they were on their way home, that she discovered the truth.

"Haven't you heard?" he asked with annoyance. "We lost the elections by ten P.M."

"What!" she exclaimed loudly and broke down in tears. The pain and confusion my victory caused all the Sandinistas was enormous.

Then at 5:30 A.M. a gaunt President Ortega came on the air. Standing beside him, overcome with grief and anguish, were his comrade in arms and wife, Chayo. He delivered a brief and poignant speech in which, with a tremulous and raspy voice, he conceded his defeat. He committed to a peaceful transition and promised to cede his position as the government leader. But he added that he would take up a new role as leader of the opposition. They were words that in any other country would have been unexceptional. But in Nicaragua, where the Sandinistas had ruled so completely, his statements were nothing short of miraculous.

So on that sunny Monday morning, I was proud of our country. We had given the world an example of civic duty in an election in which 90 percent of the country had chosen to participate and which Carter would characterize as a solemn ceremony that had the "gravity of a mass." Together, we had belied all the negative misconceptions about us. At that moment I harbored only the deepest respect for the Sandinistas.

After Ortega's announcement I met with scores of foreign correspondents, and I said to them what I was destined to repeat many times later: "There will be no victors or vanquished in this emergent Nicaraguan democracy. Violeta Chamorro may be stubborn, but she is not vindictive. And her government will not produce exiles or political prisoners. There will be no confiscations. No left-out wing of civic opposition. But most important, there will be no more war, because the people have voted freely for peace."

That morning Ortega had experienced a brief period of contrition. But by noon he was back on the stump promising his followers that he would defend the conquest of the revolution. He said, "We will rule from below."

At 2 P.M. on the afternoon of February 26, Carter called Antonio and asked him to visit him at his hotel. He said, "Antonio, now the Sandinistas have accepted their defeat. It's a great thing. However, now it's important for you to establish some kind of communication with them."

Carter asked Antonio to meet with the Sandinistas, and Antonio accepted. Later that day Carter called Antonio and told him the meeting was set up for the next day at 4 P.M. at the Carter Center offices in Managua, in Barrio Bolonia.

Antonio and Alfredo César attended the meeting. (Later, when Alfredo realized that as a result of his participation in the talks, he would have to sign an accord—the Protocol of Transition—he withdrew from the talks. Alfredo never likes to appear to give his imprimatur to anything that might be politically damaging.)

➤ ➤

They arrived a little before four. They were waiting with Carter, Elliot Richardson, and João Baena Soares when, exactly on the hour, three *comandantes* appeared, Humberto Ortega, Joaquín Cuadra Lacayo, and Jaime Wheelock.

Carter said he understood that the Sandinistas had some concerns and that he thought it would be a good idea if we knew them so we could carry out a peaceful transition in Nicaragua.

Predictably, Humberto cited as his main preoccupation the existence of the Contras as an armed group of opposition. He said that as long as the Contras had not been disbanded and repatriated, they could not hand over power, because the rebels constituted a threat to them. He also wanted to know what would happen with the army.

Antonio told him that he believed he needn't have concerns about the Contras. The Contras' reason for existence was to achieve democracy. Now that we had won, we were going to work to achieve their disarmament. Antonio, however, made it quite clear that the Sandinistas couldn't make the Contras' demobilization a prerequisite for them to recognize the legitimacy of my government, because we were not the leaders of the Contras. But he assured them that we would work full-time on this problem until it was resolved.

With regard to the army and the police, Antonio pointed out that these were national institutions, not Sandinista, and that they should function independently from the party beginning with my first day in office.

Land reform and property confiscation were other issues we agreed to work out with the Sandinistas. At the end of the meeting, Carter suggested we form two transition teams, one for each side, so we could discuss things in detail and reach an agreement. Carter offered to return to Nicaragua if we thought he could be of help in the discussions. But we felt these issues needed to be resolved among us Nicaraguans.

I can never stress enough how crucial those first forty-eight hours were in assuring that discipline and order prevailed. But the triumph of prudence over madness and of humility over arrogance was not to last. The deep wounds that existed in the left and right would soon force the two sides into a confrontation, leaving me with the difficult task of being the arbiter in their bloody match.

Almost immediately the suspicions and accusations resurfaced in my own camp. After all, we were a hastily put together coalition of opposing interests. In the days after my election the UNO organization began to come unglued. I learned quickly what politics was really about. The only thing that really interests professional politicians is power—how to attain it, how to maintain it. There were few among the UNO coalition who agreed with the policy of reconciliation I proposed. In their anger, they accused me of making a covenant to cogovern with the Sandinistas.

In fact, they had believed so little in me as their candidate that, prior to the election, I've heard, it was commonly discussed, perhaps even with Daniel, what the conditions for the loser should be. It was said that if the FSLN won, they, to give the electoral process some badly needed credibility, would grant UNO 33 percent of the vote. And so, rather than ask for cabinet positions or for a diplomatic post, the leaders of the parties that formed the UNO coalition had decided to place themselves on the ballot as candidates for the legislature. With 33 percent of the vote, they would all be assured a seat. Alfredo César was the first one to do this, Elí Altamirano was the second, Doña Miriam Argüello was the third . . . and so on. In that fashion, even if we lost they still had a quota of power, a good salary, tax exemption, a vehicle for their use, and so forth.

I, on the other hand, had only made a covenant with God, and it was to act always in accordance with my conscience. Once I was elected the leader of my nation, I felt my responsibility was not to create more division but to find a way to cut across the fault lines in my country and work so we could prosper in peace as a democratic republic.

And I felt the only way to achieve this was to take a bipartisan approach to government. I could not ignore the fact that the Sandinistas had won 41 percent of the votes. This assured them a substantial number of representatives in the legislature. All they needed was just ten UNO votes to block any legislative agenda I proposed.

Furthermore, there was the issue of General Humberto Ortega as the head of the most powerful military organization in Central America. Should I replace him, or allow him to remain? How to reduce the size of the Sandinistas' mighty military organization, disarm their paramilitary troops, and disband their secret police without the cooperation of a respected FSLN leader was a dilemma I discussed a lot with Antonio in the days following my election.

Many in the UNO coalition suggested that as the eyes of the world were upon us, there was a unique opportunity to break apart the monolithic organization of the Sandinista People's Army (EPS). But I felt such an attitude was morally wrong and would serve only to perpetuate past errors.

In addition, there were my previously stated considerations regarding reforms to the army and disarming thousands of Sandinista civilians. I was convinced that to implement these changes we needed to have on our side Humberto.

In Poland and Chile the newly elected democratic governments had sought to forge change through a slow process of transformation that required the loyalty of the armed forces.

In both cases the new government had decided that incremental reforms had to be implemented with the full cooperation of the military, which in the midst of radical changes could help maintain stability and order in the country.

I felt our situation was no different. We needed, first, to achieve a measure of order and stability so that we could concentrate our energies on addressing Nicaragua's record unemployment, poverty, and fiscal deficits.

Still, there were many who disagreed with this line of thinking. All those who had been persecuted and oppressed and whose property had been expropriated could think only of vengeance. They argued for dismantling the Sandinista party and army. When I refused to fall into the old pattern of an eye for an eye, there was talk of betrayal and of backroom deals.

This talk was fueled by the discontent of some people in the UNO coalition, who believed that my nomination had been nothing more than symbolic. I was, in their opinion, no more than a figurehead, while they, in their infinite wisdom, would lead the country.

Predictably, these disaffected followers did not respond well when I thwarted their ambitions and did not name them to my cabinet. But I had my own ideas on how to govern, and I had my own priorities. My first order of business was to demilitarize Nicaragua.

I didn't need to study economics to understand that if we reduced the size of the army, we could cut back substantially on government spending. The armed forces, left as they were, consumed one third of our national budget. Nor did I need to be a psychologist to understand how people felt toward the military. For us it had become a symbol of oppression and part of our stormy past of brutal domination.

Thus, I resolved to abolish the draft, to reduce the armed forces from eighty-four thousand to fifteen thousand, to destroy the caches of arms that were stockpiled all over the country, and to place the military firmly under the jurisdiction of the executive power. Logically, I felt, this could best be accomplished with the full cooperation of General Ortega.

My next step, then, was to propose these measures to the leader of our armed forces. So in the days that followed my election, Antonio and I met with Humberto to discuss my vision for Nicaragua and the role we felt he could play in forging a better future for all our countrymen.

Right away he seemed to understand that the Sandinista People's Army could not continue to be the repressive arm of the party. It was equally clear to him that to stage a military coup was not advisable. After the recent U.S. invasion of Panama, the perception existed that the United States was willing to use force. Furthermore, Humberto agreed that we could not continue to plunge Nicaragua into civil war. Thus, it was essential that, parallel to the reduction of the army, there be a demobilization of the Contra resistance, still poised to attack from the Honduran border.

In my judgment, there was no one in the Sandinista movement who had more power and political influence than Humberto. Without his cooperation it would have been virtually impossible to depoliticize and shrink the army peacefully. In addition, by preserving the integrity of the armed forces I was signaling to army officials that they could collaborate with and trust my new government.

Agrarian reform was a thornier issue. The situation had the potential to sink the nation into a social and political quagmire that could only serve to bog down the peace process and the economic reactivation of the country. My belief was that to roll back what had been accomplished in a decade of socialism would involve taking away land from humble campesinos and giving it back to people who were perceived by the majority as a privileged class. Nevertheless, many unjust confiscations had been enacted in the name of the revolution; they needed to be reviewed and quite possibly revoked. But in the interest of peace, what had been deeded to the poor or organized under cooperatives needed to be respected. But properties that were under the control of an anonymous state enterprise would be returned or privatized. Thirty days later the accords we discussed became the basis of the Protocol of Transition.

What we were trying to do was to make the Sandinistas commit themselves to the transition process my government was initiating on three fronts: we were moving from war to peace, from a totalitarian system to a liberal, pluralistic democracy, and from a centralized economy to a free market. These were changes we had to effect together, as Nicaraguans, gently and without foreign intervention or widespread domestic instability. This was our dream.

Chapter Thirteen

DURING THE CAMPAIGN I KNEW THAT WE would win. If the Berlin Wall could fall, why not the Sandinistas? And what haven't we achieved in these last six years! Things have been different for so long, Nicaraguans have forgotten what it was like before —the shortages, the lines, the worthless currency, the militarization, and that oppressive, ever-present Sandinista power, which was always on the attack.

I won't go into a tedious accounting of everything we've done or tell you of all the obstacles we faced. But it has been extremely hard to carry out the needed changes amidst the betrayals of all those who claimed to be our allies and who instead associated themselves with the Sandinistas to sabotage my legislative agenda.

The state of the nation was much worse than I had ever imagined. I received a country plagued by poverty and deeply polarized by hate. Contras and Sandinistas were on the alert, ready to take up arms. The first thing we needed to do was to bring order to the country.

That objective in itself was a formidable task. Without wishing to sound in any way superior to others, I can say with certainty that few people would have assumed the daunting responsibility of governing a country like Nicaragua. But I had a dream of democracy that I wanted to see realized. I refused to be intimidated. Those who were not by my side living through the difficulties don't understand what an enormous challenge it was.

After its defeat, the Sandinista party was like a wounded animal thrashing from the pain of its injuries and wreaking destruction in its path. As a matter of routine the Sandinistas staged mass public demonstrations that dissolved into riots in which they vandalized half the country. These were people who took pleasure in spreading panic and who were subversive of civil authority. Their behavior only added to the grievous conditions that already existed in the country. The voices of a few party moderates could be heard cautioning them against a possible backlash from the people for their actions. At the same time, as the mother of two idealistic Sandinistas, I understood full well that it would be unfair to define all of the FSLN on the basis of the actions of a handful of leaders. Not everyone in the movement was greedy and avid for command. There were many young revolutionaries who had not committed crimes or injustices and were in modest positions of state employment.

Many of them could be seen on the streets, dazed, wandering about in a state of bewilderment as they struggled to understand why the people (the supposed beneficiaries of the revolution) had voted to overturn the power of the FSLN. I felt that for these persons, a harsh reality awaited.

To these legions of disillusioned idealists could be added the hordes of internationalists, Sandinistas in sandals (or *sandalistas*) who had arrived in our country to experience the romanticism of a Marxist revolution. They were not quaint political hippies but earnest collaborators in what they believed was an emergent communist utopia.

All of them had their bitter disappointment etched on their young faces and seemed confused by what appeared to be a decisive repudiation of the Sandinistas.

A few, like the American Benjamin Linder, who was helping to build an electrical plant in Jinotega, were killed in cross fire between the EPS army and the Contras even before the election.

In truth, for every Sandinista who refused to acknowledge defeat there was another struggling to accept it. For those people I had great sympathy, and I wanted to contribute to their speedy adjustment.

So when Daniel Ortega in his postelectoral cordiality asked through my son Carlos Fernando to visit me in my home for the simple purpose, as he said, of paying his respects and congratulating me on my triumph, I welcomed him, hoping our meeting would convey the message that the hour had arrived for winners and losers to give each other a patriotic embrace.

At least that's the way I viewed things. But less conciliatory Nicaraguans chose to interpret it as a summit meeting in which Daniel and I divided among ourselves "quotas of power." Veteran politicians like Virgilio Godoy advanced this notion. They had a winner-takes-all mentality that I felt undermined our democratic objectives. I wanted to move away from that philosophy. In both movements, I felt, there were people who needed to be recognized for their courage, idealism, and patriotism. I refused to support the notion that those on the left were all villains and those on the right were heroes. In my view, misdeeds had been done on both sides.

As good mothers often do, I saw my job as bringing harmony and equilibrium back to the Nicaraguan family. I don't mean this facetiously. Others have said this before me. In fact I once read an article titled "Does Peace Have the Face of a Woman?" Essentially what it said was that a woman's experience as a mother makes her uniquely qualified to govern. Accustomed to administering family relations on a day-to-day basis, a mother is more apt to understand the great paradox of human emotions; for instance, that it is perfectly possible for people to behave in good *or* evil ways, depending on what level of hostility exists in the environment. Thus, I have tried to condemn not individuals but their actions. And I have worked to alter the environment that is a factor in generating evil deeds.

I suppose that's why when I saw Daniel, accompanied by my son Carlos Fernando, I followed my natural impulse to hug Daniel, as I did my own son. As he stepped into the intimacy of my front garden, he stopped to admire the flowers.

It's a practical thing, I told him. "It saves me the expense of buying the flowers that I take each week to Pedro's tomb. Plus, it gives me more privacy and protection. Though my greatest protection is God and the Virgin of Guadalupe," I said, pointing to the statue at the entrance.

I built the garden after the Sandinista *turbas* had come to paint my walls and had thrown rocks at my windows. At first it was just an unattractive chain-link fence. Afterward I planted the Santa Marta vine that now covers the fence with purple blossoms. Last I added the flowerpots.

Before entering the house I showed Daniel the ceramic tiles with my initials. "As you can see," I said, "they are *V.B.Ch.* because I am Violeta Barrios de Chamorro. And not, as it was said during the campaign, simply Violeta Barrios."

I told him, "I put them there so that my people will not be deceived.

I want them to know exactly who I am, the wife of their martyred hero, Pedro Joaquín Chamorro Cardenal."

Once inside, Daniel broke down in tears. I hugged him and said, "My muchacho, it's all right." Then I invited him to sit in a rocker by my side.

During the campaign Daniel had adopted the posture of a rock star. But now, as we sat side by side, I was struck by his obvious melancholy. The reversal of his political fortunes had apparently caused him to spend many sleepless nights.

I realized that I had before me a man who because of his own misguided behavior was but a shadow of his former self. Gone was the luster of the young revolutionary who had ridden into power less than a decade ago. Gone was the proud bearing of the leader who, until recently, had been hailed by his followers like Caesar.

As we began our conversation, somebody entered the room to tell me former president Ronald Reagan was on the line. At first I thought it was a joke, and went on talking. A little while later the same person came back to tell me President Reagan was still waiting on the line.

Hurriedly I excused myself and went to take the call. I had already received a telegram from the ex-president congratulating me for my and Nicaragua's triumph over dictatorship. But until that day, I had never had the opportunity to speak directly to Mr. Reagan.

From lack of practice, my English was not so good. So we spoke through an interpreter. But I could understand everything. He told me of the pleasure he felt at the success of my campaign, and he said that February 25 had been a blessed day for democracy.

The irony of it, I thought. Here I was speaking to Ronald Reagan while I had Daniel Ortega waiting in my office. For most of the 1980s these two men had stubbornly refused to meet and discuss a peaceful solution for Nicaragua. With their dogmatic attitude toward resolving the conflict, President Reagan and Daniel had added another bloody chapter to our history. Neither man had won. The biggest loser was Nicaragua. Had I known Ronald Reagan then, I could have been a better advocate for peace. Beginning in 1987, after I regained control of *La Prensa,* Cristiana and I as a matter of policy had opposed the armed struggle and favored the civic struggle being waged from within. From the pages of our newspaper we had lauded as heroes as yet unknown politicians like Miriam Argüello, one of the many who were repressed and jailed at a UNO rally in Nandaime. We followed this policy at great political cost. There were many within the opposition whose fondest dream was to have the U.S. Marines march into Managua and seize the bunker on the hill of Tiscapa, expelling the Sandinistas from Nicaragua forever. Within my own family I was criticized for taking the middle road—from the left by Carlos Fernando and Claudia, and from the right by Pedro Joaquín.

Many books have been written about Reagan's foreign policy toward Nicaragua. I don't have much to add, except that I don't believe the Contra war went a long way in furthering the democratic cause. Perhaps it may even have hindered democracy, because the Sandinistas tightened their grip on all of us, restricting political dissent, strangling the civic opposition, and sinking us deeper into poverty.

I do agree with President Reagan that among the Contras there were many freedom fighters, humble and honest campesinos who had joined the ranks of the resistance because they felt that all hope for a reasonable dialogue had been dashed. Lamentably, the hardening of positions also served to increase the resentment and the desire for revenge in the hearts of many Nicaraguans.

The Sandinistas laid all of the burden of guilt for the war on Ronald Reagan. But it was their love of power that made them want to fight on for as long as they had ammunition. The Soviets are to blame, as well, for continuously supplying them with arms. But it is Fidel Castro whom I hold most responsible. He made the Sandinistas, and once they were in power he used them as a springboard onto the American continent. He advised them on the hard-line polices they used to perpetuate their power. He sent General Ochoa and his troops (Ochoa fought in Angola) to help Humberto Ortega design a new and more effective military strategy in our country. He is to blame for the thousands of boys who died in Nicaragua.

Fortunately, now that dark past is behind us. The telephone call from President Reagan, which had been preceded by one from President Bush, was the beginning of good relations between our countries.

The elections proved that the will of most voters was to say no to American intervention, no to the communists, no to the madness of war. What people wanted was for reason and common sense to rule the day, two things that, unfortunately, among politicians, are about as common as alien beings.

And so it has taken patience and perseverance to transform a political culture such as ours. Changing Nicaragua will take at least a generation. Even this may be too optimistic a prediction, given our history and current behavior. To bring about a transformation I had to destroy the confrontational stereotypes with my own attitudes.

I returned to my meeting with Daniel having decided that whatever this man and the other Sandinistas had done to me, I could not allow my anger to taint the cordial civility of our relations. They deserved a second chance. I assured Daniel that he had nothing to fear from me, and that my hope was that he would use his influence to help Nicaragua. No one doubted that Daniel controlled the Sandinista masses.

But in the two months that elapsed between the February elections and my inauguration in April, I came to understand a lot about the perfidy of politicians. Soon after we met, in an apparent change of heart, Daniel abandoned his position of contrite and civic-minded statesmanship. In the last days of his presidency, instead of taking the higher ground as Humberto tried to do, Daniel sank deeper and deeper into error.

Reports were coming in that he was encouraging the looting of every nook and cranny of the government, including taking home televisions, cars, furniture. What they could not carry the Sandinistas deeded to themselves under false titles. Overnight, a huge portion of Nicaragua was privatized to a group of Sandinistas.

Then, on a higher level of pilferage, Daniel and his crony Sergio Ramírez and the legal eagles he had in congress were rapidly issuing decrees to ensure that in the end they could retain as much power as possible, if not the government itself. With a majority of the vote we could overturn later what they had done. (But Alfredo César was to split the UNO vote for his own gain, making this impossible.)

The Sandinista vandalism reached such heights that the entire period was dubbed by *La Prensa* the piñata, because it reminded us all of the fiestas in which children take turns whacking the piñata with a stick until it breaks and they scramble to the floor to gather the booty.

The abuses I witnessed in those sixty days prior to my inaugural were in stark contrast to the way my husband, Pedro, had lived his life. Pedro was a true disciple of Christ. Pedro adhered to the principle that we must "do unto others as we would have others do unto us." In Pedro's political thinking, "others" meant the people of Nicaragua.

So, in spite of the tension, I resolved to go forward with my plan to reform Nicaragua so that it could be, as Pedro and I had dreamed it, pluralistic and democratic.

But a dream is never what you think it will be. Many things happen along the way that change it.

With only about ten days left before the inauguration, Daniel had not granted permission for the ceremony to take place at the site that I had chosen. Everyone was in a quandary about what to do. Then the summit meeting of the Central American presidents was held in Montelimar, Somoza's old sugar plantation, which the Sandinistas had reportedly spent $30 million to turn into a resort hotel. A luncheon with the presidents was organized in La Casona on the hill, Somoza's old residence to which I and the Cardinal were invited. So I went on my crutches, *taca-taca-taca,* down the hall to the room where these senior statesmen were gathered. I was seated next to Oscar Arias of Costa Rica. I wasn't eating. At one point during the luncheon Oscar Arias turned to me. "Violeta, where is the inaugural going to be?"

"Well, I don't know yet. The date is getting near, but you know these people"—I was gesturing toward Daniel at the far end—"don't want to give us anything." Daniel cackled, "Ja ja," but I went on. "You know, I've tried to get permission to use the stadium. But they've offered me an enclosed space that can fit only a select few. I want all the people of Nicaragua to see what an inauguration can be like in Nicaragua. I'm sixty and I've never seen one."

Oscar Arias, Nobel peace laureate, said to Daniel, "What can we do to resolve this?" Careful not to reveal that he had been the one holding up plans for the inaugural, Daniel said, "I'll tell Sergio." But I said, "Let's send for Sergio right now, or else there won't be an inaugural." When Sergio appeared, Daniel said to him, "See to it." It was that simple.

On April 24, while Antonio was putting the finishing touches on the next day's inaugural speech, the desertions from my cabinet had already begun. Gilberto Cuadra, appointed minister of construction, and Jaime Cuadra, minister of agriculture, were dead set against Humberto's remaining in charge of the army.

As this was happening, the officers in congress were being voted on.

As expected, Miriam Argüello was elected president. But after that, a rebel faction in the UNO emerged to join with the Sandinistas to form a power bloc. Although it had been agreed that the secretary should be Jaime Bonilla, Alfredo César was instead proposed. With the Sandinista vote he was elected. The same phenomenon happened with the four remaining offices. After that day, the UNO vote in congress was split.

Alfredo maintained the allegiance of his bloc until the day he began to campaign against U.S. aid for Nicaragua, at which time he was expelled from his party.

When Alfredo was doing his mischief in parliament, Antonio and I were busy dealing with more important issues, negotiating with the Sandinista government the transfer of power and with Humberto the situation of the army.

It was resolving the latter issue that concerned me the most because politicians are slippery fish, like the *guarinas* that swim in the waters of the Great Lake Nicaragua. I needed Humberto's assurance that the army would become depoliticized and that he would respect my government and help me forward my agenda. So on the eve of my inauguration I met with Humberto once more to make sure that we had a deal to rebuild our country together and to be certain he understood what his role was to be.

Right away I told him that in spite of the opposition I was facing, I believed we could work together, but that if he did not keep his word to respect the constitution and participate fully in my program of government, he would have no future in Nicaragua because he and his brother were personae non gratae. No one believed in them. Their past deeds and betrayals had destroyed their credibility. I made him see that this was his last chance to regain the trust of the Nicaraguan people. He gave me his word.

History would prove me right.

On April 25, 1990, I awoke with the first light of morning. Anita brought me my breakfast of tea and bread. The house was deserted. The small troop of campaign aides and clerical assistants that for the past months had moved tirelessly through my home at all hours of the day, running around holding meetings and conducting interviews that could further our democratic cause, were all gone. Pedro Joaquín and Marta Lucía were asleep in one room; Claudia Lucía, who had come specially for my inauguration, stayed with a brother of Edmundo's and so was not there that morning.

The silence in the house put me in a pensive mood. I dwelt on the significance of the moment. For the first time in our history a duly elected civilian president was to receive the authority of government from a military group that had achieved power through an armed revolt. It was an important event in our lives. On that day we were agreeing to give back to the people the power to elect their leaders. For this I felt the Sandinistas had to be commended. However, when I read all the newspapers—*La Prensa, Barricada, Nuevo Diario*—except for *La Prensa* they were predicting my presidency would not last. The FSLN, they said, promises to govern from below. In Sandinista Morse code this meant, "We are going to sabotage her government."

Other stories said that the Sandinistas had pledged to defend the advances of the revolution. This was a veiled threat against any legislative proposal intended to undo the piñata.

My reading was interrupted at 9 A.M. by Cristiana and Clarisa Barrios, my late brother Raúl's daughter. They were surprised to find that I hadn't begun dressing. I had not yet chosen what I wanted to wear that morning. I'm not one who spends a lot of time thinking about my wardrobe. But I know the importance of symbolism and the value of making the right gestures. So on that day I wanted to give my clothing careful thought. I had already decided my dress should be white, the color of the garments worn to receive the sacraments, because it best symbolized the unblemished character I wanted to impart to my presidency. In addition, I felt it would reflect the blessed holiness with which I viewed our political crusade as we began a new era of democratic reordering and national reconciliation.

My confusion lay on whether to wear one of the dresses that famous designers such as Oscar de la Renta had sent me as gifts. That morning I decided that as much as I appreciated their offerings, to wear one of their dresses was to reject Aurorita Cárdenas, my loyal friend in Houston who buys some of my clothes. She knows my taste—simple, pretty, and inexpensive. It was one of her suits that I ultimately selected. As my only accessory I wore an antique cross my grandmother had given me.

When my nephew Carlos Hurtado arrived, we discussed the car I should go in. There was some concern about safety; some thought that I should be in something that gave me protection. No one was certain how the Sandinista *turbas* would behave. But I told Carlos I wanted to ride in my "convertible," the Violemobile, so people could see me as I had campaigned, fearing nothing. When you have already lived the worst day of your life, nothing can frighten you. Carlos and Antonio insisted that I go as far as the stadium in a covered car and that I switch when we got there.

I emerged from my home in Las Palmas and was immediately encircled by hordes of reporters, bodyguards, and advisers, all of whom had become part of my permanent entourage. I confess that being the object of so much attention had become a nightmare for me. It deprived me of my freedom to wander the streets like a private citizen. However, it was something I could not run away from once my political life began.

Thus, I determined to cope with my new situation with great humor, candor, and patience, especially in my dealings with the foreign correspondents who were constantly parked outside my door. I understood that, like the Sandinistas, they were stunned by the election results and needed to comprehend for themselves and for their readers "the great mystery" behind Doña Violeta's victory.

But my patience was stretched to the limit when they asked me questions like "Do you consider yourself a Margaret Thatcher, a Benazir Bhutto, or a Corazon Aquino?" To these senseless queries I would respond that, though I liked and respected all these women very much, I didn't think I was like any of them. To begin with, I lived in Nicaragua, not Great Britain, Pakistan, or the Philippines. Mrs. Aquino and I did have one common link: the fact that both our husbands had paid with their lives for their love of country.

Sometimes the questions took a feminist turn. Did I attach great significance to the fact that, as of late, there seemed to be more female world leaders? Did it herald a new era of feminine dominion in our planet? That question should be asked when the list includes twenty or forty women in the world who are prime ministers, presidents, or chiefs of state, not when there are but a paltry few. Indeed, it never occurred to me that my election could be read as part of a growing trend toward matriarchy in the halls of power. I have always felt that my candidacy was a product of my circumstances, which I embraced wholeheartedly so Pedro and Nicaragua could triumph through me.

But what I could not endure was when I had to submit to their conventional wisdom, particularly when they patronized me. On the morning of the inauguration, one of the correspondents had the audacity to suggest that my reliance on God and Pedro was excessive and could not possibly see me through my presidency.

It annoyed me no end that they had not understood that, though my faith in God gave me strength and Pedro's ideals inspired my leadership, my administration had other things to offer. I would point to my loyal cadre of assistants, who in addition to being courageous and honest possessed great intelligence and excellent academic and professional credentials, which I felt certain could lift Nicaragua from the ruins my "experienced predecessors" had left it in. Like any president I would rely on my trusted advisers and staff. "But," I added, "without leadership, ideals, and a high moral component, we will inevitably go astray."

And so I entered the Estadio Nacional aboard the Violemobile confronted with the enormous task of bringing peace to my war-torn country. Far from being dazzled by my victory, I was concerned about whether our many problems would make Nicaragua an impossible country to govern. I knew that for years to come my life was destined to be a constant struggle, in which there would be only rare instances of harmony. Chief among my concerns that day were the political fissures that were ripping our nation apart.

It was a phenomenon that was plainly discernible in the way the bleachers of the stadium appeared to be divided down the middle. On one side sat the ecstatic crowds of those who had voted for Violeta, and on the other the boisterous spectators of the FSLN. Yet I realized on that occasion that as the newly elected leader, in an invincible way I was bonded to friends and foes alike.

When the Violemobile stopped in front of the speakers' platform my children were waiting for me to give me their support. I remember thinking how fortunate I was to have such positive relationships with them in spite of our different political allegiances. Even during the dark years of Sandinista oppression, when tolerance was so difficult to attain, they never stopped coming home to share a meal with me and inquire about my health.

Away from my house, they often expressed opinions and acted in ways that would unavoidably hurt me. But Pedro and I wanted them to be this way, free and independent. We believed that we should allow their personalities to develop unhindered by our own prejudices and opinions, while we fostered in them feelings of love and respect for one another. The diversity and unity we achieved within the nucleus of our home would translate, on a national level, into pluralism and democracy.

For that reason, I had not found it surprising when Claudia announced she was coming home for my inauguration. At the time she was living with Mundo—Edmundo Jarquín—in Spain, where he was the Sandinistas' ambassador. The day she arrived we all gathered in my home and opened a bottle of champagne. Carlos Fernando was also present, though his newspaper had vilified my campaign. Both of my Sandinista children understood that, like their father before me, I felt it was my duty to fight the yoke of oppression, whether it be Somoza's or the Sandinistas'.

Claudia's presence at the podium that day strengthened my resolve to work for unity at a time when everyone wanted to act only in their own best interest or in accordance with their raging hearts.

I wondered, as I stepped up to the platform to receive the blue ribbon of the presidential sash, whether I was reaching for an impossible dream, for I could not ignore the culture of our country, which made it easier for men to succumb to greed and the lust for power rather than to do their patriotic duty.

With a mixture of anxiety and joy, I greeted all Nicaraguans without exception. And I congratulated them for joining me at "our democratic fiesta," which I said had been made possible "not by the firing of cannons but by the casting of votes."

I spoke to them as "friends, compatriots, and allies" and told them of my resolve to lead us away from greed and the "raw struggle for power" that had been consuming us for centuries. I reminded them of our dream of becoming a democracy, which, until their "vote of conscience," had remained an impossibility because of the vulgar appetites of our military leaders, who were incapable of serving their country because they preferred, instead, to serve themselves.

And those who chose to persevere in our quest for freedom and equality, such as Pedro, had been exiled, kidnapped, assassinated, or imprisoned. "Lamentably," I said to them, "we would win the war but always lose the struggle."

Until that morning, I could not help wondering if Pedro's death had been for naught. But as I looked into the jubilant faces of my people, I knew that the blood he had spilled from his martyred body was giving rise to the seeds of a new nation.

And just as Pedro had told me so many times before, I repeated to them: "There cannot be sovereignty without peace; no sovereignty without liberty." But to have liberty, I said, you must respect the "rule of the law, other people's morals and opinions and private property as well."

Then, as a symbol of reconciliation, I held out my hand to every one of my compatriots and declared a general amnesty for all. And I added that from that day forward I wanted us all to put down our guns and lay aside our partisan politics so that we could begin the difficult task of rebuilding Nicaragua.

Standing before a delirious and exuberant crowd, I explained in essence my plan of government, beginning with what I knew would be unpopular but necessary: my intention to keep Humberto Ortega as head of the army.

Conscious of the resistance with which my announcement would be met, I elaborated on my decision and explained that I felt the only way to govern Nicaragua was to break the vicious cycle of vengeance that was characteristic of all the politicians in our country. I appealed to their "noble and patriotic hearts" and asked them to help me "rescue Nicaragua from the jaws of defeat." I reminded them that as Nicaraguans we were all brothers and sisters, and on those grounds we should sweep away our political culture of patronage and punishment, put aside our ideological differences, and focus on those issues that unite us. And I promised them they would discover that reconciliation is more gratifying than victory.

As I looked around me on the podium and beyond I could tell there were many who were willing to be my collaborators.

Yet there were some who had already made it plain they would oppose me—and others who, I knew, would simply pack their bags and go elsewhere because they did not agree with my policies.

But I was prepared for this reaction. My decision not to force the resignation of General Ortega had already caused desertions from my own cabinet. Thus, I was aware that my policy of reconciliation would not encompass all Nicaraguans, only those who truly desired to "serve our country more than they wished to serve themselves."

I realize that in developed democracies, where people have liberty, there are no such dilemmas. A system of checks and balances always guarantees a peaceful transition and the ability to renew government at will. But in our Latin American cultures, things are very different. Usually a particular family or a group monopolizes authority. They perpetuate themselves endlessly, as if it were a simple issue of family patrimony, something to be inherited. My dream was to lift us, the heirs of an imperfect legacy, above the mistakes of our political heritage, and to create a democracy where a balance of power exists.

To achieve this, I said, we must "substitute our culture of confrontation with one of tolerance and a love for peace." Our society of warriors we must domesticate and turn into judicious men of letters.

Finally, I said, my dream is that if we accomplish the reforms I would propose, my presidential sash will one day be passed to a duly elected democratic successor, a tradition that I hope will go on for centuries so that Nicaragua can, at last, be a republic.

I urged everyone to take on the "national identity" that in his works our great poet Rubén Darío described. There, I felt, was the key to our success. Pride and unity of purpose were what we needed to rebuild Nicaragua and convert it into a country where there would never again be a need for generals. And in this endeavor will lie our power.

Chapter Fourteen

PEOPLE HAD VOTED FOR CHANGE, BUT A transition period in which to heal our wounds was necessary to achieve political equilibrium. So the first twelve months of my government were dedicated to bringing peace to the country.

Before the inauguration, all my efforts had been geared toward disarming the Contras. We had met with the Contras' chief commanders in Honduras. Their mission was accomplished, and now they could all go back to a peaceful and civic life. We explained that now it was my job to work for democracy. As a result of these talks they signed a letter of intent stating that they would demobilize by June. This was only the beginning of what would become a lengthy process of persuading the Contras to lay down their arms.

Now the challenge for us was to overcome the military, judicial, and trade-union influence over the government and the economy.

At the Ministry of Interior, Carlos Hurtado replaced Tomás Borge. As one of my first acts of government, I asked Carlos to instruct the ministry's employees that from now on every visitor be addressed as "Mr." or "Mrs.," and not "Comrade" as had become the custom. Among themselves they were to address one another by rank. The green military uniform of the police, we decided, would be exchanged for a blue uniform that had the colors of the Nicaraguan flag. We felt this would give policemen a more civic presence. Even the building that housed the police received a makeover. A thick cover of white paint went over the front of the building to cover the inscription that read: *Ministry of Interior—Guardians of the People's Happiness.*

In its place we painted simply *Ministry of Government.* The police, we decided, would now be called National Police, not Sandinista Police.

These changes were not as innocuous as they sound. Though the change of uniform and name was an imposed regulation that did not yet reflect their inner feelings, in time, I was certain, the newly anointed National Police would identify with these symbols and take possession of its new role as civic-minded enforcer of the nation's laws.

Soon after I assumed office, Daniel Ortega, the man who had been president for an entire decade, turned into a black-shirted party boss with a red bandana around his neck as he called thousands of Sandinista militants to defend the revolution. He demanded the Contras disarm by their deadline, June 1990. "If not," he threatened, "it will be the people with their arms who will see to their disbandment."

Furthermore, it had come to my attention that Daniel, in the previous two months, had seen to it that hundreds of public enterprises were privatized overnight to anonymous corporations whose executives were former Sandinista cabinet members.

What was already a critical situation had deteriorated even more as a result of the Sandinistas' abuses in their last sixty days of power.

Those who had portrayed themselves as opponents of private property had appropriated huge chunks of Nicaragua's patrimony. Hundreds of party leaders now hold title to thousands of acres of valuable farmland and to the most luxurious residences in Managua. To give a socialist patina to their endeavor, the Sandinistas gave tiny plots of land to the poor.

In the state coffers Daniel left me $3 million to administer the country. I concluded that these people weren't the young idealists who had marched into Managua a decade before to build a better Nicaragua. They were no better than Somoza.

Daniel had always been a talker, but since being tossed from office in a free election, he had taken to the airwaves with an unbridled passion that revealed a deep insecurity and a need to treat his bruised ego. It was also evident that he was a man whose pettiness had no limits. Though it exacted a great price on the country for us to have to replace all the assets and inventory the Sandinistas had stolen, it gave him great satisfaction to leave me nothing with which to govern.

To deal with the labor disputes caused by rampant inflation, my government began talks with the labor leaders. The salary adjustments they requested were granted to them, and everyone returned to work. But I sensed this would be only a temporary settlement. The economic crisis required that we implement a set of even tougher measures than what was originally contemplated. This, I felt, would become an opportunity for Daniel to unchain a mass reaction among his people.

Fully aware that more trouble lay ahead, my son-in-law Antonio and I tried to resolve the Contra problem as quickly as possible. Throughout the month of May we were in constant dialogue with the top brass of the Contra army and Sandinista leaders.

In previous conversations Humberto had said that he wanted us to allow him to come aboard the new train, the train of peace and reconciliation. In return, we asked him to try to exert a positive influence on Daniel. His view was that once the Contras were disarmed, things would change.

But negotiation with the Contras was a slow-moving process. They were understandably concerned with their personal security. We assured them that the government would guarantee their personal safety and we signed an agreement in which they expressed a desire to disarm.

That was the beginning of the peace process. Many more meetings came after that, in which we discussed the specifics of the demilitarization process. Throughout the negotiations there was a great deal of bad faith. Progress was constantly stymied by recriminations. The ferocious and savage conduct of a small group of FSLN members wreaked havoc on the peace process and increased the loathing each group felt for the other. Both sides were guilty of sitting at the negotiating table and committing to terms and conditions they later felt free to break.

So when the Contras were informed of my decision to keep Humberto as head of the army, they told me bluntly, "There can be no reconciliation with General Ortega commanding the military. We refuse to disarm."

But I did not lose hope. It was only a matter of time, I thought, before the rage both parties felt would dissipate and be replaced by a more reasonable attitude.

Antonio met with as many commanders as possible and tried to convince them of the gravity of their circumstances. He made them see that the humanitarian aid they were receiving was due to expire, and that a resolution had to be found before they were left homeless, hungry, and exposed to attacks from renegade elements of the FSLN.

The first group of Contras laid down their arms on May 8, 1990. We had expected disarmament to proceed at a rhythm of 150 to 200 men per day. But after the first two days, in which a total of 120 men disarmed, it became clear that our calculations were way off the mark. Israel Galeano, known among the Contras as Comandante Franklyn, whom I had appointed as a mediator, explained that it was hard to persuade his men to disarm because nothing definite had been decided by the commission in charge of delineating the areas in which to locate the development zones for the Contras. The Contras also expressed a desire to have their own medical centers and schools.

As if we were planning an independent state within the country, we assigned sixteen thousand square kilometers to the Contras, the entire Department of the Río San Juan and part of Zelaya South. Franklyn assured us that approximately half of the twenty-three thousand Contras would opt to establish themselves in the development zones, while the other half would choose to return to their old homes. This settlement would consume in the first year almost $50 million of the $300 million in aid the United States had granted us, much more than any of us had imagined. But I understood it was important for these men to know that when they traded in their swords for plowshares, their security was assured.

On May 10, during this period of intense negotiations, I had to go abroad on my first presidential trip, to the inauguration of Costa Rica's new president, Rafael Angel Calderón Fourniere. Rafael and I are blood relatives twice over. Our great-grandfathers were first cousins on the Barrios side and on the Muñoz side. He was born in Diriamba, Nicaragua. His father, Rafael Angel Calderón Guardia, arrived in Costa Rica as an exile. In time he applied for citizenship for his family.

The newspapers made much of the fact that I left Antonio in charge while I was away. By then it was common knowledge that my vice president, who had more experience in government than I, had publicly disagreed with the compromises I was making in my desire to bring peace to our country.

Though I had tried to make amends with Don Virgilio, a politician in the old style who is confrontational and at times vituperative, it was evident that he and I were not like-minded colleagues. His disloyalty to me had been proven in the many interviews in which he had accused my administration of cogoverning with the Sandinistas. Don Virgilio, breaking with the traditional role of vice presidents the world over, had decided to oppose me from within my administration. Naturally, I felt I could not leave him in charge of my government. It was Antonio, whom I most trusted to carry out my agenda exactly as I envisioned it, who had to be left in command.

Many people have resented the degree to which I have assigned matters to Antonio. But I think we complemented each other perfectly. As a mature woman I provided the pacifying skills, the sensibility, the political instincts. And he, as an engineer and a businessman, trained at Georgia Tech and the Massachusetts Institute of Technology, had an immediate grasp of what needed to be done to rescue Nicaragua from an accelerating descent into poverty.

I think what the UNO politicians liked least about Antonio was that, unlike them, he is not the kind of man whose actions are fueled by a desire to please a roomful of people. He likes to define views clearly and in no uncertain terms, regardless of the political consequences. As minister of government he wanted to use the power of office to lead, to challenge, to effect big reforms for the nation's benefit. But his job had a political dimension that required from him a certain degree of artifice, which Antonio loathes.

During the campaign the UNO leaders tried to remove him as my campaign manager, against my will. They intended to run my campaign as a committee, and if we won, run the presidency too. But Antonio made it clear that campaigns that succeed are run like businesses, with one person at the top making all the important decisions and delegating to others the various tasks.

Having seen during the Sandinista years the effects of central-committee planning, I agreed entirely with Antonio. And that's the way I wanted to run my presidency too, no matter who disagreed with me.

I had decided that reconciliation was the course to take. It was a life-or-death issue for my country. My popularity with Don Virgilio, the UNO, or even the nation was a trivial issue in the balance. I would find the strength to bear the responsibility for what I felt ought to be done.

The pacification that Contadora and Esquipulas I and II had not been able to resolve in five years of negotiations, I was expected to resolve in my first thirty days in office.

At the end of May the Sandinista labor organizations went on strike again. To pressure us, government workers took over all state offices, including the Central Bank of Nicaragua. The Ministry of Communications cut off service. The Water Department did the same. Electrical power was maintained by the Nicaraguan Institute of Energy, but all administrative functions were suspended. No railroads or buses were operating. The airport was barely functioning. Managua was paralyzed.

To sabotage my government the Sandinistas had left every state employee, from middle management down, poised to resist the new administration under the pretext that they wanted an increase in wages or improved working conditions. Within the administrative structure of the country they had left intact the basis for the continuation of Sandinista power. Their plan was to wage a bureaucratic and administrative war against the economy until my government collapsed.

It was an intimidating scenario. But I carry with me the image of Pedro's body, martyred like that of Jesus Christ, the image of the blood Pedro shed to redeem Nicaragua—and that signals to me the path to take to achieve dignity for our country. I had accepted Pedro's death long ago as a testimony to the kind of commitment to the fatherland that all of us who want a free and democratic Nicaragua must have. So I wasn't going to let a few hoodlums deter me from carrying out my promise to the Nicaraguan people. Only death could stop me. In addition, I felt that the Sandinistas, though rowdy and aggressive, were not the majority of Nicaraguans.

Well aware of the consequences, I questioned the legality of the twenty-two laws the Sandinista-controlled legislature had passed in its last two months that guaranteed the positions of state employees loyal to the FSLN, granted inordinate privileges to party members and committees, legalized their expropriation of public funds and properties, and created legal obstacles for my government. One in particular would plague my administration for my entire term in office. It granted university students (loyal supporters of the Sandinistas) the right to claim 6 percent of the nation's budget to subsidize their studies, regardless of their financial circumstances or their academic performance. During all the years in which the Sandinistas controlled the budget they had never done any such thing. It was a ridiculous proposition, especially when you consider that Nicaragua is a poor country where many are still illiterate. Priority had to be given to primary education before we could favor university students. And so I announced two decrees that would examine these laws as well as all property confiscations and a score of suspicious-looking rental agreements that gave use of state property to third parties.

The Sandinistas' response was to accuse me of being antidemocratic, of violating the constitution. I found it unbelievable to hear them speak of democracy—for the first time in a decade.

The labor crisis grew as hospital workers, teachers, construction workers, and others joined the protest. A total of thirty thousand government employees had now brought all activity in the country to a halt.

As this was happening, the Contra director, Comandante Rubén, who was negotiating with us in Managua, announced that eighteen Contras had been reported dead by the Commission on Human Rights. Immediately he ordered Contra troops to be on alert. He said he had information that government military forces were advancing toward the security zones. Rubén said that the Contras could not be held accountable if there was a resurgence of the war.

Carlos Hurtado, my new minister of government, suggested we cordon off the Hotel Las Mercedes, where the Contra directors were staying. The intention was twofold. If the story was true that Contras were being killed, then we needed to protect them. If the story was false, then we needed to make sure they were not free to join their forces in the security zones and restart the war.

The reaction of the Contra leaders was to go on a hunger strike. They said that my government was holding them hostage. It was my administration that was being held hostage. Everywhere we turned people were on strike.

I had decided that the lesson I wanted to teach my fellow Nicaraguans was peace, not violence. I wanted to completely eradicate the notion that conflict resolution could be reduced to three words: *destroy your opponent*. To the contrary, conflicts can and should be resolved through civilized discourse. We needed to make people understand that strikes and riots would only adversely affect the socioeconomic conditions of the country. In all our discussions, this was the message: "Without peace, there can be no prosperity." We gained some additional leverage by signaling to the government workers that *we* administered the national budget, not Daniel Ortega, and that their cooperation in rebuilding Nicaragua would be greatly appreciated. But it wasn't until we fired the union leaders, and in fact beheaded the labor movement, that progress was made and the situation pacified.

By June every ministry was functioning, though a great deal of mistrust existed between old and new employees. In time this would change.

Within our family nucleus, things were also shifting. My son Pedro Joaquín, who had spent the last few years involved with the Contras, now was promoting Nicaragua in Taiwan. During the campaign he had successfully raised funds among the Nicaraguan community in Miami. And so at the behest of the Taiwanese I decided to send him to Taiwan for a year to open a new embassy there.

Mundo, Claudia's husband, had a seat in the legislature. The plan was that they would resettle in Nicaragua. But in September Marcos Tolentino, ten years old, her third child, became ill. In Houston he was diagnosed with leukemia. It was a devastating blow, but at the same time Claudia discovered she was pregnant with Mateo Cayetano, my ninth grandchild, which gave us some reason to be joyful. Mundo remained in Nicaragua for a time with the other children, until he found a job at the World Bank; then the whole family moved to Washington, where Tolentino could receive the best care.

So began a period in our personal lives that centered around helping Tolentino. Cancer transforms the lives of people, especially when it is the life of a child that is threatened. At first we were told it was a mild form of leukemia; his prognosis was good. But a month later we were told that Tolentino's cancer cells had a Philadelphia chromosome, which is resistant to chemotherapy. Our only hope was to find a bone marrow donor. The search began immediately.

To my utter dismay, in Miami a Nicaraguan exile who is influential among the community began a campaign against Tolentino. He suggested it was incorrect to help my grandson because I had not responded to demands that all confiscated property be returned to its original owners immediately. To think that a child was condemned to die and they saw fit to mix this with politics . . .

A donor for Tolentino was never found. The doctors decided to transplant bone marrow from his own body. For a time he showed signs of improvement, but it soon became clear there was nothing science could do to help Tolentino except to give him a certain measure of comfort before he died. Claudia told Tolentino the truth. My grandson, like Pedro, could not tolerate lies.

Tolentino faced death with the same determination and courage that characterized his life. His resemblance to Pedro was astonishing. His maturity was such that at times I felt I was talking to an adult. He never talked for the sake of making conversation. He was a great thinker.

But he always showed great concern for my health and my political situation. At times he even tried to advise me. He had a noble heart. The thing that upset him about having to die so young was that he would never have a chance to do something for society. But as Claudia adroitly pointed out to him, there are so many who live long lives and only use them to make others miserable; Tolentino, on the other hand, was fated to have a short life but he would leave an indelible mark in our hearts. The thing I learned from my grandson is that love strengthens us and should guide all our actions.

For the next five years, until Marcos Tolentino's death, I tried to help my daughter cope with his sickness and the sorrow it brought her. In the end she was her own pillar of strength.

At *La Prensa,* Cristiana continued in her role as director of the newspaper. Eventually she would find herself in a difficult position as the daughter of an elected leader and wife of a government functionary, particularly one who was so often under attack. Like Antonio's, her objectivity was questioned when she tried to maintain the centrist position she had always held. In addition, none of the members of the board understood or agreed with my policy of national reconciliation. Their opposition to my administration they unloaded on Cristiana, as if she were part and parcel of my government and not an independent thinker as all my children are. None of them have ever changed their beliefs on my account. Through all the difficult years of Sandinista oppression it was Cristiana who was by my side fighting for *La Prensa.* After the campaign, however, this fact was completely forgotten. They pitted my son Pedro Joaquín against her for the directorship of the newspaper. In the end both my children were pushed aside. Ironically, the newspaper that Pedro made and died for and which I had personally financed when it was left in ruins by Somoza is now in the hands of people who abandoned it in its most difficult moment.

At *Barricada,* Carlos Fernando's fate was not much different. For the last decade he had had a difficult time balancing his opposing allegiances, to party and family, and party seemed to have priority. Now he experienced this situation in reverse. Party leaders like Daniel, Bayardo Arce, and Tomás Borge suggested that in Carlos Fernando's newfound objectivity there was a great deal of bias in favor of the president, his mother. They couldn't accept that Carlos Fernando firmly believes that Nicaragua has been transformed into a more open, competitive, and democratic society—and that for a daily to survive, even one as heavily subsidized as *Barricada,* it has to stop being the official voice of the Sandinista party. It has to deliver quality.

My son was evolving. He matured enormously that year. He married Desirée. They had two children, Luciana Fernanda and Andrés Fernando, who are now five and three. Every Sunday they come for dinner and meet with their other cousins, Pedro Joaquín's and Cristiana's children. In Pedro's office they share with me the week's events.

Perhaps it is owing to these family gatherings that Carlos Fernando and Desirée have changed so much; or maybe it is that they now think as parents do and ask themselves what kind of a world they are creating for their children. And so they must conclude that we need to build a lasting peace that rises above partisanship and contributes to the economic development of the country. Though still members of the Sandinista party, they belong to one of several splinter factions. I don't think they believe anymore that the National Directorate should be considered above reproach. Without a doubt, since my election to the presidency, the mystique of the National Directorate has been shattered, though they still try to cling to a leadership position in their fractured party.

On June 28, 1990, in San Pedro del Lóvago, the same place where Pedro had been rescued by the Virgin in the Olama and Mollejones invasion, eighteen thousand members of the resistance laid down their arms and the Contras as an armed movement ceased to exist. Oscar Sobalbarro, Comandante Rubén, said the Contras' new motto was "Peace and Work." He said, "From this moment on, even if the administration of Violeta Chamorro does not keep its promises to us, there will be no more war. We will defend our rights through civic and political means." In a symbolic gesture Comandante Franklyn gave me his gun. I accepted it and promised to put it in my private museum, Pedro's study.

As a mother and as a Nicaraguan I felt extremely happy such a day had finally come.

Cardinal Miguel Obando y Bravo officiated at mass. He said the time had come to bury the violence in Nicaragua. He suggested that the Contras' disarmament should be followed by that of the whole country and the reduction of the Sandinista military forces.

In the days that followed about three thousand ex-Contras established themselves in the development zones. Twenty thousand remained dispersed throughout the country, close to their families.

I invited the leaders of all parties to a national dialogue, called the *Concertación,* which means an ordering, an integrating, a making whole. The Sandinista labor organization promised that for two hundred days they would abstain from strikes or takeovers of any kind. More important, they agreed to give their support to a series of measures that would pull us out of the economic debacle we were in. Throughout 1990 we had as many as sixty devaluations of our national currency. We had an inflation rate of 55,000 percent. Our first efforts to adjust the economy had not worked.

We began 1991 by launching—with the support of the international community and the International Monetary Fund—an economic stabilization plan in conjunction with a structural adjustment plan. As a first step we devalued the cordoba by 400 percent. Then we adjusted salaries and fixed the value of the cordoba at five to the dollar.

This was followed by calling an end to government subsidies, price controls, unregulated credit, and the indiscriminate printing of money by the Central Bank to cover our fiscal deficits.

We reduced the number of people on the government payroll from seventy thousand to fifty thousand with an occupational conversion plan that gave government employees the opportunity to withdraw voluntarily in exchange for one year's pay and financing to start their own businesses. It was a slower and more expensive process than firing people outright. It cost nearly $200 million over a period of two years. But it had two benefits. One was to avoid resentment and conflict; the other was to avoid adding to the 65 percent jobless rate. Within a few months inflation dropped to 6 percent per month.

Then we moved to end state monopolies. We passed a private banking law and extended operating licenses to six new banks so that they could begin aggressively competing with the state-owned banks.

We passed a foreign investment law that assured would-be investors that they could repatriate their capital and earnings freely. We promoted exports and authorized the establishment of an industrial free-trade zone. This was followed by the privatization of 107 businesses. For a decade these businesses had been unproductive and a burden on the nation's budget. In private hands they would contribute to the creation of a more competitive and efficient business environment.

I felt at last we had the basis to begin our economic recovery. I was especially elated when Pedro Joaquín reported the interest of the Taiwanese in investing in Nicaragua in the areas of tourism, manufacturing, and lumbering.

I was full of hope for my little Nicaragua when I and my delegation of fifteen left, on April 15, 1991, on an official visit to the White House. The invitation was a gesture from President Bush rich in significance for both our countries after all the years in which Nicaragua had been unwelcome in Washington, embargoed and blockaded.

I think that Daniel, who had never received such an invitation, was understandably jealous. He said that this was proof that my administration was an agent of imperialism.

From the moment we landed in Miami I received an embarrassing, red-carpet treatment. Ernesto Palazio, our ambassador in Washington, came on an official plane to collect us. We flew to Dulles Airport in Washington, where a helicopter was waiting to fly us right into the heart of downtown. We landed in the middle of a field. Then we got into a fleet of limousines and sped off, the sirens of our police escort blaring.

I remember it was a brilliantly sunny day and it was spring, so everything in Washington was in full bloom. We passed the broad expanses of manicured lawns, the trees meticulously planted in rows along the Potomac. The people on the sidewalk waved. It was curious how they responded to the sight of the motorcade. I imagine they were thinking, from the size of our entourage, that someone important must be riding by.

I turned to Cristiana and Antonio, who were with me in the limousine, and said, "All this protection, all this being bowed to and saluted is enough flattery to spoil the humblest, most unassuming person."

We were taken to Blair House. All the walks leading up to the house had been festooned with little flags of Nicaragua. That evening I hosted a dinner at Blair House in honor of congressional leaders. It was a very elegant affair. Blair House has a homey feeling but it is also a place full of history. The busts of Lincoln and Jefferson stare down at you from their perches. Afterward, alone in my room, I wondered how many people had slept in my bed.

The following day, Tuesday, we had a full agenda. First was breakfast with the secretary of commerce and a group of American business leaders, to explore investment opportunities in Nicaragua. At 11 A.M. I addressed a joint meeting of Congress in the Great Hall of the House of Representatives. Congress, I am told, usually convenes in this way only for the president's State of the Union address.

I ended the day with a meeting at the Inter-American Development Bank. I wanted to plead Nicaragua's case personally, as deserving special consideration. I've never pleaded for anything for myself, but for my country I have done so many times.

On Wednesday, April 17, we began the day with an arrival ceremony at the White House. President and Mrs. Bush were waiting to greet me. The wind was blowing gently across the front lawn of the stately mansion. I could hear the snap of flags and the click of cameras and the gentle murmur of people as we alighted from the car.

The rest of the day was dedicated to official business at the White House with President Bush and Secretary of State James Baker. The issue at hand was a case that Nicaragua had won against the United States before the International Court in the Hague, over the mining of Nicaragua's ports. The case had been brought before this court by Daniel Ortega during his presidency. But it now fell to me to decide whether to press ahead with it or not. The United States was clearly a friendly nation to our country, so I had decided to desist from making any claims.

That evening there was a reception for me at the White House. Cristiana, Antonio, and I were invited for drinks with the Bushes in the first family's apartment. Several of the Bush children were there. Their dog was there too. At one time Pedro and I had had a pair of champion German shepherds. I love dogs, but they were never allowed inside the house. I must admit, however, that the White House was filled with a certain warmth by the presence of this furry, spotted canine. President Bush, always warm and effusive toward me, thanked me for the gift I gave him, a big rock painted in the naive style to look like a Nicaraguan village on a hilltop. Afterward he invited us with his family out onto the balcony of the south portico. I will never forget the view of the Potomac River at dusk and of the Washington Monument. But the thing that most impressed me was the Bushes' family unity.

As this was happening, the guests for the evening congregated below.

Some weeks before, I had been asked for a guest list. I don't know how the protocol office operates, but only a few of the people I wanted there were invited. One person I was particularly anxious to see did make the guest list, Marie Guarini. On one occasion on which I visited Congress before I was elected president, among the legislators there was one from New Jersey whose name was familiar to me, Frank Guarini. The man I saw and the boy I knew weren't very alike. Out of embarrassment, I said nothing. But later I learned that he did have a sister named Marie. Under such unusual circumstances, Marie and I were reunited.

There were many movie stars that evening, like Sylvester Stallone, and some of them were famous Nicaraguans, like Barbara Carrera, who was in a James Bond movie, but I had never met them. The Nicaraguan boxer Alexis Argüello was there. He had been badly treated by the Sandinistas. I imagine the people in protocol thought I would like to meet these people.

I cannot deny that the experience was interesting. A pair of young men in red jackets, like Roman soldiers, heralded our entrance into the room with trumpets. I thought the whole thing was unreal—the power, the radiance, the people who attended to us so perfectly square in their poise and their crew cuts. A traveler would take one look at the place and walk away thining, What a great society this is.

The thing about the United States that is extraordinary is that all its great leaders seem to have been concerned about tomorrow, about making their country great for their children and their grandchildren. They saw their role in a historic sense, as going beyond their lifetimes. And so every step is measured and weighed in terms of the greater good.

Even today, I think American presidents think about how they will be perceived hundreds of years from now. We die, but our acts are immortal. It is the way I see my presidency, as laying the groundwork for future generations.

I returned to Nicaragua to host an official visit from the king and queen of Spain. The motherland, as some might call that country, had been extremely cooperative with my administration. Spanish soldiers were part of the United Nations peacekeeping force, helping in the disarmament of the Contras and the pacification of Nicaragua. In addition, on the occasion of the five-hundredth anniversary of the "discovery" of America, Spain donated money for the historic preservation of architectural gems in the cities of Granada and León. Without bowing our heads—we are not, after all, subjects of the Spanish crown—we wanted to honor the royals.

In the European continent, Their Majesties, as they are called, are used to a great deal of protocol and pomp. But in the tropics we are much more informal. So when the king and queen descended from the airplane that had the Spanish crown emblazoned on its tail, I rushed out to greet them, and holding hands we proceeded to receive them with military honors, speeches, and the like. I admit this is my personal style and I can't really change it.

I've been in public life now for seventeen years. By now, everybody around me has a good idea of who I am and what I stand for. There is a kind of self-control, self-censorship among my staff. They know what I won't agree to, and it rarely gets put before me. They know the issues that I am totally unmovable on. I am not, for instance, in favor of social programs that promote family planning on the basis of abortion. I am a pacifist. I reject violence of any kind and the suffering of others. My respect for human rights is from the heart. My belief that Nicaragua must remain independent, free of intervention, is a pillar of our foreign policy. This translates into an aggressive defense of our territorial and maritime borders. At international forums I have been categorical on this. I reject foreign intervention in my country. Naturally, it follows that I do not approve of invasions into other countries, be they Panama, Grenada, or any other. I can't abide dictatorships and would rather not have relations with any. And so I pray each day that in Fidel's island a Violeta will arise and change the lives of the oppressed people. On a more personal level I feel that once I give my word, no matter how unimportant the promise, I am compelled to keep it. My aides, I am sure, are sometimes annoyed because I write down on little bits of paper reminders of things I have to do for people that I have met. I believe we have been put on this earth to help others. That is at the core of everything I do.

Like any executive, I have delegated to Antonio and my cabinet the details of government. All of them without exception are excellent professionals who came from successful careers in the private sector. I picked them because they are smart, because they have demonstrated a sense of organization, and for their efficiency. I see myself as the person responsible for setting the agenda for my administration. I provide the leadership and the inspiration. I sit in on all the big meetings, then turn to my advisers, get the consensus, and if it agrees with my own views and principles, I tell them to proceed.

I'm no intellectual. But I know a few commonsense things. I spent the years before having any power with the normal folks of my country, in Amayo and in the town of Rivas. I know how average people think because I am one of them. People want to have their plot of land, plant their corn patch, raise their cattle in complete freedom. It's a dignified aspiration. I don't need to be an economist to understand that our free-market economy is the way to ensure they have that life. To my muchachos, the young men in my economic cabinet, who understand the mechanics of making such an idea a reality, I simply say, "Work it out." They tell me what measures we need to implement and I say, "Okay, if you've studied all the alternatives and you think this is the way to go, let's do it." This is the way we work.

When we were initiating the economic stabilization program, one of the hardest things my economic cabinet asked me to do was to go out and ask for money. I'd never done it before and I still don't like it. But for my country I knew I had to. One of the important reasons for my visit to the White House was to ask President Bush for more aid in the year to come. I did, and he pretty much promised it to me. But our ambassador, Ernesto Palazio, told me later it wasn't all that certain we would get it. It seems that Congress and the State Department were upset because they believed I wasn't creating the right conditions for democracy to flourish, that I was too bland. One year into my government, Humberto Ortega was still head of the army, and Congress apparently thought that I needed to make more progress in reforming the army and the police. Bush himself never said anything to me. He was always gracious and respectful. But Dan Quayle did say to me that he believed I was allowing my government to be compromised by the Sandinistas. I explained that we were still laying people off in the army and that a set of reforms for both the police and the army was still in the works. These reforms could not be effected without the cooperation of key Sandinista figures. They had to be discussed.

I don't think people realized what a violent country Nicaragua had become. In the past months I had had to go on television to ask the people to please moderate themselves. Many innocent people were killed by accident because of the number of guns that were in the hands of the population.

The antidote to violence is not more violence. I am sure of that. Peace has to be built through daily acts of tolerance, fair play, and legality. Even if my counterparts did not follow these rules, I, as a leader, was obliged to do so. My aim was to create a country in which people respected the rule of law, and a government that operated within the strict parameters of the constitution. Even if this constitution was flawed because it had been drafted by a party whose objective was to extend its power, it still had to be respected until it could be changed by consensus. And if for this attitude people believed me to be weak, so be it.

Though we continued to make great advances in resettling the resistance, there were many who insisted on remaining at large. Eventually some, like one who came to be appropriately called the Indomitable, became delinquents who terrorized the countryside. For those who preferred to lead a disorderly life of crime, nothing we could do was satisfactory. They accused my administration of turning our backs on their needs.

The real story was quite different. By December 1991 we had formed nineteen development zones, which took up an area of approximately 410,000 hectares for a population of ten thousand ex-Contras, or forty-one hectares per man. About half of the land was in the south, half in the north.

The ex-combatants were being assisted by a civic organization that acted as technical consultants and administrators of the development zones. With the help of this group the Contras were slowly becoming farmers, producing a bountiful crop of corn, beans, and tubers and learning how to cultivate cacao and cardamom. They were also raising pigs, chickens, and cattle.

Some of the farms were organized in cooperatives; others were not. This was a strictly voluntary decision. Ex-combatants received vocational training in such skills as shoemaking and carpentry as well.

About half the Contras did not want to go into the development zones. So we had to look for land in other places and arrange for them and their families to receive pensions and free medical attention for one year. To meet those demands we invested $85 million in social programs for the Contras.

Our efforts to rebuild Nicargua's image were having an effect. In the previous months, Venezuela, Mexico, and Colombia had forgiven $1 million of the $11 million Nicaragua owed them. Then we paid $360 million to the World Bank with a short-term loan. This opened the door to fresh loans for the first time in seven years.

That same year we went before the Club de Paris (its members are the United States, France, Spain, Germany, Holland, and Italy) to rene-gotiate the $830 million foreign debt the Sandinistas had left unpaid with them. The United States forgave us its part of the debt ($260 million). Afterward we would deal with the problem of our debt to the Soviet Union, Czechoslovakia, Poland, Iran, Brazil, and Central America. Slowly we were putting together the pieces of our shattered economy.

In Nicaragua we envisioned 1992 as the year for economic liftoff—if we succeeded in bringing under control the violence that plagued our country. I declared an amnesty for all the renegade groups, Sandinista or Contra, who were living outside the law, ostensibly for political reasons. "From this moment on, anyone who breaks the law," I declared, "will be considered a delinquent and sent to jail." To make my point, the first workers who went on strike espousing violence and taking over busi-nesses were dislodged by force and temporarily jailed.

In the legislature, a group of Sandinistas, led by Sergio Ramírez, formed an independent faction, which Daniel angrily referred to as opportunists and linked to my son Carlos Fernando at *Barricada*. So a lot of pressure was being put on Carlos Fernando to resign. But he refused to leave until they fired him.

Politically I had two main challengers. Daniel Ortega continued to be a problem. On the thirteenth anniversary of the Sandinista revolution, twenty thousand people gathered in the plaza to listen to Daniel inveigh against our capitalist stabilization plan. The university students in particular responded to his speeches. No longer satisfied with 6 percent of the budget, they wanted to claim for the two state-owned universities 6 percent of the nation's gross output and of all incoming donations. My other foe was Alfredo César, who was upset by the appearance of a centrist group of the UNO and Sandinista moderates who supported my presidential agenda. Alfredo recklessly claimed that some U.S. aid was going to the Sandinistas. As a free citizen, Alfredo had the right to say what he pleased. But his remarks caused Senator Jesse Helms and a member of his staff—both rabid right-wingers— to insist that $100 million in U.S. aid be delayed pending an investigation of Alfredo's charges. Alfredo's action hurt the people of Nicaragua more than it hurt my administration. After the investigation, the much-awaited $100 million in U.S. aid was not released. The members of the investigating delegation insinuated that they wanted to see more reforms in the army and the police.

I was trying to show Nicaraguans that economic prosperity is the result of the efforts of an entire nation. Government does not achieve this on its own. I had little or no cooperation from the various sectors in our society.

Predictably, the year ended in a disastrous way. The expected year of the economic liftoff barely registered on the scale, with a reported 0.5 percent growth.

The meeting with the investigating delegation was very disappointing in terms of the results it yielded. However, it also showed Alfredo César's hand working behind the scenes with trusted members of my cabinet and diplomatic corps to undermine the actions of my government. In the Washington halls of power, they had let it be known that my government was *unwilling* to make more purges in the ranks of the police and the army, and they presented behind my back their own package of reforms, which included removing the current heads of both bodies.

It wasn't that I was unwilling; but we simply couldn't do it without consensus. The case of Nicaragua is much more complex than that of the average communist country going through a democratic transition. We are the only civilian government I know of that has attempted to reduce the size of an army that was the arm of a party defeated in a free election. Czechoslovakia, now split into the Czech Republic and Slovakia, hopes to be able to reduce the army by 5 or 10 percent a year over a period of ten years. It is a much less ambitious plan than ours. We reduced the army 80 percent in two years. When you consider that along with that reduction we professionalized and institutionalized the army, it is a miracle to have succeeded.

When one compares Nicaragua to the old Eastern bloc countries, I think it is fair to say that when they made the leap from communism to democracy, those countries did so in relative peace. Their wars and confiscations had taken place fifty years prior to their liberation, so the wounds of their social upheaval had been healed. In Nicaragua we had to effect our reforms in a polarized environment. The wounds of war were still fresh in the hearts and minds of our people. Our revolution was only ten years old. When I took office, the Sandinistas were still expropriating. The people who had suffered were alive and resentful of the injustice that had been committed against them. In Bulgaria, in East Germany, in the ex–Soviet Union, private property had been confiscated fifty years earlier. The original owners were in most cases dead. It was their children or their grandchildren who wanted to reclaim property. They were emotionally removed from the issue. There wasn't as direct a sentimental attachment as in Nicaragua.

The promise I had made throughout my campaign was that we would give legal title to plots of land to demobilized Contras and to retired members of the army. With regard to confiscations, I felt the only solution was to establish a special court empowered to review all claims. More than five thousand claims flooded the courts. All those whose property was judged to have been improperly confiscated would, if possible, have land restored; otherwise they would be fairly compensated. Compensation required two things: an office had to be established to set a fair value for confiscated land, and funds had to be raised through the sale of state assets. But who wants to buy obsolete or run-down property? The process is a lengthy one; it still goes on. Most state assets were sold at fire-sale prices.

I felt I had a moral duty to respond to the demands of those whose property had been confiscated. My administration has done everything possible to move the process along—the issue directly affects 20 percent of the population, and indirectly it affects all of us.

Over the question of property, the powers of government were pitted one against the other. The executive was against the legislative, the legislative against the judicial, and so on. While it is healthy for the powers of government to be independent of one another, the lack of consensus among us had a stagnating effect.

Everybody has his own version of how the war between the powers of government began. This is my theory. Alfredo César, an ally, turned foe chiefly because he could no longer bear the political cost of supporting my policy of reconciliation and picked up the banner of anti-Sandinism. This was a subject dear to the UNO coalition's heart, which catapulted Alfredo to the forefront of this monster coalition. Powerful once again, Alfredo began to push an aggressive legislative agenda that went against our national interests and threatened the country's stability, causing the Sandinista minority in Congress to walk out. In the days following the minority's walkout, Alfredo continued to legislate without the center and without a quorum. The minority protested. An appellate court ruled the day's legislative actions unconstitutional and ordered them annulled. Alfredo disregarded the order of the appellate court, though he was going against the rule of law. The constitution specifies that, in such instances, the executive can punish such actions by putting a freeze on all payments to the legislature or can disregard any laws issued by a parliament operating illegally. It was an action I preferred not to have to take.

Within days the supreme court reaffirmed the findings of the appellate court. Still Alfredo refused to yield.

In a bold act against the executive, Alfredo formed an alliance with my vice president, Virgilio Godoy, and Arnoldo Alemán, and proposed a referendum that dealt mainly with Humberto's departure and the property issue. They suggested that if I or anyone else in my government opposed the UNO's objectives, we should resign.

As this was happening, Antonio had been dutifully working to see to it that the $100 million in U.S. aid was released. The aid came—as a Christmas gift. In December, when the government coffers were completely empty and we were on the verge of declaring an economic emergency, I received a call from President Bush, who informed me that the $100 million was on its way.

When Alfredo César heard the news, he declared that he would see to it that our next request for aid, $300 million for 1993, was not approved unless the UNO's demands were met.

By the end of the year our nascent democracy was also threatened by the precarious economic situation. Between strikes and political maneuverings from the left and right, the expected economic liftoff did not take place. Unemployment remained at 60 percent.

It was turning out to be a turbulent year. And the question of Humberto's permanence in the army was at the center of the controversy.

Unofficially, Humberto had let it be known that he would leave in 1995. But in various private meetings with him I told him I felt the time had come for him to go. The army was reduced and professionalized; the Contras were resettled. His presence at the head of the army was only polarizing the country.

So on September 2, 1993, on the thirteenth anniversary of the army, in front of members of my cabinet, representatives of the state, other officials, army soldiers, and the diplomatic corps, I announced that General Humberto Ortega would be retiring from the army in 1994.

Officials of the army bolted from their chairs, some of them yelling. Daniel Ortega said, "Who does she think she is? She thinks she owns the place."

I was a little surprised by the reaction because I felt I had given sufficient warning to Humberto that I was going to take this step. I felt Humberto had accepted his fate. (History will show he turned the Sandinista electoral defeat into personal victory.) But on the day-to-day emotional level, I think it was hard for him to accept that there was a greater power than his. The fact that that power had been transferred to a woman with no real political experience, I am sure, did not make things any easier.

On this occasion, unfortunately, Humberto felt that I had shamed him before his men, before the whole nation, by announcing his departure without ample warning.

Putting my own wounded feelings aside, I agreed to meet with him to discuss a way out of his predicament. He did not want to go against my designs. Historically it would have been a grave error. Everything he had worked to achieve since the electoral defeat would have been seen through the lens of his rebellion against the president, the elected representative of the people. But he needed to save face. We determined that in December 1994 I would appoint a new army chief and give Humberto two months to effect a transition. He would leave office, as he had said, in 1995.

As important a problem was the property issue. When we repealed a confiscation, the Sandinista labor organization would move to occupy the farm or business. Armed and dangerous, they did not let the rightful owners take possession. For the rest of the year the army had to dislodge them by force. The constant tension this caused led to the assassination of the leader of the Expropriated People's Association.

. . .

Concerned about Alfredo's threat and the warnings of our ambassador in Washington that aid for 1993 was in danger of being suspended, I instructed Antonio to go to Washington in March 1993 and personally lobby the new Clinton administration, the Department of State, the National Security Council, the Senate, the House, and the multilateral agencies.

I couldn't understand the mixed signals coming from the United States. I felt that if, in Russia, Boris Yeltsin had managed to pacify those who opposed the kind of deep democratic transformations I was bringing about in Nicaragua, everyone would have been pleased. How satisfied the Europeans would be if the left-wingers in Russia supported the center! But where I was concerned, the fact that my policies had splintered the monolithic unity of the Sandinistas, and brought some of them to the center, was seen as a problem.

In Washington Antonio tried to explain the political effect of withholding aid in 1993. He told them,

> When an important member of the international community turns its back on the people of Nicaragua and defaults on its commitments to our country, the authority of Violeta Chamorro and her ability to effect change is substantially reduced. The extreme right and the extreme left harden their positions, and a new wave of intolerance is generated in our society. Consensus is broken and the doors are wide open for intolerance and violence.

Antonio's words were almost prophetic.

In August 1994 a renegade group of 150 ex-Contras, led by a man named El Chacal (the Jackal), took hostage forty-one people who were part of a special commission for disarmament. Among them were some Sandinista legislators. El Chacal's group demanded, among other things, the dismissal of Humberto Ortega and more assistance for the demobilized resistance.

In retaliation, a group of ex–army officers calling themselves Commandos for Dignity took hostage thirty UNO members of the legislature while they were in a private session. Among those taken hostage were Alfredo César and Virgilio Godoy.

This was proof that violence only leads to more violence. The situation we faced was sad and disappointing. I decided to address the nation and call for an end to the hate, violence, and intolerance that we had in our hearts.

In the United States a group of Nicaraguans put together a commission that petitioned the White House to intercede in the problem. They received no response, apart from expressions of solidarity from President and Mrs. Clinton. I have always maintained that problems are best resolved among ourselves. And so I called the leaders of the UNO and the FSLN, including Daniel Ortega. We agreed to jointly condemn the assaults and work together for the immediate release of the hostages.

Five days would pass before our negotiations with both opposing sides yielded results and the hostages were released. Among the last ones to be freed were Alfredo César and Virgilio Godoy. They were made to pose in their underwear as a form of humiliation.

After the legislators resumed their duties, they took on the challenge of elaborating a new constitution. For the past three years, reforming the constitution had been a subject of much controversy. Designed in 1987 by a Sandinista-controlled congress at a time when it looked as if it would be "Daniel Ortega Forever," the constitution gave the executive omnipotent powers over the legislature, the judiciary, and the treasury and it made the army constitutionally an institution of the FSLN party. The disparity of views that existed threatened to make the discussions a virtual war of opinion. So I, as the executive, and the various legislative groups agreed that the question of what laws to reform, how to reform them, when to activate these reforms would be the product of a consensus.

Soon after these meetings began, Sergio Ramírez, Alfredo César, and various other UNO leaders decided to turn their backs on the executive and vote on a constitution that granted the congress inordinate powers. This legislation would in a sense give the Sandinistas what they had always wanted, the possibility of "governing from behind the scenes."

What motivated Alfredo and the leaders of the UNO to play along with such a scheme was the possibility of hurting Antonio, who was considered a presidential hopeful in the next election. The constitution they proposed carried a set of restrictions directly affecting Antonio. The new constitution decreed that he could not run for president in a free and fair election because he was married to the daughter of the president and because he was minister of government. The implication was that he was somehow privileged. But Antonio had every intention of resigning a year in advance from his post before presenting himself as a candidate, thereby eliminating any possible conflict of interest.

In addition, these inhibitions raised a convenient smoke screen that shielded the fact that the new constitution gave so much power to the legislature that it now had the right to replace the president and the vice president of the republic. In any country this would be considered a coup d'état, an overthrow of the executive by congress.

Though I was aware that I would cause a furor and that everyone would focus on the issue of my son-in-law, I refused to ratify the new constitution. Fortunately, the legislators had made a series of legal errors in writing the new set of laws and the supreme court declared the new constitution invalid.

Always trying to build consensus, I extended my hand to the legislators, and a new set of negotiations began.

To simplify the discussion, Antonio suggested that we separate the restrictions against him from the rest of the package and that we concentrate on the issues that affected government.

In November 1994 a set of partial reforms to the constitution passed a first vote. A second vote was scheduled for the beginning of 1995. Though a substantial improvement over the first, this version had some constitutional errors, favoring the congress and weakening other powers of state.

About this time Carlos Fernando was fired from *Barricada*. I don't think it came as a shock to him. The rumor was that he was too independent, too outspoken, too critical of the Sandinista leadership. He has a talk show now, where he invites personalities to discuss political issues. He also has a foundation that does economic studies. Recently he told me he wants to go back to school. Pedro's assassination was a detour in his life. I look at Carlos Fernando and I think that maybe someday he too will go into politics. And if he does, I know that he understands now that absolute power corrupts.

In early February 1995 the new constitution was approved. Nineteen out of the forty-two Sandinistas voted in favor of the reforms. I had asked for ten days for discussion before ratifying it, but that was voted down. I still had the option to veto it. However, I chose not to exercise this right.

Humberto was retired from the army on February 21, 1995, in a quiet ceremony. To replace him I appointed General Joaquín Cuadra. He is the first chief of the army in the history of Nicaragua appointed by a civilian.

Still the notion persists in the American press that Nicaragua has not made any advances. The last time the U.S. press said anything good about Nicaragua was when it came to the passionate defense of the Sandinistas.

Nobody reported that in 1995 Nicaragua's economy grew at a rate of 3.2 percent; that our exports have increased; that Exxon Corporation has enlarged its presence in Nicaragua and Texaco too; that Motorola has invested; that Mobile University (Alabama) has opened a campus in Nicaragua; that we've privatized hundreds of businesses.

There is very little said in the U.S. press about Nicaragua these days. When the press does remember we exist, it is to report the gripes from this or that sector. I have come to think that no news is good news.

Toward the end of 1995, I made a last effort to persuade the pope to come visit us in Nicaragua. I had written many letters to him. After he had published his latest encyclical, in which he affirms life and attacks the culture of death, I asked him to please come to Central America to deliver his message in person. That's how his trip came about.

I hoped that his presence would bring hope, unity, and purpose to our country. One day in December, Cardinal Miguel Obando y Bravo came to tell me the pope had said, "Yes, I want to go to Nicaragua. God willing, I will be there on February seventh." So began our plans to receive him.

At 8 A.M. on the morning of February 7, I was at the airport with the full diplomatic corps, my cabinet, army chief General Joaquín Cuadra, and the bishops of the Episcopal Conference, awaiting the arrival from Guatemala of Pope John Paul II. Thousands of people were there with us. A huge banner read: JOHN PAUL II NICARAGUA RECEIVES YOU WITH LOVE AND OPEN ARMS.

As his plane came to a stop, the people were chanting, "One God, one love, one church."

I was waiting for the pope at the foot of the stairs, thinking, Bless the Lord, my dream has come true. I have been much criticized for an unprecedented break in Vatican protocol. The truth is, it was a sudden movement on both our parts when we embraced. I did not kiss him on the cheek, as it is said. He greeted me with a kiss on the forehead. I was embarrassed and explained to him that in Nicaragua our emotions get in the way of protocol, and I asked him to please forgive us. But he waved his aides aside and held on tightly to my hand.

The two of us, figures in white, stood solemnly listening to the hymn of our republic being played by a military band. Afterward a twenty-one-gun salute was sounded.

In my welcome speech at the airport I told the pope of the happiness we felt to be able to express at last, freely and openly, the love we felt for him as "the vicar of Christ on earth and a symbol of unity and pardon." The last time he had visited, he had been kept standing under the merciless sun as Daniel Ortega went on a long tirade about the war with the Contras.

During his homily the pope talked about the importance of family values. He said that when they are ignored, that undermined the fabric of society. Family is the human laboratory in which individuals are formed. The well-being of an entire nation is dependent on the morals we instill in our children. He talked about peace and reconciliation and encouraged us to trust in forgiveness.

I am not trying to compare myself to the Holy Father, but these were my same themes. I thought, My God, I haven't been mistaken.

At times the pope departed from his prepared text. He said that on his last visit, Nicaragua was a shooting gallery for the superpowers, that it was a great dark night . . . and that there was noise. I thought, This is a gentleman who understands our reality.

That day he celebrated the Eucharist under the sun. And when he elevated the Body of Christ, there was such silence one could hear the humming of the birds, or the fluttering of the wings of the little white dove of peace. The people did not say a word. They were all silently praying for peace and unity for all of us. It was something incredible. Tears were rolling down my cheeks. I don't know if anyone saw me, or if they criticized me for taking out my handkerchief and drying my tears, but I could not stop thinking about his last visit and the sad hour of the consecration, when the *turbas* had chorused, "They will not pass, they will not pass," with their fists extended in the air.

I never tire of repeating that throughout my life it is my faith in God that sustains me. I don't think it is a question of being Catholic or not. But faith of whatever kind has a positive impact on a person's life.

After the mass in the plaza, the pope met privately with the cardinal and other church officials until later in the afternoon, when it was time for him to go.

I asked the pope what he thought about my family. He said that what was once disunited is no longer. I said, "Thank you, thank you, Holy Father. My dreams have come true." He told me, "Don't worry, Violeta, we are together. I always pray for you, for your family, for your people." When I asked the Holy Father the question about my family, I didn't mean just Pedro Joaquín, Claudia, Cristiana, and Carlos Fernando. I was including my family of Nicaraguans. I feel that, like my own children, my compatriots are maturing and slowly developing tolerance for one another's differences.

We were so happy that day. Everything went so well that the cardinal and I could hardly believe it.

Before leaving, the pope expressed his sorrow at not being able to stay longer. He said, "I will return," and he gave me a bronze dove of peace. It says, *Nicaragua 7 Febrero 96*.

When I came to power in 1990, restoring peace was not easy to do. The Sandinistas had spent the last five years fighting a war and preparing for an American invasion. They were unified in their hatred and their fear. There was a lot of tension. Anyone who appeared to be on the side of the foreign aggressor was viewed as the enemy. After their defeat in the elections, the Sandinistas' natural instinct was to reach for their guns. The first twelve months of my administration were completely dedicated to reducing the size of the army, demobilizing the Contras, and disarming dangerous civilians. We bought as many as thirty thousand rifles to destroy. The country was a powder keg, ready to explode.

I soon realized the advantage of having Daniel Ortega assume the leadership of the enraged masses was that it gave us a central figure to negotiate with and not a cornucopia of warlords each with his own agenda. I am the last person to want to sing his praises. I had hoped Daniel would be more of a statesman. But I'll grant him this: given the power he has over the masses, he could have been worse.

Since 1990 violence has been in a steady decline. But it is by no means eradicated. There is great poverty. There is still a lot of social tension. People blame my administration. But government is not entirely to blame. Poverty, unemployment, and violence are things we must combat together.

In the north there are still small bands of delinquents who have refused to join civilian life. Some people insist on living outside the law. I have offered them ample opportunity, including three pardons. Now it is the army's job to bring these people to heel.

In my six years in office I have come to see the need for having a small army. Today we have twelve thousand enlisted men and 6,600 men in the police. Costa Rica has thirty-six thousand men in arms, almost twice what we have, although, supposedly, they do not have an army. A government without an armed force cannot assert its laws.

Last year we had to take two thousand delinquents prisoners. This year the army reports that in exchanges of fire with delinquents, seventy of their own men have been injured, and seven died; forty-nine delinquents were killed, as well as ninety-four innocent civilians. General Joaquín Cuadra Lacayo, the new army chief, tells me we are still fighting a silent war.

I have great hopes that sometime soon there will be total peace. Somoza's bunker on the hill of Tiscapa, later a Sandinista stronghold and the current site of the national army's administrative buildings, was recently turned over to the people of Nicaragua for the construction of a national park.

There was a great ceremony that day, and as I sat looking beyond the hill toward the beauty of Lake Managua and the volcanoes Momotombo and Momotombito, I remembered my sentiments of long ago, that regardless of our different political allegiances we are all bonded by the pain we endured together. The hill of Tiscapa is a symbol of that joint suffering. Now what had been a symbol of oppressive power and "a well of sorrows," as Cardinal Obando said, is for the enjoyment of the people of Nicaragua.

We have become a body of people in which there exists no greater might than the civil power.

Epilogue

On April 25, 1990, when I became president of Nicaragua, I looked out at the bleachers of the Estadio Nacional, divided by the blue-and-white banners of the UNO coalition and the red-and-black banners of the FSLN. From one side I was showered with plastic bags filled with soda pop, while from the other I received applause. The rancor, vindictiveness, and antagonism convinced me that for the well-being of our nation, my government had to rise above party interests and break the cycle of violence and intolerance that has dominated us.

I began my job certain that I had to be a president of all Nicaraguans if we were to succeed in erecting a palace on the hill where humanism and democracy could reside in a new, republican Nicaragua. More than six years later, we have surmounted incredible obstacles.

This is the Nicaragua that I leave:

Today we stand at the threshold of the palace of our dreams—democratic, pacified, reconciled, with an unshakable foundation of liberty.

The Contras have been demobilized, peacefully integrated with the rest of society.

There is not one political prisoner in our jails. Not one citation of human rights violations can be attributed to my administration. A human life is now valued in Nicaragua.

The military power is subordinate to the civilian government. It is professionalized. Officials in the army are now elected to their posts for a limited amount of time. The monopoly the Sandinista party had over the army and the police has been broken. These two bodies now serve only one interest, that of the nation.

There exists today a healthy respect for the independence of the powers of government. The people can dictate laws and they can rest assured that the laws will be implemented without being overshadowed by a dictatorial power.

Our country is solvent. Nicaragua is now eligible for fresh credit for development from international lenders. To help reactivate the economy we have invested more than a billion dollars into improving the country's infrastructure: roads, ports, telecommunications, etc.

The economy is growing. Our most recent figures show that our growth index stands at 4 percent, the highest it has been in the last eleven years. Inflation held steady at 12.2 percent. Our exports have grown 45 percent. Last year the agricultural sector grew by 8 percent. In the staples of the Nicaraguan diet, rice and beans, we experienced a growth of 30 percent. The Chinese have set up assembly plants in our free-trade zones. They say our labor force is quick to learn and much cheaper than their own. Tourism offers great hope for the future. The Costa Ricans can generate $500 million in tourism alone. So can we, who have a country that is every bit its equal in ecological beauty and diversity, only much bigger.

The expectation is that this year our growth index will reach a high of 5 percent and that inflation will drop to 10 percent. The economic crisis of the 1980s, hyperinflation and economic stagnation, is behind us.

We have invested half a billion dollars in the social sector; $68 million was spent to construct schools in the poorest regions of the country, with special emphasis in the rural areas. Our school program is free of all political indoctrination and geared toward creating civic-minded citizens. Perhaps as a result, school attendance has risen every year during my six-year term.

There are five new universities in Nicaragua, including a new technological institute for vocational training. INCAE, the graduate school for business administration, affiliated with Harvard University, has returned to Nicaragua to train our future business leaders.

When I leave the presidency, I plan to create a foundation that will launch a private initiative to educate Nicaragua by generating scholarship opportunities. I want our future leaders to spring not from the top, privileged layers of society but from a broader sector. This, I believe, can take us one step further in consolidating democracy.

We have invested $138 million to build or repair a total of six hospitals in the cities of Chinandega, Estelí, Jinotega, and Managua, and hundreds of clinics everywhere in the country. We have also invested in new hospital equipment throughout the nation. Through the Ministry of Health we have increased prenatal care for expectant mothers. Special attention was given to the prevention of transmissible diseases. We launched a national vaccination campaign that covered 95 percent of children under one year of age.

We reformed the social welfare system to discourage dependency and stimulate efficiency. Through public investment we generated a total of sixty thousand jobs, either directly or indirectly.

In the private sector investment rose in 1995 to approximately $100 million, 14.5 percent more than in the previous year. We gave $40 million in government loans for the development of small businesses. Bank deposits grew 40 percent, a sign that entrepreneurs big and small have faith in our economy.

Our thorniest issue, the problem of ownership of private property, is almost resolved. When possible we have returned property to its rightful owner or extended government bonds instead. We have resolved 100 percent of the cases brought before the government under article 85. We have resolved 89 percent of the agrarian cases. Of the 5,288 cases of confiscated properties, we have resolved 43 percent. The cases that are still pending will be resolved when we privatize the Ministry of Telecommunications.

In addition, through the Institute of Agrarian Reform we issued 6,100 new property titles for approximately 250,000 hectares, which benefited around 10,500 families.

We have returned to their legitimate owners most of the businesses previously administered by the state, and privatized the remainder. This has contributed to creating a more efficient and competitive business environment.

Things have changed in Nicaragua. War has given way to peace. Totalitarianism has succumbed to democracy, and an economy on a backward march became a stable free-market economy, experiencing a growth that is entirely dependent on private-sector investment. To put it in the words of Pope John Paul II, "Once it was a dark night in Nicaragua. Now there is a shining sun."

President Bush, who still writes to me every Christmas, confirms this. He tells me that what has happened in Nicaragua is incredible. The president of Taiwan, Lee Teng-hui, says that what has been done here is the path to follow if we want to achieve in Nicaragua the kind of growth Taiwan has attained. Enrique Iglesias of the Inter-American Development Bank says there is no other way to go than our way. The International Monetary Fund and the World Bank agree. The people who know and understand economic policy in the world and who rate our performance all believe that Nicaragua offers excellent opportunities for development.

Unfortunately we have not been as good at communicating our advances. One tends to presume that people understand what we are doing. But it is not that way at all. People pick up the newspaper, listen to the radio, or turn on their television sets, and instead of receiving accurate information, they are filled with worthless superficial comments from people who often don't comprehend or don't wish to comprehend what we are all working for. There is a lot of sensationalism in journalism today. No one wants to report about a new school we opened or the hospital we inaugurated. Who will pay attention if they write that my government has negotiated the remission of Nicaragua's foreign debt with Germany? It is more newsworthy to broadcast stories about the alleged corruption of this or that minister, and to state these things as fact without ever feeling burdened by the need to establish evidence. Sadly, what many journalists in my country are engaging in is not reporting but defamation. Though it is not responsible journalism or even moral, I understand that they are exercising a right to free speech they have never been able to enjoy so fully. And so they can't help but go to extremes. I believe it's a natural thing and it's democracy. As a leader I am proud of having fostered freedom of expression in my country even when it is unfairly launched against me. I accept it as my personal sacrifice so that freedom of expression can exist and serve as guarantor of the balance of power and of the subordination of the armed forces to a civilian government.

But on some evenings, alone in my bed, I spend hours wrestling with feelings of sadness that builds up in my heart. The hardest thing for me to accept has been to see how undervalued by my compatriots the efforts of my administration have been, how underestimated the complexities of effecting a triple transition—from war to peace, from totalitarianism to democracy, from a centrally planned economy to a free-market economy. It is particularly disappointing when I consider that some of these people suffered by my side during those long years of Somocista and Sandinista oppression. They forget that our history is rife with conflict, abuses of power, and instances of foreign intervention (in fact, invasions). These experiences create a culture that is antidemocratic, to which one must add the difficulties created by poverty.

Time will tell if there was merit to my acts of government. I've only done what I believed in accordance with my moral duty. People will write and say what they will. One or another will express frustration and perhaps discontent or an angry word or two. But why not? That is what I envision pluralism to be. It doesn't bother me.

What should never again be lost is peace. Every day I ask the Lord that my successor will not allow the peace to be destroyed and that our path toward democracy will be an irreversible one, so that our family of Nicaraguans will never be divided again. The train of unity, reconciliation, and progress that we boarded in 1990 must not be derailed. Our country must continue to progress in liberty, and each and every Nicaraguan must have a decent home, bread, and opportunities to advance.

My hope is that we will all go forward and consolidate our economic, social, and political reforms by going out to vote in the next elections with enthusiasm and vigor for the person most likely to promote Nicaragua's interest above those of any party. Remember, the only victory worth having is the one that benefits the whole nation.

Never before have we, as Nicaraguans, had an opportunity to influence our future in a climate of freedom, honesty, and peace. Nobody should sit by the wayside to wait for a better future to come.

My greatest aspiration is to live to see the day when I will place the presidential sash on the one who is freely chosen by the voters to be president of Nicaragua.

God bless all Nicaraguans.

Index